# Make the Grade.
## *Your Atomic Dog Online Edition.*

The Atomic Dog Online Edition includes proven study tools that expand and enhance key concepts in your text. Reinforce and review the information you absolutely 'need to know' with features like:

- **Review Quizzes**
- Key term Assessments
- Interactive Animations and Simulations
- Notes and Information from Your Instructor
- Pop-up Glossary Terms
- A Full Text Search Engine

D0573580

Ensure that you 'make the grade'. Follow your lectures, complete assignments, and take advantage of all your available study resources like the Atomic Dog Online Edition.

## *How to Access Your Online Edition*

**If you purchased this text directly from Atomic Dog ....**
Visit atomicdog.com and enter your email address and password in the login box at the top-right corner of the page.

**If you purchased this text NEW from another source....**
Visit our Students' Page on atomicdog.com and enter the **activation key located below** to register and access your Online Edition.

**If you purchased this text USED from another source....**
Using the Book Activation key below you can access the Online Edition at a discounted rate. Visit our Students' Page on atomicdog.com and enter the **Book Activation Key in** the field provided to register and gain access to the Online Edition.

Be sure to download our *How to Use Your Online Edition* guide located on atomicdog.com to learn about additional features!

This key activates your online edition. Visit atomicdog.com to enter your Book Activation Key and start accessing your online resources. For more information, give us a call at (800) 310-5661 or send us an email at support@atomicdog.com

# 166GLR5KJ

*Some online Editions do not contain all features.

# Hand in Hand

## Research Design and Statistics in the Behavioral Sciences

# Hand in Hand

## Research Design and Statistics in the Behavioral Sciences

## First Edition

**Sandra K. Webster**
Westminster College

**THOMSON**
™

Australia · Canada · Mexico · Singapore · Spain · United Kingdom · United States

# Hand in Hand
## Sandra K. Webster

**Executive Editors:**
Michele Baird, Maureen Staudt, and Michael Stranz

**Marketing Manager**
Mikka Baker

**Managing Editor:**
Kendra Leonard

**Marketing Coordinators:**
Lindsay Annett and Sara Mercurio

**Production/Manufacturing Manager:**
Donna M. Brown

**Production Editorial Manager:**
Dan Plofchan

**Rights and Permissions Specialists:**
Kalina Hintz and Bahman Naraghi

Cover Image:
© Getty

The Adaptable Courseware Program consists of products and additions to existing Thomson products that are produced from camera-ready copy. Peer review, class testing, and accuracy are primarily the responsibility of the author(s).

Business Protocol / David Robinson
Second Edition

BOOK ISBN 1-592-60273-8
PACKAGE ISBN 1-592-60274-6

LCCN 2006929376

**International Divisions List**

**Asia (Including India):**
Thomson Learning
(a division of Thomson Asia Pte Ltd)
5 Shenton Way #01-01
UIC Building
Singapore 068808
Tel: (65) 6410-1200
Fax: (65) 6410-1208

**Australia/New Zealand:**
Thomson Learning Australia
102 Dodds Street
Southbank, Victoria 3006
Australia

**Latin America:**
Thomson Learning
Seneca 53
Colonia Polano
11560 Mexico, D.F., Mexico
Tel (525) 281-2906
Fax (525) 281-2656

**Canada:**
Thomson Nelson
1120 Birchmount Road
Toronto, Ontario
Canada M1K 5G4
Tel (416) 752-9100
Fax (416) 752-8102

**UK/Europe/Middle East/Africa:**
Thomson Learning
High Holborn House
50-51 Bedford Row
London, WC1R 4L$
United Kingdom
Tel 44 (020) 7067-2500
Fax 44 (020) 7067-2600

**Spain (Includes Portugal):**
Thomson Paraninfo
Calle Magallanes 25
28015 Madrid
España
Tel 34 (0)91 446-3350
Fax 34 (0)91 445-621

# Dedication

*This book is dedicated to the hundreds of students who have taught me the value of struggling to master new concepts as we work together on moving from understanding how to read about psychological research to being able to conceptualize, do, and report psychological research.*

# Brief Contents

# Contents

# Preface

Congratulations! You are among the brave faculty members who are intrepid enough to teach the research design and/or statistics course in psychology. This has been, and will continue to be, my favorite course to teach precisely because the course content is so challenging for most students. They need us to motivate them to master concepts and skills that seem to them abstract and unnecessary but are in reality the very skills that will support their success in both the world of work and graduate study. Psychological research requires logical analysis of "word problems," quantitative reasoning, and clear communication. This text is designed to support your course in each of these three areas.

This text does the following:

- Integrates research design, statistical analysis, and reporting research using APA style in each chapter

- Incorporates examples of research taken from actual studies done by my students

- Uses language and examples chosen to be effective across cultures

- Illustrates statistical formulas with step-by-step examples

- Assumes no math background for students

- Begins with values of research and ethics because they are essential at every part of the research process

- Presents experimental designs before quasiexperimental designs in order to emphasize the role of the hypothetico-deductive method in making causal inferences

- Includes effect sizes with each inferential statistical technique

- Follows guidelines set forth in the *Publication Manual of the American Psychological Association*, 5th Edition, and the *APA Ethical Principles for Psychologists*

- Provides a background for students at the beginning level and may be used for undergraduate and selected graduate courses in which students have had no prior training in psychological research

## Pedagogical Philosophy

This text integrates psychology research designs with the statistics needed to carry out those designs. In keeping with the integrated approach, the text incorporates sections on APA style in each chapter as it covers the relevant material. This text is unique in covering the three aspects of psychological research—design, statistics, and scientific writing—in an integrated approach at the beginning level.

Most students who take research design and statistics in psychology do so to meet a requirement of their major or minor. Many of the students who have taken courses in mathematics are still uncomfortable with math and not confident that they really understand and can do it well. This text does not assume an affinity nor high level of initial math competence in the students. Integration of statistics with research design throughout the text is especially important for students who do not enjoy math. The integration allows them to appreciate the value of statistics as tools to understand interesting human problems. Research design allows them to ask questions that can be answered, and statistics are required to understand the answers. I often tell my students that research design without statistics is like a joke with no punch line. It leaves you hanging, waiting for the conclusion. Statistics without research design are like the punch line without the joke. They are confusing and not even funny. Together, research design and statistics still may not be funny, but they do make sense.

The largest problem facing an instructor of research methods and statistics is the students' initial attitude toward the course. Many students expect to dislike the course. Many are afraid of the statistics and do not perceive of themselves as researchers. The first task of the successful instructor is to motivate students to understand that the skills of research design and statistics are useful in all aspects of their current careers as students and even more so in their future psychology-related jobs. This is why this text begins with an explicit discussion of the values of the science of psychology, which is followed with a substantial chapter on the ethics of psychological research. These topics are less intimidating to beginning students, and they are central to the course content. Covering them first not only emphasizes their importance but also eases the students into the course content.

The second thing the successful instructor must do is move the students from their attitude of persevering through the difficult course to an attitude of mastery and competence. Life is a word problem, and the tools of research design and statistics can be used to solve many problems, both in psychological research and the rest of life. That's why the chapter on the logic of research design includes examples and exercises on step-by-step problem solving. Students should be able to apply their new skills to solve increasingly complex psychological problems.

Many students perceive statistical formulas to be the most difficult part of this course. However, that difficulty is diminished by introducing statistics gradually in their natural research design contexts. It is also diminished by showing students the math but allowing them to do the more tedious (and thus more likely to fail) statistical analyses using computer programs. When statistics are demystified and put into context as tools, much of the difficulty students have learning them is reduced.

In my experience, the most difficult concept for students to learn is that of hypothesis testing. It is introduced in this text about one third of the way in with the most simple but also strongest research design: the posttest only control group design. Hypothesis testing is reinforced and extended with each of the following chapters that focus on more complex designs so that students can practice with the concepts and learn them at a deeper level. Many of the examples of hypothesis testing that I provide come from projects that my students have accomplished over the years. These examples tend to be simple yet relevant to the interests of current students. They also provide models of how the tools of research design and statistics have been successfully employed by students. Throughout the discussions of hypothesis testing, there is a balance between the statistical concepts and the design strengths and limitations. The text focuses on evaluation skills that will aid students in understanding the published research as well as conducting their own research.

The most important changes in the field of psychology that relate to this course are the increasing emphasis on effect size in addition to significance testing, the new ethics code, and the updated APA style manual. This text addresses all three areas by including the new material in each chapter. Thus, the new ethical guidelines serve the basis of the chapter on ethics but also are incorporated through-

out the text. The methods of measuring effect size are introduced with each hypothesis test statistic. The new APA style is featured in each chapter as it relates to the content of that chapter. Another change in the field is the reliance on computer programs for statistical analysis. The text provides examples showing the math (using the simple algebraic form rather than the calculus form). However, exercises and applications may be completed with computer programs, and there is greater emphasis on correct interpretation of the statistics than on their correct calculation.

The language and examples used in this text have been selected to be cross-culturally appropriate. The first time-integrated textbook that I wrote was for use by my Nigerian students. I wrote that slim volume during my Fulbright Lectureship in 1990. Each extension and revision since then has been informed by my understanding of how to communicate to students from diverse backgrounds. Again in 2001 I was able to test how well this plan has worked when I used a greatly expanded version of that text with two South Korean classes as part of another Fulbright Lectureship.

# Online and in Print

*Research Methods/Statistics* is available online as well as in print. The online version demonstrates how the interactive media components of the text enhance presentation and understanding. For example,

- Animated illustrations help to clarify concepts and bring them to life.

- Interactive activities engage you in the learning process and give you hands-on experience in political science.

- Clickable glossary terms provide immediate definitions of key concepts.

- References and footnotes "pop up" with a click.

- Highlighting capabilities allow students to emphasize main ideas. They can also add personal notes in the margin.

- The search function allows students to quickly locate discussions of specific topics throughout the text.

- An interactive study guide at the end of each chapter provides tools for learning, such as interactive key-term matching and the ability to review customized content in one place.

Students may choose to use just the online version of the text, or both the online and print versions together. This gives them the flexibility to choose which combination of resources works best for them. To assist those who use the online and print versions together, the primary heads and subheads in each chapter are numbered the same. For example, the first primary head in Chapter is labeled 1-1, the second primary head in this chapter is labeled 1-2, and so on. The subheads build from the designation of their corresponding primary head: 1-1a, 1-1b, etc. This numbering system is designed to make moving between the online and print versions as seamless as possible.

Finally, next to a number of figures, tables, and boxes in the print version of the text, you will see an icon similar to those below. This icon indicates that this figure, table, or box in the Online Edition is interactive in a way that applies, illustrates, or reinforces the concept.

# About Atomic Dog

Atomic Dog is faithfully dedicated to meeting the needs of today's faculty and students, offering a unique and clear alternative to the traditional textbook. Breaking down textbooks and study tools into their basic "atomic parts," we were able to recombine them and utilize rich digital media to create a "new breed" of textbook.

This blend of online content, interactive multimedia, and print creates unprecedented adaptability to meet different educational settings and individual learning styles. As part of Thomson Custom Solutions (http://www.thomson custom.com), we offer even greater flexibility and resources in creating a learning solution tailor-fit to your course.

Atomic Dog is loyally dedicated to our customers and our environment, adhering to three key tenets:

- **Focus on Essential and Quality Content:** We are proud to work with our authors to deliver you a high-quality textbook at a lower cost. We focus on the essential information and resources students need and present them in an efficient but student-friendly format.

- **Value and Choice for Students:** Our products are a great value and provide students more choices in 'what and how' they buy-often at a savings of 30–

40 percent versus traditional textbooks. Students who choose the online edition may see even greater savings compared to a print textbook. Faculty play an important and willing roll-working with us to keep costs low for their students by evaluating texts online and supplementary material.

- **Reducing Our Environmental 'Paw-Print':** Atomic Dog is working to reduce its impact on our environment in several ways. Our textbooks and marketing materials are printed on recycled paper and we will continue to explore environmentally friendly methods. We encourage faculty to review text materials online instead of requesting a print review copy. Students who buy the online version do their part by going 'paperless' and eliminating the need for additional packaging or shipping. Atomic Dog will continue to explore new ways that we can reduce our 'paw print' in the environment and hope you will join us in these efforts.

Atomic Dog is dedicated to faithfully serving the needs of faculty and students—providing a learning tool that helps make the connection. [We know that after you try our texts Atomic Dog, like a great dog, will become your faithful companion.]

# Organization

| Chapter | Research Design | Statistics | APA Style |
|---|---|---|---|
| 1 | Values: Empiricism, Determinism, Organization, and Curiosity | Frequency Distribution Mean | Sections of a Research Report |
| 2 | Ethical Principles | Graphs | Citing Source APA Reference Style |
| 3 | Hypothetico-Deductive Method | Central Tendencies: Mean, Median, Mode | Literature Review |
| 4 | Dependent Variables Scales of Measurement | Selection of Parametric and Nonparametric Statistics | Method: Participants<br>Method: Materials and/or Apparatus |
| 5 | Independent Variables Within vs. Between | Dispersion: Variance, Standard Deviation, Standard Error of the Mean, $Z$-Scores | Method: Procedure |
| 6 | Control Group Posttest Only Design | Normal Distribution Hypothesis Testing: Student's Independent $t$ test<br>Cohen's $d$ | Results |
| 7 | Pretest Posttest Design Threats to Internal Validity: History, Maturation, Testing | Hypothesis Testing: Related Measures $t$ test<br>Cohen's $d$ for repeated measures | Discussion |
| 8 | One Factor Between Subjects Design | Partitioning the Variance Oneway ANOVA<br>Multiple Comparisons: Tukey HSD | Results: Reporting ANOVA Results |
| 9 | One Factor Repeated Measures Design | Repeated Measures ANOVA<br>Effect Size: Eta Squared | APA Title Page |
| 10 | Between Groups Factorial Designs | Graphing Interactions<br>Two Factors Between Groups ANOVA | APA Style Graphs |
| 11 | Repeated Measures Factorial Designs<br>Multiple Treatment Interference<br>Mixed Factorial Designs | Repeated Measured Factorial ANOVA<br>Mixed Factorial ANOVA<br>Multiple Comparisons | APA Style Tables |
| 12 | Pre-Experimental Designs: Single Subject, Case Studies, Survey Research, One Group Studies | Chi-Square | Reporting Chi-Square Results |
| 13 | Quasi-experimental Designs: Static Group Comparison<br>Threats to Internal Validity: Selection, Mortality, Selection X Maturation | Pearson's Correlation Coefficient<br>Scatter Plots | APA Style for Reporting Correlations |

# Acknowledgements

This book was instigated by my students' desire to have one book that presented research design and statistics together. I thank them for their continued feedback that psychological research methods must include statistical analysis and reporting. Thanks also to Westminster College, which provided me with the resources to develop and test this textbook. My colleagues in the Psychology Department have been a consistent source of encouragement. Most especially, I wish to thank my husband, Ronald G. Webster, who published earlier versions of the book. He also provided a working environment that enabled me to keep on task and meet deadlines. It's very good to be married to excellent tech support. I am indebted to the seven anonymous reviewers who gave me much valuable feedback. Thanks to Elaine Blevins for a thorough edit of the text and her occasional poetry about its content.

# About the Author

Sandra K. Webster is Professor of Psychology and Faculty Development Officer at Westminster College in New Wilmington, Pennsylvania. She has been teaching research methods and statistics since first entering graduate school at Southern Illinois University and volunteering to be a teaching assistant for that course. Her degrees include a Ph.D. in Experimental Social Psychology with a minor in Mathematical Statistics. Before becoming a professor, she had research positions at Masters and Johnson in St. Louis and at Associates for Research in Behavior in Philadelphia. She has taught research design and statistics in Nigeria and South Korea on two Fulbright Lectureships (1989–90, 2000–01). She has had National Science Foundation grants for equipping secondary school teachers to teach psychology as a science, and for developing cluster courses between psychology and computer science. She has been recognized for technology integration in the curriculum with a Joe Wyatt Challenge Award. Dr. Webster's current research program focuses on cross-cultural studies of emotion and coping with prolonged stress. She has been awarded two Westminster College research awards: the Henderson Award in 1998 for research on the relationship between incoming student coping styles and college success and the McCandless Scholar Award in 2004–05 for her cross-cultural research on emotion.

Dr. Webster and her husband Ronald have two grown children. She enjoys designing things in her spare time and has applied the skills of research design and statistics to her hobbies. Two examples that the application really works are her local museum exhibit, Psychocyberceramics, and the Kennedy Center Theatre Festival Certificate of Merit she received for costuming *The Baker of Madrigal,* a new play set in 16th century Spain. She and her husband Ronald keep fit with modern Western square dancing.

# Values in Science

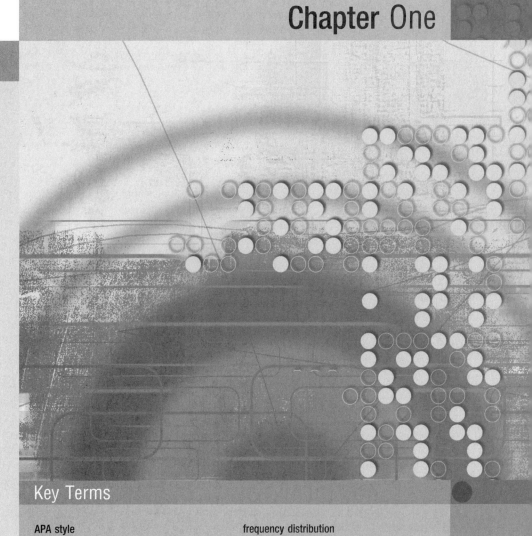

## Chapter One

## Key Terms

| | |
|---|---|
| APA style | frequency distribution |
| curiosity | implicit values |
| determinism | mean |
| empiricism | statistics |
| explicit values | values |

# Learning Objectives

- Be able to define four values of science.
- Be able to explain the role of values in science.
- Describe what differentiates science from art, philosophy, and religion.

- Give examples of the role of determinism in scientific thinking.
- Be able to explain the role of statistics in science.
- Know how to construct a frequency table and how to calculate a mean.

## Key Idea

Research design is the method of organizing empirical data to satisfy scientists' curiosity about the determination of behavior.

# 1-1 Values

**values** Beliefs held by an individual that influence the individual's thoughts, emotions, and overt behaviors.

**explicit values** Values that individuals have consciously developed and accepted as their own.

**implicit values** Values developed over time through socialization that individuals may not consciously recognize as values.

**Values** are beliefs held by individuals that influence the individuals' thoughts, emotions, and overt behaviors. They may be explicit or implicit. **Explicit values** are those that individuals have consciously developed and accepted as their own. **Implicit values** are those developed over time through socialization that the individuals may not consciously recognize as values. These implicit values are often considered to be "self-evident truths," which the individuals think that everyone shares. For example, most Americans hold an implicit value that change is not only good but also necessary. We enjoy proverbs such as "If you're not moving forward, you're moving backward." Our value for change is so deeply held that most individuals won't even recognize its importance until it is challenged. Yet individuals from other cultures hold different values about change. A traditional West African value is for constancy. Change is not desirable. A way of expressing this value from the Idoma ethnic group of Nigeria is "Man dies, and man forever comes back" (Amali, 1985). This expression implies that what was good for the ancestors is good for the living. Although the proverbs exist, individuals often do not know the strength of the values they hold in determining their own behaviors. Values serve to guide individuals in life decisions, including that of lifework (Rokeach, 1973).

It is a common myth, especially among undergraduates, that science and scientists are value free. That is, many students believe that science is carried out in an objective fashion with the values of the scientist playing no part in it. Although scientists strive for objectivity in their research, this, too, is an important value of science. Not only are scientists influenced by their own personal values in terms of the areas they choose to study, the methods of study they choose to employ, and the context in which they interpret and apply their results, but the very nature of science also is influenced by a set of shared values (Kuhn, 1970). Without these specific values, the individuals could not be effective scientists. Neither would they choose to pursue scientific research as their lifework. Four of the values that are shared by scientists and that provide the foundation for science are empiricism, determinism, **curiosity**, and organization.

**curiosity** Characteristic often found in scientists, whereby they want to know what makes things work and why.

# 1-2 Empiricism

**empiricism** The practice of relying on observable facts.

**Empiricism** is the practice of relying on observable facts. Scientists, like other scholars, base much of their work on abstract logic and thinking. They read the work of others and deduce their own conclusions from their reading and abstract analysis. However, *they do not stop at the level of abstract reasoning*. They make their conclusions in the form of hypotheses and theories, which they *test empirically*. That is, through research, they gather observable facts to determine whether the facts fit (or support) the hypotheses. If the facts fit the hypotheses, the scientists will continue to work on revising and extending those hypotheses and perhaps begin to develop a theory. One definition for a theory is a systematic explanation of a phenomenon. However, if the facts observed in the research do not fit the hypotheses, the scientists are likely to revise the hypotheses. The new hypotheses will likewise be tested with empirical research.

The basic difference between a scientific discipline and a nonscientific discipline is the central role of the value of empiricism. Philosophers traditionally depend on abstract logic alone. Scholars in the arts and humanities search for meaning through symbolism and illustration. Science relies on testing ideas against observable facts. Although all three ways of understanding are important, science is based on empiricism as a method of validating abstract logic and intuitive reactions.

An illustration of the importance of empiricism in determining a lifework was presented by Jean Piaget, as he described his early career and his decision to empirically study cognitive development:

> But from these diverse interests resulted a crisis which modified my career. On the one hand, the company of philosophers, whilst exercising its well known attractions upon me, led to a sort of misgiving; whatever his integrity, a philosopher is by training led to talk about everything and when he enters into the discussion of special questions or ones which cannot even be decided, his knowledge of texts is often enough to allay his scruples by taking precedence over his knowledge of the facts. On the other hand, I discovered in myself an undeniable leaning towards speculation, and quickly understood that my biological epistemology would be a philosophy like any other, if I confined myself, on the one hand, to pursuing my zoological research, and during my leisure hours to "reflecting" on general questions. I thus came to consider as a kind of intellectual dishonesty any of my works which were not submitted to the proof of the two methods of verification which seemed to me at that time the only valid ones: either factual verification, subordinated to a personal experimentation and not consisting merely of thinking about someone else's work, or deductive proof, subordinated to precise algorithms like those used in mathematics or in symbolic logic. (Beth and Piaget, 1966, p. 131)

As Piaget pointed out, there is a double method of verification: empiricism and logic. Thus, scientists do not deny the importance of philosophy (especially logic) as a way of knowing. Indeed, the preceding quote is taken from a collaboration that Piaget spent 10 years working on with the philosopher E. W. Beth. Furthermore, scientists do not necessarily argue that empiricism is the only way to know. They can, and do, appreciate the ways of knowing used in the humanities and arts. But, as Piaget, they subject their own work to the test of empiricism.

# 1-3 Determinism

**Determinism** is the value that every effect has a cause. Without this value, the scientific endeavor would be hopeless because the alternative to determinism is confusion. Among scientists there is a full range of types of attitudes about determinism. Some believe in evolutionary determinism. Others believe in Divine determinism (i.e., that God is in control of everything). Within psychology, you can see two extremes of determinism by comparing the radical behaviorist with the individual differences viewpoint. The radical behaviorists (Watson, 1913; Skinner, 1978) argue that behavior (human and other organisms) is determined by an individual's past reinforcement history.

**determinism** The value that every effect has a cause.

> [A] person's behavior is determined by a genetic endowment traceable to the evolutionary history of the species and by the environmental circumstances to which as an individual he has been exposed. (Skinner, 1971, p. 96)

Thus, the individual has no free will but will behave according to past conditioning. In contrast, the individual differences viewpoint is that an individual determines behavior through rational decision making and personality.

> The *reason* for a present act of conduct is to be sought in the present desires and intentions of the individual (though these in turn may arise from deep-lying personal traits and interests); but the *style of execution* is always guided directly and without interference by deep and lasting personality dispositions. (Allport, 1937, p. 466)

Again, behavior can be predicted and understood, but in this case that understanding is based on knowing how rational beings choose to use their own free will (desires and intentions). Although these two viewpoints are opposite in terms of the role of the individual in determining behavior, they agree on the fact that behavior is determined.

The basic goal of science is to understand the nature and processes of the physical universe. For psychologists, this means behavior including thoughts, emotions, motivations, as well as actions. Psychologists seek causes and effects to aid in this understanding. Therefore, one value psychologists share is their belief that behaviors are determined by discernable causes.

# 1-4 Curiosity

Not only do scientists believe that effects have causes, they also want to find them. Scientists are characterized by their curiosity. They want to know what makes things work and why. Within psychology, they want to know why individuals and groups act and think the way they do. Kuhn (1970) described normal science as puzzle solving. Science offers many puzzles in the form of unanswered questions. Scientists do not like leaving a question unanswered even though they know that answering one question will probably lead to even more unanswered questions. Instead of dreading more unanswered questions, scientists relish them as new puzzles to be solved and, more importantly, as new opportunities to seek understanding in an area of study. In my own view, wisdom is not knowing all the answers, but rather it lies in knowing what are some of the questions.

Fritz Heider (1986) described his life as a psychologist in his autobiography. In its closing chapter, he discussed retirement. From his perspective, he did not really retire although he stopped teaching students. He continued the most important part of his lifework with less interruption than before. He was able to satisfy his curiosity by attempting to solve psychological puzzles:

> The activities that have meant the most to me were centered on puzzling out problems in the theory of psychology, and most often they have consisted in attempts to bring greater clarity into the seeming confusion of commonsense notions. (p. 187)

# 1-5 Organization

Scientists are characterized by their value for organization. Bronowski (1965) gave the following definition for science:

> I define science as the organization of our knowledge in such a way that it commands more of the hidden potential in nature. (p. 7)

Scientists employ methods that are precise and meticulous in their organization. Often the individual scientist may tolerate lack of organization in other aspects of life, but within his or her research, there is organized action. The methods describing science have been developed to be both precise and concise. Precise means that the descriptions are accurate. On the other hand, concise means that the descriptions are brief. Usually, for the descriptions to be both precise and concise, scientists must resort to their own special language and to quantification, which allows precise and concise description of the empirical facts they rely on to test ideas. Nonscientists often refer to the language as *jargon,* and scientists refer to it as *technical terminology.* The quantifications used are *statistics.* Being both precise and concise allows for efficient organization.

## 1-5a APA Style

Psychologists and many other behavioral scientists demonstrate their values of organization through the use of the **APA style**. This style is described fully in the *Publication Manual of the American Psychological Association* (APA, 2001). Manuscripts that are to be published in most forms must be submitted in the format described by the APA style. Instructors also extensively require students to use APA style in research reports. Therefore, you will find explanations of APA style throughout this text.

**APA style** Specific format for manuscripts submitted to the American Psychological Association for publication.

Reports of experiments are precisely organized. Understanding the organization allows readers to quickly assimilate and interpret the information in the reports. The sections of a report are as follows:

- Abstract—Brief summary of the research described in the report.
- Introduction—Clear thesis statement, review of previous research on the topic, and hypotheses of this research.
- Method—Description of the design, participants, materials and/or apparatus, and the exact procedures used in the research.
- Results—Summary of the statistical tests of the hypotheses.
- Discussion—Nonstatistical description of the results, integration of the findings with previous research, conclusions, and suggestions for future research.
- References—A complete list of all sources referred to in the report.

## 1-5b The Abstract

Each of these sections will be described individually in the one of the chapters of this text. This chapter will begin with the abstract. The abstract of an article is a particularly good example of the scientists' value for organization and writing that is both precise and concise. The exact maximum length of an abstract is different for different journals, but all abstracts are short. The *Publication Manual of the American Psychological Association* (APA, 2001) states that an abstract should be 120 words or fewer. It should still be specific enough that a reader will know everything needed to determine whether reading the entire article will be of value for his or her specific purpose. This means that you, as a reader, can tell from a short paragraph whether a particular article is useful to you at this specific time. If the abstract does not relate to your project, then the article is almost definitely not relevant either. Careful reading of abstracts can save a lot of time. On the other hand, writing a precise and concise abstract is very difficult. It should be written last and concisely convey the specific problem, methods, results, and interpretation of the study.

The value of conciseness means that reports of experiments do not end with summaries. The summary is the abstract. It comes first. One of the rules of article writing, especially in the results section, is that you don't say anything twice. The exception is that the first part of the discussion section does repeat, in different words without statistical jargon, the major findings (i.e., results) of the study. This repetition helps students who may not understand all the statistical jargon to be confident that they understood the main points of the results. In fact, it helps a lot of psychologists and other behavioral scientists too.

Some students have told me that the prescribed format and organization of the research report inhibits their creativity. They think that having all reports in the same format is dry and boring. The format and organization are designed to be efficient. However, efficiency does not preclude creativity. Consider a coffee mug. Particular features of a coffee mug are prescribed by its function. It must hold hot fluid, be easy to drink from, be of sufficient capacity that there is enough coffee to satisfy the drinker, but not so much that the coffee cools before it is consumed. Therefore, all coffee mugs are alike. But they are also different. A tremendous amount of creativity still goes into designing and producing a functional coffee mug. The same is true with a good research report. The specific content and the way the hypotheses are formed, tested, and reported are all opportunities for creativity. Creativity is not a main goal of scientific research, but it is considered a necessary element of successful research.

## 1-6 The Use of Statistics in Science

**statistics** Tools for understanding data.

The use of **statistics** in behavioral research is related to each of the four major values discussed thus far. Statistics are tools for understanding data. It is possible to be scientific without using numbers, but it is not desirable. Remember that science is empirical. Many facts are observed, recorded, and analyzed. But science also is organized. It is very difficult to organize facts without putting them into like categories and counting them. For example, if you want to scientifically address the question "How many people fear math?" statistics will be very helpful. A simple statistical approach would be to categorize types of fears and determine which people have which fears. When the members in categories are counted, analysis will include quantitative comparisons between categories. (For example, do more people fear math than fear riding in an airplane? How many more? What is the ratio? Are more than twice as many people afraid of math than are afraid of riding in an airplane?)

A precise organization of the facts is very desirable in science. Therefore, the more precise the numbers used to describe the data, the better, up to a point. (See Chapter 4, "Operational Definitions of Dependent Variables and Scales of Measurement.") If you can measure the amount of fear to a particular stimulus, this is better than simply knowing that it causes fear. Science also strives to be concise. After facts have been coded as numbers, it is easy to describe all the facts very accurately using statistics. These statistics are called descriptive statistics. Inferential statistics are another type of statistics also essential to science. After the facts have been statistically described, the scientist is ready to make an inference about his or her hypothesis based on those statistics. To know how likely this inference is to be wrong, inferential statistics are calculated. (The major inferential statistics used in psychology are covered beginning in Chapter 6, "Hypothesis Testing: The Control Group Posttest Only Design.")

## 1-7 Using Statistics to Describe Facts: Frequency Distributions

Scientists use many different statistical tools to understand and explain behavior. Two of the basic tools for describing data are described in this section. Other common statistical tools used in psychological research are presented throughout the text.

| TABLE 1-1 | Things People Are Afraid Of | | | |
|---|---|---|---|---|
| **Amy** | **Jen** | **Juan** | **Rob** | **Nate** |
| dogs | death | dying | sharp things | graduation |
| snakes | spiders | spiders | falling | love |
| falling | snakes | | the dark | death |
| the dark | drowning | | death | |
| **Wong** | **Phillip** | **Latrice** | **Kim** | **Heather** |
| horses | dogs | snakes | public speaking | failure |
| dogs | death | bugs | falling | death |
| | | sharks | death | the dark |
| | | attack | | |

Imagine that a student researcher decided to test my son's hypothesis (see Take a Closer Look 1-1) by asking his friends to make a list of all the things they are afraid of. These lists are shown in Table 1-1. To quantify these lists, the student first categorized them into types and then counted the number of entries in each type. These counts are presented in Table 1-2. A count is also called a *frequency*. Table 1-2 shows the **frequency distribution** for each category of fears. In this imaginary survey, animal fears were most frequently mentioned (11 mentions). However, more people mentioned some fear of death (7 out of 10) than mentioned fear of animals (6 out of 10).

The student researcher also counted the total number of items listed by each person. This counting is shown in Table 1-3. One way to summarize the data in a descriptive manner is to make a frequency table of the number of items mentioned. You create the frequency table by counting each of the numbers. To make a frequency distribution, first set up a table as shown in Table 1-4. Then count the

**frequency distribution** A table showing the number of entries for each type, or category, of data.

## Taking a Closer Look 1-1 — *An Example of Scientific Thinking*

Scientists are not the only ones who use scientific thinking. One day while riding in the car, my 5-year-old son asked me what I was afraid of. After thinking about the question, I answered that I was afraid of something bad happening to my little boy. He went on to ask his father and his sister the same question. Then we asked him why he wanted to know. His friend at school had told him that everyone was afraid of something. My son was testing this "hypothesis" empirically by conducting his own survey. As a psychologist, I was proud that he chose an empirical approach. In addition, he attempted to make his "survey" more valid by asking the question in such a way that it did not reveal his hypothesis. As a child, he demonstrated two of the values central to the conduct of science: curiosity and empiricism.

His interest did not, at that time, extend to the other two values described in this chapter: determinism and organization. He did not ask the question "Why are people afraid?" Another way of asking the same question

is, "What factor determines (or causes) fear?" This question is one that has been dealt with by many psychologists. Some would look for causes in the environment (e.g., Little Albert and his conditioned fear of white, furry things; Watson and Rayner, 1920). Others would look for personality or intrapsychic causes (e.g., Freud's theory of defense mechanisms, 1946).

A scientist endeavoring to test the hypothesis that everyone is afraid of something would have used a more organized approach than did my son. First, the scientist would have developed and pretested the questions. Next, he or she would have carefully selected a sample of respondents to represent the population. Then the scientist would have collected data by asking the questions in exactly the same manner to each respondent. Answers to the questions would have been recorded. They would have been coded into categories, quantified, and analyzed. The scientist would also have presented conclusions drawn from these analyses in an organized form, generally a written report.

**TABLE 1-2**     Frequency for Categories of Fears

| Category | Frequency of Mention | | | | Total Mentions |
|---|---|---|---|---|---|
| | **0** | **1** | **2** | **3** | |
| Animals | 4 | 2 | 3 | 1 | 11 |
| Death | 3 | 7 | 0 | 0 | 7 |
| Falling | 7 | 3 | 0 | 0 | 3 |
| The dark | 7 | 3 | 0 | 0 | 3 |
| Other | 5 | 5 | 1 | 0 | 7 |

**TABLE 1-3**     Number of Fear-Inducing Items Mentioned by Each Person

| | |
|---|---|
| Amy | 4 |
| Jen | 4 |
| Juan | 2 |
| Rob | 4 |
| Nate | 3 |
| Wong | 2 |
| Phillip | 2 |
| Latrice | 4 |
| Kim | 3 |
| Heather | 3 |

**TABLE 1-4**     Frequency Distribution of the Number of Fear-Inducing Items Mentioned

| Number of Mentioned | Frequency |
|---|---|
| 0 | |
| 1 | |
| 2 | |
| 3 | |
| 4 | |

number of respondents who mentioned zero fears. There were none. Write a zero in the column under "Frequency" on the row of 0 mentions. Next, count the number of respondents mentioning 1 fear. Again there were none, so a zero also goes in the frequency column on the row for 1 mention. Count the number of respondents who mentioned 2 fears. There were 3. This number goes in the frequency column on the row for 2 mentions. Continue counting for each of the numbers of mentions. The completed frequency distribution is shown in Table 1-5. You can see that 3 people mentioned 2 fears, 3 people mentioned 3 fears, and 4 people mentioned 4 fears. The sum of the frequencies always adds up to the total number of respondents. (In this example that sum, 0 + 0 + 3 + 3 + 4, equals 10 people.) This number is usually referred to as $n$.

| TABLE 1-5 | Frequency Distribution of the Number of Fear-Inducing Items Mentioned | |
|---|---|---|
| **Number of Mentioned** | | **Frequency** |
| 0 | | 0 |
| 1 | | 0 |
| 2 | | 3 |
| 3 | | 3 |
| 4 | | 4 |

# 1-8 Using Statistics to Describe Facts: The Mean

A frequency distribution summarizes the facts in a very convenient form. However, for comparative purposes, frequency distributions are very limited. It would not be easy to compare the frequencies of fears from the student researcher's sample to those of a different set of classmates. Furthermore, frequency distributions become cumbersome when the number of different scores possible is large. If you took a 10-point quiz and wanted to know how the class as a whole performed, a frequency table could be very informative. However, such a method of presentation is still very confusing with many possible scores, say with a 100-point final exam or with a 1600-point college entrance exam. Therefore, the average of the scores is used to describe them. The average is referred to as the **mean** ($\overline{X}$). Two other measures of the center of a set of data (median and mode) will be presented in Chapter 3, "The Hypothetico-Deductive Method and Experiments in Psychology." The mean is the most often used descriptive statistic in psychology.

**mean** Average of a set of data.

The formula for the mean is as follows:

$$\overline{X} = \frac{\sum_{i=1}^{n} X_i}{n}$$

Where

$\overline{X}$      is the mean.

$\sum_{i=1}^{n} X_i$      is the sum of all the scores from the first ($X_1$) to the last ($X_n$).

$n$      is the number of scores.

Figure 1-1 shows how to calculate the mean from the raw scores.

Although you probably already know how to calculate an average, it is a good idea to study the formula and example shown in Figure 1-1 because the terminology introduced will be used throughout this book for more advanced statistical techniques.

# 1-9 Using a Calculator

While you are learning to do statistics, it is essential to use and be comfortable with a calculator. You can get by without a calculator for the first few chapters of this book.

| Step 1. | Write the formula. |
|---|---|

$$\bar{X} = \frac{\sum_{i=1}^{n} X_i}{n}$$

| Step 2. | Find the parts (data from Table 1-3). |
|---|---|

$$\sum_{i=1}^{n} X_{i_i} = \sum_{i=1}^{10} X_i = 4+4+2+4+3+2+2+4+3+3 = 31$$
$$n = 10$$

| Step 3. | Substitute quantities (Step 2) into the formula (Step 1). |
|---|---|

$$\bar{X} = \frac{31}{10}$$

| Step 4. | Calculate. |
|---|---|

$$\bar{X} = \frac{31}{10} = 3.1 \text{ mentions.}$$

| Step 5. | Evaluate. |
|---|---|

Ask yourself, does this number make sense?
Check for errors.

**Figure 1-1**
*Example of Calculating the Mean from Raw Scores*

By Chapter 3, "The Hypothetico-Deductive Method and Experiments in Psychology," however, most statistics will require the computation of square roots. If you can speedily calculate them by hand, bravo! Nevertheless, the speediest hand calculation cannot compete with the one-button ease of a scientific calculator. The square root button is a necessity. Other statistical functions may be desirable as well. Those functions include special keys for the summation of a set of numbers and the summation of the squares of a set of numbers. Scientific calculators often have buttons that automatically calculate the mean, $n$ (count of the numbers), and standard deviation (described in Chapter 4, "Operational Definitions of Dependent Variables and Scales of Measurement") of that set of data. The exact form of the buttons is different on different calculators; therefore, you'll need to read the instruction manual to learn how to produce the statistics you want.

It is very important to understand statistics, their uses, and their limitations as you think about research done by others and by yourself. To understand statistics at a very basic level, most people need to calculate them with a pencil and calculator first. In reality, researchers do calculations by computer most of the time. The computer is faster and more accurate for calculations. Understanding which statistics are appropriate and what they mean is the researcher's job. The descriptive statistics that are most frequently used are built-in functions on most data-handling software (e.g., spreadsheets, databases). However, the inferential statistics used are usually computed with canned statistical programs. That means specific software that has been developed for use with most research designs. Students can study these examples along with the hand-calculated ones.

You should be proficient doing statistics with both a calculator and computer. The former is like a pocketknife—very handy for small jobs. The latter is like a power saw, essential when you have a big job. You should learn to use both tools so that you can choose the one that fits your needs.

# Summary

Research design is directly based on the four values discussed in this chapter. Research design is the method of organizing empirical data to satisfy scientists' curiosity about the determination of behavior.

Statistics are the tools that scientists use to understand the data they collect. Designs are the questions, and statistics provide the answers. Two basic statistical tools are the frequency distribution and the mean. The remainder of this book focuses on the designs and statistics most commonly used in the behavioral sciences.

## References

Allport, G. W. (1937). *Personality: A psychological interpretation*. London: Constable.

Amali, S. O. O. (1985). *An ancient Nigerian drama*. Stuttgart: Verlag Weisbaden GMBH.

American Psychological Association (2001). *Publication manual of the American Psychological Association*. Washington, DC: Author.

Beth, E. W. & Piaget, J. (1966). *Mathematical epistemology and psychology*. New York: Gordon and Breach.

Bronowski, J. (1965). *Science and human values*. New York: Harper and Rowe.

Freud, A. (1946). *The ego and the mechanisms of defense*. New York: International Universities Press.

Heider, F. (1986). *The life of a psychologist: An autobiography*. Lawrence, KS: University Press of Kansas.

Kuhn, T. S. (1970). *The structure of scientific revolutions, Second edition, enlarged*. Chicago: University of Chicago Press.

Rokeach, M. (1973). *The nature of human values*. New York: Free Press.

Skinner, B. F. (1971). *Beyond freedom and dignity*. New York: Alfred A. Knopf.

Skinner, B. F. (1978). *Reflections on behaviorism and society*. Englewood Cliffs, NJ: Prentice-Hall.

Watson, J. B. (1913). Psychology as the behaviorist views it. *Psychological Review*, 20, 158–177.

Watson, J. B. & Rayner, R. (1920). Conditioned emotional responses. *Journal of Experimental Psychology*, 3, 1–14.

## Exercises for Application

1. Think about how your own values fit with the values of science. What importance do you place in empiricism, determinism, curiosity, and organization? How do your own values about these four areas affect your own day-to-day living? Give concrete examples.

2. Read a research report in a journal. What values can you see in the research described in the report? Are the values of the scientists clear to you? Why did the researchers choose to study the behavior they did? Why did they choose to use the scientific method to study that behavior? Why did they choose their particular methods of study? How do you think the scientists' values influenced the conclusions they drew from their data?

3. Evaluate the values presented in a research report in the popular media (newspaper, magazine, radio, Internet site, or television). How are the values of the scientists portrayed? Can you also detect any values of the reporters?

4. The following data represent the quiz scores for this chapter for one class. Make a frequency distribution and calculate the mean for the quiz.

| Quiz 1 | Quiz 2 |
|--------|--------|
| 10 | 9 |
| 8 | 7 |
| 9 | 8 |
| 10 | 7 |
| 8 | 7 |
| 9 | 9 |
| 10 | 10 |
| 8 | 10 |
| 10 | 8 |
| 10 | 10 |

5. Following are the numbers and types of dreams recalled in one week by a sample of college freshmen during their first week at college. Make a frequency

distribution for each type of dream and the total number of dreams reported. Calculate the mean for the total number of dreams reported.

| Student | Happy Dream | Neutral Dream | Sad Dream | Nightmare |
|---|---|---|---|---|
| Amy | 4 | 2 | 2 | 0 |
| Bob | 1 | 3 | 3 | 0 |
| Kim Soo | 3 | 2 | 0 | 0 |
| Deb | 1 | 0 | 1 | 0 |
| Ernie | 4 | 0 | 0 | 1 |
| Damaris | 3 | 2 | 2 | 0 |
| George | 2 | 0 | 3 | 1 |
| Helen | 1 | 2 | 3 | 4 |
| Ojiji | 3 | 0 | 2 | 2 |
| Jack | 1 | 1 | 1 | 3 |
| Kang | 1 | 0 | 0 | 1 |
| Laura | 4 | 2 | 0 | 0 |
| Juanita | 2 | 2 | 3 | 0 |
| Nate | 3 | 4 | 2 | 0 |
| Oscar | 1 | 1 | 1 | 1 |
| Patty | 3 | 2 | 2 | 2 |
| Quinn | 0 | 0 | 4 | 2 |
| Keilon | 1 | 2 | 3 | 4 |
| Sally | 4 | 0 | 1 | 0 |
| Theo | 6 | 0 | 0 | 0 |

# Practice Quiz

*Note:* You can find the correct answers to these questions by taking the quiz and then submitting your answers in the Online Edition. The program will automatically score your submission. If you miss a question, the program will provide the correct answer, a rationale for the answer, and the section number in the chapter where the topic is discussed.

1. Research design is the method of organizing empirical data to satisfy scientists' curiosity about the _____ of behavior.

   a. mysteries
   b. value
   c. determination
   d. study

2. A belief that has been consciously accepted and that influences thought, feeling, and action is a(n)

   a. implicit value.
   b. explicit value.
   c. attitude.
   d. opinion.

3. The double method of verification that Piaget referred to uses both _____ and logic.

   a. determinism
   b. rationalization
   c. empiricism
   d. statistics

4. Piaget decided to become an experimental scientist because

   a. he found abstract logic too difficult.
   b. his interest in zoology was so great.
   c. he needed to verify his reflections.
   d. he failed in philosophy.

5. Skinner believed that behavior was _____ by evolutionary history and by environmental circumstances.

   a. unaffected
   b. classically conditioned
   c. determined
   d. organized

6. For Fritz Heider, the most exciting aspect of the scientific study of psychology was

   a. puzzling out problems.
   b. applying research results to solve real-world problems.
   c. doing statistical analyses well.
   d. the elegance of good research design.

7. Scientific jargon is often used in an attempt to be

   a. objective.
   b. obscure.
   c. superior.
   d. precise and concise.

8. A simple count of the number of times each score is present in a set of data is the

   a. mean.
   b. median.
   c. frequency distribution.
   d. average.

9. In statistics, the letter $\overline{X}$ usually refers to

   a. the total of all the scores.
   b. the total number of observations.
   c. the average of all the observations.
   d. a single raw score.

10. Which statistic tells you the most about the data set in the fewest numbers?

   a. the set of raw scores
   b. the mean
   c. the frequency distribution
   d. a graph of the frequency distribution

11. The basic difference between a scientific discipline and a nonscientific one is the role of

   a. organization.
   b. curiosity.
   c. empiricism.
   d. values.

12. In an APA style paper, a brief summary of the research report is included in the

   a. abstract.
   b. introduction.
   c. methods.
   d. end of the paper.

13. Psychologists use statistics in order to

   a. prove their points.
   b. understand their data.
   c. confuse other people.
   d. appear more scientific than they are.

14. The statistics that are used to describe the data concisely are called

   a. empirical statistics.
   b. deductive statistics.
   c. inferential statistics.
   d. descriptive statistics.

15. The total number of scores described in a set of data is usually referred to as

   a. the count.
   b. the mean.
   c. the frequency.
   d. $n$.

16. Why is a calculator like a pocket knife?

   a. It is easy to carry in your pocket.
   b. It is very handy for small jobs.
   c. It was designed for one very specific purpose.
   d. It functions well even though it doesn't look very good.

# Ethical Principles for Psychological Research

## Chapter Two

## Key Terms

APA Ethical Principles
APA reference style
authorship
bar graph
citing sources
confederate
confidentiality
data falsification
debriefing
deception
demand characteristics
deprivation
ethics
frequency histogram

full citation
informed consent
Institutional Review Boards (IRBs)
line graph
minimal risk
peer reviewers
pie chart
pilot study
plagiarism
risk
risk/benefit ratio
terminate
unobtrusive research

# Learning Objectives

- Explain why ethics are important in psychological research.
- Know how to evaluate research in terms of the ethical principles.

- Describe four key principles in dealing ethically with human participants.
- Compare the ethical principles of dealing with human participants to those dealing with other animal subjects.

## Key Idea

**ethics** Principles of right action.

Experiments should meet the goals of describing and explaining behavior while treating the research participants (human or animal) with dignity and respect.

The term **ethics** refers to principles of right action. Ethical conduct of research is not an afterthought of research. Rather, ethical considerations should come first and foremost. Therefore, the ethics of research design are presented here before research design is presented in the remainder of the text.

## 2-1 General Guidelines

The suggestions presented here are based on application of the Ethical Standards for the Conduct of Research of the American Psychological Association (2002) and my experience supervising hundreds of undergraduate research projects. I offer them in the hope that they may aid students in conducting good, and ethical, research while avoiding many practical pitfalls. Please note that these principles have been developed and adopted in the United States. Students in other countries should consult with their professors to determine the appropriate ethical guidelines. Although the general principles that research participants are to be treated with respect and dignity are the same across different countries, specific implementation of those principles may differ.

All psychology experiments conducted at the beginning level should have the goal of providing students with educational benefit while treating the participants in the research (human or nonhuman) with dignity and respect. Because the major goal of the research is educational, only projects that pose no or minimal risk to participants are suggested.

**risk** The negative outcome(s) that might occur to a research subject or participant as a result of study participation.

**Risk** is an important concept in planning ethical research methods and evaluating the ethical conduct of published research. Researchers attempt to design research that minimizes the physical, emotional, and social risks involved to the research subjects. Much research has no obvious risks of participation. It is still the researchers' responsibility to carefully evaluate the potential risks to participants for all research before, during, and after data collection. An example of a no-risk experiment would be a study using anonymous student evaluations of a hypothetical description of a teacher based on the teacher's gender. **Minimal risk** research involves temporary physical discomfort, emotional stress, or social pressures. For example, participants may experience a negative physical state (a loud noise) that could produce a startle response and then mild embarrassment that the experimenter had observed the response. Frustration at being unable to perform well on an experimental task is a mild risk for many research participants. The temporary physical, emotional, and social risks should be resolved before participants complete participation. Risks are not the same for all participants. Shy participants could perceive a social risk if experimenters require that they perform any behaviors in front of observers. Researchers should evaluate the potential risks for all likely participants.

**minimal risk** The temporary physical discomfort, emotional stress, or social pressures experienced by research participants.

As research is designed, it is the researcher's responsibility to create the minimum possible risk to participants. The researcher weighs the potential benefits of the research against the potential risks of study participation. This weighing of benefits to risks is often referred to as the **risk/benefit ratio**. If the benefits do not outweigh the risks, then the study should be redesigned. The researcher is not the best person to evaluate the risk/benefit ratio for research he or she has designed. For that reason the ethics of research projects are reviewed by other researchers (peer review) and in many cases by **Institutional Review Boards (IRBs)**.

It is the responsibility of both the student and the faculty advisor to carefully evaluate the ethical acceptability of the research proposed before it is undertaken. They should continue to evaluate the welfare of participants throughout the data collection stage of the research because sometimes stress or risk to participants cannot be anticipated before the experiment is conducted. In such cases, the experiment should be stopped at the first signs of risk to participants.

According to the **APA Ethical Principles** (2002), researchers must obey the law. However the ethics code goes far beyond the law. It is not a set of legal principles, but rather a set of ethical principles that mandate avoiding harm while actively benefiting psychological clients, research subjects, and society in general. The specific features of the Ethical Principles that apply to research design will be addressed in sections 2-2 through 2-6.

## 2-2 Human Participants

The ethical goal of all psychological research should be to minimize participant risk and maximize the benefits of the research for participants and society. The specific principles are different for research involving human participant and nonhuman subjects. Sections 2-2a through 2-2f cover issues of informing human participants of the risks, their rights to confidentiality, deception in research, and special ethical concerns for research involving children.

### 2-2a Minimal Risk to Participants

Research projects should be designed to minimize the risks for all participants. The student researcher must consider the potential physical, emotional, and social risks from the viewpoint of the participants. It is always advisable to get a second opinion regarding the potential risks of what may seem to the researcher innocuous procedures. Furthermore, each college or university will have its own policy covering ethical review of research. The student researcher should carefully consider ways to minimize risks to participants before the project is proposed. Others (an instructor and possibly **peer reviewers** or an IRB) should then perform an ethical review of the proposal. Ethical reviews are safeguards, but they do not remove the responsibility of ethical conduct of research from the experimenters.

The following data collection methods usually involve risks to participants; therefore, student researchers should avoid them:

- Any research that involves the ingestion of any psychoactive substance (e.g., alcohol, nicotine, and other drugs).

- Research that involves pain or the threat of pain to the participant (e.g., electric shock or the threat of electric shock is inappropriate).

- Research that involves personality testing except in those cases in which personality profiles will not be interpreted to the participants and the personality profiles are truly anonymous. (Personality assessment is a complex skill that requires advanced training. Correct or incorrect interpretations could be very damaging to participants.)

**risk/benefit ratio** The weighing of benefits to risks in a research study.

**Institutional Review Boards (IRBs)** The formal review panels convened by a college, university, or other research supporting institution to review the ethical aspects of proposed research sponsored by the institution and/or conducted at it.

**APA ethical principles** A set of ethical principles published by the American Psychological Association that mandate avoiding harm while actively benefiting psychological clients, research subjects, and society in general.

**peer reviewers** Colleagues who review a researcher's study for potential risks of participation.

- Research that involves a special population such as the mentally ill or mentally disabled. These individuals cannot legally give their consent. They should be participants in research only if they will benefit from participation. Trained clinical staff should supervise all research with special clinical populations.

## 2-2b Informed Consent

**informed consent** The approval received after potential participants are given a clear and accurate description of the time and tasks required by participation before they decide to become involved in the research.

In most research, human participants should be given the opportunity for **informed consent**. To receive informed consent, researchers give potential participants a clear and accurate description of the time and tasks required by participation before they decide to become involved in the research. The two exceptions for informed consent are naturalistic observation that does not involve invasion of privacy nor compromise the participants' confidentiality, and anonymous surveys. For all other research, participants should know that they are participating in an experiment. They should also be informed that it is their right to withdraw from the experiment at any time without penalty. (Keeping this policy will remove risks associated with invasion of privacy and coercion of participants.)

Taking a Closer Look 2-1 contains a sample of an informed consent form that I used for one of my experiments. Notice that it states the purpose of the experiment in very broad terms. It is not necessary or desirable for participants to know the specific hypothesis to be tested. In this case, the hypothesis involved which side of the brain was processing music and the fact that the maze is a spatial task. In some experiments, exact knowledge of the hypothesis could bias participants' responses in the experiment. This is undesirable. For example, in a study of conformity, participants are not likely to conform if they are first told that the study concerns conformity. In the example on the effects of the side of the brain used to process music, even a knowledge of the specific hypothesis is unlikely to cause participants to act in a way that is in favor or against the hypothesis because they don't know enough about it to do so. Imagine trying to increase your right hemispheric activity in order to solve the maze faster. You couldn't will yourself to do it. However, such knowledge could distract you from the instructions and the main task of the experiment. Participants do not need to know the hypothesis to give informed consent. However, they do need to have a general idea of what they will be expected to do. In this example, their task was to perform a pencil maze blindfolded while listening to music.

The most important thing you usually take from your participants is their time. It is important to tell participants an accurate estimation of the time required for the experiment. In the sample experiment, I could not accurately predict how long each participant would take to solve the maze. Some people may never be able to solve

---

### Taking a Closer Look 2-1    *Sample Informed Consent Form*

This research is concerned with the effects of music on maze learning. You will be asked to learn to successfully complete a pencil maze while blindfolded. In some conditions you may be asked to listen to music while you learn the maze. After you finish the maze, you will be asked some additional questions. The entire experiment should take just over 30 minutes. All the information you provide in this experiment will be kept in strictest confidence. Your name will not be attached to the data that you provide.

There are no obvious risks involved in study participation. You are free to withdraw from the experiment at any time without penalty.

I hereby indicate that I am informed of the nature of this research and consent to the use of the results by the researchers.

Print name _____  Signed _____

Date _____

such a task. Therefore, participants who did not complete the maze in 30 minutes were stopped. There were several such participants. Their data were included in the data analysis with 30 minutes as the time required to complete the maze. When you are doing an experiment for the first time, unless you are using timed tasks, you do not know how long the tasks will take. To find the time, you must pilot test the tasks.

A **pilot study** involves conducting the experiment (or specific parts of it) to see how well the procedures work. A pilot study will help you determine whether the instructions are clear, whether particular aspects of the situation will interfere with data collection, and how long each portion of the procedure will take. The data that you collect in a pilot study are not used to test your hypothesis. The purpose of a pilot study is to assure you that the data can be accurately measured with the methods you have designed. After you have received approval from your instructor, you can begin pilot testing. To pilot your tasks, you will need several of your friends who will not be participants in the experiment. It is often a good idea to have your classmates pilot test the tasks because they have enough knowledge of what you are trying to do to give you a good critique. However, psychology majors and upper class students (juniors and seniors) will complete tasks faster, on average, than will beginning freshmen. You should also pilot test your tasks with members of the specific population from which you will obtain the participants for your experiment. If you plan to have adolescents be the participants for the experiment, pilot test the experimental tasks with adolescents and so forth.

My sample experiment involved very few risks of study participation. Nevertheless, you need to carefully consider all possible risks. Some people may have a fear of the dark or a tremendous dislike for mazes. The risk in terms of anxiety may be greater for these people. They may choose to decline participation. Do not assume that, because you would not find the study to involve any risks, there are no risks. Your instructor can also provide an ethical review of your procedures. If your friends are willing to think deeply about the potential risks of participation in your study, then they may be able to act as peer reviewers for your research project. Finally, most colleges and universities have ethical Institutional Review Boards (IRBs) that regularly review proposed research. In all events, the ethical review should come before the research is conducted.

Participants have the right to withdraw from an experiment at any time they choose, without penalty. But they may not be aware of this right if you, the experimenter, don't tell them. An example comes from the Stanford Prison Experiment (Zimbardo, 1972). Zimbardo set up a fake prison in the basement of the Psychology building on Stanford's campus. Young men were randomly assigned to role-play either prisoners or prison guards for a 2-week long experiment. Those assigned to be prisoners were under so much stress that they planned an attempt to break out of the "prison." Some even asked for outside assistance. (A priest did come.) But no one said, "As a participant of this experiment, I have the right to stop participation without penalty." No one quit the experiment although the researchers withdrew participants from the study because of their "emotional" breakdowns. In fact, the proposed 2-week experiment was stopped after only 6 days because the stress to the participants was so much greater than anticipated. One main point of this example is that participants need to be reminded of their right to withdraw without penalty. An informed consent form is an excellent place to remind participants of their rights. A second point of this example is that the researcher is responsible for evaluating the risks of participation throughout the data collection period. Risks can be higher than anticipated, as Zimbardo learned in the Stanford Prison Study.

My students often ask, "What does 'without penalty' mean?" They think it is unreasonable that a student who is participating in an experiment should get extra credit (say in an Introductory Psychology class) without doing the experiment. My solution to this problem has been fairly simple. Potential participants who refuse to participate before signing an informed consent form do not receive extra credit.

**pilot study** A part of the research study in which the researcher conducts the experiment (or specific parts of it) in order to see how well the procedures work.

Those who sign the form but then for some reason later decide they cannot complete the experiment do receive the extra credit. Neither of these cases has happened often. Only once have I, personally, come across a student who had decided "to beat the system" by showing up for experiments but not participating in them. The other extreme is much more frequent. Students in my classes often participate in research projects far above their extra credit limits. They tell me they like being in experiments, and they like helping out the psychology majors.

The informed consent form should also mention how the data will be handled after the experiment. In particular, the form should describe measures that will be taken to keep the information confidential. Methods of maintaining confidentiality will be discussed next.

## 2-2c  Confidentiality

**confidentiality** The use of data provided by research participants only for the purpose of the research and not presented as information about the participants for any other purpose.

Participants' **confidentiality** should be protected as much as possible. The behaviors that are observed in the experiment should be either public behaviors or those volunteered by the participant. Nevertheless, this information should be treated with confidentiality because it was given only for the purpose of the research project. Some strategies to maximize confidentiality are to have participants provide data anonymously or accumulate data by group only (making individual responses difficult to identify). Data should never be reported in such a way that the individual providing the data can be identified. (This includes examples given in class discussions as well. Student participants may volunteer their reactions, but the faculty advisor or student experimenter should not.)

Sometimes protecting participants' confidentiality involves more than keeping their data coded anonymously. A good example of such a study is the Asch conformity study (see Taking a Closer Look 2-2). This type of experiment uses "confederates." A **confederate** is an assistant to the experimenter who is playing the role of a research participant. The "real" participant is led to believe that the confederate is just another participant. Because both the experimenter and the confederates view the behavior in the Asch study, the confederates must also keep the information confidential. Because of the need for confidentiality, and the fact that students cannot easily be confidential with their friends, my students are required to use confederates who do not know the real participants outside the experiment. This approach ensures that participants will not be embarrassed by their behavior in the experiment in front of their friends. (This restriction is also essential for the validity of the experiment because conformity to friends is different from

**confederate** An assistant to the experimenter who is playing the role of a research participant.

**Taking a Closer Look 2-2**    *Conforming to Deception in the Laboratory*

Many students prefer to begin their research experience by replicating (repeating as exactly as possible) some classic psychology experiment. A number of them have successfully replicated Asch's (1951) study of conformity. In this study, several participants are seated together in a room. Their task is to judge sets of lines to determine which of three lines is closest in length to a standard line. Before they begin, they draw straws to determine the order they will follow in reporting their answers to the experimenter who records each answer. Then a number of repetitions with different stimulus sets are done.

The experiment involves deception because in reality all the "participants" but one are confederates of the experimenter. In this experiment the real participant always draws the short straw (has to give his or her response last). The confederates have been trained to give the wrong responses on particular trials. The measure of conformity is the number of times the participant also gives the wrong response to these trials. Asch found about 75% of his participants conformed at least once. His results have been replicated by almost all of my students who have attempted to do so. However, the deception in the study requires special attention.

conformity to strangers.) The restriction of using strangers as confederates is very difficult on many campuses. Often students have friends from home or another nearby college act as confederates. Sometimes they ask college seniors to be the confederates and have first-year student participants to minimize the chance that the confederates and participants are acquainted.

Many experiments require the work of several assistants as well as the primary experimenter. The assistants, just like the confederates described in the previous paragraph, must be trained to keep the information provided by the participants confidential. An example is from a senior thesis on restrained eating. In this study participants were videotaped having a discussion of the emotional meanings of specific situations. A team of trained raters coded the videotapes for a variety of eating behaviors. In this example the experimenter and the coders were responsible for maintaining confidentiality of the participants' behavior (including how much they ate and drank and how precisely they did it).

Whenever permanent records (videotapes, audiotapes, and writing samples) of behavior are made, participants must be informed, and they must also be informed of the methods of keeping that data confidential. Early in my career, I worked at a research institute in which therapy was also a major activity. All clients were informed on their first visit that the therapy sessions were tape recorded for future scientific analysis. The microphone was displayed prominently on the desk. However, the tapes were carefully coded and stored. These tapes provided valuable data on therapy effectiveness, but they were kept confidential as was everything else relating to clients or to nonclient research participants. Samples of behavior (videotape or audiotape) should not be used as parts of presentations of the research unless the researcher has explicit written permission from the participant and/or legal guardian.

Most behavioral research involves participants who knowingly volunteer to participate. Some research, however, involves public behaviors without the express knowledge of the participants. This type of research is called **unobtrusive research** (see Taking a Closer look 2-3). It is valued because it has fewer demand characteristics than other research. **Demand characteristics** are those aspects of the research situation that lead people to act differently than they would if they were not in the research. The difference between unobtrusive research and other research is like the difference between the old television show *Candid Camera* and a late-night talk show. On *Candid Camera* people were unaware that they were being filmed. Their behavior was natural. In contrast, on the talk show, guests are very much aware that they are being observed, not only by the people in the studio, but also by the people watching at home. They do not act in a natural way, but rather in a controlled way. They are aware of their audience and of themselves as performers. The problem with the *Candid Camera* approach is that it invades people's privacy. In research, if you obtain public data in an unobtrusive manner, you must be very careful not to invade privacy and to keep the information obtained through unobtrusive observation confidential.

**unobtrusive research**
Observation of public behaviors without the express knowledge of the participants.

**demand characteristics**
Aspects of the research situation that lead people to act differently than they would if they were not in the research.

---

> **Taking a Closer Look 2-3**  *Public Versus Private Data*

A student devised a simple, unobtrusive measures experiment to test the effects of proscriptive information on behavior. He placed a work of art prominently within a main traffic area of campus. On half the trials, a sign placed before the art said, "Do not touch." On the other half of the trials, a different sign was in front of the art. It said, "Please touch." Meanwhile, the experimenter stationed himself across the room where he could unobtrusively observe the behavior of participants. He found, as he had predicted, that more people touched the art when the sign proscribed them from doing so (Do not touch) than when it permitted touching (Please touch).

## 2-2d  Deception

**deception** The active misleading of a participant by either false information and/or the presence of confederates in the experiment.

Wherever possible, students should avoid **deception** in experiments they conduct because it raises many ethical concerns that cannot be justified for research as part of a class. Deception occurs if the participant is actively misled by either false information and/or the presence of confederates in the experiment.

Omission of information is not necessarily deception. It is not advisable to tell participants all the details of the experiment until after the data have been collected. Consider the example of an experiment that tests the effects of volunteerism on mood enhancement. Participants in one condition are given an unanticipated reward after their volunteer activity. The researcher should not tell these participants about the control group who do not receive a reward until after the experiment because these participants are likely to tell future participants about the potential for a reward. The information would bias their responses. Such omissions are essential for a good study, but they are not usually considered to be deception in research.

Whenever deception is used, its use must be justified before beginning the study. Three questions must be addressed. First is whether the deception is really necessary to the study. In the sample research described in Box 2-2, clearly some concealment was essential because people cannot, or will not, demonstrate conformity when told to do so. This is true for most behaviors that are perceived to be socially inappropriate (e.g., being aggressive, changing attitudes, cheating on a test). For the researchers to study these behaviors, it is essential that the participants do not know the real purpose of the experiment.

The second question to address before deception is justified is whether alternative procedures could be accomplished that do not involve deception. In the study of conformity, many methods can be employed. However, they tend to involve some sort of deception because it is necessary to evaluate participants' agreement with others in stating a wrong answer.

Finally, the third question is whether the deception would alter the participants' willingness to participate in the study. Researchers must not deceive participants about the risks of study participation. They should not use deception to lure participants into a study. Deception can be justified only in minimal risk studies. In summary, deception can be justified in an experiment only if it is necessary to produce the psychological phenomenon, there are no alternate procedures, and the deception does not alter participants' willingness to participate in the research.

If deception is used, the researchers must provide an explanation of the deception and its need as soon as possible. (See section 2-2e on debriefing.) Many students have found that a good debriefing is the most difficult part of conducting the conformity study. The experimenters must not make their participants feel stupid or naive because they were "taken in" by the experimenters and confederates. Participants also must not feel that their behavior (for example, conformity) has disgraced them. The researchers must follow a careful, well-staged, debriefing outline that gradually and thoroughly leads the participants through the experiment and allows them to gain maximum benefit from study participation while maintaining their dignity.

## 2-2e  Debriefing

**debriefing** Clear and complete feedback about the experiment and its results.

After the data are collected, researchers have the responsibility to provide participants with a debriefing. A **debriefing** is clear and complete feedback about the experiment and its results. This is the case for all research except no risk naturalistic observation studies and surveys. However, individuals should not be made to feel in any way inferior, insensitive, or otherwise threatened by the results of the experiment. For this reason it is a good idea not to present individual scores that participants might perceive as achievements (or failures), but rather present grouped data (averages of each group).

If participants have been deceived during the study, or if they have been subjected to stress, it is important to do a thorough debriefing immediately following the experiment. Participants' questions about the experiment should be answered. They should be encouraged to express their feelings about the experiment. If deception or stress was used, the participants should be made to understand the need for such measures in the experiment. An immediate and thorough debriefing is important if the participants' main benefit of participation is education. Students who participate in research as part of a class requirement (e.g., for extra credit) will learn more if the experimenter takes time to do a thorough debriefing that relates the research to what the participants are studying in class. The debriefing is also a good time to remind participants of resources or support personnel available (such as a college counselor) in case participation brought to mind any concerns.

If there was no deception, and if the results of the study are unlikely to need individual explanation, then the debriefing can be done in a group session or through the mail. One way to accomplish this is to ask each participant, after study participation, whether he or she would like to receive the results of the study after it is completed. If so, the participant would write his or her address on an envelope that the experimenter would use to send the results and debriefing or notice of the group debriefing. This method of debriefing, after all data have been collected, is especially useful if any knowledge of the hypothesis under study will bias results. Knowledge of the hypothesis is kept to a minimum because no participants are given a debriefing until all participants have participated in the study.

## 2-2f  Research Involving Children

Research that involves children as participants requires extra ethical consideration. The reason is that children don't have the cognitive development to give truly informed consent. They may also be more vulnerable to certain risks because of their developmental stages, thus requiring even greater ethical vigilance on the part of researchers.

Studies involving children require the informed consent of their legal guardians. In the case of adolescents, the legal guardian's consent is required, and it is good to also get the adolescent's informed consent as well. The research described in Taking a Closer Look 2-4 was completed as an undergraduate honors thesis (Mimnaugh, 1992). The ethical considerations were many. First, the researcher, Heather, had to obtain informed consent from parents. Her original experiment, which involved removing all television from the children for 2 weeks, proved impossible because parents would not give consent. They did give consent to the observational study described in Box 2-4. Because children cannot give informed consent, their parents and the preschool administrators (because they participated in the research during preschool hours) were asked to give their consent.

The ethical concerns of Heather's study included first and foremost the children's safety. They had to be allowed to play in a quiet room without dangerous

---

▶ **Taking a Closer Look 2-4**     *Ethical Issues in Research with Children*

Heather wanted to study the relationship of media violence to preschool children's aggressive play and attitudes toward violence. She devised a study in which 3- and 4-year-old children were videotaped while playing with same and opposite gender playmates. Later, she interviewed them regarding their attitudes toward violence on television, in real life, and among men and women. The videotapes were coded for aggression by trained raters, and the interviews were transcribed and coded for attitudes. The results showed that children who preferred violent television were more likely to be violent in their play.

furnishings. The average college classroom is not a safe place for a 3-year-old. To demonstrate this to Heather, I had her sit on the floor of the classroom she intended to use and pretend she was 3 years old. The perspective shift helped her to understand the potential risks from her participants' eye level. The children also had to be kept safe from potential abuse from the researcher. Although Heather and I knew that she would not abuse the children, their parents did not know this. The experimental plan had to make sure that the children were not isolated with the experimenter during any part of the study. This assured the children's safety and also protected the experimenter from false accusations that she behaved improperly with them. The children also had to be kept safe from themselves. Although Heather did not want to interfere with the children's behavior, she had to sit quietly beside the video camera with the children during their play session. In this way she could be sure that they would not be in danger from the equipment or from themselves. On several occasions she had to stop the play session before 10 minutes had elapsed because one child was about to hurt another.

There were also special considerations about confidentiality. Children's play is public behavior, but because the experimenter had placed them in a specially controlled situation, she had altered that aspect. The parents were informed before the study began that they could not view the videotapes of their children's play behavior because each tape included two children. Because the other child's parents may not want their child viewed, no videotapes would be viewed. Parents readily agreed to this condition. Three trained raters coded each tape for the aggressive behaviors the children exhibited. The raters were instructed to keep the information private and were not told the names of the children. The audio-tape interviews also presented ethical considerations. The questions needed to be thorough but not too taxing for a 3-year-old. Furthermore, the answers obtained to the questions were not always what were expected. The children became upset with some questions (e.g., what happens when a man hits a woman?). Other children gave personal answers that revealed more than Heather had hoped to learn (e.g., "When mommy hits daddy..."). The children had to be treated with sensitivity in the interview, and the information had to be kept confidential. The experimenter transcribed the interviews and coded them by number. Then, the responses were organized for further analysis by question number instead of participant. This arrangement made their responses more difficult to identify by content and context than would presentation of answers to a series of questions by a single child.

The preceding paragraph raises a very serious question. What is the ethical response for the researcher when a participant volunteers information that could indicate danger outside the experiment? The issue is important for all types of studies, and especially those involving children. First, psychological researchers, even undergraduate students, must follow the law. Most states have laws that require reporting evidence of child abuse. Second, student researchers should always consult in such issues with their instructor and other appropriate professionals. Any of my students who design studies that make them liable to such information collect their data when I am available to consult. Before student researchers collect any data, we've already included the college counselor in our project as a backup person and have specific information about community agencies that are available for the participants. Most studies do not involve potential self-disclosure, but responsible, ethical researchers are prepared in case they should occur. Topics such as restrained eating, attributions of fault to crime victims, and attitudes about abortion are more likely to evoke help seeking from participants than those on memory, cognition, or perception. Student researchers are not able to provide the help but can provide participants with the contact information for the relevant mental health professional. (Providing only services for which they have been trained and are competent to deliver is one of the major ethical principles of psychologists [APA, 2002].)

Debriefing children is also a sensitive issue. The preschool children in Heather's study were not debriefed, but their parents were. After the results of the study had been calculated, the parents were invited to a group debriefing. Because there was some potential for problems, both Heather and I, as her advisor, were present. I handled the delicate job of telling the parents what we had found. Essentially, the children who preferred violent television shows exhibited more violence in their play than did the children who preferred nonviolent television shows. We also went into more detail about the results of the interviews which showed that although preschool children engage in aggressive play, they do not approve of violence. Then the parents were encouraged to ask questions, which were answered to their satisfaction.

# 2-3 Nonhuman Research Subjects

The ethical principles for research with nonhuman subjects focus on the care of the animals before, during, and after the study.

### 2-3a Care of Animals

Care of nonhuman research subjects is described in section 8.09 of the APA ethics code (2002). It is the responsibility of both the student researcher and faculty advisor to ensure the welfare of the animals used in research and to treat them humanely. Housing and diet should be appropriate to the species. It is usually desirable to house animals individually to avoid crowding and/or aggression. Bedding should be changed regularly, as should water and food. Cages should be large enough to accommodate the animal comfortably (e.g., an aquarium is a good home for a small rodent).

### 2-3b Acquisition of Subjects

Animals used in research must be acquired lawfully, and their care and use must be in compliance with local, state, and federal laws.

### 2-3c Minimal Risks

The following types of research involve extreme risk to the animal subjects and should be engaged in only if the potential benefit of the project clearly outweighs the harm to the subjects:

- Any research involving electric shock or other presentation of a painful stimulus to an animal
- Research involving subjects ingesting any substance other than a healthy diet
- Research involving surgery or other biologically invasive procedures
- Research that places animals in an undesirable environment for long periods of time (e.g., crowding research should be avoided)

Such research must be carefully evaluated in terms of its benefits. Often research with animals uses efficient designs that guarantee the best use of an animal's life for the research. An efficient pilot study for animal research may be the replication (exact repeat) of a previous experiment. A replication demonstrates that the student researcher has competently learned the research technique. Until that has been demonstrated, it would be wasteful to conduct a new experiment. The reason is that if the new experiment failed to support the hypotheses, it would be impossible to tell whether the failure was a result of the researcher's inexperience or the phenomenon under study.

### 2-3d Deprivation

deprivation The act of withholding food or water from animals.

Research on conditioning should use positive reinforcement, time out, or removal of positive reinforcement if at all appropriate. Research that requires **deprivation** (depriving animals of food or water) should avoid depriving the animals for a period longer than 24 hours. If a longer period of deprivation seems to be needed for training, the animals must be weighed daily. The animals should not fall below 85% of their baseline weight (their weight before the training period began).

### 2-3e Termination of Subjects

terminate End study participation.

Under all circumstances vertebrate animals must be well cared for. In some cases it may be necessary to humanely terminate subjects after the research project. To **terminate** means to end study participation. For nonhuman subjects, this means that it is the responsibility of the student researcher and faculty advisor to see that the animals used in research are cared for properly after their use as research subjects. For example, mice used in experiments should not be used as food for other animals but should be placed in a good home. If such homes are unavailable, the research subjects must not be released to "the wild" because they may cause serious damage to the ecosystem. In this case the word *terminate* is a euphemism for *kill*. The APA (2002) ethical code states that when an animal's life must be terminated, it must be done quickly and in a way that minimizes pain.

Research involving invertebrate animals (e.g., planarians, fruit flies, etc.) must have an ethical plan for disposal of the subjects after the experiment is completed (e.g., students who do fruit fly experiments should not release them afterward because the fruit flies could present a public health hazard). Releasing animal research subjects into the environment is not ethical because of the dangers it poses for the ecosystem and to the research subject.

# 2-4 Ethical Uses of Statistics

Disraeli said, "There are three kinds of lies; lies, damn lies and statistics" (Adams, 1969). He implied, what many people believe, that statistics are deceptive. There are several ways that statistics can be deceptive. The first is the falsification of results or data. The Ethical Standards for Psychologists (APA, 2002) directly deals with **data falsification** (section 8.10). Falsification of data rarely happens, and when it is caught, it has serious consequences. For the professional scientist, it means the end of a career. For the student, it may mean failure in a course or even academic dismissal. Yet such cases are caught. They are caught because it is very hard to lie with statistics to the trained statistician. To a statistician, a page of numbers reads like a page of words. If those numbers are fraudulent, the reading does not ring true. Therefore, it is very difficult to lie with statistics to a person who understands them. That, alone, is one good reason to learn to be comfortable understanding and interpreting statistics.

data falsification The act of making up data to produce desired results.

It is the ethical responsibility of the researcher to report statistics accurately (APA, 2002). When errors occur, the researcher is responsible for correcting those errors. The Publication Manual of the American Psychological Association (APA, 2001) lists the policies and procedures for making corrections. It also includes the ethical principles for reporting and publishing research in Appendix C.

A misuse of statistics that is more common than data falsification or publication of errors is to represent the results in such a way that they seem to say more than they really do. For example, suppose a researcher reported a 200% increase in memory scores from a control group to a treatment group. That result sounds very good. But if you don't know the original memory scores to start with, you really do not know what the increase is. If the control group remembered nothing, then 200% of nothing is still nothing. It is important, especially when percentages are reported, to know the base of the percentage. (In this case it is important to know the control group memory score.)

Sometimes graphs are used in ways that misrepresent the information they are supposed to convey. This is especially easy to do because computer programs make graphs so easy to prepare. A graph is supposed to present a particular result in a way that is easier to understand than the numbers it represents. Section 2-5 presents principles for constructing graphs, along with some guidelines on what to avoid.

# 2-5 Clear Presentation of Results: Making Graphs

### 2-5a The Purpose of Graphs

The purpose of a graph, as stated in section 2-4, is to clarify results. Because there are so many ways to present the same information, it sometimes gets quite confusing. Statistics should be used to clarify rather than to obfuscate (make confusing). Gordon Allport (1937) has clearly stated this:

> Similar is the case of the currently popular statistical methodologies. Many believe these are indispensable in supplying the factual ground for the science of personality. Sometimes they are useful; but many times they are not. In any event, mere arrays of statistics are never capable of self-interpretation. It is for this reason that I have preferred in most cases to state the results of research as clearly as possible in words, proceeding at once to the interpretation of the results. If the argument is sound, statistics can do no more than symbolize the fact; if the argument is unsound, statistical elaboration can never make it sound and may even increase the confusion. (p. viii)

A quick glance at Figure 2-1 may lead to some confusion. However, each of the six graphs in the figure represents the same information. Each illustrates the frequency distribution for the results of a 10-point quiz on Chapter 1. In a class of 16 students, results were one 10, three 9s, five 8s, six 7s, and one 6. Although the graphs can make the information seem quite elaborate, each one contains no more information than the previous statement.

### 2-5b Bar Graphs and Frequency Histograms

A **bar graph** is shown in the upper left of Figure 2-1. This type of graph is also called a bar chart. It is very familiar. Many children now learn to construct and interpret this type of bar chart in first grade. It is customary to place the categories that have been counted on the X-axis. The X-axis, or the horizontal axis, is also sometimes called the abscissa. In the example the categories are the number of items mentioned as fears. The frequency of each item is plotted on the Y-axis. The Y-axis, or the vertical axis, is also sometimes called the ordinate. For each category, a bar is drawn to the height of its frequency.

A **frequency histogram** is like a bar graph except that the X-axis represents a continuous variable, not one that is defined in categories. The biggest difficulty in making frequency histograms is deciding on the categories to use. So far the examples have been easy. But imagine that you wanted to represent the frequency of Scholastic Aptitude Test (SAT) scores of a particular entering college class. Because the range of scores goes from 200 to 1600 (theoretically), you could have 1,401 categories. Not only would 1,401 categories be difficult to graph, but also they would not help tell anything about the scholastic aptitude of the

**bar graph** A graph in which a bar is drawn to the height of the frequency for each category.

**frequency histogram** A type of graph similar to a bar graph, except that the X-axis represents a continuous variable, not one that is defined in categories.

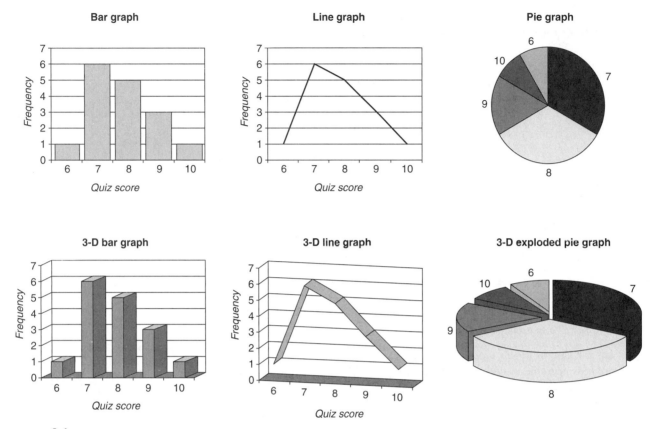

**Figure 2-1**
*Frequency of Quiz Scores on Chapter 1*

incoming class. A more meaningful approach would be to form larger categories, say every 100 points (in which case, there would be 14 categories). It is important to define categories in such a way that each score can fall into only one category.

### 2-5c  Line Graphs and Pie Charts

**line graph** A graph that shows the same information as a frequency histogram, with points placed vertically to represent the frequency for each category

In the middle of Figure 2-1 is a **line graph**. It shows exactly the same information as shown by the frequency histogram. Instead of a bar for each category, a point is placed vertically to represent the frequency for that category. Because 3 people score 9 on the quiz, a point is placed 3 units above the 9 on the X-axis that represents the score. After the frequency for each score has been represented by a point, the points are connected with straight lines. The lines serve to illustrate the points and the differences among the points. They do not allow you to make inferences about the frequencies of scores between the categories. For example, the line graph in Figure 2-1 does *not* indicate that 4 people scored 8 1/2 points. It's not possible to get half a multiple-choice quiz point.

**pie chart** A circle divided into wedges, with the area of each wedge proportional to the frequency of each category represented.

The two top graphs are the types most often used in behavioral science. However, the one on the far right is often used in the popular press, such as newspapers and magazines. The **pie chart** shows the same information as the other charts. Pie charts seem simpler to understand, but in reality direct comparisons among the pieces are rather difficult to make. Remember the last time you tried to decide who had the biggest piece of pie. It always seems to be the other guy. In both the line graph and the frequency histogram, you can more easily see that there were the same frequencies of people scoring 10 and 6 points.

## 2-5d Graph Misrepresentations

In this high-tech era, it is possible to enhance graphs in many ways. One popular way to do so is to make the graph three dimensional. Figure 2-1 shows a 3-D version of each graph type. The 3-D versions are not simpler to understand. In fact, they may lead the reader to make false conclusions about the statistics they represent because they have added unnecessary lines that can cause visual illusions. Three-dimensional graphs are seldom recommended for use in behavioral sciences. They are used for some advanced statistical measures of association among three variables. There are many opportunities in experimental research to graphically represent three variables at once. However, in these cases, two-dimensional graphs are used as the major representational tool because the three-dimensional graphs are so difficult to interpret. The method of representing three variables with graphs is covered extensively in Chapter 9, "Repeated Measures One Factor Designs."

The mean was introduced in Chapter 1, "Values in Science." It is common to present comparisons among group means in graphs. The Y-axis represents the scale of measurement, and the X-axis represents the different groups that are being compared. Sometimes the Y-axis shows only a small portion of the full scale of measurement. In fact, computer programs often automatically rescale the Y-axis so that it fits the smallest and largest means on the graph. The automatic rescaling can make small differences between groups appear very large. This is a misrepresentation of statistics. Figure 2-2 shows two graphs of the same information. Each shows the total memory score means for four groups of participants under different emotion conditions. The graph on the left seems to show that memory scores were much better for people who had been sad or disgusted as compared to those experiencing amusement or humor. However, a careful examination of the Y-axis shows that the largest difference amounts to less than one item correctly remembered. The graph on the right shows the entire range of possible memory scores (from 0 to 20). In this graph, you can easily see that the differences among the group means are very small.

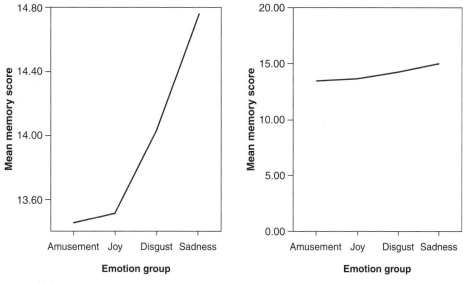

**Figure 2-2**

*Differences Among Group Means Exaggerated by Partial Y-Axis Scale*

# 2-6 Ethics of Scholarship and APA Style

According to the Ethical Principles for Psychologists (APA, 2002), it is the responsibility of the researcher to give credit to the work of others. Individuals who substantially contribute to a piece of research should be included as authors of the written report, with the major contributor being the first author. Other individuals should be acknowledged for their assistance. You will see many examples of these types of credit in the journal articles and books you read. This explains why some articles have five or more authors. It is highly unlikely that each person actually wrote the words reported. However, each person significantly contributed ideas to the work. Unlike previous versions, the current APA Ethical Principles make explicit recommendations about **authorship** for student researchers.

A second way that credit is given to the source of ideas is through **citing sources** in a paper. Most undergraduate students know that they must give credit to the source of a direct quote. However, research reports seldom have direct quotes. All sources of ideas should be cited even when the exact words from the source are not used.

**Plagiarism** occurs when another person's idea is used without giving credit to its source. The APA Ethics code defines plagiarism as presenting "...portions of another's work or data as their own, even if the other work or data source is cited occasionally" (APA, 2002, Section 8.11). In psychology, research reports (particularly the first sections) are filled with parenthetical citations (as in the preceding sentence). These citations give credit to the original source of the idea. They also allow the reader to find and evaluate the ideas presented in that source. Thus, the reference section of a research report supplies two important needs: It gives credit to the underlying sources of ideas upon which the research was built, and it provides the reader with a list for further study in the area. Too often, students do not give sufficient credit to their sources. If you read it someplace, you need to cite it, even if you have restated the idea in your own words. Failure to do so is unethical, and it is plagiarism.

A good way to avoid plagiarism and to do more efficient scholarly work is to take good notes on every research report that you read. You should carefully note the **full citation** of the source so that you may refer to it in your own reports and have all the information you need for your reference section. Even if you don't end up using the particular source in a particular paper, you may find the ideas useful in the future. Therefore, you should keep your notes so that you can refer to them in future papers. In addition to the complete citation, your notes should include the main points of the report, *in your own words*, any direct quotes you may want to use (with page numbers), and your own evaluative analysis of the report. Finally, as you read research reports, you are likely to have ideas for future research. Note them as well.

A complete citation always includes the information that another person needs in order to find the source. The author and the title are always included, but the rest of the information differs depending on the type of source. The APA publication manual (2001) includes a comprehensive chapter on the **APA reference style** that describes how to appropriately cite almost all types of sources. The two most frequently used sources are journal articles and books. The forms of both are presented as follows:

**The format for a journal article:**
Author, I. M. (Year). Title of the article with only the first word and proper names capitalized. *Full Journal Title. volume number*, first page number–last page number.

**An example using the format:**
Choi, I., & Nisbett, R. E. (2000). Cultural psychology of surprise: Holistic theories and recognition of contradiction. *Journal of Personality and Social Psychology, 79*, 890–905.

**The APA format for a book citation:**
Author, I. M. (Year). Title of the book: Capitalized the same as journal articles. Place of publication: Publisher.

---

**authorship** Inclusion as authors of the written report those individuals who made substantial contributions to a piece of research, with the major contributor being the first author.

**citing sources** Listing sources for all ideas in a research report.

**plagiarism** The act of using another person's idea without giving credit to its source.

**full citation** Complete bibliographic information, including author(s), year of publication, title, journal name or publisher, volume number and pages, or place of publication.

**APA reference style** Specific guidelines for citing sources in research published by the American Psychological Association.

**An example of a book citation**:
Allport, G. W. (1937). *Personality: A psychological interpretation*. London: Constable.

Note that the citations are double-spaced and that titles of books and journals are italicized, as are the volume numbers, but not the page numbers. Page numbers are required for journal articles but not for books. However, if you use a direct quotation from either a journal article or a book, you must include the page number(s) for the quotation in the text of your report with the quotation.

# Summary

Researchers are responsible for evaluating the ethics of their research procedures before, during, and after data collection. The APA Ethical Principles (2002) include guidelines specifically addressing the ethical conduct of research (Section 8). Research should be conducted in ways that maintain the respect and dignity of the research subjects. Researchers are responsible for designing research that minimizes potential risks to subjects. Proposed research should undergo ethical review. Student-proposed research should be reviewed by the instructor and may also undergo informed peer review and/or an Institutional Review Board.

Ethical concerns of research involving human participants include informed consent, confidentiality, use of deception, and debriefing. Participants should be informed of the general purpose of the research, the confidentiality of their data, the time and type of activities required, and their rights to stop participation before they consent to participate. Information that is obtained in research should be kept confidential by the researcher, any assistants or data coders, and other participants. Deception is sometimes used in research with minimal risks when the behavior under study is likely to be influenced by demand characteristics. When deception is used, participants must be thoroughly debriefed immediately following study participation. The debriefing completes study participation by explaining what the study was about and satisfying the participants' curiosity about it. Research involving children requires additional ethical consideration. Ethics for research with nonhuman subjects address the acquisition, care, and termination of the subjects, as well as protection of the environment.

After the research data have been collected, there are ethical ways to present them. Researchers should present results to accurately depict their findings. Graphs should not exaggerate results by using a complicated format or showing only partial scales. In research reports, it is ethical to give credit to others through authorship and citation of sources.

# References

Adams, A. K. (1969). *The home book of humorous quotations*. New York: Dodd, Mead & Co.

Allport, G. W. (1937). *Personality: A psychological interpretation*. London: Constable.

American Psychological Association. (2001). *Publication manual of the American Psychological Association*. Washington, DC: Author.

American Psychological Association. (2002). *Ethical principles of psychologists*. Washington, DC: Author.

Asch, S. E. (1951). Opinions and social pressure. *Scientific American, 193*, 31–35.

Mimnaugh, H. Q. (1992). *The relationship of preschool children's violent television preference to aggressive play and attitudes*. Undergraduate honors thesis. Westminster College, New Wilmington, PA.

Zimbardo, P. G. (1972). Pathology of imprisonment. *Transaction/Society*, April, 4–8.

# Exercises for Application

1. The following four cases describe research proposed by undergraduates. Each has one or more ethical problems. Evaluate each case in terms of ethical considerations. Determine which ethical issues need to be addressed and what, if any, modifications to the description could help overcome the ethical problems. (The researcher names have been changed.)

   a. Mary wanted to study the effects of time pressure on helping behavior. She asked participants to participate in a two-part experiment. In the first part, participants were told to either hurry to the second part in another building (time pressure condition) or that they should show up for the second part of the study in another building in about half an hour (no time pressure condition). On the way between the two buildings, Mary's confederates staged an accident. In the accident a man fell unconscious to the ground. An unobtrusive observer watched to see if and how participants helped the man. During the second stage of the experiment, a second experimenter administered a questionnaire about helping behavior and fully debriefed the participants.

   b. Bill has concluded that people with an internal locus of control will cope with stress in an adaptive way, whereas those with an external locus of control will cope with stress in maladaptive ways. He therefore has predicted that in an experiment internals who are told that the second part of the experiment, which will occur two weeks later, requires them to receive painful electric shock will have no higher stress levels after two weeks than internals who did not get threatened with painful electric shock. In contrast, he predicts that externals will feel high stress levels two weeks later if they had been told of the electric shock but not if they received no such information.

   c. Jack wants to see how children's expectations of their own competencies influence their performance on cognitive tests. He asks parents to inform their children that either they would do very well on this type of test or that they can't do well on this type of test. After giving the tests, he then debriefs the children about the experimental deceptions.

   d. Georgia has decided to study the effects of crowding on rats' aggressive behavior. She builds a closed environment to produce crowding. The animals show a high degree of unusual as well as aggressive behavior.

2. Find a graph from some nonscientific source (newspapers, magazines, etc.). Evaluate the information based on what you have learned about graphical presentation of information in this chapter. Does the graph seem to accurately represent the information, or does it exaggerate certain aspects? How does it do this?

3. Construct a frequency histogram, line graph, and pie chart for the data supplied in the exercises at the end of Chapter 1.

# Practice Quiz

*Note:* You can find the correct answers to these questions by taking the quiz and then submitting your answers in the Online Edition. The program will automatically score your submission. If you miss a question, the program will provide the correct answer, a rationale for the answer, and the section number in the chapter where the topic is discussed.

1. Who is responsible for the ethics of experiments conducted by undergraduate students?

   a. the American Psychological Association
   b. the undergraduate college or university
   c. the student researcher and faculty member
   d. the subjects of the research

2. The most important thing that is usually required of a research participant is

   a. pain.
   b. time.

   c. personal data.
   d. mental effort.

3. The use of deception in research is

   a. necessary to study some socially undesirable behaviors.
   b. never acceptable at the undergraduate level.
   c. acceptable if the deception is described in the informed consent form.
   d. no longer needed because newer simulation techniques have replaced it.

4. Potential physical, social, and emotional risks of study participation should be

   a. evaluated from the perspective of the student researcher.
   b. avoided at all costs.
   c. balanced against potential benefit to society.

d. evaluated from the perspective of the research participant.

5. When using children as research participants, the researcher

   a. has the same ethical responsibilities as when using adults.
   b. is less concerned with confidentiality because children don't know anything private.
   c. must get informed consent from their legal guardians.
   d. must get informed consent from both the children and their parents.

6. The major ethical considerations for research involving animals

   a. are the same as those for humans.
   b. assure that animals are treated humanely.
   c. were developed by animal rights advocates.
   d. have to do with deprivation training.

7. Which type of graph is most difficult to use to compare the relative frequencies of each category represented?

   a. frequency histogram
   b. line graph
   c. pie chart
   d. column chart

8. It is important to evaluate the scales of measurement used in line graphs because

   a. the data may be fraudulent, and a careful inspection of the scale of measurement could reveal the deception.
   b. they show the base for comparisons.
   c. the scale of measurement may be altered to exaggerate differences between means.
   d. the X-axis must always equal the Y-axis.

9. Participants are likely to learn more from an experiment if

   a. the experiment has many parts to it.
   b. they are given their own scores as part of the debriefing.
   c. they receive the results of the study as a debriefing.
   d. they receive an immediate and thorough debriefing.

10. The right of a participant to withdraw from an experiment without penalty means that

   a. people who sign an informed consent form receive extra credit for study participation.
   b. the researcher is freed of the responsibility of monitoring risks to the participant during the study.

c. many participants will complete only a small portion of the experiment.
   d. participants may not sue the experimenter.

11. Which of the following was *not* listed as a type of research to be avoided by student researchers because it is likely to involve too much risk to participants?

   a. research involving the ingestion of psychoactive substances
   b. research that uses deception
   c. interpretation of personality profiles to participants
   d. threatening pain, or actually causing pain to participants

12. An assistant to the experimenter who is acting a role in the experiment, often as a "fake" participant, is called a(n)

   a. false positive.
   b. itinerant.
   c. confederate.
   d. grad assistant.

13. One way to avoid demand characteristics in research is to use

   a. a detailed informed consent form.
   b. unobtrusive measures methods.
   c. participants who already know the hypothesized results.
   d. less demanding procedures.

14. A well-organized debriefing allows participants to understand the _____ of the study while maintaining their _____.

   a. purpose, dignity
   b. results, comfort
   c. deception, honor
   d. methods, confidentiality

15. In order to maintain confidentiality of videotaped behavior, it is important to

   a. train coders to treat all information on the tapes as confidential.
   b. code the responses using an ID system that doesn't associate the names with the data.
   c. refrain from using samples of the videotapes as examples for public presentations without permission from the participants.
   d. all of the above.

16. Plagiarism can be avoided by

   a. never using direct quotes in a research report.
   b. making sure to copy things correctly.
   c. giving credit to all sources for ideas as well as quotes.
   d. having at least one source cited in each paragraph.

# The Hypothetico-Deductive Method and Experiments in Psychology

**Chapter** Three

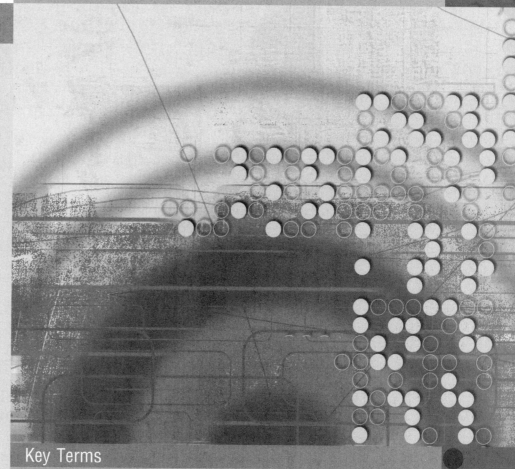

## Key Terms

atheoretical
Boolean search
deduction
dependent variable
descriptive statistics
experimental design
hypothesis
hypothetico-deductive method
independent variable
induction
inferential statistics
key word searches
literature review
measures of central tendency
median

mode
operational definition
paradigm
peripheral search
population
premise
*PsychInfo*
*Psychological Abstracts*
samples
skew
subject search
syllogism
theory

# Learning Objectives

- Be able to illustrate the roles of induction and deduction in the hypothetico-deductive method.
- Be able to use both inductive and deductive logic.
- Explain the role of theory in the research hypothesis.

- Deduce a hypothesis from a theory.
- Illustrate the research process with an example.
- Be able to calculate and interpret three measures of central tendency.

## Key Idea

The hypothetico-deductive method is the use of both inductive and deductive logic to derive hypotheses from theory, design experiments to test those hypotheses, and analyze and interpret the results of the experiments in order to build new theories and applications.

## 3-1 The Hypothetico-Deductive Method

**hypothetico-deductive method** A method used in science to test the ideas that derive from our curiosity in an organized way.

The **hypothetico-deductive method** is the method used in science to test the ideas that derive from our curiosity in an organized way. It involves an organized step-by-step process of using the two types of logic—inductive and deductive—in deriving hypotheses from theories, testing those hypotheses, and interpreting the results.

John Stuart Mill (1874) was the first to write thoroughly about the hypothetico-deductive method. He originally described it as the deductive method:

> The mode of investigation which ... remains to us as the main source of the knowledge we possess or can acquire respecting the conditions and laws of recurrence, of the more complex phenomena, is called, in its most general expression, the *Deductive Method*; and consists of three operations: the first, one of direct induction; the second of ratiocinations; the third, of verification. (p. 325)

For more than a century, philosophers, logicians, and mathematical epistemologists have debated the validity of Mill's methods. Meanwhile, scientists have whole-heartedly endorsed them. The methods rely on the combination of logic and verification of the conclusions of logic with empirical data. Much of the debate over Mill's methods has, in fact, revolved around the inclusion or omission of data in the testing of hypotheses. Empiricism was introduced in Chapter 1 "Values in Science," and the remaining chapters of this book deal with methods of data collection (empirical evidence). Therefore, this chapter will deal mainly with the logic in the hypothetico-deductive method.

## 3-2 Logic

Professors and other teachers from time to time consider the question, "Can we ever teach a person to be logical, or is logic an individual difference in personality?" Students, also, tend to classify themselves into two categories: those who are logical and all the rest. However, since Aristotle, people have indeed been teaching the "science of logic."

Lewis Carroll, most famous as author of *Alice in Wonderland*, was in reality Charles Lutwig Dodgson. He was a mathematician who spent a large part of his life developing a system of symbolic logic. He attempted to popularize its practice in the "Game of Logic" and in his book *Symbolic Logic* (1977), which he addressed to children. Lewis laid many claims for the power of logic, as the following quote illustrates:

Once master the machinery of Symbolic Logic, and you have a mental occupation always at hand, of absorbing interest, and one that will be of real *use* to you in *any* subject you may take up. It will give you clearness of thought—the ability to *see your way* through a puzzle—the habit of arranging your ideas in an orderly and get-at-able form—and, more valuable than all, the power to detect *fallacies*, and to tear to pieces the flimsy illogical arguments, which you will so continually encounter in books, in newspapers, in speeches, and even in sermons, and which so easily delude those who have never taken the trouble to master this fascinating Art. *Try it.* That is all I ask of you! (p. 53)

The claims that Lewis Carroll made for logic seem to be demonstrated in our popular culture, again and again, as some of our most enduring heroes rely on logic to find the murderer (Sherlock Holmes, Miss Marple, etc.) or even save the universe (Mr. Spock of the original *Star Trek* series). These cases show the entertainment value of logic. But for behavioral scientists and students of behavioral science, logic is the essential tool of their trade. Mill (1874) described it as follows:

Logic, then, is the science of the operations of the understanding which are subservient to the estimate of evidence: both the process itself of advancing from known truths to unknown, and all other intellectual operations in so far as auxiliary to this. (p. 23)

The students who have classified themselves as the nonlogical type often despair when they arrive at a course in research methods and statistics. Fortunately, the world is not really divided into two types of people—the logical and the others. In reality, most people are very logical in many different practical aspects of life. Some have never learned to speak about those logical activities in any language of logic or other symbolic form. Nevertheless, each day, they make many correct uses of logic. To illustrate this, consider the problem of determining how many and what types of pizzas should be ordered for a party. This particular problem is familiar to many undergraduates, who make these determinations as a very routine matter. However, solving the problem requires many logical steps. These steps include determining how many people are likely to eat how much of each different kind of pizza. Because the pizza toppings can be ordered in any combination, the logical problem is very complex. Yet, in the United States and many other places in the world, pizza is a favorite party food. Obviously, many people are able to solve this complex logic problem without necessarily recognizing it as such.

Students can, and do, learn to improve their application of logic in research methods and statistics. I base this assertion on the improvement in logic that I have witnessed in many students over the years. Jean Piaget, who developed the stage theory of cognitive development, collaborated with E. W. Beth on a book titled *Mathematical Epistemology and Psychology* (1966). Piaget described the development of cognition in the same terms that Beth described the rules of logic. The first thing covered in logic textbooks is the set of rules for naming. Early in life, children develop schema through their experience with the environment. There is a correspondence between the rules of naming and rules for existence and the development of cognitive schema. A second level of logic is the development of new information from a combination of what has been accepted previously. Piaget's concept of accommodation and of concrete operations is applied to this area. The final stage of cognitive development, according to Piaget, is that of *formal operations*. This stage is characterized by many attributes, but the main relevance here is that in this stage abstract logic can be symbolically applied. Piaget even called the method by which children discover the world (and develop cognitively) the *hypothetico-deductive method*.

## 3-2a Induction

**Induction** is the form of logic in which a general conclusion is drawn from the observation of many specific events or facts. It is the type of logic used when an

**induction** A form of logic in which a general conclusion is drawn from the observation of many specific events or facts.

individual observes the behavior of many others and puts together conclusions based on the similarities between those others. Mill (1874) defined it as follows:

> Induction, then, is that operation of the mind, by which we infer what we know to be true in a particular case or cases, will be true in all cases which resemble the former in certain assignable respects. (p. 210)

Consider the following example of induction. When going to a new university, a psychology student may want to understand the characteristics of students at that school. To determine the common characteristics, the student investigator could spend time observing other students and noting how they are similar and how they differ from one another. After making many careful observations of these "facts," the student could induce some general conclusions about his or her classmates. Such an induction might be that students at the university are generally physically attractive and healthy.

A second example of induction is the work of the botanist who discovered the general categories for plants. Imagine the first botanist. To understand the vast array of plant life, the botanist needed to understand the features of plants and their kinds. The botanist first observed the many characteristics of a large number of plants. By noting what was similar among those plants, the botanist was able to develop categories of kinds of plants. Some were trees, and others were bushes. Some plants were grouped through induction into the category of fruits, whereas others were typed as vegetables based on their shared characteristics. In this task, the botanist used induction by observing many specific facts and using those facts to derive general rules of the basic kinds of plants.

The inductive form of logic is often used in personality research as psychologists try to understand what the basic dimensions of personality are. The psychologists measure and compare personality traits of many individuals for similarities and differences. Based on those comparisons, they draw inductions to describe a particular personality dimension (for example, extraversion) by the traits associated with it. Extraversion is described through induction. A person high on the dimension labeled extraversion is outgoing, sociable, talkative, and he or she likes to be in groups. This example of induction does not address many important questions about extraversion. For example, what produces extraversion? Under what conditions is extraversion likely to result in successful behavior? What are the consequences of extraversion? Using induction is a good way to describe commonalities. It can be used to answer the question, "How are these things alike and different?" It is very valuable because you need to know *what* something is before you know *why* it is. In the case of extraversion, you need to know that it is a basic dimension of personality that can be described by a set of traits before you can understand its causes and consequences.

As hinted at in the preceding paragraph, inductive logic is a rather weak form of logic in that it allows you to draw only generalizations about associations. That is, you cannot show a cause/effect relationship using inductive logic alone. This failing is illustrated by the old saying "the exception proves the rule." An exception occurs when a general rule doesn't hold for a specific individual. That individual is the exception. The saying "the exception proves the rule" applies only to inductive logic, not to deductive logic. Induction involves observing similarities among many individuals in the same group. For example, consider the generalizations that could be made of students at your college or university. Are they all considered nice? Perhaps you attend a college or university where it's assumed that every student spends a lot of time enjoying parties. Or maybe women at your institution have a reputation for being shy and fashionable. In this case, induction was used to make the label of "typical" student at a particular college or university. That does not mean every individual at the school fits the label (the induction rule). A single case (or several) that does not fit the label will in no way influence your faith in the label. If a few students don't fit the label, the conclusion that generally the university students are as labeled stays strong. In fact, the exceptions are noticed only because they stand out from the other students by their difference. Only if the students generally are nice will discourteous behavior be particularly noticeable. Likewise, if the students have the label "fashionable but shy," there is likely to be some student who is outspoken and cares nothing for the dictates of fashion. Does the existence of this student mean that the label about students in general doesn't apply? No. But the fact that the student is noticed as an exception, an atypical case, means that the rule generally does hold. When the saying "the exception proves the rule" is used, it does not mean literally that an exception proves the rule. It merely means that, with inductive logic, an exception is to be accepted and perhaps even expected. In fact, the exception would not be noteworthy unless the general induction held.

Induction is used extensively within statistics. In fact, most statistical analysis is really formalized induction. Survey research relies exclusively on inductive logic in drawing general conclusions from a sample to a population. The many facts (survey data) are compiled statistically to allow researchers to logically induce the general characteristics of the population. As with all induction, the research associates similarities between facts. But, as in the preceding paragraph, it cannot show a cause/effect relationship.

The statistics commonly used in experimental research are also formalized induction. Data are collected in an experiment. These data form the "facts" for induction. Statistics are used to summarize the data and to draw inferences from the summaries. That is, the statistics enable the researcher to go from the specific facts to a general conclusion. Again, this example illustrates induction. The superiority of using statistical analysis to formalize the induction process is that it allows the scientist to estimate the probability that the induction is wrong. In informal induction, there is less precision.

## 3-2b  Deduction

**Deduction** is the logical process of going from a general rule to specific applications. In this way, it is the reverse of induction. The most famous example of deduction is the following:

> All men are mortal.
> Socrates is a man.
> Therefore, Socrates is a mortal.

**deduction** The logical process of going from a general rule to specific applications.

The first two statements are premises upon which the conclusion (the third statement) is based. The first statement is the general principle or rule. The second premise is the relation of a specific individual to the general rule. The conclusion logically follows from the two premises by the process of deduction. (The entire set of statements is referred to as a *syllogism*.)

In the case of deduction, unlike induction, if the conclusion is not the case (i.e., exceptions), then the premises or the logic linking them must be false. In deduction, the exception disproves the rule. Given the classic example, suppose Socrates did not die. Then either the first premise is false (all men are not mortal), or the second premise is false (Socrates is not a man). The conclusion made by one student—that if Socrates did not die, then he was a woman—is a humorous misapplication of deductive logic. Clearly, if the conclusion is shown to be false, then something must be changed.

Deductive logic, going from general principles to specific applications, is the kind used most in philosophy and in the popular culture examples cited in section 3-2. Mr. Spock, from *Star Trek* (or Data from *Star Trek: The Next Generation*), uses his knowledge of scientific theories (the general rule) and the specific facts of the situation (which relate to the general rule) to conclude that a current course of action will result in the destruction of the universe in approximately 10.2453 seconds. Likewise, the sleuth Sherlock Holmes (the fictional invention of Sir Arthur Conan Doyle) uses his own theories of criminal and other human behavior (general rules) and his observations of a specific case (its relation to the general rules) to identify and capture the crook (conclusion). Readers delight in following along to see whether they, too, can deduce the solution to the crime. This can be accomplished only if all the premises are supplied to the reader (those premises are provided with much irrelevant information). Sometimes Holmes doesn't reveal his key information until after he has revealed the criminal. In these cases, readers are helpless to deduce the criminal from the evidence because the evidence was not available to the readers until after the "crook" was announced.

There are many rules of deductive logic. In fact, it is a good idea for science students to study both philosophy (especially logic) and higher mathematics because those disciplines provide practice in application of symbolic logic. For the meantime, consider some more entertaining examples. The following discourse on logic, between a fairy and a child, is from the pen of Lewis Carroll (1889):

> "For a *complete* logical argument," Arthur began with admirable solemnity, "we need two prim Misses __"
> "Of course!" she interrupted. "I remember that word now. And they produce __?"
> "A Delusion," said Arthur.
> "Ye—es?" she said dubiously. "I don't seem to remember that so well. But what is the whole argument called?"
> "A Sillygism." (p. 259)

This excerpt is humorous because of the child Arthur's malapropisms. He uses words that sound like the technical logic terms in place of those words. The "two prim Misses" are, of course, the *premise*. A **premise** is a general rule or a specific fact. The premises could be in the symbolic form of

All X are Z.
All Z are Y.

**premise** A general rule or a specific fact that is used in logical deduction.

Arthur's term "delusion" should have been *deduction*. Deduction applied to the preceding symbolic statements would yield this conclusion:

Therefore, all X are Y.

The entire argument is called a **syllogism**, not a "sillygism." The technical terminology may not be easy to understand at first. But you can overcome that difficulty by substituting meaningful terms for the symbols X, Y, and Z. For example,

**syllogism** The combination of premises and deduction that lead to a logical conclusion.

All psychology students are industrious.
All industrious people are successful.
Therefore, all psychology students are successful.

Often, the misapplication of logic is used to produce humor. Mark Twain (1924) did this repeatedly in his book, *Tom Sawyer Abroad* and Other Stories. The excerpt from this book in Taking a Closer Look 3-1 provides several examples of misused logic on the part of Huckleberry Finn. Huck, Tom Sawyer, and the freed slave, Jim, find themselves afloat over the Midwest in a balloon. Huckleberry Finn uses deductive logic. The premises for his first argument are as follows:

The map represents the states as they are (it's the truth).
The states are the same color "out-of-doors" as they are on the map.
The state of Illinois is green.
The state of Indiana is pink.
The land below the balloon is green.
Therefore, the land below the balloon is Illinois, not Indiana.

Huck's logic is faultless, but his premises are not. A deductive argument can be valid only if the logic and the premises are correct. Tom pointed out the weak premise, but Huck was also able to "prove" that premise logically. He accepted his general principle based on other general principles. He, in fact, overgeneralized. The

## Taking a Closer Look 3-1 — *The Logic of Huckleberry Finn*[1]

There was one thing that kept bothering me, and by and by I [Huckleberry Finn] says:

Huck: "Tom, didn't we start east?"
Tom: "Yes."
Huck: "How fast have we been going?"
Tom: "Well, you heard what the professor said when he was raging round. Sometimes, he said, we was making fifty miles an hour, sometimes ninety, sometimes a hundred; said that with a gale to help he could make three hundered any time, and said if he wanted the gale, and wanted it blowing in the right direction, he only had to go up higher or down lower to find it."
Huck: "Well, then, it's just as I reckoned. The professor lied."
Tom: "Why?"
Huck: "Because if we was going so fast we ought to be past Illinois, oughtn't we?"
Tom: "Certainly."
Huck: "Well, we ain't."
Tom: "What's the reason we ain't?"
Huck: "I know by the color. We're right over Illinois yet. And you can see for yourself that Indiana ain't in sight."
Tom: "I wonder what's the matter with you, Huck. You know by the color?"
Huck: "Yes, of course I do."
Tom: "What's the color got to do with it?"
Huck: "It's got everything to do with it. Illinois is green, Indiana is pink. You show me any

pink down there, if you can. No, sir; it's green."
Tom: "Indiana *pink?* Why, what a lie!"
Huck: "It ain't no lie; I've seen it on the map, and it's pink."

You never see a person so aggravated and disgusted. He says:

Tom: "Well if I was such a numskull as you, Huck Finn, I would jump over. Seen it on the map! Huck Finn, did you reckon the states was the same color out-of-doors as they are on the map?"
Huck: "Tom Sawyer, what's a map for? Ain't it to learn you facts?"
Tom: "Of course."
Huck: "Well, then, how's it going to do that if it tells lies? That's what I want to know."
Tom: "Shucks, you muggins! It don't tell lies."
Huck: "It don't, don't it?"
Tom: "No, it don't."
Huck: "All right, then; if it don't, there ain't no two states the same color. You git around that, if you can, Tom Sawyer."
Huck: "He see I had him, and Jim see it too; and I tell you I felt pretty good, for Tom Sawyer was always a hard person to git ahead of...."

*Source:* Twain, M. (1924). *Tom Sawyer abroad* and other stories (p. 22–24). New York: Grosset & Dunlap.

[1]The character names, Huck (Huckleberry Finn) and Tom (Tom Sawyer), have been added to aid in your reading.

need to avoid overgeneralization is one reason that the hypothetico-deductive method relies on logic and empirical verification. Empirical verification would reveal that the states are not all different colors "out-of-doors" as they are on a map.

In experimental research deductive logic is applied to deduce a hypothesis from a **theory** (or set of theories). A psychological theory is an organized, systematic explanation of behavior. From it, many, many different hypotheses can be drawn. A **hypothesis** is a more specific application of a theory to predict a particular outcome. The form of deductive logic in this case is

Theory: The cause leads to the effect.
Specific application of the cause is present.
Therefore, the effect should occur.

Deductive logic is also used to derive the specific research design from the hypothesis. As with theories leading to hypotheses, it is also the case with hypotheses being tested by experiments. For any single hypothesis, many, many different experiments can be designed through the process of deduction. The simplified form of this deductive logic is

**theory** An organized, systematic explanation of a phenomenon.

**hypothesis** A more specific application of a theory to predict a particular outcome.

The independent variable (cause) leads to the dependent variable (effect).
All other things are equal (held constant by experimental control).
The experimenter changes (manipulates) the independent variable.
Therefore, the dependent variable must show a change.

If the results of the experiment are consistent with the conclusion, they are said to support all of the premises, most importantly the first, which is the hypothesis of the experiment. If, however, the results of the experiment do not support the conclusion, the experimenter must reevaluate the research design and the hypothesis. The experimenter will be confident in the validity of the third premise because he or she manipulated it. If the change in the dependent variable did not occur, the experimenter must carefully scrutinize the second premise. Were all other things equal? Or were there other causes that changed along with the independent variable (were confounded)? If the second premise has no fault, then the researcher must reject the first premise; i.e., the hypothesis is wrong. However, the results of the study are based on induction. The experimenter evaluates the conclusion that the dependent variable showed a change through statistics. The statistics are formalized induction. In any single experiment the dependent variable could remain unchanged just from chance. Therefore, the researcher estimates the probability that the conclusion was wrong before giving up the hypotheses altogether.

Now let's see how deductive logic can be applied to the three examples used in section 3-2a on induction. As a new student in a college or university, you still want to know about the other students. With deduction, you start with a general rule, add a specific fact, and then deduce a conclusion. If you know that your college or university accepts only people in the top 50% of their secondary school graduating class, and you know that your roommate was accepted into your college, you can deduce that your roommate was in the top half of her secondary school graduating class. You have gone from general to specific using deductive logic.

Again imagine yourself to be the early botanist. Now that you have a classification system, you want to determine which class a new plant belongs to. The general rule in this case is the set of characteristics for the class. The specific facts are the characteristics of the particular plant, a tomato in this case. The conclusion is the deduction about whether or not the tomato belongs to the class:

Vegetables have edible seed pods produced by vines, tubers, or bushes.
Tomatoes are edible seed pods produced by a vine or bush.
Therefore, tomatoes are vegetables.

You can try making the syllogism that shows why tomatoes are not fruits, as many people believe, even though they share some characteristics with fruit.

The third example in section 3-2a on induction dealt with the personality dimension of extraversion. You could use deduction to make a prediction about how a person is likely to react in a specific situation. The general rule is that extraversion makes people more comfortable in a social situation. The specific facts you need include how extraverted the person is and how social (how many people) the situation is. If you know the person is not very extraverted and the situation involves close contact with many people, you can deduce that the person won't be comfortable in that situation.

# 3-3 The Research Process

Induction and deduction are both used throughout the research process. Neither type of logic alone is sufficient. Induction is weak in terms of showing cause, but deduction is weak in making generalizations. Therefore, these two types of logic go hand in hand in the research process. Sections 3-3a through 3-3e provide an outline of the typical process of experimental psychology as both types of logic are used. The outline is necessarily simplified. In reality, the use of logic is complex, and induction and deduction are both used at all parts of the process.

The hypothetico-deductive method as it is applied in experimental research is illustrated in Figure 3-1 The first step is the inductive evaluation of many facts. The box labeled "Facts" at the bottom left of the figure can represent observations of participants in survey research and other observational, inductive types of studies. It can also represent all the previous research in the area of behavior to which the hypothetico-deductive method is applied. Thus, it represents the literature review (empirical and theoretical) and the researcher's own empirical experience. It includes the theories of behavior relevant to the study.

The process of induction is used to move from the level of theory to the hypothesis level. Deduction is used to derive from the hypothesis a specific **experimental design** to test it. The data are collected, analyzed, interpreted, and reported. Then the process begins anew, with the results of the first experiment as part of the information upon which to base future hypotheses. Each specific step in the process is outlined in sections 3-3a through 3-3e.

**experimental design** The plan of an experiment that includes how the cause will be manipulated, how the effect will be measured, and how other variables will be controlled.

## 3-3a Theory

Most research starts from the level of theory. The researcher reads reports of previous research and theory and, based on a thorough evaluation of that literature, uses deduction to form his or her own hypotheses. This process is called the **literature review**. It is the first step in an organized, scholarly pursuit of knowledge. To deduce sound conclusions, the researcher must have sound premises. The best source of sound premises comes from a careful evaluation of previous research.

Sometimes research is approached from an **atheoretical** (no theory) point of view. Very rarely, there are researchers who do not accept any of the previous research and theories and want to start "with a fresh outlook." These researchers tend to take a very inductive approach. They measure many different aspects of behavior and search for statistical associations among those variables. By relying solely on inductive methods, they run the risk of capitalizing on chance findings, and they limit their conclusions to associations rather than to explanations. Although some famous psychologists have taken an atheoretical approach, I do not advocate it. To me, it is like going on a search without knowing what you are looking for and with no idea of where to search for it. With such a method, you may find something worth finding, but even then, you may not know what it is when you find it.

**literature review** The process of reading and evaluating reports of previous research and using deduction to form hypotheses. Also used to describe the portion of a research report introduction that summarizes the previous research and theory relevant to the hypotheses tested in that report.

**atheoretical** No theory.

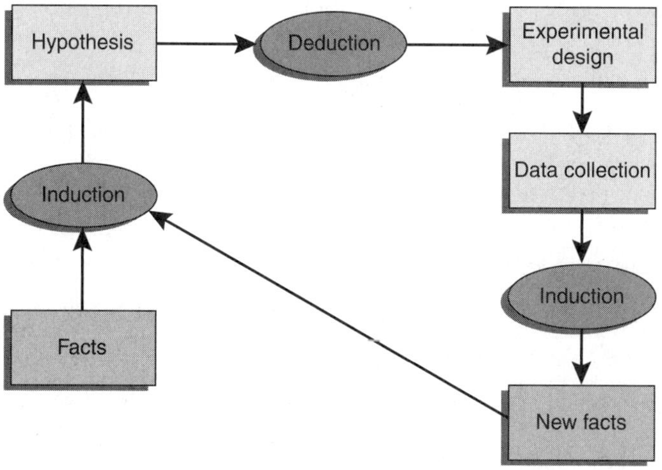

**Figure 3-1**
*Hypothetico-Deductive Method*

A second reason that some research is carried out from an atheoretical perspective is that no previous research and theory exist in that area. In this case it may be better to do research not based on theory than to do no research at all. However, this argument is usually very weak. A lot of research and theory was developed in psychology in its first century. Usually, when students say there is no research or theory on a particular area, the truth is that they simply haven't found it. Another reason students may not find research on a particular topic is that the research was conducted but not published. In the past it was the policy of many journals to publish only studies with statistically significant results. Therefore, many areas of psychology have been studied but not published because the hypotheses remained unsupported by evidence and were probably wrong. Even the early pioneers of psychology did not base their research in a vacuum. They started with theories from the related disciplines of philosophy, anthropology, and biology.

A third reason for atheoretical research is that the tool of the experiment is very useful to answer very specific curiosities about behavior. As noted in Chapter 1, "Values in Science," curiosity is a shared value among scientists. Thus, it is not surprising that students of experimental design are also curious about many things. Experimental design seems to offer an easy and quick way to satisfy that curiosity because it is a direct step from the curiosity of "I wonder if X causes Y?" to the experimental hypothesis. It is possible to skip the theory and previous research entirely. However, doing so is not advisable. The researcher misses out on the benefit of the experience of others and is likely to select the first hypothesis that comes to mind rather than the best one. The researcher will have to invent each and every aspect of the research **paradigm**. A research paradigm is a standard method of conducting research that has been developed over a number of studies as demonstrated to be effective. In most areas of psychological research, beginning without the benefit of previous research and theory is akin to "reinventing the wheel." It's really a great waste of time and effort. Finally, in my experience, this type of "I wonder what..." research seldom yields significant results. Because the benefits of past experience were ignored, it's not surprising such studies yield little information for future use.

Throughout the remainder of this chapter, a specific research example will be used to illustrate the application of the hypothetical deductive method. Taking a Closer Look 3-2 introduces the example and describes the first stages of the research process for investigating two types of memory, acoustic and visual.

The extensive discussion of the atheoretical research approach should serve to underscore the important role that theory plays in the majority of experimental research. As you begin to read psychological theories, it is good to have some ways of evaluating them. Some of the characteristics of a good theory are as follows:

- Systematic and well organized
- Comprehensive, in that it covers a lot of behavior
- Useful for both future research and theory development and for practical applications
- Testable

**paradigm** A standard method of conducting research that has been developed over a number of studies as demonstrated to be effective.

---

**Taking a Closer Look 3-2**   *Research Example: Acoustic Versus Visual Working Memory*

A researcher who is interested in working memory would first review all the available theory and empirical findings on working memory. After carefully evaluating and synthesizing that literature, the researcher would select the theory (or theories) to pursue in his or her own research. For example, the researcher might decide to pursue research using the theory that working memory uses acoustic (auditory) storage.

The last characteristic in the list, testable, means that the theory can produce specific, clear predictions (hypotheses) that can be put to the test in empirical research. The theories can be verified. Theories that are so vague that they seem to explain almost any result are not testable. To be testable, a theory must be the kind of general rule that supports the use of deductive logic to derive specific hypotheses.

## 3-3b Hypothesis

The hypothesis is deduced from the theory. An experimenter will arrive at many hypotheses as he or she reads the literature. Some researchers write down such research ideas as they occur. Others keep them in mind for later improvement and selection. Students often fear that they will not be able to deduce a hypothesis from a theory. They are so anxious that they try to come up with their own hypothesis before they read the literature. This is getting the cart before the horse, so to speak. Most students are able to develop many good hypotheses after they have completed their literature review. Then they face the problem of selecting which of the many hypotheses to pursue in their own experiment. In both developing hypotheses and selecting which ones to test, the logical process used is deduction. Box 3-3 shows some sample hypotheses.

Box 3-3 shows only a few of the many hypotheses that can be deduced from the theory proposed in Box 3-2 Researchers must select from among them because no research can adequately test all hypotheses at once. Students often want to solve their selection problem by designing research that will attempt to test all their hypotheses at one time. Such a broad, shotgun approach makes the research complicated, and this complexity is likely to make the results difficult or impossible to interpret. Experienced scientists will select among the hypotheses and carry out a series of studies to progressively test hypotheses, using the result of each experiment to further fine-tune the hypotheses for the subsequent research. This approach is called a *program of research*, and it is far superior to attempting to answer all the questions that arise with a single experiment. In sections sections 3-3c through 3-3e the last hypothesis will be used: Stimuli that sound alike will cause greater interference in working memory than those that look alike.

## 3-3c Experimental Design

After the experimenter has selected the hypothesis, he or she is ready to use the logic of deduction to design the experiment. Experienced researchers do much of this process almost automatically. However, student researchers lack the experience to do so and often have problems at points that the experienced researcher seemingly doesn't even think about. For example, in designing the experiment, students first must determine what is the **independent variable** (cause to be manipulated by the

**independent variable** A cause to be manipulated by the experimenter.

*Research Example: Hypothesis About Working Memory*

If you start from the theory that working memory is acoustically stored, you can deduce many hypotheses. Examples include:

- Working memory will be better for information that is presented acoustically than that which is presented visually.

- Working memory will be better for items that can be represented as sound than those that cannot.

- Working memory will be better for nonsense syllables that can be pronounced than those that are difficult to pronounce in the participant's language.

- Stimuli that sound alike will cause greater interference in working memory than those that look alike.

**Figure 3-2**
*Cause and Effect*

**dependent variable** An effect to be measured by the experimenter.

experimenter) and what is the **dependent variable** (effect to be measured by the experimenter). See Figure 3-2.

Although these variables are obvious to the experienced researcher, they often are not to student researchers. I have known students who designed studies in which they manipulated the hypothesized effect and measured the cause. This is like putting on your clothes before taking a bath. Everything is backward. After the students who reversed their variables collected and analyzed their data, they had great difficulty interpreting the results, and at this point, they discovered the flaw in their design. Unfortunately, in these cases it was impossible to salvage the research. This type of problem underscores the importance of student researchers seeking and using the advice of an experienced researcher about the design of their research before they begin data collection. I have often had the opportunity to alert students to design errors before they attempted data collection, including the error of manipulating the dependent variable and measuring the independent variable. Those students were able to correct the design and conduct valid research.

In an experimental hypothesis, the cause is the independent variable. It is manipulated by the experimenter. If it is truly the cause, then there should be a resulting change in the effect. In the sample experiment, acoustic similarity should affect memory interference, as shown in Figure 3-3 If the words used for an interference task are acoustically similar to the words used for the memory task, then they should produce more errors in retrieval than would visually similar words, or than would words that neither sound nor look like the target words.

**operational definition** A definition that is specific enough to be used to actually perform an experiment.

In addition to deducing the variables, researchers use deduction in the **operational definition** of those variables. An operational definition is one that is specific enough to be used to actually do an experiment. It's a definition that you can "operate" with. If you understand the abstract principles of driving a motor vehicle, you still need to know exactly how to operate a vehicle. Likewise, you may know general principles of research, but you must have specific definitions of variables to "operate" an experiment. Operationally defining the independent variable is the topic of Chapter 5. In this example the independent variable is the mode of similarity of words (acoustic vs. visual). The dependent variable is the interference effect on working memory. Operationally defining dependent variables is the topic of Chapter 4. To do an experiment, you must clearly define the variables in terms that you can operate (operational definitions). As with the selection of theory and hypothesis, this step is also aided by knowledge of the literature. Often a standard order and method of collecting data have been developed for a particular research area. This standard form of operating is called a *paradigm*. There are usually many variations of a paradigm, but the paradigm itself has been deduced to maximize a researcher's confidence in the validity of the premises of the research, namely:

**Figure 3-3**
*Cause and Effect Example*

The independent variable was manipulated by the experimenter.
The dependent variable was measured by the experimenter.
And all other things were equal.

A paradigm for studying interference in memory involves developing an interference task. First, participants are to study a list of target words. Then they are given a list of other words that form the interference task. Next, they are asked to remember the original words. The number of interference task words that are erroneously remembered is used as a measure of memory. This paradigm is illustrated in Figure 3-4 To manipulate the acoustic similarity of the words in the interference task, an operational definition of acoustic similarity is needed. In this example, the acoustically similar words all have one syllable with the long *o* vowel sound (e.g., *Sew, Dough*). Two comparison lists are defined. The list with visually similar words contains words that have the same shapes (e.g., *Fog, Pop*). The control list has words that neither look nor sound like any of the target words (e.g., *Ice, Kite*). The dependent variable must also be operationally defined. In this example, a free recall task will be used in which participants are given a blank sheet of paper and asked to write all the target words that they can recall.

The first premise in an experiment is that the experimenter manipulated the hypothesized cause. The second is that the experimenter measured the hypothesized effect. The third premise, that all other things were constant, is the major goal of experimental design. Various designs are employed to reduce chances of other things (besides the hypothesized cause) producing the effect. Figure 3-5 illustrates two common designs that could be used. A between groups design is one in which different participants receive each of the comparisons. This design is also called an *independent groups design* or a *between subjects design*. In the example, a group of participants would receive the acoustically similar words, a different group of participants would receive the visually similar words, and a control group (again different people) would receive the dissimilar words. To repeat, the groups would be made up of different people. That's why it's called a *between groups design*. To try to make all things constant between the groups, the experimenter would randomly assign participants to groups. (Chapter 6, "Hypothesis Testing: The Control Group Posttest Only Design," describes this type of design in detail.)

The lower portion of Figure 3-5 illustrates a repeated measures design (also called a within subjects design). In this design, each person experiences each different condition of the independent variable. The conditions are the ways that the cause is defined. In the simplest experiment the independent variable has two conditions. The hypothesized cause is present, or it is absent. The example illustrated in Figure 3-5 has

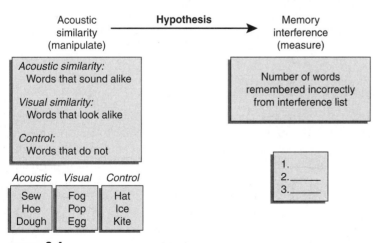

**Figure 3-4**
*Research Example Process*

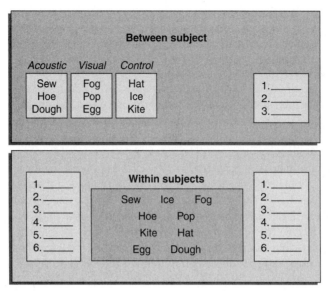

**Figure 3-5**
*Research Example Designs*

three conditions for the independent variable. A participant could be given the target words, presented with all the interference words (acoustic, visual, and control), and then asked to recall the target words. The interference measures would show separately the number of acoustically similar words, visually similar words, and control words that were erroneously recalled as target words. Because each participant experienced all three interference types, the results are calculated by looking for differences in memory within each person's scores. That's why it's called a within subjects design. It's also called a repeated measures design because for each person there are repeated measures of the dependent variable (memory interference). In this example each person produced three memory interference scores. The within subjects design purports to keep everything controlled besides the hypothesized cause because the same participants are compared to themselves. However, as shown in Chapter 7, "Hypothesis Testing: Pretest Posttest Design and Related Measures t Test," using a participant as his or her own control is no guarantee of keeping all other things constant.

Students often want to be able to select whether to use a between subjects versus a within subjects design in research after reading this section. To make the best selection, you need to know much more about research design. It is not possible to make a good choice among designs without knowledge of the particular research area and hypotheses to be tested. Be patient. We'll cover between groups and repeated measures designs in greater detail in Chapters 6 through 9.

### 3-3d  Data Collection

The data collection stage of the research involves induction. That is, data collection is the collection of the many facts with which to test the hypothesis. In an experiment it is essential to collect the data in exactly the same way for each and every data point. This is to assure the "all things being equal" premise in the design of the experiment. In Chapter 7, "Hypothesis Testing: Pretest Posttest Design and Related Measures *t* Test," and Chapter 10, "Where There Is More Than One Cause: Between Groups Factorial Experiments," we will discuss the issues of demand characteristics, experimenter effects, and other threats to the validity of an experiment. It is essential that the data are collected in a very precise and controlled manner.

### 3-3e Data Analysis

As stated in section 3-2a, data analysis is formalized induction. The first step is to organize and summarize (describe) the data. The **descriptive statistics** include frequency distributions, measures of central tendency (e.g., the mean), and measures of variation. The second step in statistical analysis is to calculate **inferential statistics**. Inferential statistics are used to find the estimated probabilities of getting the specific results by chance alone. In the sample experiment illustrated in Figure 3-4 the data collected for visually similar, acoustically similar, and control conditions represent three different **samples** of the **population** of all possible memory interference scores. Sampling from a specific population multiple times could produce very different sets of data. Then the descriptive statistics obtained in the experiment would be the result of chance, and not necessarily the result of the hypothesized cause. Inferential statistics provide probability estimates the researcher uses to infer either that the results were not likely to occur by chance or that they were. That's why these numbers are called *inferential* statistics. If the probability that the results would occur by chance is very low, the experimenter infers that they occurred because of the hypothesized cause/effect relationship.

**descriptive statistics** Summaries of the data in terms of central tendencies and spread.

**inferential statistics** Probability estimates of obtaining the specific results by chance alone.

**samples** The individuals selected from a population to be included in research.

**population** The group of individuals to whom research can be generalized.

## 3-4 Descriptive Statistics: Measures of Central Tendency

**Measures of central tendency** are statistics that describe the center of the data. Think of the center of the data as the most typical or average score. The three most frequent of these measures will be presented in sections 3-4a through 3-4c They are the mean (average), median (mid-point), and mode (most frequent).

**measures of central tendency** Descriptive statistics such as the mean, median, and mode that describe the center of a set of data.

### 3-4a Mean

The mean ($\overline{X}$) is used in almost every behavioral research project. It is a measure of the central tendency of the data. In other words, it gives an estimate of the middle. The procedure for calculating the mean was presented in section 1-8, "Using Statistics to Describe Facts: The Mean." Let's review by calculating the mean for some sample data from the memory interference experiment presented in Figure 3-4 Imagine that we had completed a between groups experiment with 10 participants per experimental group (acoustic interference, visual interference, and control). In the actual experiment there were 20 words in the original lists and 20 interference words. The dependent variable was how many of the interference words were incorrectly remembered as being in the first list. Table 3-1 shows the data for each group.

Each number in Table 3-1 represents a different person's interference score. The higher the number, the more interference that individual experienced. Remember that to calculate the mean of each group of data, you must simply sum the scores and then divide by the number of scores. The sum of the acoustic group interference scores is 66. A mean of 6.6 is produced by dividing 66 by 10.

Chapter 2, "Ethical Principles for Psychological Research," described how to make graphs. This section will describe graphing group means in more detail. Figure 3-6 shows a bar graph of the means of the memory interference data presented in Table 3-1 Each bar represents the mean for that group. The vertical axis (Y-axis) represents the amount of memory interference. You can see by looking at the graph that the control group had lower interference scores on average than did the acoustic or visual interference groups. Notice the scale of measurement in the graph. It starts at 3.5 and ends at 7.0. In actuality, the interference scores could have ranged from 0 to 20. It is possible to misinterpret trivial differences among group means by not paying attention to the scale of measurement of the dependent variable.

| TABLE 3-1 | Sample Data from the Memory Experiment | |
|---|---|---|
| | **Interference Condition** | |
| **Acoustic** | **Visual** | **Control** |
| 7 | 6 | 4 |
| 9 | 6 | 4 |
| 5 | 7 | 2 |
| 7 | 5 | 6 |
| 5 | 3 | 2 |
| 10 | 5 | 0 |
| 2 | 7 | 5 |
| 7 | 5 | 8 |
| 8 | 6 | 2 |
| 6 | 6 | 6 |

Up until about the past 10 years, a frequently used type of graph in behavioral research has been the line graph (see Figure 3-7 It looks similar to the bar graph. A point is drawn for each group mean, and then lines are drawn connecting the points. The greater the difference between the means, the steeper the slope of the line that connects their points. There is one important problem in the interpretation of statistical results with the line graph. Sometimes people attempt to interpret the lines to represent what the means would be between the points. What would happen if half the interference words were acoustical and half were visual? Some people would interpret the graph to imply that in such a case the mean interference score would be 6.1 on the graph. This is a wrong interpretation of the graph because no such condition was in the experiment. To avoid incorrect interpretations, the *Publication Manual of the American Psychological Association* (2001) specifies that you should use line graphs only when both the X- and Y-axes represent quantitative variables. There are exceptions to this general rule for graphs that involve more than cause (see Chapters 10,

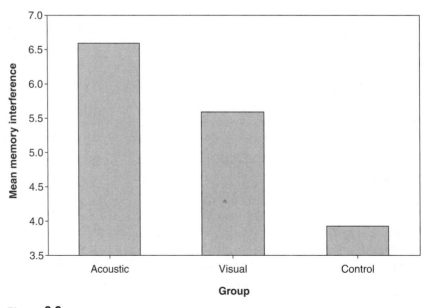

**Figure 3-6**

*Mean Memory Interferency for Each Interference Condition*

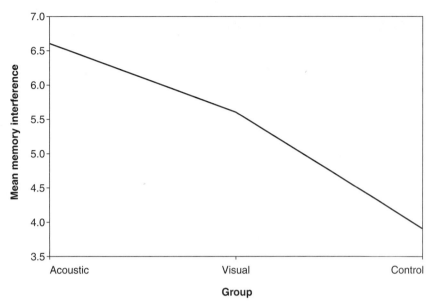

**Figure 3-7**
*Mean Memory Interferency for Each Interference Condition*

"When There Is More Than One Cause: Between Groups Factorial Experiments," and "Repeated Measures and Factorial Experiments").

### 3-4b Median

Generally, the mean is the best estimate of the middle. However, in some cases, other measures of central tendency give better or different information. The **median** is the middle score from a set of data. Thus, it is also a measure of central tendency. The median is easy to determine from a cumulative frequency table. Table 3-2 shows the frequencies for a variable LOT. This variable represents the length of treatment required for psychotherapy patients before discharge. The first column on the table, called the "Value," is the actual number of days of therapy. These values are presented in numerical order, with the lowest (23 days) at the top and the highest (1129 days) at the bottom. The second column includes the frequency of each value in the sample of 40 psychotherapy cases. As you can see, only one of the values was present more than once in the data (i.e., 2 people had 648 days of therapy).

The third column of Table 3-2 represents the percent of the total sample with that specific length of therapy. The fourth column, "Valid Percent," is the same as the third column, except that only cases with some data are used to calculate the percentage. If, for example, there were incomplete data from some participants, then they would not be included in total number of participants used to compute the percentages. In this example, all the data were complete; therefore, the percent and valid percent are the same. Let's consider another example, with the percent and the valid percent being different. Say that in a class of 40 students, there were 6 A's, 10 B's, 12 C's, 5 D's, 2 F's, and 5 people who withdrew. The percentage of students who scored a B would be 25% (10/40). However, the valid percentage that scored a B would be higher because counting the students who withdrew from the course is not valid. The valid percentage of B students would be 28.57% (10/35).

The last column in Table 3-2 is labeled "Cumulative Percent." It contains the percentage of the sample that had the particular score, or a lower score. For example, if you want to know how many people in the sample had 100 or fewer days of therapy, you look for the row closest to but not higher than 100. That length of therapy was 97 days. Following across that row to the last column, you can see that

**median** The middle score from a set of data.

| TABLE 3-2 | Variable Length of Treatment Frequencies | | | |
|---|---|---|---|---|
| **Value** | **Frequency** | **Percent** | **Valid Percent** | **Cumulative Percent** |
| 23 | 1 | 2.5 | 2.5 | 2.5 |
| 24 | 1 | 2.5 | 2.5 | 5.0 |
| 38 | 1 | 2.5 | 2.5 | 7.5 |
| 59 | 1 | 2.5 | 2.5 | 10.0 |
| 60 | 1 | 2.5 | 2.5 | 12.5 |
| 74 | 1 | 2.5 | 2.5 | 15.0 |
| 81 | 1 | 2.5 | 2.5 | 17.5 |
| 93 | 1 | 2.5 | 2.5 | 20.0 |
| 97 | 1 | 2.5 | 2.5 | 22.5 |
| 105 | 1 | 2.5 | 2.5 | 25.0 |
| 109 | 1 | 2.5 | 2.5 | 27.5 |
| 114 | 1 | 2.5 | 2.5 | 30.0 |
| 131 | 1 | 2.5 | 2.5 | 32.5 |
| 139 | 1 | 2.5 | 2.5 | 35.0 |
| 154 | 1 | 2.5 | 2.5 | 37.5 |
| 157 | 1 | 2.5 | 2.5 | 40.0 |
| 176 | 1 | 2.5 | 2.5 | 42.5 |
| 194 | 1 | 2.5 | 2.5 | 45.0 |
| 212 | 1 | 2.5 | 2.5 | 47.5 |
| 213 | 1 | 2.5 | 2.5 | 50.0 |
| 215 | 1 | 2.5 | 2.5 | 52.5 |
| 230 | 1 | 2.5 | 2.5 | 55.0 |
| 233 | 1 | 2.5 | 2.5 | 57.5 |
| 239 | 1 | 2.5 | 2.5 | 60.0 |
| 282 | 1 | 2.5 | 2.5 | 62.5 |
| 388 | 1 | 2.5 | 2.5 | 65.0 |
| 475 | 1 | 2.5 | 2.5 | 67.5 |
| 502 | 1 | 2.5 | 2.5 | 70.0 |
| 509 | 1 | 2.5 | 2.5 | 72.5 |
| 526 | 1 | 2.5 | 2.5 | 75.0 |
| 551 | 1 | 2.5 | 2.5 | 77.5 |
| 567 | 1 | 2.5 | 2.5 | 80.0 |
| 612 | 1 | 2.5 | 2.5 | 82.5 |
| 648 | 2 | 5.0 | 5.0 | 87.5 |
| 652 | 1 | 2.5 | 2.5 | 90.0 |
| 755 | 1 | 2.5 | 2.5 | 92.5 |
| 879 | 1 | 2.5 | 2.5 | 95.0 |
| 937 | 1 | 2.5 | 2.5 | 97.5 |
| 1129 | 1 | 2.5 | 2.5 | 100.0 |

22.5% of the 40 people in the sample had therapy for 100 or fewer days. Another example of cumulative percents that many students are familiar with are the percentile scores that accompany feedback on standardized college entrance exams such as the SAT or ACT. Each cumulative percentile represents the percentage of students who took the test who scored at or below the particular score.

To find the median, you look in the cumulative percent column to find the value at which the sample is evenly divided with 50% below that value and 50% above that value. In Table 3-2 the cumulative 50% occurs for the value of 213 days of therapy. This means that 50% of the sample (20 people) had therapy lengths of 213 or fewer days. Because the number 213 is included in this 50%, it is not the median. The next value, 215, represents the beginning of the top half of the data. This means that 50% of the sample (the other 20 people) had therapies of 215 or more days. Again, the number 215 is not the median because it is included in the upper half. The median is the number between the lower limit of the upper half (215) and the upper limit of the lower half (213). Therefore, the median is 214.

For most research the median and the mean are very close to each other. However, in some cases this is not so. The median will be different from the mean when there are some extreme scores on either the low or high end of the distribution being measured. For example, income is usually described with a median because the few individuals with very high incomes tend to *inflate the mean*. The mean could then be interpreted to indicate that most people earn more money than they, in fact, do. The median is not affected by extreme scores. Therefore, it is used to describe distributions of data that are liable to contain extreme scores (like income). The therapy length frequencies presented in Table 3-2 do contain some extreme high scores (e.g., 1129 days). These scores do inflate the mean. In fact, the mean of days of therapy for the sample is 330.75 days (116 days higher than the median). An incorrect interpretation from the mean would be that, on average, the participants spent 11 months in therapy. Examination of Table 3-2 reveals that only 35% of the sample had 11 or more months of therapy. In this case the median (214 days) is a better estimate of the central tendency of the data. The frequency histogram in Figure 3-8 shows how the extreme scores can inflate the mean, thus making the median a better indicator of the center.

### 3-4c  Mode

In addition to the mean and median, sometimes the **mode** is used to describe the central tendency of the data. The mode is simply the most frequent score. Although according to this statistical definition of the mode, there can be only one mode, some distributions of data are described better with multiple modes. They do not all have to have the same frequency, but they must be relatively more frequent than other scores. Although the computer analysis of the length of therapy data presented in Table 3-2 shows 648 days as the mode, this is not really so. Two occurrences of the same data point don't really qualify it as the mode. However, it is possible to describe

**mode** The most frequent score from a set of data.

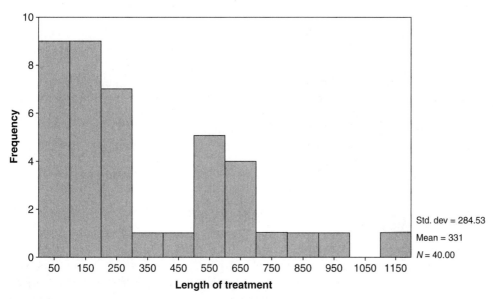

Std. dev = 284.53
Mean = 331
N = 40.00

**Figure 3-8**
*Length of Treatment Frequency Histogram*

**skew** The effect of extreme scores on the mean and variance.

the central tendency of the data by producing a frequency table that categorizes the data into broader categories. Figure 3-8 shows a frequency histogram produced with the Statistical Package for Social Sciences (SPSS). The length of therapy variable has been put into categories in which 100 days of treatment are included in a level. (The first category includes all 5 lengths of therapy between 1 and 100 days.) Examination of this histogram shows that there are modes for therapy stays between 1 and 100 days, and between 101 and 200 days. Nine of the 40 participants fit these two therapy length categories.

Modes are useful in understanding what is common in a sample of data. This is often beneficial for applications resulting from research. Figure 3-8 illustrates what is often the case when data are skewed. Skewed data are those that include a few extreme scores in one direction (either a few very high scores *or* a few very low scores). When the data are skewed, the median is always on the side of the mean away from the **skew** (extreme scores), and the mode is usually even farther away from the skewed end.

In this section, you learned how to describe the center of quantitative data. Chapter 4, "Operational Definitions of Dependent Variables and Scales of Measurement," covers the different types of data, including categorical data as well. Category variables are those that can be counted but not quantified. Many important attributes of participants are measured with categories. Examples of category participant variables include gender, ethnicity, occupation, religion, and political party affiliation. The mode is the best description of the most typical response for categorical scales.

# 3-5 Synthesis and Explanation of the Results

Students often think that their research is finished after they have calculated the statistics. That is not the case. After the data have been analyzed, the results must be interpreted. The experimenter will use deduction to relate the results of the experiment to previous research and current theory as well as to applications and generalizations. Finally, the researcher must use a combination of deduction and induction to draw implications of the experiment's results to potential future research.

# 3-6 APA Style: The Introduction

The introduction to a research report has three parts. The first section is basically the statement of the thesis. It presents the broad topic and some background information that explains why the topic is relevant for study. The second part, and the bulk of the introduction, is the literature review. This part is an integrated, evaluative summary of previous published research relevant to the topic. The literature review should lead your reader logically from the general topic to your specific hypotheses. The last portion of the introduction is the statement of the hypotheses. Because this organization is followed so regularly, research reports in APA style do not have separate headings for each part. An experienced reader will expect the organization of the report to be thesis statement, literature review, and then hypotheses.

### 3-6a  Choosing a Topic

Experienced researchers choose topics for research based on their previous research and their extensive reading of psychological research reports. Students, especially those who are just beginning to think about research, don't have the advantage of previous experience. The following suggestions may help you to find a good topic for research:

- Review the text from your favorite psychology class. What topics were most interesting to you?

- Browse some general psychology journals or magazines such as *The American Psychologist, Current Directions in Psychological Science*, and *Psychology Today* for summaries of interesting research reports.

- Select a journal that publishes research in an area of interest to you. Then read all the abstracts of research reports for the past several years.

- Based on your browsing, read the articles that seem to be most interesting. Keep a list of all the ideas for additional research that you have as you read these articles.

A good topic for research should be one that is not only interesting to you, but also relevant to current psychological science. A research topic that is to be a class project poses some practical limitations. For example, I recommend that students do their first experiment on a topic that can be studied with adult participants in a laboratory or other controlled environment. I used memory extensively for examples in this chapter. It is a good general area for beginning research. However, it is not specific enough to be a topic of research. A topic should be more specific than a broad area, but less specific than a hypothesis. Examples of topics for research on memory include level of processing, interference, retention techniques, and the relationship between mood and attention. Some memory topics are not advisable for beginning research projects. Such topics include the development of memory in preschool children, drug effects on memory, memory loss associated with disease (e.g., Alzheimer's), and the effects of sleep on memory consolidation. They are all great topics for research, but they also have practical limitations that make them difficult for a first research project. Sometimes a topic that seems to require research with a special population or professional training not available to a beginning researcher can be revised to a related topic. For example, students interested in the psychology of eating disorders have been able to study related topics of restrained eating, body image, and the influence of thinness on person perception.

## 3-6b  Searching the Literature

After you identify a topic, your next job is to find the appropriate research literature on which to base the introduction. Plan to read at least twice as much material as you will eventually include in your report. Everything that you read will provide a context and improve your understanding of the topic. You should include only those reports that directly relate to your eventual research project as citations in your report.

One of the most efficient ways to find the appropriate research literature is to use *Psychological Abstracts*. Each year a new multivolume set of *Psychological Abstracts* is published. The set includes thousands of abstracts of psychological reports published in the previous year. In addition, the set includes two great indexes (subject and author). Each index includes a set of abstract numbers for the abstract volumes in the same set. A **subject search** is the main way to access *Psychological Abstracts*. If you don't know the correct subject terms, you can look in the beginning of the subject index for the list of acceptable subject headings. The author index is very good to use when you know the author of a research report, but not the full citation. That could happen if you remember a name from a class or have read about the research in the popular press (e.g., newspaper or magazine) and only the author's name was given.

*Psychological Abstracts* is available in most college and university libraries. There is also an electronic form on the Internet that is called *PsychInfo*. It is available to enrolled students through many colleges and universities and to members of the American Psychological Association by personal subscription. The electronic version allows for **key word searches** in addition to subject and author searches. Key word searches can yield many results. In addition, the *PsychInfo* search engine allows Boolean searches. A **Boolean search** connects a set of key words with the Boolean

*Psychological Abstracts* Sets of thousands of abstracts of psychological reports published each year.

**subject search** A search of the subject index.

*PsychInfo* An electronic form of *Psychological Abstracts* available on the Internet.
**key word searches** Searches of *PsychInfo* or *Psychological Abstracts* using key, or relevant, words.

**Boolean search** An online search that connects a set of key words with the Boolean operators (and, or, not) to limit the search to specific interests.

operators (and, or, not) to limit the search to your specific interests. If you know exactly what you are looking for, and if you know the correct key words, a search of *PsychInfo* is likely to yield useful results quickly. If you don't have a specific set of key words and limiters, you may find hundreds of abstracts and be overwhelmed with only slightly relevant information. If you use the wrong key words (or spell them incorrectly), you may not find any relevant sources. The electronic search engines are great to use when you are searching for specific types of information. Using them is like looking for a needle in a haystack. If you know the right haystack and the exact properties of the needle, then you can search effectively.

Given the speed and power of the electronic version of *Psychological Abstracts*, why would anyone use the print version? A major advantage of the print version is that doing a **peripheral search** is easier because abstracts of similar research are grouped together. A peripheral search is examining the items near to the one you've located in case they are useful too. After you have used the abstract number to find the abstract in the volume of abstracts, you should also read the titles of the nearby abstracts. This type of search is a little bit like shopping in a department store. You can use the directory to know where in the store you need to go to get the shirt you want. When you get to the rack, you may find exactly what you want with the first shirt on the rack. Probably, though, you will search around for others that are similar and may find another shirt on the same rack that's just what you really wanted. Looking on the rest of the rack is a peripheral search. When you use an online electronic search, you can find a lot more, but you lose the peripheral search opportunities.

**peripheral search** An examination of the items near to the target. For example, reviewing those surrounding one located in *Psychological Abstracts* in case they also are useful.

# Summary

The research process is based on the hypothetico-deductive method. It involves the use of two main types of logic at each of its stages. Inductive logic is the process of making generalizations from many observations. Deductive logic is the combination of general rules and specific facts to come to specific conclusions. The research process involves both types of logic in the development of hypotheses, the design of research to test those hypotheses, data analysis, and the interpretation of the research results. Statistics represent one method of using inductive logic to draw generalizations from data. Three statistics that measure the central tendency of a set of data—the mean, median and mode—were described in this chapter. These three statistics summarize the data by describing its center (average or typical score). A literature review is an organization of the previous research facts that are relevant for developing the hypotheses and designing the experiment. *Psychological Abstracts* and *PsychInfo* can be used to locate relevant research literature.

# References

American Psychological Association. (2001). *Publication manual of the American Psychological Association.* Washington, DC: Author.

Beth, E. W. & Piaget, J. (1966). *Mathematical epistemology and psychology.* New York: Gordon and Breach.

Carroll, L. (1889). *Sylvie and Bruno.* London: Macmillan.

Carroll, L. (1977). *Lewis Carroll's symbolic logic* (W. W. Bartley, III Ed.). New York: Clarkson N. Potter, Inc.

Mill, J. S. (1874). *A system of logic, ratiocinative and inductive: Being a connected view of the principles of evidence and the methods of scientific investigation,* 8th Edition. New York: Harper & Brothers.

Twain, M. (1924). *Tom Sawyer abroad and other stories.* New York: Grosset & Dunlap.

## Exercises for Application

1. Describe how you could use inductive logic to solve the problem of what is the best food for a college student to eat.

2. Describe how you could use deductive logic to solve the problem in question 1.

3. Compare and contrast the use of deductive and inductive logic in problem solving. Evaluate the strengths and weaknesses of each.

4. The following data represent the Graduate Record Exam Psychology Subtest scores for 16 college seniors. TOT stands for the total score, EXPER stands for the experimental subtest, and SOCIAL stands for the social psychology subtest. Calculate the mean and median for each subtest score. Determine what, if any, are the modes. Make an interpretation of these statistics in words only.

| NUM | TOT | EXPER | SOCIAL |
|---|---|---|---|
| 1.00 | 7.00 | 40.00 | 39.00 |
| 2.00 | 17.00 | 43.00 | 48.00 |
| 3.00 | 33.00 | 54.00 | 48.00 |
| 4.00 | 12.00 | 47.00 | 40.00 |
| 5.00 | 17.00 | 49.00 | 44.00 |
| 6.00 | 26.00 | 50.00 | 50.00 |
| 7.00 | 84.00 | 64.00 | 60.00 |
| 8.00 | 15.00 | 44.00 | 45.00 |
| 9.00 | 10.00 | 41.00 | 44.00 |
| 10.00 | 96.00 | 72.00 | 71.00 |
| 11.00 | 12.00 | 41.00 | 47.00 |
| 12.00 | 33.00 | 53.00 | 51.00 |
| 13.00 | 41.00 | 48.00 | 54.00 |
| 14.00 | 45.00 | 51.00 | 55.00 |
| 15.00 | 26.00 | 52.00 | 44.00 |
| 16.00 | 9.00 | 39.00 | 44.00 |

## Practice Quiz

*Note:* You can find the correct answers to these questions by taking the quiz and then submitting your answers in the Online Edition. The program will automatically score your submission. If you miss a question, the program will provide the correct answer, a rationale for the answer, and the section number in the chapter where the topic is discussed.

1. John Stuart Mill said that the deductive method consisted of three operations. They were direct induction, ratiocinations, and
   a. verification.
   b. deduction.
   c. experimentation.
   d. explanation.

2. Statistics that organize and summarize data are called
   a. descriptive statistics.
   b. inferential statistics.
   c. hypothetico-statistics.
   d. deductive statistics.

3. The ability to use logic, as explained by Piaget,
   a. develops during childhood.
   b. is genetically determined.
   c. is greater for men than for women.
   d. can be fully developed in only a small portion of the population.

4. Which type of logic is weak because it does not allow you to draw a cause/effect conclusion?
   a. induction
   b. deduction
   c. hypothesizing
   d. experimentation

5. The process of going from general rules to specific applications is called
   a. induction.
   b. deduction.
   c. hypothesizing.
   d. experimentation.

6. To be correct, a deduction must be
   a. inferred from many observations.
   b. based on sound premises.
   c. complicated enough to represent reality.
   d. less than the total income.

7. Researchers who choose to use an atheoretical approach tend to rely mainly on
   a. induction.
   b. deduction.
   c. theory.
   d. empirical verification.

8. In an experiment the researcher manipulates the

   a. independent variable.
   b. dependent variable.
   c. control variable.
   d. intervening variable.

9. Statistics which estimate the probability that the results could happen by chance are called

   a. descriptive statistics.
   b. inferential statistics.
   c. hypothetico-statistics.
   d. deductive statistics.

10. If the median is very different from the mean, then the data are

    a. normal.
    b. inductive
    c. variable.
    d. skewed.

11. The final stage of the hypothetico-deductive method is

    a. induction through inferential statistics.
    b. new facts that can be used to generate more inductions.
    c. design of an experiment to test a hypothesis.
    d. a general theory that can be used deductively.

12. A standard method of conducting research that has been developed over a number of studies and demonstrated to be effective is called a(n)

    a. paradigm.
    b. operational definition.

    c. experimental design.
    d. hypothetico-method.

13. To be testable, a theory must be a general rule that can be used to derive

    a. statistics.
    b. inductive conclusions.
    c. research designs.
    d. specific hypotheses.

14. The precise method by which a researcher will measure the effect in an experiment is the

    a. hypothetico-deductive method.
    b. operational definition of the independent variable.
    c. operational definition of the dependent variable.
    d. inferential paradigm.

15. The middle score in an ordered set of scores is the

    a. mean.
    b. median.
    c. mode.
    d. skew.

16. What is one way that the *Psychological Abstracts* print version is superior to an electronic search using *PsychInfo*?

    a. You can find your key terms more easily.
    b. You can search by author.
    c. It is easier to go to the library than access a computer network.
    d. It allows for a peripheral search of similar research.

# Operational Definitions of Dependent Variables and Scales of Measurement

**Chapter** Four

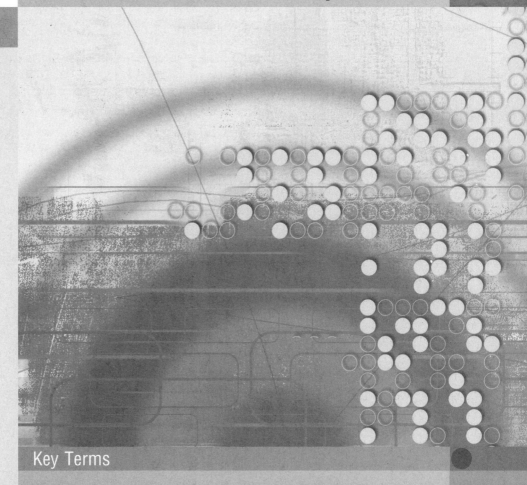

## Key Terms

bipolar
cell frequency
cross-tabulation table
dichotomy
interval
interval scale
ipsative
Likert scale
marginal frequencies
materials and/or apparatus
methods section
nominal scale

nonparametric statistics
ordinal scale
parameter
parametric tests
participants
power
ranking scale
ratio scale
reliable
scales of measurement
valid

# Learning Objectives

- Know how to operationally define a dependent variable.
- Be able to identify each of the four scales of measurement used in defining dependent variables.
- Be able to apply each of the four scales of measurement to operationally define any given dependent variable.

- Select the most appropriate scale of measurement for defining a particular dependent variable.
- Select the appropriate type of statistic to analyze data for each of the four different scales of measurement.
- Construct a cross-tabulation table for two nominal variables.

## Key Idea

Dependent variables are operationally defined in terms of how they are measured. A researcher should use the most precise scale of measurement that still retains validity for the concept being measured.

## 4-1 From Hypothesis to Design

In Chapter 3, you learned about the hypothetico-deductive method. After a researcher has deduced a hypothesis, he or she is then ready to design an experiment to test that hypothesis. One of the first steps in designing an experiment is to operationally define the variables. Those variables include the cause (the independent variable), the effect (the dependent variable), and all the things held constant (the control variables). This chapter will deal with operationally defining the dependent variable. The next chapter will deal with the operational definition of the independent variable. The hypothesis that will be used as an example in this chapter is shown in Taking a Closer Look 4-1.

## 4-2 Operational Definition

An **operational definition** is an explicit definition of a psychological concept in terms that can be used to operate the research design. This means that an operational definition for the dependent variable is a precise description of how it is to be *measured*. An operational definition must be so clear that anyone reading it knows exactly what was measured. It should also be clear enough that other researchers could read the definition and then measure the same variable in the same way.

Remember that part of the research design is the analysis of the data. The data are the outcomes of the operational definition of the dependent variable. Most computer programs require that you assign a numeric value to each data point. One way that

---

**Taking a Closer Look 4-1**    *Sample Hypothesis*

The hypothesis is attitude will be more influenced by a person who smiles while presenting a persuasive communication than by one who does not. In this case, the independent variable is the amount of smiling, and the dependent variable is the attitude. All other variables must be held constant.

you can tell whether your operational definition is precise enough is that you know exactly what number would be assigned for each possible outcome. Each number should represent a distinct, mutually exclusive set of responses. If the behaviors that you observe don't fit neatly within the definition, you won't know what number to assign them for the data analysis. You must consider this before collecting the data to avoid wasting time with useless data. You cannot do anything to correct a faulty operational definition *after* you have the data.

It is important to make sure that operational definitions are strong before you start data collection. In reality, the best way to determine that the definition of the dependent variable is strong is to use one that is "tried and true." Such a definition has been used before with good results. A survey of the research literature reveals the paradigms used for hypotheses of the kind you are studying. That survey shows you the results of the previous research and the methods. Those methods are likely to follow a specific paradigm. The paradigm will include the standard ways of operationally defining the variables under study. The paradigm may include the best scale of measurement for the research topic and the statistics to apply.

Sometimes new operational definitions are invented. At other times the standard definitions are adapted for a particular research context. In both of these cases, it is very important to do a pilot test of the definition to make sure that it is strong. The definition is operational if the numbers that result from it cover the entire behavior range likely to be demonstrated without ambiguity. A strong operational definition also has the characteristics of being **reliable** and **valid**. A reliable measurement scale is one that gives the same result every time. A valid measurement scale really measures what it is designed to measure. There are several different kinds of reliability and validity. Reliability and validity are two important attributes of good operational definitions. They will be discussed in more depth in Chapter 5, "Operationally Defining the Independent Variable," and Chapter 10, "When There Is More Than One Cause: Between Groups Factorial Experiments."

**reliable** Gives the same result every time.

**valid** Measures what it is designed to measure.

Operationally defining variables is easy to read about but hard to do. At this point it would be good to attempt to write your own operational definition of attitude. Attitude will be used as an example with each of the four kinds of measurement scales. After you write your definition, put it aside to evaluate once you have read the remainder of this chapter. You can then compare it to the examples provided here.

# 4-3 Scales of Measurement of the Dependent Variable

When operationally defining a dependent variable, you can choose from one of four different **scales of measurement**. These four scales differ in the level of their precision, going from the least precise nominal scale to the most precise ratio scale. It would seem obvious that you would always want to define variables with the most precise scale of measurement. However, sometimes the concept being measured can best be addressed with a less precise measurement scale because the less precise scale more correctly assesses actual experience of the research participants. This trade-off of precision versus reality should become clearer as you read about each of the four scales of measurement. The research sample used in this chapter is a study of the effects of verbal disfluencies on hiring decisions. Taking a Closer Look 4-4 through 4-5 show examples for each of the four levels of measurement.

**scales of measurement** Types of measurement used, whether nominal, ordinal, interval, or ratio.

## 4-3a Nominal Scale

The word nominal refers to naming. A **nominal scale** of measurement is one in which the variable is defined according to different "names." This type of scale is also called a *categorical scale* or a *class scale*. The data are differentiated according to type,

**nominal scale** Scale of measurement in which the variable is defined according to different "names."

not amount, so the information is sorted into different types (classes, categories, names). A nominal scale is not quantitative. However, the categories are often labeled with numbers for the purposes of coding data and statistical analysis.

Let's consider a cooking example. If a new cook were to attempt to make a salad, she or he would need to follow a recipe. The recipe is the operational definition. If the new cook could watch an experienced cook, perhaps the new cook could get by with the experience alone. However, even in this case the new cook would probably write down the recipe as the old cook prepared the food in order to have an accurate operational definition if the old cook is gone. Some types of recipes are made in terms of nominal scales of measurement. For example, a recipe for a salad may say to combine lettuce, tomatoes, carrots, and onions. It does not specify the amount but does specify the types of vegetables to be included. The type of vegetable is a nominal scale.

Now let's return to the example of the effects of smiling on attitude from Box 4-1. If you wanted to operationally define attitude with a nominal scale, you would have to do it in terms of the different types of attitude. The simplest type of nominal scale is a **dichotomy**. A dichotomy occurs when you can divide any variable into two, and only two, classes. In this example, then, you could operationally define attitude as the participant's agreement or disagreement with the communicator after the persuasive communication has been given. This, however, is too vague to be a good operational definition. A better definition would be: "Attitude is measured by the participant's answer to the following question presented immediately after the persuasive communication: Do you agree or disagree with the communication?" You could label the responses with numbers to make coding and statistical analysis easier. The labeling is arbitrary. For example, "Agree" could be 1 and "Disagree" could be coded as 2. You also could reverse the labels or could even use different numbers (such as 0 and 1). The researcher decides on the numeric labels for the categories but remembers that the categories differ in kind, not amount. In this example, coding "Disagree" with a 2 does not make disagree more than "Agree" (coded with a 1) even though $2 > 1$.

Dichotomies are only one type of nominal scale. Any time the dependent variable is measured according to kind (type, class, or category) of response, the variable is measured on a nominal scale. I did a study of the ways Korean students say they would resolve a conflict situation. I presented the students with a conflict situation involving a friend. They were to imagine that the friend had borrowed class notes to prepare for a big exam. Then the friend failed to return the borrowed class notes in time for the student to get ready for the exam. As a consequence, the student was unprepared for the exam. The students wrote essays describing how they would react to the conflict situation. I categorized the reactions that they wrote and then coded the essays using an operational definition of the different kinds of reactions. The numbers I used and their labels are as follows:

1 = Took notes from the friend
2 = Friend returned the notes
3 = Studied with the friend
4 = Copied notes for the friend
5 = Got notes from another source
6 = Nothing, it's not important
7 = Other
8 = No mention of reaction

To operationally define reaction to conflict, I had to develop categories. The categories had to be clear so that a different reader could easily classify each reaction in the essay into one, and only one, category. The categories needed to be mutually exclusive so that a specific answer wouldn't fit partly into one category and partly into another. The categories also needed to cover all the conflict resolution outcomes in the

**dichotomy** Type of nominal scale in which you can divide any variable into two, and only two, classes.

essay. That's why I used the code 7 = Other. I used the code 8 = No mention of reaction for essays that did not mention any reaction to the conflict. Some essays avoided the topic of conflict altogether. Notice that the categories are all different from each other, but you can't say which is the most. They are types, not amounts. Nominal scales involve qualitative differences in responses, not quantitative. Taking a Closer Look 4-2 presents the simplest type of nominal measure, a dichotomy, for the example of hiring decisions.

Many demographic variables are important in psychology and are necessarily measured on nominal scales. They include ethnic group, religion, and gender. In all of the cases, the statement that one type is more or less than another doesn't really make sense. Male is not less than female; they are categorically different and can't be evaluated quantitatively. Of course, none of the demographic variables described in this paragraph can be dependent variables in an experiment. You can't study them as the effects of causes. For example, manipulating an independent variable in an experiment will not result in a change of gender. The concept of scale of measurement applies to all variables, whether they are dependent, independent, or control variables.

## 4-3b Ordinal Scale

An **ordinal scale** of measurement is one that does allow quantitative comparisons in terms of which is more. That is, the data have an order (hence, the term *ordinal*). Like the nominal scale, the ordinal scale has clear categories. However, each category can be compared to the other categories. The numbers that are assigned to each category can be ordered in a meaningful way from low to high.

**ordinal scale** Scale of measurement that allows quantitative comparisons in terms of which is more.

An ordinal recipe for salad would be one that specified not only which vegetables to include but also specified the relative amounts of those vegetables to include. Such a recipe might go like this: Put in mostly lettuce, some tomatoes and carrots, and a scant amount of onion. It is not clear exactly how much of any one vegetable should be included, but which is more is very clear.

In psychology researchers often use ordinal measures of dependent variables in the form of **Likert scales**. They tend to be in the form of degree of agreement. For example, rather than asking participants whether they agree or disagree with the persuasive communication, you could ask them to indicate whether they

**Likert scale** Ordinal scale that requires ratings organized in order of strength—e.g., strongly agree, somewhat agree, neither agree nor disagree, somewhat disagree, or strongly disagree.

- Strongly agree
- Somewhat agree
- Neither agree nor disagree

---

**Taking a Closer Look 4-2**    *Example: Nonverbal Communication and Hiring Decisions*

A student researcher investigated the effects of verbal disfluencies on hiring decisions. To do this, she produced audiotapes of interviews. Audiotapes were selected based on the number and types of speech disfluencies present. There were three levels of disfluency: none, moderate, and high. A fourth comparison condition was a written transcript of the interview. These four levels represent the independent variable. The dependent variable, hiring decisions, was actually a set of dependent variables. Hiring decisions can be measured in many ways, and many of them were used in the study.

If you're a job applicant, it may be nice to know that you have a high ranking, your skills are rated highly, and the salary offered is high, but all of this is relative to the bottom line: Would you be hired or not? In the experiment participants were asked both how likely they would be to hire the individual (ordinal scale) and whether they would hire or not hire the applicant. The latter is a dichotomous nominal scale, even though "Hire" is definitely more positive than "Not hire." A mean hire (average hire) doesn't make sense. It is important to know how many participants said they would hire the applicant and how many said they would not (frequency).

- Somewhat disagree
- Strongly disagree

In this type of scale, it is clear that Strongly agree is more agreement than Somewhat agree, which is more than Neither agree nor disagree, and so forth. However, you don't know that the amount of difference between Strongly agree and Somewhat agree is the same as the difference between Somewhat agree and Neither agree nor disagree. In this example, you know the order but don't know the interval between points. This is the essential difference between an ordinal scale and the next level of measurement, the interval scale.

The study of Korean student conflict resolution, described in section 4-3a, also provides an example of an ordinal scale. In this case the variable of interest is how directly the student would confront the friend who had failed to return the class notes in a timely manner. Again, I read the essays for the types and range of responses and then developed categories. But in this case the categories do have an order, as you can see by examining the following code definitions:

1 = Directly asked for notes
2 = First indirectly asked, then directly asked
3 = Indirectly asked for the notes
4 = Not ask for the notes
7 = Other
8 = Not mentioned

Begin by looking again at the order in the first four categories. The most assertive response is 1, which is more assertive than 2. A response coded as 2 is more assertive than a response coded as 3. To be coded as 4, the student essay had to explicitly state that the student would not ask for the notes. Ideas in the essay that were about asking but didn't fit the ordered categories were coded as 7. This category would not be used for some statistical analyses because Other (7) is not more or less assertive than the responses coded 1 through 4. In this case it simply means that other possibilities existed and were counted. The same is true for those participants who did not mention asking their friends for the notes (directly or indirectly). The code 8 was given so that all responses could be coded. The first four codes, 1 through 4, represent the ordinal variable of assertiveness in asking for the notes from one's friend. Taking a Closer Look 4-3 presents an ordinal measure of hiring decision confidence.

**ranking scale** Scale in which participants are asked to rank their preference for a number of different objects or alternatives.

A particular type of ordinal scale is a **ranking scale**. In this type of scale, participants are asked to rank their preference for a number of different objects or alternatives. Researchers use ranking scales when they feel that the important thing to measure is not the absolute strength of a concept, but rather the relative strength. For example, values researchers such as Rokeach (1973) argued that a person's behavior would be most influenced by those values that are strongest relative to other values. Therefore, Rokeach measured values by having participants rank values in terms of their importance to the participants. Ranking is also used when psychologists study decision-making rules and the psychology of voting. In

---

> **Taking a Closer Look 4-3**    *Speech Disfluencies and Hiring: Ordinal Scale*

| | |
|---|---|
| After indicating whether or not they would hire the applicant in the interview they heard or read, participants were asked how confident they were in their decision. The measure of confidence was done with an ordinal scale as follows: | 1 = Not at all confident<br>2 = Somewhat confident<br>3 = Fairly confident<br>4 = Very confident<br>5 = Extremely confident |

these cases a ranking procedure more closely parallels the behavior being studied because usually people are allowed to select only one from among their top-ranked choices. Ranked data must be dealt with statistically in a different manner than other numeric data.

## 4-3c Interval Scale

An **interval** is the amount of space or distance between two things. The time that a lecture takes is the interval between the beginning of the lecture and the end of the lecture. An interval scale of measurement is like an ordinal scale, in that there is a clear order among the different points on the scale. In addition, the intervals between the points are known. That is why it is called an **interval scale**.

In a recipe the temperature that will be used to bake a cake is measured on an interval scale. The recipe may specify to preheat the oven to 350 degrees Fahrenheit or 200 degrees centigrade. The interval of degrees is specified, and the distance between each degree in terms of temperature is equal.

Attitude can be measured on an interval scale taking the **bipolar** measurement approach. Instead of labeling the response options as in section 4-3b, you would ask the participants to indicate the degree of agreement by circling the number that best represents their opinion, as shown here:

| 1 | 2 | 3 | 4 | 5 | 6 | 7 |
|---|---|---|---|---|---|---|
| Strongly disagree | | | | | | Strongly agree |

The labels at the ends of the scales are the two opposite "poles." That's why it's called a *bipolar scale*. The difference between each point on the scale is the interval of 1 unit. Thus, it is an interval scale. However, it is also clear from this example that the numbers must be limited in their interpretations. A score of 6 does not represent "twice" as much agreement as a score of 3. That is, the ratios aren't meaningful. The reason is that there is no true zero on the scale. Without a true zero, ratios are meaningless. The presence of a true zero in a scale is what differentiates the next level of measurement from the interval scale. The interval scale does not specify the true zero point for the quantity being measured.

The Korean student conflict resolution study was an extension of a senior thesis that Sara Rothenberger did with me (Rothenberger & Webster, 1998). Measuring students' conflict resolution styles used a standard paradigm. The measures were interval scales. Students were asked how likely they would be to use a particular conflict resolution technique for particular situations. For example, "How likely would you be to resolve the conflict by directly asking your friend to return the notes?" Instead of using an ordinal likelihood scale (Very likely, Somewhat likely, A little likely, Not at all likely), we used an interval scale that provided six equal intervals with no middle response:

Not at all likely ___ ___ ___ ___ ___ ___ Extremely likely

Participants placed a check mark on the line between the two scale ends that most closely represented their response. We scored the response by counting the numbers of lines from the left side of the scale (the left "pole"). The scores could range from 1 to 6. When defining a bipolar scale, the researcher has to decide whether to have an even or odd number of intervals. The researcher uses an even number of intervals if he or she hopes to force people away from the center, toward one end or the other of the continuum. If a middle response option is important, the scale should have an odd number of intervals. Taking a Closer Look 4-4 presents three of the interval scales used to measure perceptions of the job applicant. Note that these examples are 7-point scales with a middle, neutral option.

**interval** Amount of space or distance between two things.

**interval scale** Scale of measurement in which the intervals between the points are known.

**bipolar** Measurement approach in which labels at the ends of the scales are the two opposite "poles."

*Speech Disfluencies and Hiring: Interval Scale*

The participants were asked to rate the applicant presented in the taped or transcribed interview on a number of bipolar adjective scales.

Examples of these scales include:

| | | | | | | | | |
|---|---|---|---|---|---|---|---|---|
| Attractive | 1 | 2 | 3 | 4 | 5 | 6 | 7 | Unattractive |
| Honest | 1 | 2 | 3 | 4 | 5 | 6 | 7 | Dishonest |
| Shy | 1 | 2 | 3 | 4 | 5 | 6 | 7 | Outgoing |

Sometimes the bipolar approach is used with scale (pole) ends that aren't really opposite. Such definitions are confusing and lead to bad conclusions. From the Korean student conflict resolution example given for ordinal measures in section 4-3b, you can see that different results would have occurred if participants were forced to choose between directly asking their friend or indirectly asking:

Indirectly ask ___ ___ ___ ___ ___ ___ ___ Directly ask

In this case the scale has an odd number of intervals, but responses in the middle are ambiguous. They could mean that the students would both directly ask and indirectly ask. They could just as well mean that the students would do neither, not ask at all. For unambiguous interpretation, the poles of the scales must be true opposites and mutually exclusive. In the follow-up study conducted with American students, both essays and the interval scales were used. The interval scales included the likelihood of 12 different types of resolution responses, including one for directly asking, one for indirectly asking, and one for not asking at all.

### 4-3d Ratio Scale

**ratio scale** Scale that has equal intervals between its points and that contains a true zero.

A **ratio scale** of measurement is one that has equal intervals between its points and that contains a true zero. To understand this scale, you must appreciate the concept of a true zero. Section 4-3c showed Fahrenheit and centigrade scales for measuring temperature as examples of interval scales. Each of these scales has a zero point. However, neither of these zero points is a true zero. A true zero is the measurement of the total absence of the quantity being defined. Because 0 degrees centigrade is 32 degrees Fahrenheit, it is clear that it is not the absolute lowest temperature possible. Neither is 0 degrees Fahrenheit. Scientists who study the effects of temperature needed to have the power and precision of a ratio scale. Therefore, they developed the Kelvin scale. In the Kelvin scale, 0 represents the absence of all molecular movement (the molecular movement produces heat). It is a true zero.

Consider again the need for a true zero in order to make statements about ratios. A ratio can be used to describe one quantity in terms of relative amount of another, such as two to one, or one-fourth. If you were using an interval scale, the conclusion you would draw about relative temperature would be wrong. For example, with a Fahrenheit scale, you might be tempted to say that 66 degrees is twice as hot as 33 degrees. This is not true because the zero is not a true zero, but rather an arbitrary point on the scale. On the other hand, if you were measuring in Kelvin degrees, you could correctly say that 66 is twice as hot as 33, and conversely, 33 is half as hot as 66 degrees.

In cooking, ratio scales are often applied. The typical measures of quantities in terms of liters, cups, teaspoons, etc., are all ratio scales. Thus, you can easily double a recipe by making a ratio of 2 to 1 for all the ingredients. Some recipes are given only as ratios. For example, to reconstitute powdered milk, you follow this recipe: Mix 3 parts water for 1 part milk powder. This is a ratio definition, and in this case, the exact units are unnecessary. The milk will be right regardless of whether you add 3 teaspoons of water to 1 teaspoon of milk powder or you add 3 liters of water to 1 liter of milk powder.

Attitude agreement can be operationally defined using a ratio scale if you ask the participants to estimate the strength of their agreement on a scale from 0 to 5, where 0 indicates no agreement and 5 indicates total agreement. In this case the 0 could be called a *true zero,* and the ratios would make sense; e.g., 4 would indicate twice as much attitude as 2. However, the example points to a problem with a ratio scale. It is doubtful whether the participant is able to actually assess his or her own degree of agreement in such a precise manner. The numbers here are probably no more accurate than those obtained with an interval or perhaps an ordinal scale of measurement. In selecting a scale of measurement, you should choose the most precise level that makes sense for what you are measuring. It doesn't make sense to measure the distance between continents in inches. Nor does it make sense to measure psychological concepts more precisely than the participants can conceive of them. Consider the likelihood ordinal and interval scales for conflict resolution described in sections 4-3b and 4-3c. Instead, you could ask participants to rate their likelihood of using a particular conflict resolution as an odds ratio—for example, 2-to-1 odds. Or they could rate it on a 100% scale of 0% chance to 100% chance. Each of these is a ratio scale. But neither is superior to the simple ordinal scale because people don't actually know their behavioral likelihood as this level of precision. On the other hand, people do know some things very precisely. People who are accustomed to defining their weight using the ratio scale of pounds and ounces would have a hard time switching to the less precise ordinal scale of underweight, average, and overweight. The variable is measured more accurately in this case with the ratio scale. (Asking weights is advisable if you are studying self-disclosure. If you really need to know weight, then you need a scale to actually weigh the participants. Some people "misremember" their own weight. It's also good to use the same scale to have a more reliable measure because not all bathroom scales have the same accuracy.)

The admonition to avoid overly precise scales refers mostly to the measurement of perceptions, attitudes, and other self-reports. Many of the dependent variables that psychologists measure can and should be measured with ratio scales. They include reaction times, counts of choices or items remembered, number of problems solved correctly, etc. Whenever the quantity is a count, time, score correct or incorrect, length, or weight, then it is a ratio scale. Taking a Closer Look 4-5 shows an example of a ratio scale, proposed starting salary, that was used in the hiring study.

A class experiment on memory of emotional and neutral words provides a good example for a ratio measure of the dependent variable of memory. In the study both free recall and recognition memory were measured. To measure free recall, participants wrote down all the words they remembered from a list of 64 stimulus words that had been presented during an acquisition period. To measure the recognition memory, participants marked a list of 124 words indicating whether or not they remembered the word. Several different ratio measures resulted. They included

---

**Taking a Closer Look 4-5**         *Speech Disfluencies and Hiring: Ratio Scale*

It is difficult for participants to think about hiring decisions in terms as precise as a ratio scale. However, there is one way of valuing a potential employee that is measured with a ratio scale. That aspect is the proposed starting salary. Participants were asked how much money, to start, the applicant should be paid. This amount is a ratio scale.

- Number of words correctly recalled from the list (hits)
- Number of words forgotten from the list (omissions)
- Number of words falsely recalled (not on the original list)
- Number of words correctly recognized from the list
- Number of words not recognized from the list
- Number of words incorrectly recognized from the list
- Number of words correctly identified as not being on the list

Because the number of words on the list was 64 for everyone, the scores for remembering and forgetting are essentially the reverse of each other. If a person correctly recognized 35 of the words, then that would leave 29 that weren't correctly recognized. Hence, you can choose to define memory in terms of remembering or forgetting. It's redundant to do both. What's important with this example is seeing how the use of a ratio scale can aid in interpretation. You can say that almost twice as many emotion words ($\overline{X} = 6.2$) were recalled on average than neutral words ($\overline{X} = 3.15$). You can even make comparisons between the recall and recognition memory scores in terms of ratios. The results of the class experiment showed that the average recognition score was 5 times the average recall score.

# 4-4 Selection from among the Four Scales

As mentioned in section 4-3, the researcher should choose to operationally define a dependent variable with the highest (most precise) level of measurement possible with two additional considerations. First, the operational definition should not be more precise than can be actually measured. People will give numbers as answers to any question. But if I tell you my belief that it will rain today is a probability of 55.5462%, you would be mistaken to interpret that as anything more than a slightly greater belief that it will rain than not rain. From a subjective point of view, it would have been just as accurate for me to say, "I don't know. It might rain." The researcher can ask the participant to use a more precise scale of measurement but should take care not to conclude that the scale is how the participant actually perceived the judgment.

Second, practical considerations often influence the decision to use a particular level of measurement. If you study helping behavior, it is one thing to know how likely a person is to help, and yet another to know whether or not the person will help, and finally another thing to determine how much help the person will give. The examples of measuring conflict resolution in this chapter so far have all been particpant propensities. People were asked to say what they might do or how likely they would be to do a certain thing. The measures provided good numbers but didn't really answer the question, "How would the participant resolve the conflict?" Laura Grove and I (Grove & Webster, 1999) did answer that question in a study of conflict resolution among romantic couples. Laura assigned volunteer couples to mild conflict situations and videotaped their resolution styles. The coders of the videotapes were trained in applying a specific operational definition to identify behaviors as 14 categories of conflict resolution styles for both participants. We were able to describe how the romantic partners resolved their conflict in the experiment.

There is a drawback in defining dependent variables in terms of the "bottom line." As mentioned in section 4-3a, dichotomies such as "help" and "not help" are very weak measures of behavior. The statistical analysis of nominal data is not as powerful as that for ordinal, interval, or ratio scale data. Statistical **power** refers to the ability to find relationships among variables. The more precise the measurement scale, in general, the more powerful the statistical analysis. Of course, no statistical analysis can be powerful if the scales used for measuring the variables are not reliable as well. In Laura's study, we could know which of the 14 conflict resolution

**power** Ability to statistically find relationships among variables.

strategies was employed most often (Grove & Webster, 1999). In fact, we discovered that almost none of the partners used the demand-withdraw strategy that Laura predicted. However, this particular measure was not useful in testing our complex hypothesis about the causes of conflict resolution style. Researchers can measure the same concept with both the nominal scale and with a more precise scale. In the case of helping behavior, the help/not help dichotomy can be augmented by using a ratio scale to also measure how many minutes and seconds were spent helping. Laura and I used interval scales like those Sara used in her conflict resolution study (Rothenberger & Webster, 1998). After the partners had actually resolved their conflict, we asked them their likelihood of using a set of different conflict resolution methods. Those interval scale measures were very useful in testing our complex causal hypotheses.

When selecting the scale of measurement, the new researcher (any researcher for that matter) does not have to invent each operational definition alone. Like the new cook, the new researcher can benefit from the experience of the seasoned researchers. Tried and true operational definitions for cooking are put into cookbooks. Paradigms for research (recipes for operationally defining variables) are presented in research reports in journals. Not only is it essential to carefully review the previous research to deduce a good hypothesis based on carefully evaluated theory, but that review also provides the recipes (paradigms) for this research. The skillful researcher will take the information provided in those "recipes" and, if necessary, adjust them to fit the particular hypothesis and data collection conditions. Always remember to evaluate the research literature to find the operational definitions used in previous studies.

# 4-5 Scale of Measurement and Statistics

This section will outline the relation between scale of measurement and the selection and use of statistics. You should always select statistics to test hypotheses before collecting the data! This is an additional check that the design will indeed test the hypothesis. You should state the hypothesis in terms of predicted results using actual numbers if at all possible.

The first question that you must ask in determining what statistics to use is, "What is the scale of measurement of the data?"

### 4-5a Nominal Scales

If the data are nominal, then you should present the descriptive statistics in terms of frequency tables, percents, bar charts, or pie charts. (Note: Use only one form. To present all of them is redundant because they all give exactly the same information. Remember psychological writing always strives to be precise and concise.)

The most descriptive statistic for a nominal scale is the frequency distribution. After constructing a frequency distribution, you can use it to identify the mode (most frequent category). The mode is the only measure of central tendency that can describe nominal scales. Table 4-1 shows the SPSS output from a frequency analysis of the conflict outcome variable. The table shows the frequencies of each type of response to the conflict scenario.

You can see from Table 4-1 that less than three-fourths of the essays (73.8% of the total sample) mentioned a specific outcome to the conflict. Among the 48 who did mention something, the modal response (41.7%) was that the student would copy the notes for the friend (this involved tracking down the friend, getting the notes, making a copy). One-fifth of the participants wrote that their friend would return the notes. This example illustrates the value of the Valid Percent column in interpreting the results because it includes only those people who wrote something about the conflict outcome. The final column, Cumulative Percent, isn't very useful for

| TABLE 4-1 | | Outcome of Conflict Frequency | | | |
|---|---|---|---|---|---|
| | | Frequency | Percent | Valid Percent | Cumulative Percent |
| Valid | Took Notes from Friend | 3 | 4.6 | 6.3 | 6.3 |
| | Friend Returned the Notes | 10 | 15.4 | 20.8 | 27.1 |
| | Studied with Friend | 5 | 7.7 | 10.4 | 37.5 |
| | Copied Notes for Friend | 20 | 30.8 | 41.7 | 79.2 |
| | Got notes from another source | 7 | 10.8 | 14.6 | 93.7 |
| | Nothing, not important | 3 | 4.6 | 6.3 | 100.0 |
| | Total | 48 | 73.8 | 100.0 | |
| Missing | No Mention | 17 | 26.2 | | |
| Total | | 65 | 100.0 | | |

nominal variables. Saying that 79.2% or fewer of the participants copied the notes for their friends just doesn't make sense. Remember to avoid drawing incorrect quantitative conclusions from nominal data.

**parameter** Numeric value used in a formula.

Inferential statistics are divided into two classes: parametric and nonparametric. The terminology comes from the word **parameter**. A parameter is the numeric value used in a formula. For example, the formula Y = 2X + 3 can be evaluated for X equal to any number. If X = 4, then Y = 11. But the formula doesn't apply when the values for X aren't numbers. How could you evaluate the equation Y = 2X + 3 if X equals "studied with friends"? When nominal variables are coded with numbers, parametric statistics are inappropriate. The inferential statistics to use are the **nonparametric**

**nonparametric statistics** Statistics that are used on nominal data.

**statistics**. The most commonly used nonparametric statistic in psychology is the chi-square statistic ($\chi^2$), which is a measure of association between two (or more) categorical variables. In an experiment the independent variable is usually defined by different categories of the hypothesized cause. Therefore, it is treated as a categorical variable in the chi-square analysis. Consider the speech disfluency example from Taking a Closer Look 4-2. There were four conditions of the independent variable: no disfluency, moderate disfluency, high disfluency, and transcript. To see whether these conditions had an impact on the hiring decision, researchers calculated a chi-square. A chi-square statistic is calculated from a **cross-tabulation table** (also

**cross-tabulation table** Frequency table that shows the counts in the cells based on two variables (rows and columns).

called a *contingency table*). This is one way to present the descriptive statistics for a nominal variable. The $\chi^2$ statistic is presented in Chapter 12, "When the Cause Cannot Be Manipulated: Pre-Experimental Design and Chi-Square."

### 4-5b Constructing a Cross-Tabulation Table

Cross-tabulation tables are constructed by making rows and columns representing the two different nominal variables being tabulated, as shown in Table 4-2. Boxes represent the intersection between the two categories. For example, Table 4-3 shows the results for the speech disfluency study described in Taking a Closer Look 4-2 through 4-5. The number of participants who listened to the no disfluency applicant and decided to hire him or her is placed inside the top-left box. That places it under the No Disfluency column and in the Hire row. This number is called the **cell frequency.**

**cell frequency** Count (frequency) that occurs in one cell of a cross-tabulation table.

There are as many cell frequencies as there are cells in the table. The product of the number of columns and the number of rows ($c \times r$) is equal to the number of cells.

**marginal frequencies** Frequencies for the two nominal variables, without regard to their cross tabulation.

The cross-tabulation table also provides the frequencies for the two nominal variables, without regard to their cross tabulation. These frequencies are called the **marginal frequencies**. The frequencies in the final column are called the *row totals* (one kind of marginal frequency). You can see the number of participants who thought the applicant should be hired summed across all four of the treatment

| TABLE 4-2 | A Cross-Tabulation Table |
| --- | --- |

| | Variable A | | |
| --- | --- | --- | --- |
| **Variable B** | *Category 1* | *Category 2* | |
| *Category 1* | Cell frequency | Cell frequency | Row 1 Total |
| *Category 2* | Cell frequency | Cell frequency | Row 2 Total |
| *Category 3* | Cell frequency | Cell frequency | Row 3 Total |
| | Column 1 Total | Column 2 Total | Grand Total |

| TABLE 4-3 | Speech Disfluency by Hiring Cross-Tabulation Table |
| --- | --- |

| | Treatment Condition | | | |
| --- | --- | --- | --- | --- |
| **Decision** | *No Disfluency* | *High Disfluency* | *Transcript* | |
| *Hire* | 17 | 8 | 20 | 45 |
| *Not Hire* | 3 | 12 | 0 | 15 |
| | 20 | 20 | 20 | 60 |

conditions in the top row of the last column in Table 4-3. The last row on the bottom of the table shows the column totals (the other kind of marginal frequency). You can see how many participants received the transcript condition by looking at the bottom of the table. Of course, all the cell frequencies in that column must add up to the column total. The sum of the column totals will always be equal to the size of the total sample ($n$). The sum of the row totals will also always equal the size of the total sample. If either of these situations is not true, then there is an error in the table.

### 4-5c Ordinal Scales

Usually, it is informative to describe ordinal data in terms of a frequency distribution. Although it is possible to use mean, median, and mode for most ordinal variables, they will be easier to interpret if you first understand the frequency distribution. Recall the ordinal example of asking for the notes from the Korean conflict resolution study from section 4-3b. The scale was defined as 1 = Directly asked; 2 = Indirectly asked, then directly asked; 3 = Indirectly asked; and 4 = Did not ask. The mean for the 62 people who said something about asking their friend for the notes was 1.45. Now, 1.45 asking just isn't very informative. Because the scale is ordinal, there's no unit of measurement. If you had an interval scale, you would know the unit of measurement. With an ordinal scale, you don't know what unit goes with the 1.45. For the asking variable, the mode was 1 and so was the median. That helps the interpretation somewhat because now you know that the most frequent response was to directly ask the friend (mode) and that more than half the participants did so (median). Compare the description of the data given in the preceding sentences to that provided in Table 4-4.

Table 4-4 shows that 73% of the participants who said anything about asking their friend about the notes said that they would directly ask. Only 3 said that they would only indirectly ask, whereas 10 said they would start indirectly but then directly ask for the notes if they needed to. In this case the Cumulative Percent column can be useful because the codes are ordered in terms of assertiveness.

| TABLE 4-4 | | Asking for Notes Frequencies | | | |
|---|---|---|---|---|---|
| | | Frequency | Percent | Valid Percent | Cumulative Percent |
| Valid | Directly ask for notes | 45 | 69.2 | 72.1 | 72.6 |
| | First indirect then direct asking | 10 | 15.4 | 16.1 | 88.7 |
| | Indirectly ask for notes | 3 | 4.6 | 4.8 | 93.5 |
| | Not ask for notes | 4 | 6.2 | 6.5 | 100.0 |
| | Total | 62 | 95.4 | 100.0 | |
| Missing | Other | 2 | 3.1 | | |
| | No mention | 1 | 1.5 | | |
| | Total | 3 | 4.6 | | |
| Total | | 65 | 100.0 | | |

**parametric tests** Tests that require data (the parameter) that have been measured with quantitative scales.

The inferential tests used with most ordinal dependent variables will be **parametric tests**. Most inferential statistical tests are parametric because they require data (the parameter) that have been measured with quantitative scales. Because they are so common, they are seldom referred to as parametric statistics. The inferential statistics most commonly used in psychology for ordinal scales are the *t* test and analysis of variance. Special nonparametric statistics may be appropriate for some ordinal scales. They include the Wilcoxin rank-sum test and the Kruskal-Wallace analysis of variance.

**ipsative** Within any individual participant, the scores sum to a constant.

There are special problems with analyzing ranking data. Ranking produces **ipsative** scores. The scores are called *ipsative* because within any individual participant, the scores sum to a constant. Imagine that you are participating in a conflict resolution study. You are asked to rank order the following ways of resolving the conflict:

- Do nothing, just wait.
- Ask a mutual friend to negotiate.
- Discuss the conflict calmly with your friend.
- Use physical force to get what you want.
- Engage in a battle of words with your friend.

Your responses to each of the items depend on how you rank the other items. They are not independent. Your average ranking across all five options is 3.0. No, I'm not psychic; I'm not reading your mind in the future as I write this text. Your mean is a consequence of the ipsativity of the ranks. Not only is your mean rank 3.0, so is everyone else's.

A frequency table is the best descriptive statistic for ranking data. The descriptive statistics you can use include the mean, median, mode, and variance for each item ranked (not for each person doing the ranking). If you present the mean of all the participants' rankings, it will always be the middle rank, so be especially careful to remember what the data represent as you analyze and interpret them. There are special inferential statistical procedures for ranking data. Greer and Dunlap (1997) claimed that with proper care they can be analyzed with analysis of variance.

### 4-5d Ratio and Interval Scales

Ratio and interval data are analyzed in the same ways. The statistics of mean, median, and mode are descriptive of ratio and interval scale data. The difference between the interval and ratio scale statistics lies in the interpretation. It is often very descriptive to compare one treatment group to another in terms of a ratio. For example, participants in the smiling condition showed twice as much agreement as participants in the nonsmiling conditions. Such a conclusion would be warranted only if you measured agreement with a ratio scale.

Both ratio and interval scale data can be analyzed with parametric statistics. As with the ordinal scales, the most commonly used inferential statistics for these scales of measurement are the *t* test and analysis of variance.

Now get out your own operational definition of attitude. Check it against these questions:

- What scale of measurement are you using?
- What are the units used?
- What statistics can be applied?
- Is it clear enough that some other person could accurately measure the same thing with no further instructions?

If you can answer all these questions satisfactorily, then you have an operational definition of a dependent variable.

# 4-6 APA Style: The Method Section, Part 1

The second major section of a research report is the **methods section**. It has at least three main subsections: the participants or subjects, the materials and/or apparatus, and the procedure. *The Publication Manual of the American Psychological Association* (APA, 2001) describes the method section in detail. Section 4-6a and 4-6b will deal with the first two subsections. The procedure subsection will be discussed in Chapter 5, "Operationally Defining the Independent Variable."

**methods section** Section of an APA style paper that describes the participants, materials and/or apparatus, and the procedures of the study.

### 4-6a Participants or Subjects

In reports of single experiments, the method section typically begins with a description of the **participants** or subjects of the research. For complex research, the methods section may begin with a subsection labeled "Design."

The heading of this section should be "Participants" if the research involved people. It should include the number of participants and the participant attributes that are important for determining the appropriate applications of the research results. Examples of potentially relevant participant attributes include gender, age group, occupation, and marital status. You should also describe any incentives that were used to encourage study participation in this section.

If the study involved nonhuman subjects, the heading should be "Subjects." Again, you should describe the relevant attributes of the subjects. In the case of animal subjects, these attributes include genus, species, and other particulars that make it clear what types of animals were studied. Also, describe the particular animal care practices that were used so that readers can successfully replicate the study under the same conditions.

**participants** Human subjects of the research.

### 4-6b Materials and/or Apparatus

You should present an exact description of the **materials and/or apparatus** required to conduct the experiment in enough detail that another researcher can use the same operational definitions as you did. Standard laboratory equipment (e.g., stopwatch) can be described without further detail. Specialized equipment should be identified by name and manufacturer (e.g., Marrietta Millisecond

**materials and/or apparatus** Questionnaires, scales, equipment, and so forth that are needed to conduct research.

Timer). You should describe an apparatus that has been constructed based on previous research and cite the previous research report. You also should describe in great detail any apparatus that was specially designed and constructed for the purpose of the study.

When the research involves only materials (e.g., conflict scenarios and essay forms), then the heading for this section should be "Materials." You should describe standardized measurement scales by name and include a citation to the published form of the scale. The nature of the instrument, its subscales, if any, and the type of items it includes should all be described. The reliability and validity statistics associated with the instrument should be described if they are available.

Any materials that have been developed for the experiment and not previously published should be described in great detail. It may be appropriate to include the entire set of materials in an appendix. The materials section should contain a clear, complete description of the materials.

Some of the apparatus and materials used in the experiment can be implied. For example, participants need a writing tool to write answers. It is not important whether they do so with a pencil or a fountain pen. They may need to write the answers while sitting at a table. The precise type of chair and table are probably not crucial to the study. Generally, you do not need to mention the typical office supplies and furnishings used in conducting the experiment. However, in some studies, these items may be important. What you include in the apparatus and materials section depends on the specific experiment. You should include anything that is important to replicating the experiment (operationally defining the variables in the same way).

## 4-6c  APA Style Headings for the Method Section

The method section follows the introduction. It does not start on a new page but begins directly after the introduction, under the heading "Method." Five levels of headings are used in APA format (APA, 2001). You can write most reports of a single experiment with only two or three heading levels. You use the level 1 heading for the major sections of the article. Thus, "Method" is a level 1 heading. Level 1 headings are centered. The headings for the subsections are level 2 headings; they are left justified and italicized. If the subsections have multiple parts, then you may also use level 3 headings. A level 3 heading begins a paragraph; it is italicized and followed by a period. Only the first word and proper names are capitalized in a level 3 heading. The exact APA heading format is shown in Figure 4-1. The level 3 headings are optional and depend on the complexity of the experiment. The level 1 and 2 headings are required for any report of an experiment.

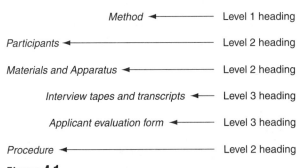

**Figure 4-1**
*APA Style Headings for the Method Section*

# Summary

The dependent variable in an experiment must be operationally defined with a precise scale of measurement. There are four levels of measurement scales. A nominal scale is used if the dependent variable is best measured in terms of categories. Nominal scale measures are best described with frequency tables and modes. They must be analyzed with nonparametric inferential statistics such as the chi-square.

Ordinal scales measure the dependent variable in terms that can be ordered but that do not have the other quantitative properties of numbers. Examples of ordinal scales are rankings and Likert scales (e.g., strongly agree, somewhat agree, neither agree nor disagree, somewhat disagree, and strongly disagree). Ranking data must be carefully analyzed and interpreted because of ipsativity. Other ordinal scale data may be described by means and medians and analyzed with parametric statistics such as the $t$ test and analysis of variance. Great care must be taken to avoid misinterpreting the statistics from ordinal measures because the numbers assigned represent only relative order and not amount.

Interval scales are basically ordinal scales with the added benefit of having equal intervals between each measurement point. An example of an interval scale is the IQ.

Ratio scales are true quantitative scales. They have all the benefits of the interval scales, and they contain a true zero. Examples of ratio scales are times, counts, and lengths. Both interval scales and ratio scales are analyzed with parametric statistics such as the $t$ test and analysis of variance.

Researchers should operationally define their dependent variables with the most precise level of measurement they can to maximize the power of their design. At the same time, they should select measurement scales that are both reliable and valid for the psychological variable under study.

# References

American Psychological Association. (2001). *Publication manual of the American Psychological Association.* Washington, DC: Author.

Greer, T. & Dunlap, W. F. (1997). *Analysis of variance with ipsative measures.* Psychological Methods, 2, 200–207.

Grove, L. B. & Webster, S. K. (1999, April). *Couples in conflict: An examination of relationship, power and gender.* Poster presented at the annual meeting of the Eastern Psychological Association, Boston, MA.

Rokeach, M. (1973). *The nature of human values.* New York: Free Press.

Rothenberger, S. & Webster, S. K. (1998). *Gender, group status and importance as determinants of conflict response.* Resources in Education, CG029219.

# Exercises for Application

1. Make an operational definition for measuring the perception of the Mueller-Lyer illusion using a nominal scale of measurement.

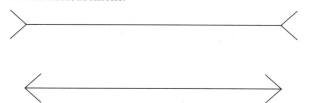

2. Make an operational definition for measuring interpersonal attraction using an ordinal scale.

3. Make an operational definition for measuring learning using an interval scale.

4. Make an operational definition for measuring memory using a ratio scale.

5. Describe the types of data analyses that are appropriate for each of the operational definitions you wrote for exercises 1 through 4.

6. Imagine that the following data represent a set of color-blind individuals by type of color blindness and gender. Construct the cross-tabulation table. What percent of the sample are red-green color-blind males? What percent of the sample are females? What percent are totally color-blind?

| Gender | Type of Color-Blindness |
|--------|-------------------------|
| Male | Red-green |
| Male | Red-green |
| Female | Blue-yellow |
| Female | Red-green |
| Male | Total |
| Male | Blue-yellow |
| Male | Red-green |
| Female | Red-green |
| Male | Total |
| Male | Red-green |
| Female | Blue-yellow |
| Male | Blue-yellow |
| Female | Red-green |
| Male | Red-green |
| Male | Total |
| Male | Red-green |
| Female | Blue-yellow |
| Female | Total |
| Male | Red-green |
| Male | Red-green |
| Male | Red-green |
| Male | Total |
| Female | Blue-yellow |
| Male | Total |
| Male | Red-green |

## Practice Quiz

*Note:* You can find the correct answers to these questions by taking the quiz and then submitting your answers in the Online Edition. The program will automatically score your submission. If you miss a question, the program will provide the correct answer, a rationale for the answer, and the section number in the chapter where the topic is discussed.

1. The scale of measurement that is not quantitative is the
   a. nominal scale.
   b. ordinal scale.
   c. interval scale.
   d. ratio scale.

2. Academic major is a variable that should be measured on a(n)
   a. nominal scale.
   b. ordinal scale.
   c. interval scale.
   d. ratio scale.

3. A scale of measurement that has only two categories is called a
   a. nominal scale.
   b. dichotomy.
   c. disjoint variable.
   d. yes-no scale.

4. A scale that clearly shows only the order of the data is called a(n)
   a. nominal scale.
   b. ordinal scale.
   c. interval scale.
   d. ratio scale.

5. A dating service asked its clients to rate descriptions of prospective dates as either good, acceptable, so-so, or no way. The scale it used was a(n)
   a. nominal scale.
   b. ordinal scale.
   c. interval scale.
   d. ratio scale.

6. An IQ score is an example of a(n)

   a. nominal scale.
   b. ordinal scale.
   c. interval scale.
   d. ratio scale.

7. A measurement scale that contains a true zero is a(n)

   a. nominal scale.
   b. ordinal scale.
   c. interval scale.
   d. ratio scale.

8. The most precise scale of measurement is the

   a. nominal scale.
   b. ordinal scale.
   c. interval scale.
   d. ratio scale.

9. A cross-tabulation table should be used to describe data measured on a(n)

   a. nominal scale.
   b. ordinal scale.
   c. interval scale.
   d. ratio scale.

10. The statement "The treatment tripled the amount of memory produced" implies that memory was measured on a(n)

    a. nominal scale.
    b. ordinal scale.
    c. interval scale.
    d. ratio scale.

11. You have a(n) _____ definition if it is so clear that other researchers could read the definition and measure the variable in the same way as you did.

    a. operational
    b. implicit
    c. ideological
    d. hypothetical

12. A scale in which participants are asked to indicate how strongly they agree with a specific statement selecting from the options strongly agree, somewhat agree, neither agree nor disagree, somewhat disagree, or strongly disagree is a

    a. rational scale.
    b. reliable scale.
    c. valid scale.
    d. Likert scale.

13. A scale with opposite words on each end of a set of marking lines or numbers is called a(n)

    a. Likert scale.
    b. bipolar scale.
    c. open-ended scale.
    d. dichotic scale.

14. The ability of statistics to show relationships among variables is called

    a. reliability.
    b. generalizability.
    c. inherent stability.
    d. power.

15. The decision to use the term *subjects* or *participants* in the methods section of an APA style report is determined by

    a. the preference of the researcher.
    b. whether the research design is a true experiment.
    c. whether the study is theoretical or hypothetical.
    d. whether the research involves nonhumans or humans.

16. Nonparametric statistics should be used with variables measured on a(n)

    a. nominal scale.
    b. ordinal scale.
    c. interval scale.
    d. ratio scale.

# Operationally Defining the Independent Variable

## Chapter Five

## Chapter Outline

## Key Terms

between subjects
concomitant variation
control
counterbalancing
dispersion
experimental treatment
external validity
internal validity
levels of the independent variable
matching
multiple treatment interference
normal distribution
random assignment

random number table
$s$
$s^2$
standard deviation
standard error of the mean
standard scores
treatment
uniform distribution
variability
variance
within subjects
$z$-score

# Learning Objectives

- Know how to operationally define an independent variable.
- Be able to determine the correct number of levels of an independent variable needed to test a hypothesis.
- Explain the purpose of a control condition.
- Differentiate a between subjects experimental design from a within subjects experimental design.

- Know how to best assure that experimental treatment conditions are equivalent.
- Know when and how to use repeated measures, match participants in groups, or use random assignment to treatment conditions.
- Calculate the variance for a set of data.
- Be able to calculate and interpret a z-score.

## Key Idea

The operational definition of an independent variable is the precise description of how the researcher will manipulate it at each of its levels.

The second step in moving from a hypothesis to the design after operationally defining the effect (dependent variable), as described in Chapter 4, "Operational Definitions of Dependent Variables and Scales of Measurement," is to operationally define the cause (independent variable). An operational definition for an independent variable is one that specifies exactly how the independent variable will be manipulated in the experiment. To manipulate an independent variable, the experimenter must produce it in different conditions. That is, the experimenter must be able to present it to participants in changed form.

## 5-1 Manipulating the Cause

The concept of manipulating a cause to determine its effect is based on the fourth of Mill's Canons of Proof. The philosopher John Stuart Mill (1874) stated the following proofs that are necessary to prove causation:

1. Where there is the effect, there must also be the cause.
2. Where there is the cause, there must be the effect.
3. Where there is no cause, there should be no effect.
4. When there is a change made in the cause, there should be a resulting change in the effect.

**concomitant variation**
Change in one variable that occurs as a result of a change (manipulation) in the other variable.

The last principle is called the principle of **concomitant variation**. The first three principles are necessary, but they are not sufficient to prove a causal relationship. They can be shown to be the case for events that are correlated but that are not causally related. The principle of concomitant variation is both necessary and sufficient to prove causation. It forms the basis of the experimental method. The experiment is to change the cause (manipulate the independent variable) and observe the resulting effect.

Before going on, let's consider a humorous example by applying Mill's Canons of Proof. Suppose that we wanted to know why the chicken crossed the road. There are many answers to that straight line of the old, old joke. What's your favorite? Is it "to get to the other side"? That answer and all the others that I've heard don't address the underlying causal relationships. Let's try Mill's Canons of Proof with the motivational answer, "because it was there." Does this causal explanation show agreement between the cause (the road was there) and the effect (the chicken crossed the road)? Yes. When the chicken crossed the road (effect), the road was there (cause). Therefore, the first canon is satisfied. Also, when the cause was present (the road was there), the chicken crossed it (effect). At least this was the case during the episode described in the joke. The third canon would be applied to say that when there is no road (cause absent), the chicken would not cross it (effect absent). By the first three canons, the evidence for a causal relationship is sound. All these things would have to be true for the causal relationship to hold. If they were not so, then we would not believe that the chicken crossed the road *because* it (the road) was there. But just because the first three canons are satisfied, we, as scientists, are not. The first three canons are necessary to prove a causal relationship, but they are not sufficient.

The fourth canon is that a change in the cause should result in a corresponding change in the effect. That means we, as the researchers, must make a change in the cause (the road is there) and measure a change in the effect (whether the chicken crosses it). We would need to collect some data under different road conditions (the road is there or the road isn't there). Then we would need to observe the chicken's behavior. Obviously, when there was no road, the chicken could not cross it. However, our chicken is plucky, and she did find other roads to cross some of the time. When we removed the chicken from the road, she still walked the distance to find a road 4 times out of 10. But what about the change in the cause when the road was present? Did the chicken always cross the road when it was there? Imagine that our test chicken crossed the road only 3 times out of 10 when we brought it to different roads. Our experiment would not support the causal statement that the chicken crossed the road because it was there. Say, on the other hand, our results showed that when we removed the chicken from the road, she never crossed any road, and that when we presented the chicken to the road, she always crossed. Then we would be justified in believing that the chicken crossed the road because it (the road) was there. We would have satisfied the fourth of Mill's Canons of Proof.

Some hypotheses involve more than one cause. Perhaps the chicken crosses the road because it is there and because she is motivated to do so by another cause (the other chickens are all on the other side). In these cases the experiment will be designed with as many independent variables as there are hypothesized causes. Each one will be operationally defined separately. These types of designs, called *factorial designs*, will be covered in detail in Chapter 10, "When There Is More Than One Cause: Between Groups Factorial Experiments," and Chapter 11, "Repeated Measures and Factorial Experiments." This chapter will focus on operationally defining one independent variable. Taking a Closer Look 5-1 presents the variables and hypothesis that will be used to illustrate different methods of defining the cause, emotion.

# 5-2 Levels of Cause

Manipulating an independent variable in an experiment means presenting at least two **levels of the independent variable** to the participants. Levels refer to different amounts or types of the cause. Hence, the "change" in the independent variable needed for the fourth Canon of Proof is accomplished when the experimenter changes from one level to the other level. In the simplest case, this refers to comparing the presence of the cause (**treatment**) to the absence of the cause (**control**). The levels are also called the *conditions* or *treatments*. The condition in which

**levels of the independent variable** Different amounts or types of the cause.

**treatment** Presence of the cause.

**control** Condition in which the cause is absent.

---

**Taking a Closer Look 5-1**          *Sample Hypothesis: Emotion Produces Arousal*

In this hypothesis, the independent variable is emotion, and arousal is the dependent variable. Assume you have already operationally defined arousal. The next step is to operationally define emotion. That is, you must specify exactly how it is to be manipulated.

**experimental treatment**
Condition in which the cause is present.

the cause is present is the **experimental treatment** or condition, and the condition in which the cause is absent is called the *control treatment* or *condition*. If the independent variable is really the cause of the effect, then there should be a different measurement of the dependent variable in the experimental condition than in the control condition.

### 5-2a  Experimental Versus Control Conditions

Let's consider the simplest case first. In this case your task is to define an experimental condition in which emotion is present and a control condition in which no emotion is present. To make it operational, you must specify exactly how you will induce emotion in the participant. Say you have decided to use the emotion happiness. Perhaps you could induce happiness in most participants by giving them some good news. An operational definition must include the timing, a description of the nature of the good news, and so forth, like the example shown in Taking a Closer Look 5-2.

The placebo condition is a special kind of control condition. The placebo has all the external features of the treatment condition, but it lacks the critical causal property. A classic example of the placebo is the sugar pill. It was used to determine whether a drug was effective in alleviating symptoms or if the patient's expectation for treatment provided the relief. Thus, some participants were given the real pills, whereas others received pills that looked exactly the same but didn't contain the drug. None of the patients knew whether they were taking the real pills or the placebos. If the real pills improved the patients' physical conditions but the placebos did not, then the researchers could conclude that the drug was effective. The placebo condition can be applied to many kinds of treatments. Whenever the control condition appears to have all the features of the treatment condition except the hypothesized cause, it is a placebo condition.

### 5-2b  Multiple Treatment Conditions

In many experiments, you will have more than two levels of the cause. There are two clear reasons for this. First, the independent variable may have different effects at different amounts. You could hypothesize that weak emotion produces weak arousal and that stronger emotion produces stronger arousal until an upper limit is reached (at which no more arousal can be produced even though the emotion is stronger). To test this hypothesis, you would have to operationally define emotion according to several different magnitudes. For example,

- Control condition: Participant has no knowledge of the random drawing.
- Weak emotion condition: Participant wins $0.50 in the random drawing.
- Moderate emotion condition: Participant wins $5.00 in the random drawing.
- Strong emotion condition: Participant wins $50.00 in the random drawing.
- Extreme emotion condition: Participant wins $500.00 in the random drawing.

**Taking a Closer Look 5-2**

*Operational Definition of the Manipulation of the Emotion Happiness*

Happiness condition: As part of the experimental procedure, the participant is told that he or she has won a random drawing for a prize of $50.

Control condition: The experiment proceeds with no mention of a random drawing for $50.

In this example five different *amounts* of emotion are defined. The definition is operational because it can be manipulated exactly as described. The type of random drawing is not important except that it is the same in each case. It is also not important that all participants value money in the same way. That criticism does not affect the operational definition. It does, however, bear on the **external validity** of the study. The external validity of an experiment is how well its results may be applied outside the experimental setting. An experimental design has **internal validity** if the only logical explanation for the effect observed (dependent variable) was the manipulation of the cause (independent variable). Internal validity results from being able to logically rule out all other alternative explanations. Both internal and external validity are important in research design. If the experiment has internal validity, you can be confident of the cause-effect conclusions drawn from it. On the other hand, if the experiment also has external validity, you can make better applications of the results. Therefore, you try to operationally define variables in ways that maximize their external validity as long as the internal validity criteria are fulfilled first. Internal validity is the first requirement for external validity. If the results of the experiment cannot be unambiguously explained by the hypothesized cause, then those results should not be applied outside the experimental setting either.

A second reason to have multiple levels of the independent variable in one experiment is that the independent variable's effect depends on its *type*. For example, you could have hypothesized that different types of emotion produce different amounts of arousal. In that case you might operationally define emotion by having the participant view films of the following:

- Happiness condition: A person wins $50.00 in a random drawing.
- Sadness condition: A person has to pay an unanticipated extra $50.00 fee.
- Disgust condition: A person is eating rotting food.
- Control condition: A person is walking around a track.

These four different conditions are qualitatively different. They are aimed at producing different types of emotion. It is very difficult to produce different types of emotions because people react differently to different stimuli. For example, winning a contest can produce pride in some people and anxiety in others. Another technique that is often used to produce emotional response is to have participants remember and describe in writing a typical happy, sad, or average day.

You could ask the participants to describe when they felt joy, fear, anxiety, surprise, and other types of emotion as well. The act of recalling and describing an emotion usually produces that same emotion, although in lower amounts.

# 5-3 Within Subjects Versus between Subjects Designs

When defining the independent variable, you need to determine whether you will use a within subjects or between subjects design. A **within subjects** design is one in which each participant receives all the levels of the independent variable. Thus, each participant acts as his or her own control or baseline. This type of design is called either a *within subjects design* or a *repeated measures design* (the terms are synonymous). A **between subjects** design is one in which each participant receives only one treatment. This means that each condition is given to different groups of participants.

## 5-3a Within Subjects Designs

One major aim of designing the research is to assure that the treatment conditions are the same on all aspects except the independent variable. With this in view, it

**external validity** Degree to which results may be applied outside the experimental setting.

**internal validity** Ability to logically rule out explanations for the effect observed (dependent variable) other than the manipulated cause (independent variable).

**within subjects** Experimental design in which each participant receives all the levels of the independent variable.

**between subjects** Experimental design in which each participant receives only one treatment.

might seem better always to use a within subjects design. The reason is that the participants in the different treatment conditions will always be equivalent because they are the same participants. However, the process of the experiment itself could make the conditions nonequivalent, even though the same participants are in each condition. Consider the last operational definition given for emotion in section 5-2b. Suppose you first have the participant view the happy condition film and then measure arousal. Next, you have the same participant view the sadness condition film. It is unlikely that the participant is in the same psychological condition as he or she was prior to the happiness treatment. Thus, the experience of being in the experiment has altered the participants, and participants are not psychologically equivalent with even themselves.

It is difficult to understand how a participant can be different from himself or herself as a result of experiencing one level of the cause. Therefore, let's look at a second example. Think about the chicken that crossed the road again. By now, you probably have a name for her. In a repeated measures design, Clarice Chicken would receive both the treatment (be presented with the road) and the control (be placed where there is no road). Clarice may get to the other side of the road on the first trial (the treatment) and be no longer motivated to look for a road to cross on the second treatment (the control). She's not really the same chicken, psychologically, as she started out. Her motivation has changed. Because participants may learn or change from experiencing one level of the cause, repeated measures research is usually restricted to those variables that will not have any residual effects. That is, participating in one condition is known to have no effects on participation in other conditions. Repeated measures designs are good when there are no **multiple treatment interference** effects.

The sample research in Taking a Closer Look 5-3 illustrates some of the considerations that must be taken into account with a repeated measures design. The number of stimulus sets (12 pairs of speeches) was fairly small, but the experiment required about an hour to complete. The time for the experiment was limited to 1 hour in order to avoid participant fatigue. Presenting the pairs of speeches in the right order was very important to rule out the effect of learning over time. For example, the participants may improve over the 12 trials so that if the women target speeches were presented first, the results would appear to support the hypothesis, but the real explanation would be improvement during the experiment. That's why there were three repetitions of each gender of speaker and a randomized order of presentation between the male and female speakers. Keeping the conditions ordered in this way over a set of trials is called **counterbalancing**.

## 5-3b  Between Groups Designs

The between groups design avoids the problem of multiple condition interference because each participant experiences only one condition (level of the cause). However, there remains the problem of how to make the groups of participants equivalent so that they are similar on everything except the independent variable. Remember that in order to satisfy the fourth Canon of Truth, only the cause should change, while everything else remains unchanged. Then the resulting change in the effect (dependent variable) can be explained as a result of the cause (independent variable). You can take two approaches to assure that the individuals in different treatment groups are equivalent in a between subjects design. One is matching the participants in the different conditions, and the other is random assignment to treatment group.

**Matching** refers to the practice of determining, before the experiment is conducted, which psychological variables are important for the particular causal relationship under study and matching the participants on those variables. For example, in studies of the effects of emotion on arousal, you might consider it important that the groups be composed of individuals who are similar in terms of age, gender, education, and openness. To match participants on these variables, you would first have to

**multiple treatment interference** Threat to internal validity of an experiment that occurs when multiple treatments are present and interfere with each other.

**counterbalancing** Keeping the numbers of participants with a particular attribute equivalent across the treatment conditions.

**matching** Determining, before the experiment is conducted, which psychological variables are important for the particular causal relationship under study and matching the participants on those variables.

> ## Taking a Closer Look 5-3    *Sample Research*
>
> Daryl, a former student of mine, hypothesized that people can detect men lying more often than they can detect women lying because of men's nonverbal leakage. He designed a repeated measures experiment by manipulating the gender of the speaker as follows. Three men and women were recruited to act as the target individual. Each was instructed to describe his or her academic major and reasons for it to another individual. The target speakers were then asked to lie about the same information to a different individual by presenting someone else's information (one of the other speakers) as their own. Each speech lasted about 2 minutes and was videotaped. The tapes showed only the head and shoulders of the target individual. Because the study was concerned with nonverbal communication, there was no sound.
>
> A stimulus tape that contained 12 pairs of 2-minute speeches was constructed. Each target person's speeches were paired (his or her own opinion and the opinion of another presented as his or her own). The participants were asked to identify which of the two speeches was the deceptive one. The two pairs of speeches were randomly ordered with the constraint that half the false statements came first and half came second in the pairs. Furthermore, the order of male and female speakers on the tape was random.

measure all the participants on each variable. Then you would attempt to match them according to their scores so that you could place participants who are most similar into matched pairs (for a two-group experiment). You would have to find matches of four persons for the four-group experiment suggested in section 5-2b. In that example the four emotion treatment conditions were happiness, sadness, disgust, and control. Each participant of the matched set would be randomly assigned to a different one of the treatment conditions. Therefore, the participants in each treatment condition should be equivalent at least on the variables that were used in the matching.

A more routine example of matching is the process that is often used to divide children into teams for spontaneous sporting activities. Assume that you want to have children play a game of basketball. Furthermore, you want the teams to be fairly composed (i.e., equivalent). You would first match children based on height and then assign one child from each matched pair to Team A and the other to Team B. You might argue that, even with matching on height, the two teams may not be equivalent because they could differ on experience, skill, intelligence, and drive. Because none of these qualities were used for matching, the groups may not be equivalent on them. If you had matched on these variables, other variables that were not considered still could influence the abilities of the groups for basketball. Thus, matching cannot guarantee the total equivalence of the basketball teams. Neither can it guarantee total equivalence of treatment groups in an experiment.

**Random assignment** is another technique used to make treatment groups as equivalent as possible. It rests on the assumption that a truly random process will result in an equivalent overall distribution of participant attributes in each group. Assignment to treatment condition is random if each participant has an equal chance of being assigned to each treatment condition. Although in common usage, the word *random* can connote *haphazard, unpredictable, and uncontrolled*, random assignment in an experiment is just the opposite. It is very precise. It must be done in a very controlled manner. Random assignment to a treatment group allows the researcher to have confidence that the attributes of the group, on average, are equivalent.

Random assignment works best with large sample sizes. If you were to test the hypothesis that the chicken crossed the road because it was there, you would need to get another chicken. If you had only Clarice Chicken and her shy friend Celia, you could not be confident that randomly selecting one of them for the control condition (no road) and the other for the treatment condition (road present) would make the

**random assignment** Method by which each participant has an equal chance of being assigned to each treatment condition.

two chickens equivalent. Clarice is more adventurous and active. She crosses more of everything than does the shy Celia. Therefore, a difference in behavior between the two conditions is more likely to be the result of differences in the individual chickens than the hypothesized cause. If you had all the chickens from the coop and could randomly assign half of them (say 15) to the control condition and the other half (15) to the treatment condition, then you could assume that the two groups are equivalent. The larger the groups, the better randomization is able to accomplish group equivalence.

Many students confuse the concepts of random assignment and random sample. Random assignment to treatment condition occurs when each member of an available sample has an equal chance to be assigned to each treatment condition. A sample is random when each member of a population has an equal chance of being included in the sample. A random sample increases the validity of survey research because the sample is more representative of the population. A random sample does not increase the internal validity of experimental research because the purpose of the experiment is to demonstrate a cause-effect relationship with the given sample. The most important consideration for the internal validity of an experiment is that everything is controlled other than the manipulated cause (independent variable) and the measured effect (dependent variable). In between groups designs, random assignment is the best way to assure equivalence of treatment groups and is therefore one of the best ways to make the experiment internally valid.

The between subjects experiment described in Taking a Closer Look 5-4 required that 72 participants be randomly assigned to the 6 treatment conditions. In addition, Amy had to counterbalance the design for participant gender because another student researcher had previously discovered a gender effect in a similar type of experiment. Counterbalancing means to keep the numbers of participants with a particular attribute (gender in this case) equivalent across the treatment conditions. This meant that participants were randomly assigned to treatment condition, with the constraint that as closely as possible, the ratio of men to women was the same in each condition. Ideally, there would be 6 men and 6 women in each of the conditions. The men and women would be randomly assigned, except that when a particular condition was filled up (had its 6 participants), then participants would be randomly assigned to the remaining treatment conditions. In reality, it was not possible for Amy to recruit as many men for her study as women. She randomly assigned the 47 women to the 6 conditions and the 25 men to the 6 conditions. As you can deduce, it was impossible

---

**Taking a Closer Look 5-4**     *A Between Subjects Experiment in Rhythm and Emotion*

A former student, Amy, hypothesized (Webster, Radjenovic & Woods, 1992) that the complexity of rhythm affects emotional arousal. Low complexity (very simple rhythm) music was hypothesized to produce a small negative emotion. Moderately complex rhythms were hypothesized to be easily accommodated and thus produce a positive emotional response. Overly complex rhythms were hypothesized to produce negative emotion because they could not be accommodated into existing musical schema by the participant.

To test this hypothesis, Amy operationally defined the complexity of rhythm defined as follows:

- Control: No music
- Level 1 (Simple): Quarter; rest; 8th; 8th

- Level 2 (Moderate):8th; 8th; 8th; 16th; 16th
- Level 3 (Complex): Changing patterns with 8th and 16th notes
- Level 4 (Very complex): Add syncopation and 8th rests
- Level 5 (Extremely complex): Add triplets and 16th rests

A musician played each of the rhythms on a drum machine. One-half-hour tapes were made and played at the highest volume level in the adjoining room while participants wrote about their day as part of the experiment. Participants were randomly assigned to one of the six treatment conditions.

| TABLE 5-1 | Random Number Table |
|---|---|

| | | | | | | | |
|---|---|---|---|---|---|---|---|
| 15376 | 14350 | 45084 | 82430 | 36474 | 71060 | 74603 | 74516 |
| 57146 | 10723 | 24447 | 80321 | 24533 | 28165 | 84737 | 20030 |
| 12268 | 15041 | 56816 | 77388 | 80642 | 05028 | 78501 | 20531 |
| 28064 | 58542 | 26171 | 33616 | 33180 | 64875 | 44687 | 21763 |
| 28006 | 51176 | 33646 | 04003 | 53723 | 65324 | 24070 | 20843 |
| 13877 | 38330 | 47278 | 05174 | 30426 | 05678 | 11615 | 80758 |
| 57450 | 36685 | 57180 | 65352 | 21361 | 58504 | 02832 | 53017 |
| 51203 | 76231 | 46366 | 70678 | 82067 | 37854 | 85550 | 13122 |
| 51061 | 12637 | 42380 | 72547 | 25325 | 70736 | 48811 | 51702 |
| 50768 | 50388 | 07381 | 26605 | 28072 | 18211 | 71537 | 81423 |
| 40571 | 85336 | 57140 | 81307 | 70445 | 01443 | 41675 | 37453 |
| 88232 | 40057 | 76055 | 56347 | 14470 | 42115 | 08720 | 41332 |
| 52072 | 36587 | 40242 | 05514 | 65865 | 30718 | 88167 | 72643 |
| 44057 | 36101 | 00612 | 35640 | 23560 | 71815 | 26506 | 64044 |
| 68473 | 64616 | 04528 | 11654 | 35845 | 56624 | 14747 | 41013 |
| 08416 | 20460 | 56441 | 83315 | 67860 | 35224 | 41872 | 15470 |
| 30336 | 15217 | 53827 | 11737 | 68414 | 21077 | 38112 | 08331 |
| 48222 | 80373 | 57464 | 24584 | 11665 | 40158 | 07401 | 45843 |
| 52415 | 86678 | 32061 | 52023 | 67042 | 88352 | 40354 | 20402 |
| 22580 | 15870 | 37658 | 50041 | 25245 | 42717 | 87287 | 05842 |
| 43547 | 66145 | 76528 | 82356 | 34700 | 72084 | 23307 | 20868 |
| 85536 | 77320 | 15072 | 40383 | 05856 | 56463 | 22585 | 36186 |
| 03406 | 13258 | 10563 | 72330 | 24724 | 18123 | 34145 | 52068 |
| 35638 | 67684 | 05074 | 56373 | 85130 | 47238 | 48730 | 54118 |
| 36084 | 15015 | 16748 | 68448 | 51035 | 13331 | 45284 | 43785 |
| 51808 | 22652 | 71264 | 23262 | 37635 | 58187 | 04842 | 41711 |
| 50882 | 52054 | 06288 | 71441 | 15726 | 60145 | 10712 | 68672 |
| 03742 | 65517 | 24554 | 05226 | 33412 | 60746 | 42270 | 28210 |
| 36715 | 26246 | 77357 | 40337 | 85240 | 57850 | 54133 | 11153 |
| 51133 | 64287 | 52671 | 56240 | 30233 | 52761 | 15830 | 35846 |
| 27412 | 72237 | 31401 | 45723 | 41807 | 41476 | 88176 | 22472 |
| 80314 | 37682 | 83032 | 32523 | 20481 | 74244 | 73768 | 50427 |
| 24311 | 45550 | 24461 | 38052 | 28742 | 57686 | 45703 | 68107 |
| 71307 | 21102 | 43365 | 88415 | 42510 | 47054 | 64123 | 53281 |
| 38448 | 48808 | 58324 | 10666 | 22432 | 87770 | 28417 | 12088 |
| 33410 | 78185 | 40755 | 56330 | 37621 | 82220 | 61873 | 38741 |
| 76166 | 23274 | 35842 | 45844 | 13560 | 32658 | 28418 | 35061 |
| 54885 | 71854 | 61140 | 81884 | 11328 | 20485 | 74765 | 00778 |
| 36610 | 28715 | 25263 | 72386 | 46252 | 85756 | 28540 | 06366 |
| 03236 | 71485 | 44273 | 20310 | 60272 | 33217 | 52574 | 27688 |

to have the same numbers of men and women in each condition because neither 47 nor 25 is evenly divisible by 6. Amy kept the numbers as balanced as possible.

### 5-3c Random Assignment Method A: The Random Number Table

Table 5-1 is a small **random number table**. This table can be useful in making random assignments. People have different methods of entering the table (i.e., finding the starting place). Some close their eyes and place the point of a pencil on the page. They start where the pencil is positioned. I like to determine my starting point by selecting the row and column by opening a different book to any page.

**random number table** Table of numbers that has been derived through a random process and that can be used for random assignment.

I take the first number I find on that page as the column, open to another page and find the first number to be the row, and finally, use the first number on a third page as the position within the set of numbers. The table of random numbers can be used in any order—left to right, top to bottom, bottom to top, etc. Before using a random number table to make assignments to condition, determine the decision rules. For example, if there are two treatment conditions, experimental and control, then odd numbers could indicate the experimental, and even numbers could indicate the control condition. It would be just as effective to have the numbers 1, 2, 3, 4, 5 represent the experimental group and the numbers 6, 7, 8, 9, 0 represent the control group. If you have three treatment groups, you use different decision rules. You then assign the conditions according to the decision rules.

### 5-3d Random Assignment Method B: Computer Assignment

Many computer programs can set up the random assignment for experimental designs. Computers cannot be truly random, but they can approximate randomness. To add the element of randomness to the design, most programs either ask for a starting number (which the experimenter supplies through a random process) or take a starting number from the computer's clock. Each program has its own directions. These programs are very useful for complex designs that require counterbalancing.

### 5-3e Random Assignment Method C: The Shuffle

Sometimes all the participants complete the experiment at about the same time, and they participate by completing questionnaires or surveys. Often in these cases the independent variable is manipulated by changes in the written material. A thorough shuffling of the materials can be a random process. This is especially true because the experimenter does not control the order in which participants enter the experiment and take up the materials.

### 5-3f Random Assignment Method D: The Gambler's Devices

Any truly random process, such as the flip of a coin, throw of the dice, or draw of a card, can be used for random assignment. One teacher I know likes to use a deck of playing cards to demonstrate random assignment. The deck makes assignment to two groups easy because there are two colors, red and black. It also works for four groups because there are four suits (hearts, spades, diamonds, and clubs). You also can use it for three-group designs by using only the face cards (king, queen, and jack). You can obtain virtually any number of treatments (up to 13) by retaining that number of cards and shuffling. This method works for my fellow teacher because he is demonstrating a process, and he can really shuffle the deck. It doesn't work for me because I have yet to master the art of shuffling.

In real research, dice, coins, and cards are seldom used for random assignment. They may not really be random, and using them to make an assignment takes more time than the other methods.

## 5-4 APA Style: The Method Section, Part 2

The first two parts of the method section for a research report were described in Chapter 4, "Operational Definitions of Dependent Variables and Scales of Measurement." The next part of the method section is the procedure (APA, 2001). It is covered in this chapter because the procedure section of a research report generally contains the operational definition for the independent variables. The procedure immediately follows the description of materials and/or apparatus and uses the same level heading. It contains a description of the exact procedures for the experiment. It usually begins with a summary of the information that was given to the participants during the consent process and as instructions. It also contains descriptions of each experimental condition, including the control condition if there is one. Any information on the procedure for measuring the dependent variable that was not already described in the materials and apparatus section is also described in the procedure. The procedure usually ends with a description of the debriefing for studies involving humans, or a description of the postexperiment procedures used for nonhuman subjects.

You can use two common organizational styles for the procedure. One is to describe each aspect of the experiment as it occurred chronologically. Consider the experiment on rhythm complexity. A chronologically ordered procedure would have this basic form:

- Informed consent and general task instructions
- Independent variable manipulation described
- Control
- Simple
- Moderate
- Complex
- Very complex
- Extremely complex
- Measurement of emotion
- Debriefing

The second common organization is to describe the control condition (or one of the treatments in an experiment without a control condition) first and then describe how each of the other treatments differs from it. In that case the organization would look like this.

- General procedure for control condition
- Informed consent and general task instructions
- Control condition described
- Measurement of emotion
- Debriefing
- Differences from general procedure for the other levels of the independent variable
- Simple
- Moderate
- Complex
- Very complex
- Extremely complex

You should describe the procedure in enough detail that someone else can replicate the study using the same procedures as you did. It can contain references to the methods described in published research reports. Summarize those procedures and cite the sources. Be sure to include the full citations in the reference section of the paper. The procedure subsection describes your operational definitions for the independent variable and the ways you designed the study to control other possible influences. It should contain everything that was important to the internal validity of your design.

# 5-5 Descriptive Statistics: Measures of Variability

Chapter 3, "The Hypothetico-Deductive Method and Experiments in Psychology," covered measures of the central tendency of a set of numbers. In that chapter, you

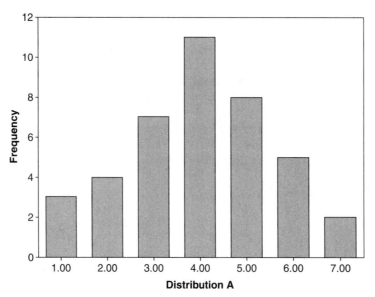

**Figure 5-1**
*Frequency Distribution A*

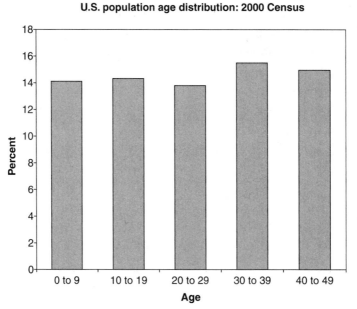

**Figure 5-2**
*Frequency Distribution B*

**variability** Amount of difference within a data set.

**dispersion** Spread of the numbers that make up the data within a data set.

**normal distribution** Hypothesized probability density function that resembles the bell-shaped curve and is assumed to represent the measurement of a variable in a population.

saw how to describe the center of a set of data with the mean, median, and mode. You also can describe a set of data in terms of **variability** or dispersion. **Dispersion** is another word for spread. Measures of dispersion describe the spread of the numbers that make up the data. Figures 5-1, 5-2, and 5-3 show three distributions that have the same mean and median but have different dispersions. Figure 5-1 shows Distribution A. It is most like the **normal distribution** of scores in behavioral science. Most of the scores are near the center. The farther away from the mean, the less frequent is any given score. There are very few really low scores or really high scores. Consider the example of children's heights discussed in section 5-3b. In a given class,

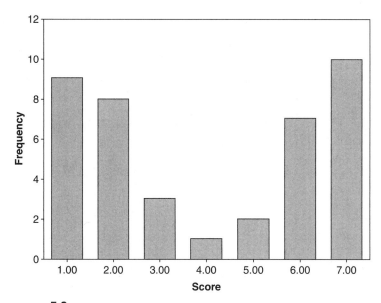

**Figure 5-3**
*Frequency Distribution C*

some of the children will be tall and some short, but most will tend to be close to the average height for children their age. In many cases, behavioral data are normally distributed.

Distribution B is more spread out than Distribution A. In fact, it is almost a flat distribution. A totally flat distribution is called a **uniform distribution**. Each score occurs with about equal frequency. The mean and median do not really describe a central tendency because the scores are so widely dispersed. In this example there is more variance because there are more extreme high and low scores than in Distribution A, and there is no tendency for more people to score near the center of the distribution. An example of an almost flat distribution is the age of the U.S. population as reported in the 2000 national census, as shown in Figure 5-2. There are roughly equal proportions of the population in each 10-year category of ages up to the age of 50.

Distribution C is the most diverse of the three. It shows the greatest variance. Instead of having most scores tending to be around the mean and median, the most extreme scores are also the most frequent ones. This type of distribution almost never occurs in behavioral science. If it does, the distribution may in reality represent two different distributions. A bimodal distribution like the one shown in Figure 5-3 has occurred on tests occasionally. When there are very many A's and F's with few grades in the middle, it generally means that the class is made up of two groups of students who differ on motivation, background, or aptitude.

**uniform distribution** Flat distribution in which each score occurs with about equal frequency.

## 5-5a  Measuring the Variance

The variance is used to measure the dispersion of a set of scores. The term **variance** refers to many measures of dispersion as well as to the specific statistic called the *variance* ($s^2$). It is like the term *Biro* that is used to refer to all ballpoint pens and to the Biro brand of ballpoint pens. It also is like the use of the term *Coke* to refer to any soft drink and to the particular brand of cola produced by Coca-Cola. Thus, variance refers to measures of dispersion in general and to $s^2$ in particular. After introducing the particular $s^2$ statistic called *variance* (in this case for a sample of data), this section will cover other forms of the variance (generic term) as well.

**variance** Measure of how all the scores in a set of data deviate from the mean.

$s^2$ Statistical notation for the variance.

| | Raw score X | Deviation score $X(X_i-\overline{X})$ | Squared deviation score $X^2(X_i-\overline{X})^2$ | |
|---|---|---|---|---|
| | 7 | −1 | 1 | Variance = average squared deviation |
| | 8 | 0 | 0 | $s^2 = \dfrac{\sum\limits_{n}^{i=1} X_i^2}{n-1}$ |
| | 7 | −1 | 1 | |
| | 8 | 0 | 0 | $s^2 = \dfrac{12}{10-1} = \dfrac{12}{9} = 1.33$ |
| | 9 | 1 | 1 | |
| | 10 | 2 | 4 | |
| | 6 | −2 | 4 | |
| | 8 | 0 | 0 | |
| | 9 | 1 | 1 | |
| | 8 | 0 | 0 | |
| $\sum$ | 80 | 0 | 12 | |
| $n$ | 10 | 10 | | |
| $\overline{X}$ | 8 | | | |

**TABLE 5-2**   Ways of Looking at Deviations from the Mean

The variance is defined as a measure of how all the scores in a set of data deviate from the mean. The term *deviate* means how they differ. Table 5-2 contains a set of scores. Imagine that they represent the quiz scores for 10 students. The first column contains the raw scores. The bottom of that column shows the sum of the scores (80) and the number of scores (10). The mean of the scores is 8. The second column shows the deviation scores. It is traditional to use X (standard font) to represent the raw scores and $X$ (italics) to represent the deviation scores. The deviation score is the raw score minus the mean. Deviations scores have signs. They are positive if the raw score is higher than the mean, and they are negative if the raw score is below the mean. The bottom of the deviation scores column shows the sum of the deviation scores (0) and the number of deviation scores (10). Calculating the average deviation score from those two quantities should be easy. But it is not! The sum of the deviation scores is always zero. This is true, by definition, for all data sets. Therefore, it is useless to calculate the average deviation.

The third column in Table 5-2 shows how statisticians decided to deal with the problem resulting from the fact that the sum of the deviation scores is always zero. Before the deviation scores are summed, they are squared. Squaring gets rid of the negative deviations but maintains the information of distance from the mean. The sum of the *squared* deviation scores is used to calculate the variance in the data. The variance is defined as the average squared deviation. Notice the definitional formula for the variance ($s^2$) is as follows:

$$S^2 = \frac{\sum\limits_{i=1}^{n} X_i^2}{n-1}$$

Where $X_i$ is the deviation score for subject i

$$(X_i - \overline{X})$$

$n$ is the number of scores.

This formula looks very much like the formula for calculating the mean, with two exceptions. The first exception is that deviation scores are squared (before they are summed). The second is that the denominator is not the number of scores, but the number of scores minus one. The second exception is called the *correction for sampling error.* The denominator is reduced by one because the data are from a sample, not the entire population. Reducing the denominator by one makes the variance estimate a little bit larger for a sample than if that same data represented an entire population. The difference is small when the number of scores is large.

Although the definitional formula for the variance seems very simple, it is not the most efficient way to calculate the variance. It is quicker and requires fewer calculations to use the calculational formula for the variance ($s^2$), which follows:

$$s^2 = \frac{\sum_{i=1}^{n} X_i^2 - \frac{\left(\sum_{i=1}^{n} X_i\right)^2}{n}}{n-1}$$

Where $X_i$ is the score for subject i
  $n$ is the number of scores.

This formula is based solely on the raw scores, number of scores, and the mean. It provides the same answer as the definitional formula. Figure 5-4 contains the step-by-step method for calculating the variance. Figure 5-5 shows how to apply the formula to the sample quiz data.

## 5-5b The Standard Deviation

The variance is a measure of the dispersion of a set of data. However, because all the deviations were squared, it is really a measure of the squared dispersion. It is not in the same unit of measurement as were the original scores. This is cumbersome for interpretation of the variance. To improve communication about the variance, you use the standard deviation as follows:

**Step 1.**

  Write the formula.

$$s^2 = \frac{\sum_{i=1}^{n} X_i^2 - \frac{\left(\sum_{i=1}^{n} X_i\right)^2}{n}}{n-1}$$

**Step 2.**

  Make a column of raw scores and determine *n* by counting the scores.

**Step 3.**

  Find $\sum_{i=1}^{n} X_i$ by summing all the scores.

**Step 4.**

  Find $\sum_{i=1}^{n} X_i^2$ by
      a. making a column of all the scores squared.
      b. summing the squared scores.

**Step 5.**

  Substitute the quantities found in Steps 2, 3, and 4 into the formula (Step 1).

**Step 6.**

  Calculate and interpret.

**Figure 5-4**
*Step-by-Step Method for Calculating the Variance*

**Step 1.**

Write the formula.

$$s^2 = \frac{\sum_{i=1}^{n} X_i^2 - \frac{\left(\sum_{i=1}^{n} X_i\right)^2}{n}}{n-1}$$

**Step 2.**

Make a column of raw scores.
Find $n$ by counting the scores.

$n = 10$

| X | X² |
|---|-----|
| 7 | 49 |
| 8 | 64 |
| 7 | 49 |
| 8 | 64 |
| 9 | 81 |
| 10 | 100 |
| 6 | 36 |
| 8 | 64 |
| 9 | 81 |
| 8 | 64 |

**Step 3.**

Sum the raw scores to find $\sum_{i=1}^{n} X_i$.

$$\sum_{i=1}^{n} X_i = 80$$

**Step 4.**

Make a column of all the scores squared.

Sum the squared scores to get $\sum_{i=1}^{n} X_i^2$.

$$\sum_{i=1}^{n} X_i^2 = 652$$

Sums:    80        652

**Step 5.**

$$s^2 = \frac{652 - \frac{80^2}{10}}{10-1} = \frac{652 - \frac{6400}{10}}{9} = \frac{652 - 640}{9} = \frac{12}{9} = 1.33$$

**Figure 5-5**
*Step-by-Step Example of Calculating the Variance*

$$s = \sqrt{s^2}$$

**standard deviation** Square
root of the variance.

**s** Statistical notation for the
standard deviation.

The **standard deviation** is referred to as $s$. It is simply the square root of the variance. Because the variance was in squared units, the standard deviation is in the original units used for the scores.

### 5-5c The Standard Error of the Mean

**standard error of the mean**
Measure of variance equal to
the standard deviation divided
by the square root of $n$.

A third statistic that is used to measure variance is the **standard error of the mean** or SE. This measure of variance is in units corrected for sample size. It is equal to the standard deviation divided by the square root of $n$. A main benefit of the standard error of the mean is that it can easily fit on graphs as well as describe the dispersion of

| TABLE 5-3 | Population Parameters and Sample Statistics | |
|---|---|---|

| | Population | Sample |
|---|:---:|:---:|
| Mean | $\mu$ | $\overline{X}$ |
| Size | $N$ | $n$ |
| Variance | $\sigma^2$ | $S^2$ |
| Standard deviation | $\sigma$ | $S$ |
| Definitional formula | $\sigma^2 = \dfrac{\sum\limits_{i=1}^{N}(X-\mu)^2}{N}$ | $S^2 = \dfrac{\sum\limits_{i=1}^{n} X_i^2}{n-1}$ |

the sample mean. In this way both the group mean and the group variance (in SE units) can be compared between groups.

# 5-6 The Population and the Sample

Thus far, this chapter has dealt with the three major ways of describing the dispersion in a sample of data. In experiments you always use a sample. In some other applications you may have all the scores for every member of the population. In that case the statistics have different terms and are calculated in a slightly different way. Table 5-3 shows the terms used to refer to the mean and variance for populations and samples. The population mean is referred to as $\mu$ (sounds like *mew*) and the standard deviation as sigma. When calculating the variance or standard deviation for an entire population, you use the number of scores in the entire population ($N$) as the denominator. In contrast, you reduce the denominator by one ($n - 1$) when only a sample of scores is available in order to correct for sampling error. In experimental research, you always use the sample statistics.

# 5-7 Calculating the Standard Deviation

This section and sections 5-8 and 5-9 illustrate the calculation of the standard deviation for each of the three distributions in Figures 5-1, 5-2, and 5-3. You should first attempt to calculate the standard deviation for Distribution A yourself. Compare your results to those in Table 5-4. If the results do not agree, look for the error. After you are certain that you understand the example for Distribution A, go on to Distributions B and C. It is essential to be able to calculate and understand the concept of variance before you go on to the next chapter.

# 5-8 Graphing Group Means and Variance

Now that you have begun to work with both measures of central tendency and dispersion, you should put them together on a graph. The three distributions are shown in Figure 5-6. The mean is represented by the height of the bar. In the sample distributions, the means were all the same, by my design. However, the variances were very different. The small lines that extend above each bar show the variances. These are the SE bars (standard error of the mean bars). You can see that the variance for Distribution B is much greater than that for Distribution A and much less than that for Distribution C. You draw conclusions about the differences between groups of data based both on the patterns of means and the variance within the groups.

**TABLE 5-4**   Calculation of Standard Deviation Sample Distribution A, B, and C

**Distribution A**

| Score X | Frequency f | Frequency × score (f × X) | X² | Frequency × score² (f × X²) |
|---|---|---|---|---|
| 1 | 3 | 3 | 1 | 3 |
| 2 | 4 | 8 | 4 | 16 |
| 3 | 7 | 21 | 9 | 63 |
| 4 | 11 | 44 | 16 | 176 |
| 5 | 8 | 40 | 25 | 200 |
| 6 | 5 | 30 | 36 | 180 |
| 7 | 2 | 14 | 49 | 98 |
| | n = 40 | ΣX = 160 | | ΣX² = 736 |

$$s^2 = \frac{\sum_{i=1}^{n} X_i^2 - \frac{\left(\sum_{i=1}^{n} X_i\right)^2}{n}}{n-1} = \frac{736 - \frac{160^2}{40}}{40-1} =$$

$$\frac{736 - \frac{25600}{40}}{39} = \frac{736 - 640}{39} = \frac{96}{39} = 2.46$$

$$s = \sqrt{s^2} = \sqrt{2.46} = 1.57$$

**Distribution B (Note: This uniform distribution is similar to Figure 5-2.)**

| Score X | Frequency f | Frequency × score (f × X) | X² | Frequency × score² (f × X²) |
|---|---|---|---|---|
| 1 | 5 | 5 | 1 | 5 |
| 2 | 6 | 12 | 4 | 24 |
| 3 | 6 | 18 | 9 | 54 |
| 4 | 6 | 24 | 16 | 96 |
| 5 | 6 | 30 | 25 | 150 |
| 6 | 6 | 36 | 36 | 216 |
| 7 | 5 | 35 | 49 | 245 |
| | n = 40 | Σ = 160 | | ΣX² = 790 |

$$s^2 = \frac{\sum_{i=1}^{n} X_i^2 - \frac{\left(\sum_{i=1}^{n} X_i\right)^2}{n}}{n-1} = \frac{790 - \frac{160^2}{40}}{40-1} =$$

$$\frac{790 - \frac{25600}{40}}{39} = \frac{790 - 640}{39} = \frac{150}{39} = 3.85$$

$$s = \sqrt{s^2} = \sqrt{3.85} = 1.96$$

**Distribution C**

| Score X | Frequency f | Frequency × score (f × X) | X² | Frequency × score² (f × X²) |
|---|---|---|---|---|
| 1 | 9 | 9 | 1 | 9 |
| 2 | 8 | 16 | 4 | 32 |
| 3 | 3 | 9 | 9 | 27 |
| 4 | 1 | 4 | 16 | 16 |
| 5 | 2 | 10 | 25 | 50 |
| 6 | 7 | 42 | 36 | 252 |
| 7 | 10 | 70 | 49 | 90 |
| | n = 40 | ΣX = 160 | | ΣX² = 876 |

$$s^2 = \frac{\sum_{i=1}^{n} X_i^2 - \frac{\left(\sum_{i=1}^{n} X_i\right)^2}{n}}{n-1} = \frac{876 - \frac{160^2}{40}}{40-1} =$$

$$\frac{876 - \frac{25600}{40}}{39} = \frac{876 - 640}{39} = \frac{236}{39} = 6.05$$

$$s = \sqrt{s^2} = \sqrt{6.05} = 2.46$$

A final example shows some of the data that Amy collected on the effects of type of rhythm on positive mood (Webster, Radjenovic & Woods, 1992). Figure 5-7 shows the means and the standard error of the mean for the control group and each of the five rhythm complexity groups.

# 5-9 The Z-Score

**z-score** Form of individual score that has a mean of zero and standard deviation of one.

**standard scores** Scores that have been made uniform in terms of center and variance.

A **z-score** is a form of individual score that takes into account the center and variance of a distribution. It is one of a set of **standard scores**. One way to think about a z-score is as the number of standard deviations away from the mean an individual score is. Thus, if the original score (the raw score) was exactly the same as the mean, the z-score would be 0. A raw score above the mean would have a positive z-score, and one that is below the mean would have a negative score. The z-score takes into account the dispersion of the sample data. A z-score of 1 results from a raw score exactly one standard deviation above the mean. If the standard deviation is 2.5 and the mean is 12, a z-score of −2.0 would mean that the raw score was two standard deviations below the mean. That raw score would be 7.0 (= 12 − (2 * 2.5)).

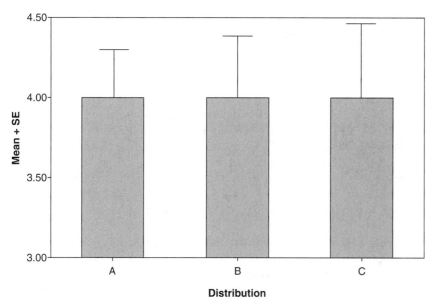

**Figure 5-6**

*Three Distributions with the Same Means and Different Variance*

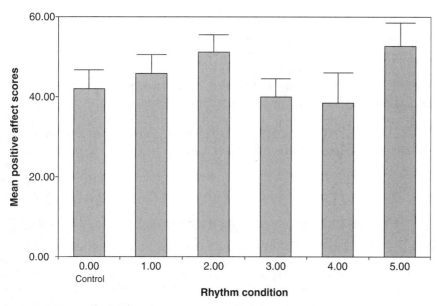

**Figure 5-7**

*The Effects of Rhythm Condition on the Change in Positive Mood*

The formula for the $z$-score is $Z = (X - \overline{X})/S$, where $\overline{X}$ is the sample mean and $s$ is the standard deviation for the sample of data. There is a $z$-score for each raw score. By definition, the mean of all the $z$-scores in a set of data is zero and the standard deviation of the $z$-scores is one.

Standard scores are useful for making comparisons across measures. Many students have taken achievement tests with results that are reported as standard scores. For example, the SAT math and verbal scores are standard scores. Even though the tests have different numbers and types of items, it is possible to make comparisons between the scores. Percentile scores are another type of standard score. They represent the percentage of individuals in the sample who scored at or below a specific raw score. The $z$-score is a very useful score for understanding the relationship of a single score to the entire sample of scores and also for making comparisons to other types of scores.

# Summary

Independent variables are operationally defined by describing the procedures for manipulating them at different levels. The levels may be the presence versus the absence (control condition) of the hypothesized cause, different amounts of the hypothesized cause, or different types of the hypothesized cause. A placebo is a control condition that appears to be identical to the treatment, except the hypothesized cause is absent.

The decision to operationally define an independent variable using a within subjects or a between subjects design is based on the way multiple treatments are likely to interfere with each other. If the different levels of the independent variable are unlikely to interfere with each other, a within subjects design may be the best way to keep everything constant between the different treatments because each participant acts as his or her own control. Often it is impossible to rule out multiple treatment interference, so between subjects designs are more likely to produce internally valid experiments. In a between subjects design, a different group of participants experiences each level of the independent variable. The treatments can't interfere with each other because each participant has only one treatment. The biggest challenge with between subjects designs is to have groups of participants who are equivalent on all important psychological variables. Matching and random assignment are two ways to attempt to make the treatment groups equivalent.

Descriptive statistics include both measures of central tendency and dispersion (variability). Measures of variability are important to describe the groups of data from within or between subjects designs. Measures of variability include the variance, standard deviation, and standard error of the mean. Distributions of data that have the same centers (means) can have very different variances. Examples are presented for normal, uniform, and bimodal distributions. The $z$-score is the number of standard deviations away from the mean of any individual score.

# References

American Psychological Association. (2001). *Publication manual of the American Psychological Association.* Washington, DC: Author.

Mill, J. S. (1874). *A system of logic: Rationative and inductive.* New York: Harper & Brothers.

Webster, S. K., Radjenovic, L. & Woods, A. M. (1992, June). *The connections between music, cognition and emotion.* Paper presented at the Annual Nebraska Symposium on Motivation, Lincoln, NE.

# Exercises for Application

1. From the theory that arousal produces emotion, deduce a hypothesis.

2. Identify the independent and dependent variables in the hypothesis you wrote in question 1.

3. Operationally define the independent and dependent variables you identified in question 2.

4. What is the scale of measurement used in your dependent variable?

5. Would you use a between subjects or within subjects design to test your hypothesis? Why?

6. In an experiment how can you know that the independent variable was the cause of the dependent variable?

7. If the mean of a set of test scores is 82 and the standard deviation is 10, what did you score if your $z$-score is −0.8? What is your score if your $z$-score is 0? What if the $z$-score is 1.4?

8. Calculate the mean and variance ($s^2$ and $s$) for each of the groups of data presented in the following table. They represent the number of hostile adjectives checked by participants in each of the different rhythm complexity conditions presented in Box 5-4.

| Rhythm 0 | Rhythm 1 | Rhythm 2 | Rhythm 3 | Rhythm 4 | Rhythm 5 |
|---|---|---|---|---|---|
| 57 | 75 | 44 | 83 | 44 | 76 |
| 71 | 57 | 44 | 42 | 44 | 68 |
| 42 | 57 | 44 | 57 | 44 | 44 |
| 77 | 44 | 42 | 44 | 102 | 44 |
| 44 | 44 | 44 | 69 | 42 | 44 |
| 42 | 44 | 44 | 70 | 95 | 44 |
| 44 | 46 | 44 | 70 | 45 | 42 |
| 42 | 44 | 44 | 42 | 45 | 50 |
| 42 | 57 | 44 | 44 | 56 | 42 |
| 44 | 44 | 42 | 44 | 44 | 83 |
| 65 | 75 | 44 | 117 | | 51 |
| 44 | 44 | 75 | 64 | | 65 |
| | | 44 | 42 | | |

# Practice Quiz

*Note:* You can find the correct answers to these questions by taking the quiz and then submitting your answers in the Online Edition. The program will automatically score your submission. If you miss a question, the program will provide the correct answer, a rationale for the answer, and the section number in the chapter where the topic is discussed.

1. The principle of concomitant variation states that
   a. when there is a change in the cause, there should be a resulting change in the effect.
   b. where there is no cause, there should be no effect.
   c. where there is a cause, there must be an effect.
   d. when there is a change in the effect, there must also be a resulting change in the

2. In an experiment with two levels of the independent variable, the condition in which the treatment is absent is called the
   a. experimental condition.
   b. treatment condition.
   c. hypothesis condition.
   d. control condition.

3. Repeated measures designs are good when
   a. it is known that the treatments will have no residual effects.
   b. it is essential to make the treatments equivalent on all subject factors.
   c. the data collection requires little time.
   d. there are only two treatments.

4. Matching is used in order to
   a. guarantee total equivalency of treatment groups.
   b. reduce bias in a repeated measures experiment.
   c. provide equivalence among treatment groups on the matching variable.
   d. avoid the unfairness of random assignment to treatment condition.

5. Random assignment to treatment condition occurs when
   a. each member of a population has an equal probability of being included in the sample.
   b. each member of the sample has an equal probability of being assigned to each treatment condition.
   c. the subjects in each treatment are not matched.
   d. the assignment has been done is a haphazard manner.

6. A random number table is used to
   a. test statistical hypotheses.
   b. determine the number of treatment conditions used in an experiment.
   c. counterbalance a design.
   d. assign subjects to treatment condition.

7. It is important to measure the dispersion in a set of data because
   a. it provides important information about the mean.
   b. many different distributions can show the same measures of central tendency.
   c. if the data are too disperse, they must be transformed.
   d. it should be normal to be valid.

8. The dispersion of a set of scores is called the
   a. central tendency.
   b. deviation.
   c. variance.
   d. average deviation.

9. The average deviation of any set of scores is

    a. the best measure of dispersion.

    b. the central tendency.

    c. the variance.

    d. always zero.

10. Variance is the

    a. average of the deviation scores.

    b. average of the squared deviation scores.

    c. the square of the average deviation score.

    d. the best measure of central tendency.

11. The hypothesized cause and hypothesized effect are often present together, and when the hypothesized cause is absent, the hypothesized effect also tends be to absent. In this case, you can be fairly confident

    a. the hypothesized causal relationship is true.

    b. the effect may be caused by other variables.

    c. the hypothesized cause and effect are correlated.

    d. John Stuart Mill would conclude causation.

12. A _____ is a special control condition in which the participants receive a treatment that has all the external features of the hypothesized cause, but not the actual hypothesized causal mechanism.

    a. concomitant

    b. null treatment

    c. experimental treatment

    d. placebo

13. The section of an APA research report that describes exactly what was done in the experiment in enough detail that someone could read it to replicate the study is the

    a. introduction.

    b. materials and apparatus.

    c. procedure.

    d. results and discussion.

14. The denominator used to calculate the variance, $s^2$, is $n-1$ in order to

    a. make the number smaller.

    b. remove the inflation from squaring the scores.

    c. give the formula symmetry.

    d. reduce sampling error.

15. One reason to calculate the standard error of the mean is that

    a. it is more accurate than the standard deviation.

    b. it is in the same units as the raw scores.

    c. it is convenient to represent dispersion on a graph.

    d. it provides additional information to the standard deviation.

16. The number of standard deviations an individual score is from the mean of the group of scores is the

    a. deviation score.

    b. stanine.

    c. z-score.

    d. skew.

# Hypothesis Testing: The Control Group Posttest Only Design

## Chapter Six

## Key Terms

a priori hypothesis
alpha
alternative hypothesis
beta
Cohen's *d*
confidence interval
control group
degrees of freedom
magnitude of effect
null hypothesis
odds
one-tailed hypothesis
one-tailed test
placebo
pooled standard deviation
post hoc hypotheses
posttest only design

probability
probability density function
replicate
results section
sampling distribution of the mean
significance level
statistical inference
statistical power
statistical precision
Student's *t* test
subject variance
treatment group
treatment variance
two-tailed hypothesis
two-tailed test
Type I error
Type II error

101

# Learning Objectives

- Be able to specify both null and alternative hypotheses.
- Explain the process of statistical inference.
- Apply statistical inference to a two-group experiment.
- Illustrate the two types of experimental errors.
- Calculate and interpret Student's *t* test for a between groups experiment.

## Key Idea

Statistical inference is the process of using statistics to make decisions about hypotheses based on the data collected in an experiment. In a control group posttest only design, the main statistical decision is whether the differences observed between the treatment group and control group were due to chance.

The purpose of psychological research is to empirically provide evidence for or against hypotheses that have been logically deduced from theories and previous empirical research. After the researcher finds support for these hypotheses from the data, he or she may apply the hypotheses in describing, predicting, explaining, and controlling behavior. As a science, psychology advocates the application of hypotheses only *after* they have been tested. This chapter will explain the process of hypothesis testing with the most simple and the most powerful of the experimental designs.

## 6-1 Control Group Posttest Only Design

**control group** Group of participants who are equivalent to a treatment group except that they do not receive the independent variable.

**treatment group** Group of participants who receive the independent variable.

As described in Chapter 5, "Operationally Defining the Independent Variable," a **control group** is a group of participants who are equivalent to a **treatment group**. The control group receives exactly the same experimental instructions in exactly the same situation and is measured on exactly the same dependent variable. The only difference between the control group and treatment group should be the independent variable. Thus, the control group is the group that "controls" for all other factors. The treatment group receives the independent variable, and the control group does not. For example, if you were studying the influence of the ability to pronounce syllables on memory for those syllables, you would give the treatment group participants syllables that they can pronounce. On the other hand, you would give the control group participants syllables that are similar except that they cannot be pronounced. All other things in the experiment would be equal between the control group and treatment group. That is why the control group is called *control* group: It controls for the influence of all considerations other than the independent variable.

**posttest only design** Design that involves measuring the dependent variable only once, after the treatment has been presented to participants in the treatment group.

**placebo** Treatment that has every appearance of the cause, but not the hypothesized causal agent.

A **posttest only design** is one that involves measuring the dependent variable only once, after the treatment has been presented to participants in the treatment group. The dependent variable is measured for the control group with the same sequence of events as for the treatment group, with the exception that the "treatment" this group undergoes is a control treatment. In some cases that treatment would be a **placebo**, as in the cases of giving inert substances (e.g., sugar pills) as a control for the study of drug effects. In other cases the control treatment is a filler task that takes the same amount of time and involvement of the participant but lacks the hypothesized cause (e.g., showing a travel film as a control for a violent film when studying the effects of violent film on aggression).

Campbell and Stanley (1963) designated the different designs with symbols:

R: Random assignment to treatment condition

O: Measurement of the dependent variable (observation)

X: The treatment (the independent variable)

With this set of symbols they described the control group posttest only design as follows:

Treatment Group          R: X O
Control Group            R: O

This is a between subjects design because different participants are assigned to the two conditions, treatment and control. One example that will be used throughout this chapter has the hypothesis that it is easier to remember syllables that can be pronounced (e.g., gax) than sets of letters that cannot be pronounced (e.g., gfx). Twenty volunteers were recruited. Ten were randomly assigned to receive the treatment (a list of 20 pronounceable syllables). The remaining 10 participants received a list of 20 unpronounceable letter sets using the same letters that comprised the treatment list but in a different order. This group acted as the control.

This chapter will focus on the control group design. Sometimes you will have two-group experiments in which you compare two levels of an independent variable and in which neither level could be called a control group. The two-group design and the statistics to test it are identical to the posttest only control group design.

# 6-2  Hypothesis Construction

Experimental hypotheses come in two forms: null and alternate. Each will be described in this section. The two forms of the hypotheses are connected. Section 6-2a describes the null hypothesis. It is necessary for statistical inference. Section 6-2b describes the alternate hypothesis. The alternate hypothesis is what you expect to happen in the experiment. In some ways the two forms of hypotheses are like the two sides of a coin. When the coin is flipped, either one side or the other will land facing up. Like the null and alternate hypothesis, the head and tail of a coin are directly related, and only one will be supported by the experiment (tossing the coin in that case).

### 6-2a  The Null Hypothesis

Before conducting an experiment, you must specify the hypothesis in testable form. A hypothesis that is made before data collection is called an **a priori hypothesis**. For each experiment there are at least two a priori hypotheses: the null hypothesis and alternative hypothesis. Sometimes new hypotheses are created after the data have been collected and analyzed. Such hypotheses are called **post hoc hypotheses**.

The hypothesis that the independent variable has no observable effect on the dependent variable is called the **null hypothesis**. The word *null* means zero or nothing. Thus, the null hypothesis is the hypothesis of no effect. If researchers really expected to get data in support of the null hypothesis, they probably would not do the research. However, the null hypothesis is essential because of the nature of statistical inference. Statistically, the null hypothesis can either be rejected, or it can't be rejected. You can get evidence against the null hypothesis. That is, you can determine the probability that the data obtained in an experiment were due to chance alone. If the null hypothesis is true (the hypothesized cause has no influence on the hypothesized effect), then the data are due to chance alone. Inferential statistics allow you to determine the exact probability of obtaining the data by chance. Thus, if the data are very unlikely by chance, researchers can reject the null hypothesis.

In actual practice, deducing a null hypothesis is very easy. With any experiment, the null hypothesis is always the same: The independent variable has no effect on the

**a priori hypothesis**
Hypothesis that is made before data collection.

**post hoc hypotheses**
Hypotheses created after the data have been collected and analyzed.

**null hypothesis** Hypothesis that a change in the independent variable has no observable effect on the dependent variable.

dependent variable. For a two-group experiment, you often state the null hypothesis as follows:

$$H_0 : \overline{X_t} = \overline{X_c}$$

This brief form simply means that according to the null hypothesis the mean for the treatment group will be equal to the mean for the control group. In the example of the effects of being able to pronounce syllables on memory, you could state the null hypothesis as follows:

$H_0$   Average free recall for the group who practiced pronounceable syllables will equal the average free recall for the group who received unpronounceable combinations of letters.

In other words, $H_0 : \overline{X}_{pronounce} = \overline{X}_{not\,pronounce}$

### 6-2b  The Alternative Hypothesis

**alternative hypothesis**
Hypothesis that the cause has an effect.

For each experiment there is also at least one hypothesis that is the alternative to the null hypothesis; it is called the **alternative hypothesis**. The alternative hypothesis also must be determined a priori (before the data are collected). The exact form of the alternative hypothesis will depend on the theory and previous research. With the two-group experiment, there are three possible alternative hypotheses:

$H_1$   The independent variable *affects* the dependent variable.

$H_2$   The independent variable *increases* the dependent variable.

$H_3$   The independent variable *decreases* the dependent variable.

Because there are two groups, the alternative hypotheses are usually stated in terms of the hypothesized relationship between the means of the two groups. In those terms, you could state the alternative hypotheses as follows:

$$H_1 : \overline{X}_t \neq \overline{X}_c$$
$$H_2 : \overline{X}_t > \overline{X}_c$$
$$H_3 : \overline{X}_t < \overline{X}_c$$

There are three possible alternatives to the null hypothesis that the ability to pronounce a set of letters (pronounceability) has no effect on memory. They are

$H_1$   Pronounceability affects memory.

$H_2$   Pronounceability improves memory.

$H_3$   Pronounceability reduces memory.

Although the two-group experiment has three possible alternative hypotheses, the researcher must select only one of them to test, a priori. Before you begin data collection, you must decide which alternative hypothesis you expect to occur based on theories and previous research. In the example of the effects of pronounceability on memory, you can easily deduce from both the theory of memory and previous research that pronounceability should improve memory. Thus, a priori, you select $H_2$ as the alternative hypothesis to be tested in the experiment.

Look at the three possible alternative hypotheses again. The first one basically says that you expect a difference due to the treatment, but the difference could go either way. The treatment could improve or impair whatever effect you are studying. This type of alternative hypothesis is called *nondirectional* because a difference in either direction will be accepted as a change in the effect. A nondirectional hypothesis is also called a **two-tailed hypothesis** in many statistics books. The second and third alternative hypotheses represent directional hypotheses because the treatment is

**two-tailed hypothesis**
Alternate hypothesis that specifies the means will be different, but not in which direction.

hypothesized to either improve (the second alternative) or reduce (the third alternative) the effect, not both! A directional hypothesis is also called a **one-tailed hypothesis**. Having a directional hypothesis is usually better than having a nondirectional hypothesis because it is more specific and therefore stronger. Sometimes the past research evidence upon which to base your hypothesis is either absent or contradictory. That's when a nondirectional test is appropriate.

> **one-tailed hypothesis**
> Alternate hypothesis that specifies the direction of the difference between the means.

# 6-3 Statistical Inference

**Statistical inference** is the process of using statistics to make decisions about the hypotheses (null and alternative) based on the data collected in the experiment. An inference is defined as drawing meaning from something. The experimenter draws meaning from the data. To do this, the experimenter uses inferential statistics.

> **statistical inference** Process of using statistics to make decisions about the hypotheses (null and alternative) based on the data collected in the experiment.

Remember that there are two types of statistics: descriptive statistics and inferential statistics. Descriptive statistics are those that summarize and describe the data. They include those that summarize the central tendencies of the data (such as mean, median, and mode) as well as those that summarize the dispersion of the data (variance, range, and standard deviation).

Inferential statistics are those that estimate the **probability** that the data could be obtained by chance alone. Probability theory is about the likelihood of a certain event, or set of events, occurring given a specific set of conditions. In a control group posttest only experiment, the set of events are the observed data for both the control group and treatment group. The specific conditions are the methods of the research that allowed everything else (besides the treatment) to be equal between the groups. Therefore, the experimenter can use inferential statistics with the data from the two groups to refute the null hypothesis, or not. If the probability is high that the data could have occurred by chance alone, the experimenter would infer that the null hypothesis is likely to be true. That is, if the data are likely to be the result of chance fluctuations, then probably the independent variable did not cause the dependent variable. On the other hand, if the probability of getting the observed data by chance alone is quite low, then the experimenter can infer that the null hypothesis is probably false. This means that the experimenter can infer that the alternative hypothesis is probably correct. Of course, the inferences in any experiment depend both on statistical hypothesis testing and on a careful evaluation of the research design to rule out alternative explanations for the effects observed. The statistical test answers the question: Did these results occur by chance? Evaluation of the design answers the question: Are these results due to the manipulated cause?

> **probability** Likelihood of anything happening.

## 6-3a Estimating Probability

Statistical inference can be considered the scientist's form of gambling. Just as a gambler takes into consideration the **odds** before making a bet, the researcher considers the odds before inferring support for the hypotheses. "Odds" here can be defined as the probability of an outcome to occur in a given situation. The difference between the process a gambler uses and a researcher uses is not in type, but more in precision.

> **odds** Probability of an outcome to occur in a given situation.

Inferential statistics have been developed so that the researcher can know the odds that the data occurred by chance alone at a very high degree of confidence. Different inferential statistical procedures have been developed for different experimental designs. A gambler deciding whether to place a bet, say on the outcome of the roll of two dice, would want to know the odds of the particular outcome. Assuming that each of the dice is fair, then the gambler would be making a good bet by choosing the most likely total. Experimenters also have to figure the odds. They need to know how likely their experimental results were, given all the possible results that could occur for a given experimental design.

The way you calculate the probability of an outcome is to count the total number of ways the *desired* outcome can occur and compare that to the total number of *possible* outcomes. With two dice, the following outcomes are possible:

Total: spots on first die + spots on second die

2 : 1 + 1
3 : 1 + 2, 2 + 1
4 : 1 + 3, 2 + 2, 3 + 1
5 : 1 + 4, 2 + 3, 3 + 2, 4 + 1
6 : 1 + 5, 2 + 4, 3 + 3, 4 + 2, 5 + 1
7 : 1 + 6, 2 + 5, 3 + 4, 4 + 3, 5 + 2, 6 + 1
8 : 2 + 6, 3 + 5, 4 + 4, 5 + 3, 6 + 2
9 : 3 + 6, 4 + 5, 5 + 4, 6 + 3
10 : 4 + 6, 5 + 5, 6 + 4
11 : 5 + 6, 6 + 5
12 : 6 + 6

The gambler would be wise to bet on 7 because it is the most likely outcome. How likely is an outcome of a total of 7 on two dice? You can find that probability by using the following formula:

$$\text{Probability of Event} = \frac{\text{Total number of ways the event can occur}}{\text{Total number of possible outcomes}}$$

By examining this dice example, you can see that there are 6 ways to get a total of 7 from the roll of two dice. It is also clear that there are 36 possible outcomes from the roll of two dice. Therefore, the probability of rolling a total of 7 is

Probability (7) = 6/36 = 1/6 = 0.17

Although 7 is the most frequent outcome, it is likely to occur only 1 time in 6, and the unfortunate gambler doesn't know which time that will be. Furthermore, even though it is likely to occur once in 6 throws, because dice is a game of chance, that outcome may not occur in any particular 6 throws, or even in any particular 60 throws. That's why gambling is considered a risky business. It is based on chance, and chance cannot be predicted with certainty.

### 6-3b Probability in Hypothesis Testing

**probability density function**
Set of probabilities calculated for each possible result in a particular experimental design.

Most experiments have considerably more complicated outcomes than a game of dice. Nevertheless, experimenters calculate the odds for the particular outcome assuming it was due to chance. They do that by employing the **probability density function** known to correspond to the particular experimental design they are using. That means, for each experimental design, based on probability theory, a set of probabilities have been calculated for each possible result (the probability density function). It also means that researchers do not have to be experts at probability theory. They must merely be able to apply probability theory to the interpretation of the results (i.e., inferences drawn from the data). In practical terms, researchers must be able to select the appropriate inferential statistics, calculate them, and be able to interpret their results.

Each gambler will decide personally what odds are sufficient basis to place a bet. Some gamblers will bet only on a sure thing, which to them may mean an odds of greater than .9 (9 chances in 10 of winning). Others will bet on the long shot, which might be considered the bet on odds of 1000 to 1 (.0001). Behavioral scientists in practice do not choose the odds on which they infer their conclusions. Instead, there is a standard odds ratio that is accepted in the profession: That is .05. It is usually referred to as **alpha** ($\alpha$). Some researchers are more conservative and use alpha levels of .01 or .001. The choice of alpha is determined by the research paradigm. In some research areas a wrong conclusion has a devastating effect if the error is to claim a difference that was really due to chance. In these areas a more conservative alpha level (.01 or .001) is typically used. In other research areas it may be worse to make the error of failing to detect a real difference between the treatment and control means. In these areas a more liberal alpha (.10) could be used. In actual practice, alpha is very seldom greater than .05.

**alpha** Accepted level of probability of a Type I error, typically .05.

Statistical theory was developed on a set of assumptions that make it impossible to prove the null hypothesis. It would be good to be able to say that two groups are equal. That's the same thing as saying that the hypothesized cause isn't the cause. The results could appear to be the same by chance alone. Statistical hypothesis testing is focused on estimating the probabilities that they are different by chance alone. By setting alpha at .05, researchers accept a difference if it could occur by chance alone less than 5 times in 100 (.05). The statistical theory of hypothesis testing is based on the premise that the null hypothesis can be rejected, but it can never be accepted. Instead, statisticians must say, "fail to reject the null hypothesis." That's why the confusing statement "the experimenter can't infer that the results didn't occur by chance" cannot be rephrased as "the experimenter infers the results occurred by chance." That would be proving the null hypothesis. It's impossible to prove the null hypothesis with statistics based on assumptions that it can only be rejected, or not rejected.

If the probability that the data obtained in the experiment could have happened by chance alone is less than .05 (alpha), then researchers will infer that the results were probably not due to chance (reject the null hypothesis). If the null hypothesis is rejected, then researchers can conclude that the results were probably due to the independent variable (support the alternative hypothesis). Researchers are basically making a bet on the data. In this case, researchers are like gamblers deciding to play the lottery based on the current odds of winning. There are some differences, however. Researchers are more conservative in betting on their hypotheses than gamblers are on lotteries. Researchers will make the bet that the data really represent the underlying hypothesized cause with odds of 19/20. Think about it. If the alpha level means that researchers are willing to take a .05 risk (1 in 20) that the results were due to chance, it means that there is a 19-in-20 likelihood that the results are due to the independent variable. Researchers are much more conservative with their bets on the data than gamblers are with their bets on lotteries. A second difference between statistical inference and gambling is that gamblers will eventually know the real outcome. Researchers don't get to know the reality of the cause-effect relationship from the data. The best knowledge researchers can get is confirmation when other researchers **replicate** their research results. Replication is the duplication of an experiment with the same results.

**replicate** To duplicate an experiment with the hope of obtaining the same results.

# 6-4 The Normal Distribution

In many psychological experiments, statistical inference is based on the normal distribution. The word *normal* in this context refers to the statistical normal, not to what is healthy or good. Thus, a normal distribution of neuroticism scores for a population of schizophrenic patients would be what statistically describes them.

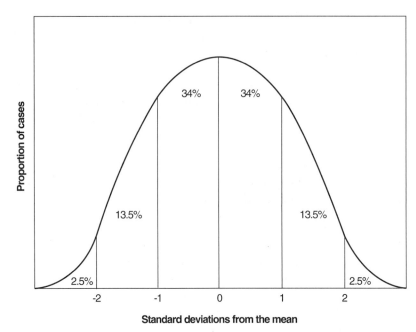

**Figure 6-1**

*The Approximate Percent of Sample Falling under the Standard Normal Distribution*

Most psychological variables are normally distributed. The characteristics of a normal distribution include the following.

The mean, median, and mode are the same. In other words, the most common (mode), center (median), and average (mean) scores are all the same.

Most individuals score near the middle of the distribution. In fact, for the normal distribution the spread of scores is known, as shown in Figure 6-1. More than 2 in 3 individuals would be expected to score within 1 standard deviation from the mean. Fewer than 5% would be expected to score more than 2 standard deviations away from the mean.

The distribution is symmetrical about the mean, which means that the amount of spread in scores above the mean is the same as that below the mean. Alternatively, the extremity of scores above the mean will be equivalent to the extremity of scores below the mean.

### 6-4a Comparing a Sample Mean to a Population

If you take the normal distribution to be the assumed underlying distribution for a behavior, then you can compare the results of the sample to what you would expect based on it. Suppose that you wanted to estimate the IQ of university students. You might do so by taking of sample of five students and measuring their IQ. The average IQ of the five students would then be the estimate of the IQ of all the students in the university. This estimate might represent the actual mean, or it might not. If you took another sample of five students, you are likely to get a different mean IQ. Which one is closest to the true population mean? You don't know. But you do know that if you continue to take samples of five students and calculate their IQ scores, the means of these samples will be normally distributed about the population mean. You can also use what you know about the normal distribution to estimate what the actual population mean is within certain limits (**confidence interval**) at given odds.

The set of all possible samples of a given size (*n*) from a population is called the **sampling distribution of the mean**. It tends to have a normal distribution. The sample means are not all exactly the same as the population mean. Some are higher

**confidence interval** Range within which a statistical result is confidently accepted as probably not due to chance.

**sampling distribution of the mean** Set of all possible samples of a given size (*n*) from a population.

and some are lower and most are near the center. The mean of all possible random samples from a population is the population mean, $\mu$. The variance of the sample means is less than the variance within each sample. Think about it. The mean of a sample must be less than its highest score and more than its lowest score so that the means of a set of samples will show less dispersion than the scores within the samples. The standard error of the mean for all possible random samples of size $n$ taken from the population is defined as $\sigma_{\overline{X}} = \frac{\sigma}{\sqrt{n}}$ where $\sigma$ is the standard deviation of the population.

### 6-4b Comparing One Sample to a Population Mean

Just as you learned to compare a single score to a sample mean using the $z$-score in Chapter 5, "Operationally Defining the Independent Variable," it is possible to compare a single sample mean to the population mean with a $z$ test. The form is the same:

$$z_{\overline{X}} = \frac{\overline{X} - \mu}{\sigma_{\overline{X}}}$$

The $z$-score for the sample mean can be used to compare it to the population. The larger the $z$-score for the sample mean, the farther it is from the actual population mean. An extreme difference could result because of the random process of sampling. An alternative explanation is that the sample mean represents a different population. Consider the example of students who have applied for a special scholarship. One of the criteria for the scholarship is grade point average. If you know that the sample has a mean grade point average of 3.7, you can use the $z$ test to see how far away from the population average the sample mean is. Imagine that the mean grade point average of all students is 2.7 and the standard deviation of all the students' grades is 0.5. If there are 25 students in the sample, then you calculate the $z$-score for the sample as follows:

$$z_{\overline{X}} = \frac{\overline{X} - \mu}{\sigma_{\overline{X}}} = \frac{3.7 - 2.7}{.5 / \sqrt{25}} = \frac{1.0}{.5/5} = \frac{1.0}{.1} = 10$$

The interpretation is that the sample mean is 10 standard deviations above the mean of the sampling distribution. Such a difference is highly unlikely. It is more likely that the sample of students who applied for the scholarship is not a random sample of the student population.

One-sample $z$ tests are seldom used in experimental hypothesis testing. One reason is that to complete one, you must know the population mean and standard deviation. You seldom know both. The second reason that such tests are seldom used in hypothesis testing is that according to Mill's Canons of Proof (1874), you should be looking for a change in the effect as a result of a change in the cause. That implies at least two samples of data to compare. I included this section because some people find the concept of the $z$ test for a one-sample mean to be a useful bridge to the statistical tests used to compare two sample means.

### 6-4c Comparing Two Groups

There are many applications of the normal probability density function to experimental psychology. In this chapter we will focus only on its application to the two-group experiment. Recall the null hypothesis:

$$H_0 : \overline{X_t} = \overline{X_c}$$

In terms of the normal distribution, you can state the null hypothesis that the mean of the treatment group and the mean of the control group simply represent

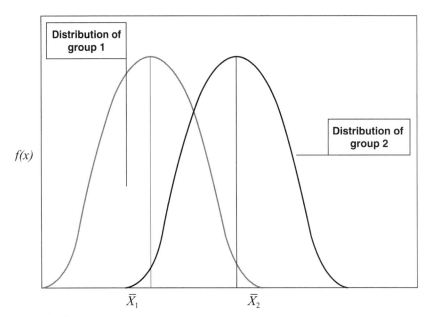

**Figure 6-2**
*Distribution of Two Samples Representing the Same Underlying Populations*

two different *samples* from the same underlying population, which has a mean ($\mu$). This is illustrated in Figure 6-2.

The alternative hypothesis was

$$H_2 : \overline{X}_t > \overline{X}_c$$

In terms of the normal distribution, the alternative hypothesis is that the mean of the treatment group represents a different *population* than the mean of the control group represents. Thus, for example, if you had not only sampled university students, but also sampled high school dropouts, you might expect their IQ scores to be different. The application of the normal distribution to this problem would let you estimate the probability that the means for the university students and for the high school dropouts represent the same population. If the difference between the means is so great that would occur by chance alone fewer than 5 times in 100, then you can infer they come from different populations (see Figure 6-3). You can apply the same type of procedure to the control group posttest only design. The control and treatment group participants are randomly assigned from the same sample. The process of the experiment changes the treatment group, but not the control group, so that the cause produces a different population, so to speak. If the difference between the treatment group and control group is greater than you would expect from taking different samples from the same population, and you can eliminate all the other alternative explanations, then the difference must be due to the treatment (independent variable).

Consider the sample experiment in which the treatment group received pronounceable syllables, while the control group members were presented with unpronounceable sets of letters. You know that the participants originally came from the same population because you randomly assigned them to treatment groups. Therefore, if the difference between the treatment mean and the control mean is greater than you would expect by chance alone (at the .05 **significance level**), you infer that the independent variable changed the participants from one population to another. It didn't literally change them from one demographic group to another, but rather it changed the distribution of the dependent variable from the distribution of the control group to a new distribution; i.e., the independent variable caused an effect.

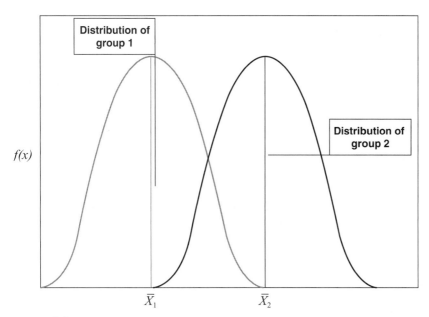

**Figure 6-3**
*Distribution of Two Samples Representing Different Populations*

# 6-5 Student's *t* Test

To determine the probability that two groups are from different populations, you employ a statistical test. The most frequently used test for the difference between two means is the **Student's *t* test**. "Student," in actuality, was named Gosset, but when he first published his statistical test, his employer prohibited him from working on scholarly problems. Therefore, he published under a pseudonym, "A. Student." This cost him the chance to have his name attached to one of the most frequently used of all inferential statistics.

The *t* test is the statistical test used to determine whether the means of two groups are significantly different. You can apply it if the following assumptions hold:

- The dependent variable has been measured on at least an ordinal scale (interval, ratio, and some ordinal scales).
- The dependent variable is normally distributed.
- Only two groups are to be compared.

It is always important to evaluate the assumptions before using an inferential statistic. For example, it is incorrect to use a *t* test for nominal data. It is also incorrect to use a *t* test on many kinds of ordinal data, especially ranks. However, *t* tests are often used with Likert scale ordinal data. The results may be incorrect if the dependent variable isn't normally distributed. Finally, using a *t* test multiple times to compare more than two means changes the alpha level of the experiment. That's no good.

The basic form of the *t* test is to compare the difference between the means of the experimental groups (treatment vs. control) to the differences among all the scores within the groups. The differences between the groups are thought to represent the effect of the treatment, assuming all other things were held constant. You can think of this difference as the **treatment variance**. The differences among the scores within each group are attributed to individual differences and chance fluctuations. Sometimes this fluctuation is referred to as the **subject variance** (also the error variance or residual variance). It is basically all the variance that is not due to the treatment. The *t* test takes the form of a ratio between these two variances:

**Student's *t* test** Statistical test used to determine whether the means of two groups are significantly different.

**treatment variance** Variance due to the independent variable.

**subject variance** Variance due to individual differences in the subjects.

| TABLE 6-1 | Data from Pronounceability Experiment |
|-----------|---------------------------------------|

**Condition**

| Pronounceable | Not Pronounceable |
|---------------|-------------------|
| 12 | 7 |
| 15 | 9 |
| 14 | 8 |
| 13 | 10 |
| 10 | 6 |
| 16 | 8 |
| 15 | 7 |
| 14 | 10 |
| 17 | 8 |
| 14 | 7 |

$t$ = treatment variance / subject variance

The data shown in Table 6-1 were collected in an experiment to test the effects of pronounceability on recall of syllables. The group of participants who could pronounce the syllables later recalled an average of 14 of the 20 syllables correctly. The control group, who could not pronounce the syllables, recalled on average only 8 syllables. Because everything besides the pronounceability of the syllables was held constant, you can infer that the difference of 6 more syllables for the average of the treatment group was due to the independent variable. However, how can you be sure that the difference was not just due to chance fluctuation? You can never be 100% sure, but you can estimate the probability for the difference being due just to chance. To calculate that probability, you use the $t$ test.

### 6-5a  Calculating the *t* Test

The formula for the between groups $t$ test is as follows:

$$t = \frac{\overline{X}_t - \overline{X}_c}{\sqrt{\left[\dfrac{\sum X_t^2 - \dfrac{(\sum X_t)^2}{N_t} + \sum X_c^2 - \dfrac{(\sum X_c)^2}{N_c}}{N_t + N_c - 2}\right]\left[\dfrac{1}{N_t} + \dfrac{1}{N_c}\right]}}$$

Note that the numerator for the formula is the estimate of the treatment variance (between groups variance). If the mean of the treatment group is greater than the mean of the control group, the numerator will be a positive number. If, on the other hand, the mean of the treatment group is less than the mean of the control group, the numerator will be negative. The sign (positive or negative) of the $t$ test is important because it tells you whether the data are consistent with the alternative hypothesis. (Statisticians say, "Whether the effects are in the direction of the hypothesis.") If the alternative hypothesis was nondirectional (two-tailed), then either a positive or negative $t$ test can support it. If, however, the alternative hypothesis was that the treatment group would improve scores on the dependent variable (one-tailed), only a positive $t$ test result will support it. Likewise, if the alternative hypothesis was that the independent variable will reduce scores on the dependent variable (one-tailed), a negative $t$ test result is needed to support it.

The denominator of the $t$ test is an estimate of the variance within the groups. You actually obtain it by pooling the differences of each participant's score to the group mean for that participant's group across both groups. It is always a positive number.

Figure 6-4 illustrates the step-by-step process of calculating the between groups *t* test. After you compute the test statistic, you refer to it as the obtained *t*. By using the probability density function for the *t* distribution, you could calculate the exact probability of obtaining a *t* as large as this, or greater, by chance alone. Note that for the *t* test, the size of the *t* value is determined by its absolute value (absolute means to disregard the sign). The larger the *t* value, the less likely that the data represent a chance finding and the more likely the difference between the group means is due to the independent variable.

### 6-5b Determining Whether the *t* Statistic Is Significant

To calculate the probability of an obtained *t* value, you must know something about the experiment. For a *t* test, you need to know the number of participants. In other types of statistics, you also need to know the number of groups, but because the *t* test can be applied to only two group experiments, this is built into the calculation of probability. You use the number of participants in the experiment to determine the **degrees of freedom** *(df)*. The degrees of freedom basically represent the number of different ways that the data could have produced the group means that were obtained simply through random sampling from a population. Determining the degrees of freedom is similar to determining how many ways there were to roll two dice and come up with a 7. In an experiment with two groups, the degrees of freedom represent how many ways you could randomly select a score and still come up with the specific group means. You find the degrees of freedom for a two-group experiment by using the following formula:

$$df = (n_1 - 1) + (n_2 - 1) = n_1 + n_2 - 2$$

> **degrees of freedom** Number of different ways that the data could have produced the group means that were obtained simply through random sampling from a population.

Where $n_1$ is the number of participants in the treatment group and $n_2$ is the number of participants in the control group.

Suppose you had two groups with means of 4 and 5, respectively, and there were three numbers in each group. Now imagine that you wanted to come up with those same means by randomly selecting scores. First, you select a score of 2. Next, you select a score of 5. Now if the mean of the entire set of three scores is 4, you know that the third number is 5. You can only randomly select two out of three scores if the mean of those scores is already determined. That's where the $(n_1 - 1)$ comes from. You likewise determine the degrees of freedom for group 2 with a mean of 5. If the first two scores are selected randomly, then the final one is fixed. There are $(n_2 - 1)$ ways to randomly come up with the mean of 5. Thus, if you randomly drew 5 and 7, you can deduce the third score. The degree of freedom in this example is $(3 - 1) + (3 - 1) = 4$. The degrees of freedom are used in the statistical process to determine how many ways the results could occur.

Using the obtained *t* value and the degrees of freedom, the statistician can calculate the probability of obtaining by chance alone a *t* as high or higher than the one observed from the data. This is what computerized *t* test programs present as the *p* value. If that probability is less than alpha (.05), then the researcher can infer that the difference between the means is due to the treatment, and not due to chance at a 95% level of confidence. Remember that there is always a chance that the difference was due to random fluctuation, no matter how large the *t* statistic is.

In actual practice, you don't have to be a statistician or rely on computers to use the *t* test. Most researchers use computer output or statistical tables to determine the significance of the obtained *t*. Table 6-2 is an excerpt of a table of critical values for the *t* function. Notice that across the top of the table are columns for different levels of alpha (.10, .05, .025, and .01, for example). To determine which column to look in, you must determine first whether the alpha levels are given for a one-tailed or a two-tailed hypothesis. Some tables present alpha levels for a **two-tailed test**. Because a one-tailed test is concerned with the differences between the means in only one direction, the probabilities are only in one tail of the probability density function.

> **two-tailed test** Statistical inference technique used for a two-tailed hypothesis.

| | |
|---|---|
| Step 1. | Write the correct formula. |

$$t = \frac{\bar{X}_t - \bar{X}_c}{\sqrt{\left[\dfrac{\Sigma X_t^2 - \dfrac{(\Sigma X_t)^2}{N_t} + \Sigma X_c^2 - \dfrac{(\Sigma X_c)^2}{N_c}}{N_t + N_c - 2}\right]\left[\dfrac{1}{N_t} + \dfrac{1}{N_c}\right]}}$$

| | |
|---|---|
| Step 2. | Determine which quantities are needed to calculate the formula. |

They are:

| | |
|---|---|
| $\bar{X}_t$ | $\bar{X}_c$ |
| $\Sigma X_t^2$ | $\Sigma X_c^2$ |
| $\Sigma X_t$ | $\Sigma X_c$ |
| $N_t$ | $N_c$ |

| | |
|---|---|
| Step 3. | Calculate the quantities determined in Step 2 from the data. |

| | |
|---|---|
| $\bar{X}_t = 14$ | $\bar{X}_c = 8$ |
| $\Sigma X_t^2 = 1996$ | $\Sigma X_c^2 = 656$ |
| $\Sigma X_t = 140$ | $\Sigma X_c = 80$ |
| $N_t = 10$ | $N_c = 10$ |

| | |
|---|---|
| Step 4. | Substitute calculated quantities into the formula and compute it. |

$$t = \frac{14 - 8}{\sqrt{\left[\dfrac{1996 - \dfrac{(140)^2}{10} + 656 - \dfrac{(80)^2}{10}}{10 + 10 - 2}\right]\left[\dfrac{1}{10} + \dfrac{1}{10}\right]}}$$

$$= \frac{6}{\sqrt{\left[\dfrac{1996 - 1960 + 656 - 640}{18}\right]\left[\dfrac{2}{10}\right]}}$$

$$= \frac{6}{\sqrt{\left[\dfrac{52}{18}\right]\left[\dfrac{2}{10}\right]}} = \frac{6}{\sqrt{[2.889][0.2]}} = \frac{6}{\sqrt{0.5778}}$$

$$= \frac{6}{0.76} = 7.893$$

| | |
|---|---|
| Step 5. | Evaluate the significance of the obtained $t$ value (Step 4). |

| | |
|---|---|
| A. | Determine if the alternative hypothesis is on a one-tailed or two-tailed hypothesis. In this case it is one-tailed. |
| B. | On the table of critical $t$ values, find the column that corresponds to $\alpha = .05$ for a one-tailed test. |
| C. | Calculate the degrees of freedom, $df = N_t + N_c - 2 = 10 + 10 - 2 = 18$. |
| D. | Find the row of the table for 18 degrees of freedom. |
| E. | Determine the critical $t$ value from the row and column selected. It is 1.734. |
| F. | Observe the means. Are they different in the hypothesized direction? If not, use a two-tailed test. |
| | $t_{critical}\,(df = 18),\;\; \alpha = .05,\; \text{(two-tailed)} = 2.101$ |
| G. | Compare the obtained $t$ test results to the critical $t$ from the table. |
| | If the $t_{obtained} > t_{critical}$ then the difference between the two groups is statistically significant (reject $H_o$). |
| | In this example $7.893 > 2.10$; therefore, the difference between the treatment groups is statistically significant at the .05 level. |

| | |
|---|---|
| Step 6. | Interpret the results. |

Present the two group means and describe the difference. In this example you would write, "The nonpronounceable words produced significantly lower recall ($\bar{X} = 8$ words) than did the pronounceable words ($\bar{X} = 14$ words)."

**Figure 6-4**

*Step-by-Step Procedure for Calculating a Between Groups* t *Test*

| TABLE 6-2 | Excerpt of Table for Critical Values of *t* Student's *t* Statistics |
|---|---|

| | α (alpha) | | | | |
|---|---|---|---|---|---|
| | .05 | .025 | .01 | .005 | (one-tailed) |
| *df* | .10 | .05 | .02 | .01 | (two-tailed) |
| 10 | 1.812 | 2.228 | 2.764 | 3.169 | |
| 12 | 1.782 | 2.179 | 2.681 | 3.055 | |
| 14 | 1.761 | 2.145 | 2.624 | 2.977 | |
| 16 | 1.746 | 2.120 | 2.583 | 2.921 | |
| 18 | 1.734 | 2.101 | 2.552 | 2.878 | |
| 20 | 1.725 | 2.086 | 2.528 | 2.845 | |

You can accomplish a **one-tailed test** by selecting the column that has two times the alpha level if the table is presented for the two-tailed test. Therefore, if the table presents two-tailed alpha values, and you are testing a one-tailed alternative hypothesis, select the column with alpha equal to 10.

The second step in using the table of critical values for *t* is to select the correct row by calculating the degrees of freedom. In the example, each group has 10 participants, so you obtain the degrees of freedom by calculating

$$df = 10 + 10 - 2 = 18$$

You find the critical *t* value for the experiment by looking in that row and under the column for the alpha level. In most cases that alpha level is .05, but for some research paradigms, an alpha level of .01 or even .001 is appropriate. In this experiment, that value is *1.734*. You write the critical value along with its parameters as follows:

Critical *t* (*df* = 18, α =. 05, one-tailed) = *1.734*

The next step is to compare the obtained *t* value to the critical value. If the obtained *t* has a greater absolute value than the critical *t* and is in the direction of the alternative hypothesis, then the null hypothesis is rejected in favor of the alternative hypothesis. You would say that there is a statistically significant difference between the means. If the critical value for *t* is greater than the obtained *t*, then you fail to reject the null hypothesis. Finally, if the absolute value of the obtained *t* is greater than the critical *t*, but in the direction opposite the null hypothesis, then you must construct and test a second post hoc hypothesis. *Post hoc* means after the fact. Because the results are opposite to the prediction, they must be tested with a two-tailed test. If the obtained *t* is greater than the two-tailed critical *t* value, then the null hypothesis is rejected in favor of the new post hoc alternative hypothesis. In experimental research you don't always find what you expect, which is why there are post hoc hypotheses and analyses.

**one-tailed test** Statistical inference technique used for a one-tailed hypothesis.

# 6-6  Statistical Decision Making

Section 6-5 illustrated how to make a statistical decision using the *t* test. Whenever a statistical decision is made, it always has one of two outcomes:

- Reject the null hypothesis.
- Fail to reject the null hypothesis.

There are also two possible outcomes for reality. The null hypothesis can in reality be true (that is, the independent variable is not a cause of the dependent variable), or the null hypothesis can be false (the independent variable does cause the dependent variable).

| TABLE 6-3 | | Statistical Decision Making and the Two Types of Errors | |
|---|---|---|---|
| | | Reality | |
| | | $H_0$ True | $H_0$ False |
| **Statistical Decision** | Reject $H_0$ | Type I error $\alpha$ | "True" significant result |
| | Fail to Reject $H_0$ | "True" nonsignificant result | Type II error $\beta$ |

The combination of the possible outcomes of statistical decisions and reality produces the four alternatives illustrated in Table 6-3. Each time you reject the null hypothesis, it can in reality either be true or false. Because your knowledge of reality is imperfect and based only on data, you never know for sure whether or not the null hypothesis is true. If the null hypothesis is false and you rejected it, your experiment is a success. You could call that the truly statistically significant result. If, on the other hand, the null hypothesis is true and you rejected it based on the statistics of the experiment, you have made an error. This type of error is called the **Type I error**. A statistical test is very precise if it shows only true differences to be significant. The lower the Type I error rate, the higher the **statistical precision**. Although you can't know whether or not you made a Type I error, each time you reject a null hypothesis, you do know the probability of making a Type I error. It is always equal to alpha. Thus, with alpha equal to .05, there is a 5% chance of making a Type I error. Another way of looking at it is that for every 20 experiments with statistically significant results, one is likely to be due to chance factors and not a real treatment effect. You never know which experiment produces a Type I error. This is one of the major reasons that researchers try to replicate results. If a finding is a Type I error, it is unlikely to be shown in the same way in a second experiment. If the result is truly significant, it should be possible to replicate that result in another experiment.

The preceding description applies to experiments with statistically significant results. Suppose the results of the experiment were not statistically significant. Then the researcher would fail to reject the null hypothesis. Again, in reality the null hypothesis can be either true or false. If the null hypothesis is true and you fail to reject it, you have again met the goals of experimental research. You could call this a true non-significance. If, however, the null hypothesis is false and you failed to reject it with your statistics, you have made the second type of error (Type II). The probability of a **Type II error** is called **beta** ($\beta$). It can be estimated by advanced statistical tests. The lower the beta, the more powerful the statistical test. **Statistical power** is the ability of the statistical test to reveal differences that actually exist. However, there is a trade-off between statistical power and precision. Usually, high precision leads to lower power. In statistical terms, alpha and beta are inversely related. Researchers generally prefer to make Type II errors to Type I errors. Therefore, they usually maintain alpha at .05 and try other methods of increasing the power (reduce Type II errors). Those methods involve having an adequate size sample and defining the independent and dependent variables in ways that are likely to show the maximum effects. The larger the number of participants, the lower the probability of a Type II error.

A Type II error is like fishing in a particular lake. In reality there is a huge fish in the lake. After not catching any fish, the fisherman says, "There are no fish in this lake." That would be a Type II error. The fisherman should have continued to fish. You can also see that this analogy supports the idea of never accepting the null hypothesis. Just because the fisherman didn't catch a fish doesn't mean that there are no fish in the lake. To carry the analogy to the extreme, the Type I error would be fishing in a different lake with no fish, but catching an old boot and saying, "What a fine fish for dinner tonight!"

**Type I error** Null hypothesis is true and based on the statistics of the experiment it was rejected.

**statistical precision** Ability of a statistical test to reveal only differences that actually exist, thus avoiding Type I error.

**Type II error** Null hypothesis is false and was not rejected with the statistics of the experiment

**beta** Probability of a Type II error.

**statistical power** Ability of the statistical test to reveal differences that actually exist.

# 6-7  Magnitude of Effect

Statistically significant results do not necessarily imply the differences between two means are practically significant. In fact, according to a statistical principle called the *law of large n*, as the sample sizes increase, even very small differences between their means will be statistically significant. Therefore, it is always important to look at the size of the difference between the means when interpreting a *t* test or any other statistical test of the differences among means. The measure of the size of the differences is called the **magnitude of effect**. The first thing to do is to consider the actual means. To understand how large their difference is, you also need to understand the variability within the groups. Cohen (1988) developed a standard way of doing this that is very much like the *z*-scores and *z* tests described in Section 6-4b. You remember that a *z*-score is the number of standard deviations away from the mean of any individual score. Likewise, a *z* test for a sample mean measures how many standard errors of the sampling distribution it is from the population mean. **Cohen's *d*** is the number of standard deviations between two sample means. In this case the standard deviation must be estimated from both samples; therefore, it is called the **pooled standard deviation**. There are two ways to calculate the *d* for a *t* test. The first is a definitional formula:

**magnitude of effect** Measure of the size of the differences.

**Cohen's *d*** Number of standard deviations between two sample means.

**pooled standard deviation** Standard deviation estimated from two samples.

$$d = \frac{\overline{X}_1 - \overline{X}_2}{S_{\text{pooled}}}$$

where

$$S_{\text{pooled}} = \frac{n_1 - 1}{n_1 + n_2 - 2}(S_1) + \frac{n_2 - 1}{n_1 + n_2 - 2}(S_2)$$

The second method of calculating *d* is based on the computations already accomplished with the *t* test:

$$d = \frac{t(n_1 + n_2)}{\sqrt{n_1 + n_2 - 2}\sqrt{n_1 n_2}}$$

The second method is much easier and will be illustrated for the *t* test calculated in Figure 6-4. In that example each group had 10 participants. The obtained *t* was 7.893. Therefore, the calculation of *d* is as follows:

$$d = \frac{7.893(10 + 10)}{\sqrt{10 + 10 - 2}\sqrt{10 \bullet 10}} = \frac{7.893(20)}{\sqrt{18}\sqrt{100}} = \frac{157.86}{4.24(10)} = \frac{157.86}{42.4} = 3.72$$

The interpretation of *d* is that there are about 3.7 pooled standard deviations between the mean of the first group (14) and the mean of the second group (8). This is a large effect. Cohen (1988) recommended interpreting *d* =.20 to .50 as small effect sizes; *d* =.50 to .80 as medium effect sizes; and *d* > .80 as large effect sizes.

# 6-8  APA Style: Writing Results

The **results section** of a research report contains all the descriptive and inferential statistics needed to test the hypotheses. In each of the following chapters, you will find examples showing how to write the results for the particular designs as they are introduced. You can state the results in many ways, but all of them include the following:

**results section** Section of a research report that contains all the descriptive and inferential statistics needed to test the hypotheses.

- The inferential statistic that was used
- The degrees of freedom
- The obtained test statistic
- Alpha and the critical value of the statistic or significance level

**significance level** Probability of obtaining the results by chance alone.

---

Results

The hypothesis that pronounceable syllables would be remembered better than would be unpronounceable sets of letters was tested with an independent groups $t$ test. The group receiving the pronounceable syllables ($M = 14$, $SD = 2$) did remember significantly more of the letter sets than did the control group ($M = 6$, $SD = 1.33$) ($t(18) = 7.89$, $a < .05$, two-tailed, $d = 3.72$).

---

**Figure 6-5**
*Sample APA Style Results Section*

- Descriptive statistics for any statistically significant results.

  In the case of a between groups $t$ test, the results should include the following:

- An independent groups $t$ test
- The degrees of freedom
- The calculated $t$ statistic
- The alpha level and/or critical $t$ value (or significance level if using a computer) and whether it was a one- or two-tailed test
- The means for each group, their standard deviations, and Cohen's $d$

The *Publication Manual of the American Psychological Association* (APA, 2001) gives some conventions that make it easier to write the results section with fewer words. For example, the degrees of freedom are usually presented in parentheses with the statistic name, $t(df)$ = calculated value; alpha = .05. The Publication Manual also includes a list of statistical abbreviations and symbols (Table 3-9) that can help you to describe the statistics. The uppercase letter $M$ is used for the mean because it's easier to write than

$$H_3 : \overline{X}_t < \overline{X}_c.$$

Figure 6-5 shows how the results of the sample experiment on pronounceability could be presented in the results section.

As you can see from Figure 6-5, the format for the results section is similar to that for the rest of the report. The heading, "Results," is centered at the beginning of the section. Paragraphs are double-spaced. Subheadings are used in long results sections following the same rules as in the method section.

# Summary

The control group posttest only design is one of the best designs to test an experimental hypothesis. The treatment is the hypothesized cause. It is given to the treatment group. The control group experiences everything in the same way as the treatment group, except the hypothesized cause. Participants are randomly assigned to either the treatment group or the control group in an attempt to produce groups of individuals that are equivalent on average over many different attributes.

The null hypothesis is that the independent variable has no effect. In contrast, the alternative hypothesis is that the independent variable has an effect. If the alternative hypothesis is directional, then the treatment group is expected to have a mean more or less than the control group mean. If one direction is expected, the hypothesis is called a one-tailed hypothesis. An a priori hypothesis is made before the data are collected. A post hoc hypothesis is made after the data have been analyzed and the results don't fit the first hypothesis.

Statistical inference is a way of estimating the odds of obtaining the results of the experiment by chance alone. If the odds are less than a certain percentage (alpha level) that the results could happen by chance alone, researchers reject the null hypothesis. Statistical distributions are used to estimate the probability of obtaining the results by chance alone. The normal distribution fits much psychological data. It is symmetrical with the mean, median, and mode at the center. The sampling distribution for the mean is also normally distributed. It's useful for determining the likelihood that a particular sample was drawn from a specific population, or if two samples were drawn from the same population.

Comparison of two groups of data is accomplished with Student's independent groups *t* test. If the *t* test is statistically significant, there is a probability of a Type I error equal to alpha. A Type I error occurs if the results were really due to chance but are interpreted as significant. If the *t* test failed to show statistically significant results, there is the probability of a Type II error equal to beta. A Type II error occurs if the hypothesized cause is truly the cause of the effect measured but the experiment failed to reveal it. Experiments that are low in Type I error rates have high statistical precision. Those that are low in Type II error rates have high statistical power.

In addition to statistical significance, the magnitude of the effect is also necessary for a good interpretation of the statistical results. The effect size is a measure of the difference between the two group means in pooled standard deviation units.

## References

American Psychological Association. (2001). *Publication manual of the American Psychological Association.* Washington, DC: Author.

Campbell, D. T. & Stanley, J. C. (1963). *Experimental and quasi-experimental designs for research.* Chicago: Rand McNally.

Cohen, J. (1988). *Statistical power analysis for the behavioral sciences.* Hillsdale, NJ: Erlbaum.

Mill, J. S. (1874). *A system of logic: Rationative and inductive.* New York: Harper & Brothers.

## Exercises for Application

An experimenter wanted to test the effect of visual imagery on memory. He presented participants in the treatment group a list of 20 words with associated pictures and presented the control group with the same 20 words, but with no pictures. The experimenter hypothesized that the images would improve memory. He measured memory through a free recall test. The data he collected are as follows:

1. State the null hypothesis.
2. State the alternative hypothesis.
3. What is the correct inferential statistic to test the hypothesis?
4. Calculate the statistic.
5. Present the descriptive statistics.
6. Make a statistical conclusion based on the data analysis.
7. Interpret the results in one nonstatistical sentence.
8. What is the probability of a Type I error?

| Control Group | Treatment Group |
|---|---|
| 14 | 9 |
| 12 | 11 |
| 9 | 8 |
| 15 | 10 |
| 14 | 7 |
| 19 | 9 |
| 17 | 8 |
| 14 | 10 |
| 11 | 12 |
| 15 | 7 |

## Practice Quiz

*Note:* You can find the correct answers to these questions by taking the quiz and then submitting your answers in the Online Edition. The program will automatically score your submission. If you miss a question, the program will provide the correct answer, a rationale for the answer, and the section number in the chapter where the topic is discussed.

1. The only difference between the control group and the treatment group should be
   a. the situation.
   b. the dependent variable.
   c. the independent variable.
   d. the standard deviation.

2. A hypothesis made before the data is collected is called a(n)
   a. a priori hypothesis.
   b. null hypothesis.
   c. alternative hypothesis.
   d. random hypothesis.

3. Statistics that are used to estimate the probability that the data could occur by chance alone are called
   a. standard deviation.
   b. descriptive statistics.
   c. inferential statistics.
   d. alternative statistics.

4. The standard odds used by scientists in testing hypotheses are
   a. .5.
   b. 1 in 1000.
   c. 8.
   d. .05.

5. Another way of stating the null hypothesis is to say that the means of two samples
   a. are statistically different.
   b. are from normal distributions.
   c. represent different underlying populations.
   d. come from the same underlying population.

6. The basic form of the *t* test is as a
   a. difference between the treatment and control means.
   b. sum of the variances between the two means.
   c. ratio of treatment variance to subject variance.
   d. total of all the variances in the experiment.

7. The parameter that must be calculated to determine the probability of an obtained *t* value is the
   a. degrees of freedom.
   b. alpha.
   c. mean.
   d. standard deviation.

8. The probability of obtaining a *t* value as high or higher than the one observed from the data is the
   a. *p* value.
   b. alpha.
   c. beta.
   d. standard deviation.

9. The null hypothesis is rejected in favor of the alternative hypothesis if the obtained *t* value is
   a. greater than the critical *t*.
   b. equal to the critical *t*.
   c. less than the critical *t*.
   d. in the direction of the one-tailed test.

10. A major reason for replicating experiments is to discover if
    a. you obtained a true significant result.
    b. you made a Type I error.
    c. you made a Type II error.
    d. you obtained a true nonsignificant result.

11. A nondirectional hypothesis is also called a(n)
    a. a priori hypothesis.
    b. post hoc hypothesis.
    c. two-tailed hypothesis.
    d. one-tailed hypothesis.

12. A set of probabilities for each possible result for a given research design is known as
    a. the normal distribution.
    b. alpha.
    c. beta.
    d. a probability density function.

13. Which of the following is *not* a characteristic of the normal distribution?
    a. The mean, median, and mode are all the same.
    b. Most scores are near the center of the distribution.
    c. The distribution is symmetrical about the mean.
    d. There are at least two modes.

14. The number of standard deviations between two means is referred to as
    a. Cohen's *d*.
    b. Student's *t*.
    c. alpha.
    d. *z*-score.

15. In the following text, what does the number 18 represent? ($t(18) = 7.89$, $p < .05$., two-tailed, $d = 3.72$)
    a. The mean
    b. The degrees of freedom
    c. The significance level
    d. The magnitude of effect

16. If the power of a statistical test is high, then the probability of _____ is low.
    a. rejecting the null hypothesis
    b. failing to reject the null hypothesis
    c. a Type I Error
    d. a Type II Error

# Hypothesis Testing: Pretest Posttest Design and Related Measures *t* Test

**Chapter** Seven

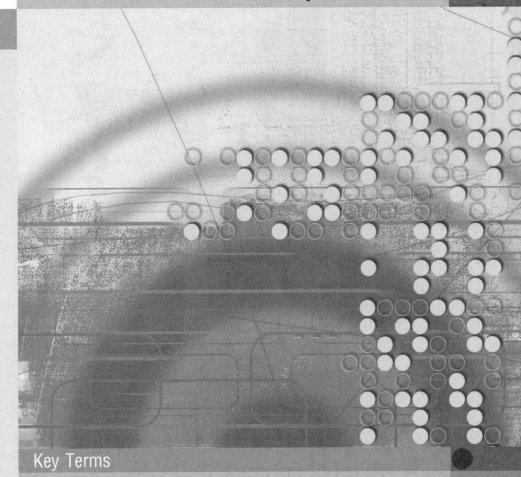

## Chapter Outline

## Key Terms

| | |
|---|---|
| confound | pretest posttest design |
| discussion section | related measures *t* test |
| history | testing |
| maturation | threats to internal validity |

# Learning Objectives

- Define internal and external validity of an experiment.
- Identify confounding in experiments and know how to design experiments that avoid confounding.
- Explain why history, maturation, or testing can make an experiment invalid.
- Know how to control the threats to validity of an experiment from history, testing, and maturation.
- Be able to apply statistical inference to the pretest posttest design.
- Know how to calculate and interpret the related measures $t$ test.

## Key Idea

The pretest posttest design uses each subject as his or her own control. This design should be used only when the threats to internal validity of history, maturation, and testing can be minimized.

## 7-1 Pretest Posttest Designs

**pretest posttest design** Design that uses each participant as his or her own control.

In Chapter 6, "Hypothesis Testing: The Control Group Posttest Only Design," we looked at the posttest only design with a control group. This chapter will focus on an alternative design that uses each participant as his or her own control: the **pretest posttest design**. At first consideration, it seems to be the ideal design: You know that the participants in the control condition (pretest) are equivalent to the participants in the treatment condition (posttest) because they are the same participants. You can notate this design using the Campbell and Stanley (1963) symbols as follows:

$$O_1 \; X \; O_2$$

Where $O_1$ stands for the pretest, X stands for the treatment, and $O_2$ stands for the posttest. This design is the simplest of the class of within subjects designs introduced in Chapter 3, "The Hypothetico-Deductive Method and Experiments in Psychology." Consider the following question: Does requiring students to engage in community service increase or decrease their likelihood to volunteer in the future? The question relates to the theory on motivation and reward, and specifically to the relationship between intrinsic (personally determined) and extrinsic (given by others) reward. The question could be answered by a pretest posttest experiment. All the students in a first-year required liberal studies course could be the participants. On the first day of the semester, all the students could complete an assessment form that details the type and amount of volunteer work they participated in during the previous 12 months. The volunteerism assessment is the pretest ($O_1$) for the experiment. During the first year of college, all students would be required to participate in 30 hours of community service as a class project. The required community service is the treatment (X). During senior testing right before graduation, the students would again complete the assessment form that measures the type and amount of volunteerism they had done during the previous 12 months. This volunteerism assessment is the posttest ($O_2$).

## 7-2 Internal and External Validity of an Experiment

A pretest posttest design overcomes the problem of individual differences among the people in a treatment group and a control group because each person is his or her own control. Each individual is tested before and after receiving the hypothesized cause. Although the participants at the two testing times are the same people, the conditions of testing may not be equivalent. In fact, the pretest posttest design poses three serious problems. Each one of these problems is a threat to the internal validity of an experiment.

The validity of an experiment was described in Chapter 6, "Hypothesis Testing: The Control Group Posttest Only Design." It is essential to evaluate the internal validity of all research designs. Therefore, we will review the concepts here. Commonly, the term validity refers to the strength or soundness of an idea. Something is valid if it is legitimate and true. An experiment can be valid in the following two senses:

- *Internal validity:* The independent variable in the experiment is the cause of the dependent variable in the experiment.

- *External validity:* The results of the experiment can be applied to populations and situations outside the experiment.

The internal validity of an experiment depends on the design and care taken in data collection. If the design is improper or the data were collected with carelessness, then some other factor besides the independent variable could be responsible for the results. If this is the case, the experiment is not valid. Some relationships are particularly difficult to study. Even with great care in design and conduct of the research, there are still alternative explanations for the results. In these cases, the researchers will design the best study possible to minimize the threats to internal validity and be sure to recognize the alternative explanations in the interpretations of their results. The relationship between community service and future volunteerism was chosen as an example for this chapter because it is one of the difficult relationships to study.

Remember that the first prerequisite for the external validity of an experiment is that the experiment be internally valid. If the results of the experiment are really due to the treatment (independent variable), then application of those results may be appropriate. If, however, the results were not valid within the experiment, it would be wrong to try to apply them to situations outside the experimental context. For example, consider new product testing. Manufacturers make changes to their products and then must test whether a change is really an improvement. A poorly designed study could lead to an invalid conclusion that the change was an improvement. Would you like to use a product tested with a poorly designed experiment that wasn't really a valid test of the product's claims? Stronger internal validity supports better external validity. This is one of the main reasons that persons whose major occupation is to apply research results, and not conduct it themselves, must be knowledgeable about research design. They must be able to evaluate the internal validity of research before they decide to apply it. If research is internally valid, it may be externally valid. Other considerations in evaluating the external validity of research will be covered in Chapter 12, "When the Cause Cannot Be Manipulated: Pre-Experimental Design and Chi-Square." This chapter will focus on some of the main problems for internal validity because it is very difficult to design an internally valid pretest posttest experiment.

# 7-3  Threats to Internal Validity of an Experiment

Any factors that are confused with the independent variable in an experiment can pose **threats to internal validity**. When some other factor varies systematically with the treatment, the independent variable is said to be *confounded*. The problem with confounded designs is that the researcher cannot know whether the results of the experiment were due to the treatment or due to the confounding factor. Consider the following analogy to get a better appreciation of confounding. Suppose you

**threats to internal validity**
Any aspect of the research design that produces a confound with the independent variable that weakens the logical link between it and the hypothesized effect.

wanted to know which of two types of flour produced a better cake. You know that Mrs. Smith uses brand X, and she makes very good cakes. On the other hand, Mrs. Jones uses brand Y, and her cakes are never as good as Mrs. Smith's cakes. Can you conclude that brand X flour is better than brand Y flour? No! You can't know anything about the flour because not only is the flour in the cakes different, but also the cake bakers are different. The type of flour is confounded with the baker of the cakes. The clearest conclusion that you could draw is that either brand X flour is better than brand Y flour, or that Mrs. Smith is a better baker than Mrs. Jones, or that brand X is better than brand Y and Mrs. Smith is a better baker than Mrs. Jones, or even that brand X is worse than brand Y but Mrs. Smith's superior baking makes the difference. Thus, you can see in this analogy, when factors are confounded, you really don't know about their individual contributions to an effect. It is the same in experiments. Confounded experiments give no clear evidence about cause and effect. Therefore, they should be avoided. The best way to avoid confounded experiments is to carefully think through the design of an experiment and all the likely confounding factors before collecting the data. This way, you can design an experiment that will minimize potential confounding factors.

Campbell and Stanley (1963) outlined nine major threats to the internal validity of an experiment. Three of these threats are particularly liable in the pretest posttest design. These three—history, maturation, and testing—will be covered in sections through sections 7-3a–7-3c.

### 7-3a History

**history** "The specific events occurring between the first and second measurement in addition to the experimental variable" (Campbell & Stanley, 1963, p. 5).

Campbell and Stanley (1963) define the threat of **history** to the internal validity of an experiment as follows:

> *History,* The specific events occurring between the first and second measurement in addition to the experimental variable. (p. 5)

Threats from history are particularly problematic with the pretest posttest design. Consider, for example, an experiment to test the effects of a specific cognitive training program on problem-solving ability. The typical pretest posttest design has three parts. First, all participants take a pretest. The pretest provides the baseline for the skills to be trained by the program. Second, all participants take the training program. The training program is supposed to cause an improvement in their skills. Third, after the training program all participants take the posttest. The posttest should show how much their skills improved from their baseline levels. The pretest posttest design is used in hopes that any differences observed between the pretest and the posttest will be due to the treatment (cognitive training program). However, consider the potential for events to occur between the pretest and posttest that could influence the results. The longer the delay between a pretest and a posttest, the greater the chance of a history effect. History effects could be due to actual historical events, such as the impact of an attempted coup on the study of attitudes toward democracy. More often, however, they are the result of more mundane interruptions of the experiment. Examples of history effects that could threaten the validity of the cognitive training experiment include

- A noisy piece of equipment being operated during the posttest
- A power failure resulting in lower light levels during the posttest than during the pretest
- An individual interrupting the experiment during either the pretest or posttest session
- Someone giving the answers to the posttest to participants between the pretest and the posttest

Now think about the sample field experiment on community service that was introduced in section 7-1. A threat from history occurs when any event, in addition to the experimental treatment, that can influence the effect (volunteerism in this case) occurs between the pretest and posttest. Because the pretest occurred at the beginning of college and the posttest occurred almost 4 years later, right before graduation, many things that influence volunteerism could occur. How many events can you think of that would be likely to increase or decrease volunteerism among college students in addition to required community service? All of those would be history threats to the internal validity of the experiment.

To reduce history effects, the experimenter may attempt to reduce the time between the pretest and the posttest. This approach will not work when the treatment is presumed to take a specific amount of time to have its effect (e.g., training programs take time). A second way to attempt to minimize the threats from history is to keep the situation very controlled during the entire experiment so that external events cannot interrupt. This is similar to sequestering a jury to ensure that influences outside the trial do not affect their verdict. However, as with juries, sequestering in experiments can have a negative effect on the results simply through changes that occur with the passage of time. This effect will be covered in section 7-3b.

## 7-3b Maturation

Campbell and Stanley (1963) define **maturation** as follows:

> *Maturation,* Processes within the respondents operating as a function of the passage of time per se, including growing older, growing hungrier, growing more tired, and the like. (p. 5)

The maturation threat is also a very great problem for the pretest posttest design. Maturation is especially a problem for two areas of research that often employ a pretest posttest design and that also always involve the participants' maturation. The first of these two areas is educational research. Often a pretest is administered and then participants are given some form of education (e.g., educational enhancement program); then a posttest is administered. If the posttest results are better than the pretest results, this outcome is taken as evidence that the treatment was effective. However, the participants are maturing on the variable being tested; therefore, there would have probably been a difference between the pretest and posttest even without the treatment. Consider, for example, a study of the efficacy of cognitive training of the memory of children with learning disabilities. Again the typical research design would be to pretest participants' memory, give them the training program, and finally assess their memory again (posttest). There is no reason to believe that the children would not be developing their memories independently during the training period. Therefore, any improvement could be due to the maturation or to the training program. The research design is confounded. Both training and maturation occur at the same time. That means the experiment's internal validity is threatened.

The second area of research that is particularly likely to employ the pretest posttest design and that is liable to maturation effects is therapy research. It is clear that individuals who seek therapy develop (or mature) in their illnesses/problems over time. Some individuals may progressively worsen, whereas others may progressively improve without the therapy. The pretest posttest design applied to therapy cannot untangle the effects of therapy from those of maturation.

The reason that educational programs and therapies are so often tested with the pretest posttest design, even though the threat from maturation is great, is that there is a great reluctance to have a control group in these two areas. The treatment is hypothesized to help the participants. Therefore, no one wants any participants to be in the control group. However, this thinking neglects the fact that without a valid test, the therapy or educational program cannot be shown effective. In other words, unless some participants act as a control and do not receive the program, the actual

**maturation** "Processes within the respondents operating as a function of the passage of time per se, including growing older, growing hungrier, growing more tired, and the like" (Campbell & Stanley, 1963, p. 5).

efficacy of the program cannot be demonstrated. Nevertheless, often there are strong ethical problems of denying a beneficial program to a control group. When the pretest posttest design is used, the results can be interpreted only as the combined effects of the treatment and maturation. There is no way with the simple pretest posttest design to determine how much of the result was due to the treatment and how much was due to maturation.

One way to attempt to overcome this problem and still be ethical is to ensure that all participants in the control group will receive the treatment if it is proven effective in the experiment. This strategy is good only if the treatment can be delayed and still provide the same benefit. Still another approach is to test a treatment against another treatment. For example, the comparison of an alternative classroom approach should be made to the standard classroom approach, not to a no education control. Both of these strategies involve the use of a control group.

Before moving to the third threat to internal validity, let's return to the required community service experiment example. The length of time between the baseline measure of volunteerism in the year before starting college and the measure of volunteerism during the year preceding college graduation is quite long. It is guaranteed that the majority of the students have matured during the almost four years of college attendance regardless of their required community service in the first year of college. How do you think maturation would affect volunteerism? Would it increase, decrease, or stay the same? Clearly, the experiment has a **confound** between the treatment (required community service) and the students' maturation during college. The experiment's internal validity is threatened by maturation.

So far the examples of maturation involve fairly large amounts of time. But maturation effects can occur within short periods of time as well. For example, right now I'm not as focused on writing this text as I would like to be because it's 12:08 and I'm being distracted by hunger. The desire for lunch is interfering with my cognitive performance. If I had taken a pretest an hour ago when I wasn't hungry and was to take the same test now, I might not do as well just because of the maturation effect of hunger. Fatigue, hunger, boredom—anything that changes as a function of time per se—can produce a maturation threat to the internal validity of an experiment.

**confound** Factor varies systematically with treatment of the independent variable.

### 7-3c  Testing

The third of the threats to internal validity of an experiment that is particularly liable in the case of the pretest posttest design is **testing**. It was defined by Campbell and Stanley (1963) as follows:

**testing** Effects of taking a test upon the scores of a second test.

*Testing,* The effects of taking a test upon the scores of a second test.

It is quite likely that participants will either learn from the pretest or that they will remember their responses on the pretest and attempt to maintain consistency from the pretest to the posttest. There are two main methods to avoid a testing effect. The first one is to use alternate forms of the measurement device during the pretest and posttest. Form A could be used for the pretest and Form B for the posttest. This strategy can be used only if the two forms have been demonstrated to reliably measure the same things and the first form produces no carry-over effect. Such an effect can occur even if the forms of the test are different.

An example of the testing effect occurred to me in the first experiment I participated in as an undergraduate student. I was given a pretest of memory and discovered during the pretest that the memory task was more difficult than I had anticipated. So before I took the posttest, I changed my memory strategy. The change in strategy was confounded with the treatment. I never learned what the treatment was, but it was obviously supposed to reduce my memory because, during the debriefing, the graduate student researcher was very interested in why my memory had improved. In this case the testing effect worked against the treatment effect. The testing effect can work to increase or decrease the behavior measured, but in either case the research results are invalid. In this example using a different form of the memory test wouldn't have helped. Instead, the research should have been designed to reduce the effects of testing by not having a pretest (use the posttest only control group design).

The required community service experiment design is unlikely to have a threat from testing even if the same form is used to assess volunteerism both at the pretest and posttest because the length of time between the tests is so great. The students are unlikely to remember what they wrote on a form almost four years earlier. When the time between pretests and posttests is long, the threat of testing is reduced, but the threats of history and maturation are increased. You or your friends may have prepared for your college admissions exams by taking practice tests. People take practice tests to produce the testing effect. Students who take them want to improve their scores on the real entrance exam just through the practice.

# 7-4 Hypothesis Testing with the Pretest Posttest Design

If the history, maturation, and testing threats to internal validity can be minimized, then the experimenter may choose to design the experiment involving both a pretest and posttest. The process of statistical analysis is similar to that used in the two group experiment.

Continuing the example of the community service field experiment would be interesting. However, because the threats to its internal validity from history and maturation are so great, I don't recommend using the pretest posttest design that was described. Therefore, this section has a new example that is less liable to the threats of history, maturation, and testing.

Have you ever been annoyed by constant interruptions while attempting to complete a task. Your annoyance might have shown itself in your bodily arousal. The remainder of this chapter will rely on the following sample experiment that tested the effects of interruption on arousal. A researcher wanted to determine the effects of cognitive interference on arousal. Twenty participants were first acclimated to the cognitive task by spending 5 minutes completing a question-and-answer task. Next, the participants were pretested on arousal for a period of 5 minutes while continuing with the question-and-answer task. The treatment involved interrupting the participants from the question-and-answer task by requiring that they stop the task and turn off a light each time the light came on. The light was programmed to come on intermittently 10 times during the 5-minute posttest interval. The arousal scores for the pretest and posttest phases are shown in Table 7-1. In the actual experiment the scores would be in terms of galvanic skin response (GSR). The numbers have been simplified here to make the statistical analysis examples easier to follow. Higher scores indicate higher arousal levels.

## 7-4a Null Hypothesis

The null hypothesis in a pretest posttest design is the same as in the posttest only control group design; that is

$H_o$: The treatment does not cause the effect.

| TABLE 7-1 | Data from Experiment on the Effects of Interruption on Arousal | |
|---|---|---|
| | **Arousal Scores** | |
| **Participant** | **Pretest** | **Posttest** |
| 1 | 20 | 25 |
| 2 | 18 | 21 |
| 3 | 23 | 19 |
| 4 | 22 | 27 |
| 5 | 19 | 23 |
| 6 | 21 | 21 |
| 7 | 24 | 28 |
| 8 | 22 | 30 |
| 9 | 23 | 27 |
| 10 | 19 | 23 |
| 11 | 18 | 23 |
| 12 | 20 | 24 |
| 13 | 22 | 23 |
| 14 | 21 | 26 |
| 15 | 20 | 20 |
| 16 | 21 | 25 |
| 17 | 17 | 20 |
| 18 | 19 | 22 |
| 19 | 22 | 23 |
| 20 | 24 | 21 |

In this case we will again compare the means of the two conditions. However, the means represent scores from the same participants, not from different groups of subjects. The statistical way of writing the null hypothesis is

$$H_o: \text{Pretest } \overline{X} = \text{Posttest } \overline{X}$$

### 7-4b Alternative Hypothesis

The alternative hypothesis is based on the conceptual hypothesis of the experiment. Again, because we are comparing two means, there are three possible alternative hypotheses. The experimenter must choose, a priori, the one that best fits the conceptual hypothesis. Recall from Chapter 6, "Hypothesis Testing: The Control Group Posttest Only Design," that the three possible alternative hypotheses are

$H_1$: The treatment affects the effect.

$H_2$: The treatment improves the effect.

$H_3$: The treatment reduces the effect.

The first of the alternative hypotheses is a two-tailed hypothesis. The last two are one-tailed hypotheses. In the sample interruption experiment the alternative hypothesis is

$H_1$: Interruption increases arousal.

It can be stated statistically as follows:

$$H_1: \text{Pretest } \overline{X} < \text{Posttest } \overline{X}$$

# 7-5 Data Collection Procedures

During the data collection period, the researcher must be very careful to maintain consistency of the conditions. The only thing that must change is the introduction of the treatment at the appropriate time (to reduce history effects). Furthermore, it is essential that the length of the experiment not be long enough to fatigue the subjects (a maturation effect). Finally, it is necessary to make sure that the measurement of the dependent variable during the pretest does not affect it during the posttest (testing effect).

The researcher conducted the sample experiment in a quiet room that was removed from visual distractions and outside interruptions to reduce potential history effects. She also designed the experiment so that its length did not fatigue the participants. Allowing participants to complete the question-and-answer task in 15 minutes prevented their fatigue or boredom (both possible maturation effects). Finally, the measure of arousal did not sensitize the participants from the pretest to the posttest. For this reason a self-report measure of arousal was not used. It might have produced erroneous results on the posttest because the participant was able to remember the pretest score and may have wanted to remain consistent. In this experiment GSR (galvanic skin response) was used as the measure of arousal because it is not very liable to testing effects.

# 7-6 Data Analysis: Within Subjects $t$ Test

In a pretest posttest design, the data from the two treatment conditions (pretest and posttest) come from the same subjects; consequently, the sets of data are not independent. Therefore, you should not do the independent groups $t$ test presented in Chapter 6, "Hypothesis Testing: The Control Group Posttest Only Design." Instead, you should employ a **related measures $t$ test**. This type of $t$ test is also called a repeated measures $t$ test, a within subjects $t$ test, or a paired samples $t$ test. It is appropriate under the following conditions:

**related measures $t$ test**
Inferential statistic to test the difference between two means that are related by being from the same participant (repeated measures) or in some other way (e.g., matching).

- The dependent variable has been measured on interval or ratio scale (and some ordinal scales, such as Likert scales).

- The scores from one condition are related to the scores from the other condition in some way.

Note that the related pairs $t$ test is appropriate with the pretest posttest design. The pretest scores are related to the posttest scores because they come from the same subject. This $t$ test is also appropriate in designs that involve the matching of subjects in groups or the comparison of two groups of subjects who are related in some other way (e.g., parents' behavior to that of their children).

The formula for the within subjects scores $t$ test is as follows:

$$t = \sqrt{\frac{N-1}{\dfrac{N \sum D^2}{(\sum D)^2} - 1}}$$

This formula is substantially different from the independent groups $t$ test formula. First, notice that this formula will always produce a positive result, unlike the independent groups $t$ test that can, and often does, result in a negative obtained $t$. Second, notice that the formula is based on difference scores ($D$). The difference score is simply the difference between the posttest and pretest on the dependent variable. A larger effect of the treatment will produce larger differences between the pairs of scores. The within subjects $t$ test is a measure of the difference between the posttest and pretest relative to the variation within the pretest and posttest taking into account their shared variance. They have shared variance due to their relationship (pairing of scores). The third difference between the related measures $t$ test and between groups $t$ test formula is the meaning of $N$. In this formula $N$ still refers to the number of subjects, but there are two scores from each subject (pretest and posttest). $N$ represents the number of differences between the paired scores. In the between groups design, $n$ is the number of subjects and is also the number of data points (one from each subject). You will remember from the independent groups $t$ test formula that $n$ was used to find the degrees of freedom ($n_1 + n_2 - 2$). $N$ is also used to find the degrees of freedom for the within subjects $t$ test. In this case, the degrees of freedom are the number of ways the mean for the difference between the pairs of scores could be arrived at by chance alone. Because the mean difference score is the goal, then the number of pairs of scores, $N$, is used to determine the degrees of freedom. There are $N - 1$ ways to randomly select differences between pairs of scores and still produce the observed difference between the pretest and posttest. Therefore, the degrees for freedom for the pretest posttest design is $N - 1$.

Figure 7-1 shows the calculation of the within subjects $t$ test for the sample experiment.

# 7-7 Interpretation of Results

The interpretation of results of the paired scores $t$ test is parallel to that in Chapter 6, "Hypothesis Testing: The Control Group Posttest Only Design." It follows this procedure:

1. Determine whether the alternative hypothesis is a one-tailed or two-tailed hypothesis.
   a. If one-tailed, examine the means from the pretest and posttest conditions to determine whether they are consistent with the alternative hypothesis.
   b. If the means obtained for the pretest and posttest are opposite in direction from those predicted by the alternative hypothesis, you must reject that alternative hypothesis and construct a new post hoc two-tailed alternative hypothesis.
2. Using the table of critical values for the $t$ distribution, determine the critical $t$ by
   a. Selecting the column based on the one-tailed or two-tailed alpha (.05).
   b. Selecting the row based on the degrees of freedom of the design. (The degrees of freedom for a paired scores $t$ test is the number of subjects [not scores!] minus 1.)
3. Compare the obtained $t$ value (calculated with the formula) to the critical $t$ value (from the table of critical values).
   a. If the obtained $t$ > critical $t$, then you reject the null hypothesis in favor of the alternative hypothesis. The difference between the pretest and posttest means are statistically significant.
   b. If the obtained $t$ < critical $t$, then you fail to reject the null hypothesis. The results are not statistically significant.

In the sample, interruptions caused a statistically significant effect on arousal as demonstrated by the obtained $t$ value being greater than the critical $t$ value. The probability of a Type I error is alpha.

# 7-8 Magnitude of Effect for Pretest Posttest Designs

Interpretation of a statistically significant within subjects $t$ test should take into account the size of the significant effect. You can compute the effect size, $d$, based

A.  Calculate mean arousal for pretest and posttest conditions.

Pretest $\overline{X} = \dfrac{415}{20} = 20.75$

Posttest $\overline{X} = \dfrac{471}{20} = 23.55$

B.  *t* test procedure.

Step 1.  Calculate the difference scores (*D*) by subtracting each participant's pretest score from his or her posttest score. (See column under Step 1 in data for *t* test procedure in B.)

Step 2.  Add all the difference scores. $\Sigma D = 56$

Step 3.  Square the difference scores.

Step 4.  Add all the squared difference scores. $\Sigma D^2 = 314$

Step 5.  Substitute the values into the formula.

$$t = \sqrt{\dfrac{N-1}{\dfrac{N\Sigma D^2}{(\Sigma D)^2}-1}} = \sqrt{\dfrac{20-1}{\dfrac{20 \times 314}{56^2}-1}}$$

Step 6.  Calculate.

$$t = \sqrt{\dfrac{19}{\dfrac{6280}{3136}-1}} = \sqrt{\dfrac{19}{2.003-1}} = \sqrt{\dfrac{19}{1.003}} = \sqrt{18.952} = 4.353$$

C.  Evaluate significance of the obtained *t* value.

Step 1.  Determine if the alternative hypothesis is one-tailed or two-tailed.
$H_1: \overline{X}_{\text{pretest}} < \overline{X}_{\text{posttest}}$
This is consistent with obtained means; therefore, one-tailed test of significance will be used.

Step 2.  Determine degrees of freedom.
$df = N - 1$          $df = 20 - 1 = 19$

Step 3.  Determine critical *t* value from the table.
Critical *t* (*df* = 19, $\alpha$ = .05, one-tailed test) = 1.729

Step 4.  Compare obtained *t* to critical *t* and make the statistical inference.
Obtained *t* = 4.353 > 1.729 = Critical *t*
Therefore, reject $H_0$.

Step 5.  Make conclusions. The interruptions produced a statistically significant increase in arousal from the pretest ($\overline{X} = 20.75$) to the posttest ($\overline{X} = 23.55$) ($t$ (19) = 4.353, $\alpha$ < .05).

Data for *t* test procedure in B
Calculation example for the Paired Scores *t* Test using the data from Table 7-1

|  | Arousal scores | | Step 1 | Step 3 |
|---|---|---|---|---|
| Subject | Pretest | Posttest | D | D² |
| 1 | 20 | 25 | 5 | 25 |
| 2 | 18 | 21 | 3 | 9 |
| 3 | 23 | 19 | −4 | 16 |
| 4 | 22 | 27 | 5 | 25 |
| 5 | 19 | 23 | 4 | 16 |
| 6 | 21 | 21 | 0 | 0 |
| 7 | 24 | 28 | 4 | 16 |
| 8 | 22 | 30 | 8 | 64 |
| 9 | 23 | 27 | 4 | 16 |
| 10 | 19 | 23 | 4 | 16 |
| 11 | 18 | 23 | 5 | 25 |
| 12 | 20 | 24 | 4 | 16 |
| 13 | 22 | 23 | 1 | 1 |
| 14 | 21 | 26 | 5 | 25 |
| 15 | 20 | 20 | 0 | 0 |
| 16 | 21 | 25 | 4 | 16 |
| 17 | 17 | 20 | 3 | 9 |
| 18 | 19 | 22 | 3 | 9 |
| 19 | 22 | 23 | 1 | 1 |
| 20 | 24 | 21 | −3 | 9 |
| Sums | 415 | 471 | 56 | 314 |
| $\overline{X}$ mean | 20.75 | 23.55 | Step 2 | Step 4 |

## Figure 7-1

*Calculation Example for the Paired Scores t Test*

on the difference scores. It is the ratio of the difference between the means for the pretest and posttest to the standard deviation of the difference scores. The formula is

$$d = \frac{\overline{X}_{\text{pretest}} - \overline{X}_{\text{posttest}}}{S_{\text{difference\_scores}}}$$

In the example of the effects of interruption on arousal, the difference between the pretest and posttest means was 2.8. The standard deviation of the differences between the 20 pairs of scores was 2.88. Their ratio is the effect size, which follows:

$$d = \frac{2.8}{2.88} = 0.97$$

The effect of disruption on arousal was large in the sample experiment. In fact, you could interpret this to mean that the average difference between the pretest before the disruption and the posttest after the disruption is almost one standard deviation of the difference scores.

# 7-9 APA Style: Results and Discussion

The final two sections of the body of an APA style research report are the results and discussion sections. In brief articles, the two sections are sometimes merged into one. Chapter 6, "Hypothesis Testing: The Control Group Posttest Only Design," introduced the APA style results section with an example of the between groups $t$ test. In this chapter, section 7-9a describes the results section that reports a related measures $t$ test. Section 7-9b describes the discussion section.

### 7-9a Writing the Results for a Pretest Posttest Design

The results for the pretest posttest design are written in the same format as those for the posttest only control group design. In both cases the descriptive statistics (means and standard deviations or standard errors) and the inferential statistics are presented ($t$ test results). The only difference is in the name of the inferential statistic. For the pretest posttest design, any of the following names refers to the same $t$ test: within subjects, related groups, paired samples, or correlated samples. The following example shows one way to report the statistical results computed for the sample experiment on disruption and arousal:

A related measure $t$ test was used to test the hypothesis that disruption increases arousal from the pretest to the posttest. The posttest mean arousal level of 23.55 ($S = 2.95$) was statistically significantly higher than the pretest mean of 20.75 ($S = 2.02$) ($t(19) = 4.35$, $p < .05$, $d = .97$).

### 7-9b The Discussion Section

discussion section Section of a research report in which the results of the research are discussed.

The last section of the body of a research report in APA style is the **discussion section** (APA, 2001). As you would guess from the heading, this section is a discussion of the results of the research. It usually contains at least three parts. First, you state the results of the experiment again, but this time without numbers or statistical terms. This is a clear statement of the support or failure to support of the results of the experiment for your research hypotheses. Second, you compare the results of this experiment to previous research. You should make connections between your study results and those of other studies that you have read (be sure to cite them in the discussion section). Finally, you can draw applications and implications from your results if they warrant it. If the results were not statistically significant, you can discuss why that might be the case, but you should not explain how to apply the results as if they were significant. The implications of the research results can be for understanding basic theory, specific applications, and questions for future research.

# Summary

A pretest posttest design uses each subject as his or her own control through the pretest. This design is good if the threats to internal validity of history, testing, and maturation can be minimized. A history threat occurs when some event in addition to the treatment occurs between the pretest and posttest and the event can be responsible for change between them. Maturation is the threat that occurs due to the passage of time such as growth, development, fatigue, and so forth. The maturation process is confounded with the treatment effect so that the researchers can't be sure how much of the change between the pretest and posttest was due to maturation and how much was due to the treatment. The third major threat to the internal validity of a pretest posttest design is called testing. It is the effect of taking a test upon taking it again.

The within subjects *t* test has many names. It is a measure of the average of the difference between the pretest and posttest taking into account the variation of the differences of the scores. The within subjects *t* test is interpreted and reported in the same way as the independent groups *t* test. The effect size for the within subjects *t* test is the ratio of the average difference to the standard deviations of the differences between pairs of scores.

## References

American Psychological Association. (2001). *Publication manual of the American Psychological Association*. Washington, DC: Author.

Campbell, D. T. & Stanley, J. C. (1963). *Experimental and quasi-experimental designs for research*. Chicago: Rand McNally.

## Exercises for Application

The following data were collected in an experiment on the use of monocular and binocular cues in depth perception. Each participant viewed an object first with both eyes and estimated the object's distance from a control point (binocular condition). Then the participant viewed the object again (at a different position) with the nonpreferred eye covered and estimated its distance from the control point (monocular condition). The data presented in the following table represent the difference between the estimated distance and the actual distance (in absolute value terms).

1. State the null hypothesis.

2. State the alternative hypothesis.

3. What is the correct inferential statistic to test the hypothesis?

4. Calculate the statistic.

5. Present the descriptive statistics.

6. Make a statistical conclusion based on the data analysis.

7. Interpret the results in one nonstatistical sentence.

8. What is the probability of a Type I error?

| Subject # | Distance Scores | |
| --- | --- | --- |
| | Monocular | Binocular |
| 1 | 2 | 4 |
| 2 | 3 | 5 |
| 3 | 1 | 3 |
| 4 | 2 | 4 |
| 5 | 0 | 3 |
| 6 | 3 | 5 |
| 7 | 1 | 3 |
| 8 | 2 | 5 |
| 9 | 1 | 4 |
| 10 | 2 | 6 |

## Practice Quiz

*Note:* You can find the correct answers to these questions by taking the quiz and then submitting your answers in the Online Edition. The program will automatically score your submission. If you miss a question, the program will provide the correct answer, a rationale for the answer, and the section number in the chapter where the topic is discussed.

1. An experiment is said to have internal validity if
   a. the independent variable is the cause of the dependent variable.
   b. the results of the experiment can be applied to situations outside the experiment.
   c. the results of the experiment can be replicated in another experiment.
   d. there is significant confounding in the experimental design.

2. When some other factor varies systematically with the independent variable, the study is
   a. confounded.
   b. internally valid.
   c. externally valid.
   d. within subjects.

3. A power failure resulting in lower light levels during the posttest than during the pretest is an example of a
   a. maturation effect.
   b. testing effect.
   c. selection effect.
   d. history effect.

4. A process within the respondents operating as a function of passage of time is called a
   a. maturation effect.
   b. testing effect.
   c. selection effect.
   d. history effect.

5. Alternate forms are used during the pretest and posttest to reduce a possible
   a. maturation effect.
   b. testing effect.
   c. selection effect.
   d. history effect.

6. In a pretest posttest experiment, the null hypothesis is that
   a. the treatment affects the effect.
   b. the treatment improves the effect.
   c. the treatment reduces the effect.
   d. the treatment does not cause the effect.

7. A paired data *t* test should be used instead of a between subjects *t* test whenever
   a. the dependent variable has been measured on at least an ordinal scale.

   b. the scores from one condition are related to the scores from the other condition in some way.
   c. there are more than two conditions to compare in the experiment.
   d. there is no a priori two-tailed hypothesis.

8. If the means obtained for the pretest and posttest are opposite to those predicted by the a priori hypothesis,
   a. there is no need to do the *t* test.
   b. the experiment was not internally valid.
   c. a two-tailed post hoc hypothesis should be tested.
   d. the Type I error probability must be doubled.

9. In a pretest posttest design, the degrees of freedom are
   a. number of scores minus 1.
   b. number of subjects minus 1.
   c. number of groups minus 1.
   d. alpha minus 1.

10. If the obtained *t* is less than the critical *t*, then
    a. the null hypothesis is rejected.
    b. the probability of a Type I error is alpha.
    c. the difference between the pretest and posttest means are statistically significant.
    d. the results are not statistically significant.

11. The magnitude of effect for a pretest posttest design is just like that for the posttest only control group design *except* that
    a. the numerator is based on difference scores.
    b. it takes a larger difference to have the same magnitude.
    c. the denominator is the standard deviations of the difference scores.
    d. the lower degrees of freedom result in a larger magnitude of effect.

12. The first part of the discussion section in a research report should be
    a. the statistical results of the study, including inferential statistics and means.
    b. the results summarized without statistical terms or numbers.
    c. a brief description of the procedures of the study.
    d. suggestions for future research.

13. The hand calculation of a related measures *t* test using the formula presented in the text will result in a negative number if
    a. the pretest is greater than the posttest.
    b. the posttest is greater than the pretest.
    c. there is no difference between the pretest and posttest.
    d. you made an error in calculating the formula.

14. Changes that occur in a pretest posttest design that result from the subject being more hungry at the posttest (and therefore more easily distracted) than at the pretest can produce a

  a. history effect.
  b. maturation effect.
  c. testing effect.
  d. confederate effect.

15. If a study has high external validity, then

  a. it doesn't have internal validity.
  b. it is probably confounded.
  c. the results can be applied to other populations.
  d. it was a pretest posttest design.

# One-Factor Between Groups Design and One-Way ANOVA

## Chapter Eight

## Chapter Outline

## Key Terms

analysis of variance
ANOVA
ANOVA summary table
experiment-wise error
*F* ratio

HSD
mean squares
multiple comparisons
partitioning the variance
sums of squares

# Learning Objectives

- Identify research designs that require the use of analysis of variance (ANOVA).
- Explain why Student's *t* test is inappropriate for experiments with more than two treatments.
- Be able to partition the variance for a one-factor between groups experiment.
- Calculate and interpret the analysis of variance.
- Apply a statistical test for multiple comparisons.

## Key Idea

Research designs that involve more than two treatment conditions rely on analysis of variance to make statistical inferences about the effects of those conditions. Analysis of variance is the statistical comparison of all the variance in the data that can be attributed to the independent variable compared to all the remaining variance in the data.

# 8-1 One-Factor Between Groups Designs

Chapters 6, "Hypothesis Testing: The Control Group Posttest Only Design," and 7, "Hypothesis Testing: Pretest Posttest Design and Related Measures *t* Test," dealt with the methods of statistical inference that can be employed in a two-treatment experiment. However, often more than two levels of the independent variable must be manipulated in an experiment. The reason is that the cause may be too complex to understand with just two levels, the treatment and control. Consider an experiment that is aimed at investigating the relationship between arousal and cognition. The researcher may operationally define arousal at two levels (control and treatment). A better experiment would be one that had several different levels of arousal. In this chapter we will use the sample experiment in Taking a Closer Look 8-1 to illustrate a one-factor between groups design and the analysis of variance.

### 8-1a Hypotheses in the One-Factor Between Groups Design

After the data have been collected from a multiple group experiment, the researcher must determine whether or not the data support the hypothesis. Because there are more than two groups, there is also more than one comparison between groups.

---

**Taking a Closer Look 8-1**      *Arousal Sample Experiment*

The researcher hypothesized that certain low levels of arousal were necessary to motivate cognitive performance but that as arousal continued to grow beyond an optimal point, it would decrease performance. Arousal was induced by having participants walk on a treadmill for 1 minute at different speeds. Four levels of arousal were manipulated:

- No arousal (control condition; treadmill is motionless)
- Low arousal (treadmill is on the low setting)

- Moderate arousal (treadmill is on the moderate setting)
- High arousal (treadmill is on the highest setting)

Participants were randomly assigned to one of the four treatment groups (with a total of 8 participants per group). After being subjected to the arousal treatment, participants' cognitive performance was measured on a 20-problem test. The higher the score, the better the performance. The scores are presented in Table 8-1.

| TABLE 8-1 | Data from the Experiment on the Effects of Arousal on Cognitive Performance |
|---|---|

**Treatment Groups**

| No Arousal | Low Arousal | Moderate Arousal | High Arousal |
|---|---|---|---|
| 11 | 14 | 15 | 9 |
| 12 | 15 | 17 | 13 |
| 11 | 17 | 20 | 14 |
| 13 | 13 | 17 | 11 |
| 14 | 15 | 18 | 10 |
| 10 | 16 | 16 | 12 |
| 12 | 14 | 19 | 11 |
| 13 | 16 | 18 | 12 |

With a multiple group experiment, the null hypothesis is still the hypothesis of no difference. However, this time it is the hypothesis of no difference among groups rather than between two groups:

$$H_o: X_1 = \overline{X}_2 = \overline{X}_3 = \ldots = \overline{X}_k$$

when there are k different treatments.

The alternative hypothesis is that the treatments will produce different means:

$$H_1: \overline{X}_1 <> \overline{X}_2 <> \overline{X}_3 <> \ldots <> \overline{X}_k$$

In the sample experiment, the null hypothesis is that the arousal level will not affect cognitive performance. In other words,

$$H_o: \overline{X}_{no} = \overline{X}_{low} = \overline{X}_{moderate} = \overline{X}_{high}$$

The alternative hypothesis is that both no arousal and high arousal will reduce performance. This hypothesis can be stated in terms of the means as follows:

$$H_o: \overline{X}_{no} < \overline{X}_{low} < \overline{X}_{moderate} > \overline{X}_{high}$$

### 8-1b Statistical Inference for the One-Factor Between Groups Design

After the experiment has been conducted and the means are known, the experimenter must decide if the differences among them are large enough to be due to the treatment and not due to chance alone. The sample experiment produced means that support the alternative hypothesis. The no arousal group averaged 12 problems correct, whereas the high arousal group averaged 11.5 problems correct. These average cognitive performance scores were lower than those obtained by the low arousal group ($M = 15$) and the moderate arousal group ($M = 17.5$). But the question is, are the differences really due to the arousal, or are they due to chance factors? How much difference between the means is enough to conclude that arousal level is the cause of the cognitive performance?

One obvious approach to trying to know how much difference between treatment means is enough to reject the null hypothesis is to use the Student's t test. With it, you could test the difference between each pair of means. Figure 8-1 shows the comparisons that would be required for the four-group experiment. Each t test has a 5% chance of a Type I error associated with it. (Remember that a Type I error occurs if you erroneously conclude that a chance result is a real effect of the treatment.) The total experiment-wise probability of a Type I error is the total across all the statistical tests of the hypothesis using the same data. The experiment-wise alpha level is still

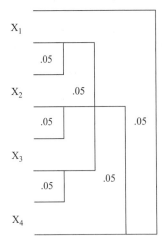

**Figure 8-1**
*All Possible Comparisons Between Four Group Means, Taking Two at a Time*

.05, even if there are more than two treatment conditions. In the case of a two-group experiment, only one *t* test is needed; therefore, the probability of a Type I error is kept within acceptable limits (.05 or less).

If there are more than two groups, the number of pair-wise comparisons can become large. Think about your friends. You have two extra free tickets to a great concert. All you have to do is figure out which two friends you should ask to go with you. Instead of choosing the two you enjoy most, you realize that you need to think about how the two of them get along. Therefore, you go through the pair-wise comparison process of checking the compatibility of each pair of your friends. If you have only two friends, say Bill and Hong, you're done. But if you have a third friend, Tania, you need to compare Bill and Hong, Bill and Tania, and Hong and Tania. Think about four friends! You would have to make six comparisons among your four friends. Because you probably have more than four friends, by now you're happy that you don't have two free tickets to give away. Pair-wise comparisons add up quickly.

A one-factor between groups experiment could be analyzed by a series of pair-wise comparisons. However, with a three-group experiment, there are a total of three two-group comparisons (Group 1 to Group 2; Group 1 to Group 3; and Group 2 to Group 3). This means that for a three-group experiment using three *t* tests, the probability of a Type I error is 3 × .05, or .15. This is much too high! The problem of increasing the Type I error rate as the number of groups increases cannot be ignored. As illustrated in Figure 8-1, with only four groups, there are six possible two-group comparisons; therefore, the chance of a Type I error is 6 × .05, which is .30! The **analysis of variance** was developed to be able to test the effects of multiple treatments while keeping the **experiment-wise error** rate for Type I errors down to alpha. Analysis of variance is often called by its acronym, **ANOVA**. An additional benefit is that doing an ANOVA is more efficient than doing a series of *t* tests.

# 8-2 Partitioning the Variance

The term *analysis of variance (ANOVA)* draws attention to the concept of variance. Variance is the total of all the differences in the data. All of these differences in individuals' scores can be considered the total variance of the data. The total variance can be divided into different sources for the variance. Dividing the variance according to source is called **partitioning the variance**. Partitioning is dividing something into

**analysis of variance** Statistical comparison of all the variance in the data that can be attributed to the independent variable compared to all the remaining variance in the data.

**experiment-wise error** All the sources of error (e.g., Type I) that can occur in one experiment with multiple statistical tests.

**ANOVA** Acronym for analysis of variance.

**partitioning the variance** Dividing the variance according to source.

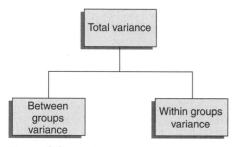

**Figure 8-2**
*Partitioning of Variance for a Between Groups Experiment*

parts. Room dividers are sometimes called partitions. When the variance is partitioned, it is systematically divided into different parts. The way the variance is partitioned depends on the design of the experiment. Figure 8-2 illustrates the partitioning of the variance for a one-factor between groups design. As you can see in the figure,

Total variance = Between groups variance + Within groups variance

The between groups variance is attributed to the treatment, because if the experiment was well designed, the only differences among the various treatment conditions were the treatments (the experimenter controls all other things). There are additional sources of variance between the groups as well. You need to use good design to try to reduce these sources of systematic variance between the groups. There may also be additional unsystematic variance between the groups besides the treatment.

The within groups variance is attributed to all the other things that could affect behavior in the experiment such as subject factors (personality, experience), external factors (noise, distractions), or errors (measurement or subject). These are the unsystematic sources of variation mentioned in the preceding paragraph. Within groups variance has been called the *error variance* or the *residual variance*. The terms are both synonymous with the within groups variance. Because there is unsystematic variance in both the between groups and within groups variance, forming the ratio of the two cancels out this source of variance. Systematic variance due to confounds or other threats to the validity of the experiment is not "cancelled" out and can be addressed only through design and appropriate interpretation of the statistical results. More on this concept will be presented in section 8-6, "Interpretation of the Results of ANOVA."

In the sample experiment, the between groups variance would be the differences among the means of the four treatment groups. Those differences reflect both the differences due to the arousal manipulation and to the individual differences of the participants within the groups. The within groups variance would be the differences among participants in the no arousal group compared to each other, combined with differences among participants in the low arousal group compared to each other, combined with differences among participants in the moderate arousal group, combined with differences among participants in the high arousal group. In effect, this is the variance within each group, pooled together for all groups.

The goal of the analysis of variance is to produce an inferential statistic that will allow the researcher to estimate the probability of getting the obtained results by chance alone (i.e., a Type I error). This statistic is called the **F ratio**. It is called *F* in honor of its developer, R. A. Fisher. It is called a *Ratio* because it is the ratio of two variances:

$$F = \frac{\text{Between group variance}}{\text{Within group variance}}$$

**F ratio** Inferential statistic that will allow the researcher to estimate the probability of getting the obtained results by chance alone.

| TABLE 8-2 | Analysis of Variance Summary Table |
|-----------|-----------------------------------|

| Source | Sums of Squares | Degrees of Freedom | Mean Square | F |
|--------|-----------------|--------------------|-------------|---|
| Between Groups | | | | |
| Within Groups | | | | |
| Total | | | | |

The higher the F ratio, the greater is the variance due to the treatment relative to all other variance. That is, the higher the F ratio, the greater the effect of the treatment. As mentioned previously in this section, the unsystematic sources of variance in the numerator (between groups variance) and denominator (within groups variance) cancel out. For example, if the control group happened to have a problem-solving champion in the group—let's call her Jen—then Jen's high score could be due to both her arousal level and her individual ability on the test. Her score would increase the mean for the control group, thereby increasing the between groups variances. Her score would also increase the within group variance for the control group (the control group would have a higher standard deviation). Therefore, it would increase the within groups variance as well. The effect of the arousal manipulation can be seen clearly, because the unsystematic variation due Jen's high aptitude for problem solving, for example, cancels itself out through the ratio formula for F.

# 8-3 Analysis of Variance Summary Table

In understanding exactly how to calculate and interpret an analysis of variance, it is better to start at the end and work backward. That is, it is better to set up the table that summarizes the analysis of variance and then calculate its parts. Table 8-2 shows the organization of an analysis of variance summary table. Notice the rows of the table. Each row is for one of the sources of variance within the experiment:

- Between groups
- Within groups
- Total

Now notice the columns. The far right column is the column for the F ratio. The F ratio is calculated by taking the ratio of the estimate of between groups variance to the estimate of within groups variance. These variances are estimated as the **mean squares** (MS) and are placed in the next column. You calculate the MS by dividing the second column (**sums of squares**, also called SS) by the degrees of freedom (df) for each source (in the third column). The mean squares are basically the variances due to each of the sources.

Calculating the SS is the first step in calculating the analysis of variance. You can think of them as the sum of the variance for each source. The degrees of freedom indicate how many different ways there could have been to randomly get the particular variances. *Degrees of freedom* here has the same meaning as it did in the t test, except here there are degrees of freedom associated with each source of variance: between groups, within groups, and total. Thus, if you divide the sum of the variance from a source by the degrees of freedom for that source, you get an average variance for the source, which is called the *mean square*.

**mean squares** (MS) Sums of squares divided by the degrees of freedom for each source of variance.

**sums of squares** (SS) Sums of the squared scores for each of the sources of variance.

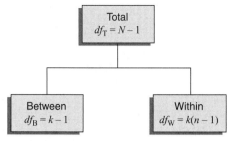

**Figure 8-3**
*Partitioning of Degrees of Freedom for a Between Groups Experiment*

The degrees of freedom can be partitioned in the same manner as the variance. Figure 8-3 shows the degrees of freedom being partitioned. You use the following formulas to obtain the degrees of freedom:

- $df_B = k - 1$, where $k$ is the number of treatment groups
- $df_W = k(n - 1)$, where $n$ is the number of subjects per group
- $df_T = N - 1$, where $N$ is the total number of subjects

It will always be the case that the sum of the $df$ between and the $df$ within will be equal to the $df$ total. Consider an experiment that has five treatment groups with six participants in each treatment. The $df_B$ will be 4, the $df_W$ will be 25, and the $df_T$ will be 29.

# 8-4 Calculation of the Sums of Squares

After you have set up an analysis of variance summary table, you need to be able to fill in the blanks. That means you must be able to first calculate the sums of squares for each source. Table 8-3 shows some basic formulas that will be used in calculating the SS. Notice that to calculate these formulas, you must either sum and then square or square and then sum. That's why they are called the sums of squares. But doing the operations in the right order is essential. Figure 8-4 shows, step by step, how to calculate the sums of squares for the sample experiment.

After calculating the sums of squares, check them. The sum of SS between and SS within must add to SS total. Also, all the quantities must be positive. If you get any negative numbers with an analysis of variance, you have made a mistake. Variances are always positive; therefore, it is not possible to have a negative sum of squares. If you do have a negative SS, correct your mistake before completing the **ANOVA summary table**.

Fill the SS into the analysis of variance summary table. Then you can calculate the df, MS, and finally the F statistic in short order. Table 8-4 shows the completed ANOVA summary table for the sample experiment.

**ANOVA summary table**
Table that shows the sources of variance for a given experiment, estimates of those variances *(SS, df, MS)*, and the ratios of the variances *(F)*.

# 8-5 Significance of *F*

The calculated F statistic is an inferential statistic. Given any calculated F statistic, the probability of that F occurring by chance alone can be estimated based on the F distribution. As with the t test, the researcher does not have to apply advanced mathematics to estimate the probability. Rather, the researcher may use a table of critical values for the F distribution. Table 8-5 is an excerpt of the F distribution table. In the case of the F distribution, three pieces of information must be considered. They are

| TABLE 8-3 | Analysis of Variance Summary Table |

| Source | Sums of squares | Degrees of freedom | Mean square | F |
|---|---|---|---|---|
| Between Groups | $SS_B$ | $df_B$ | $MS_B$ | F |
| Within Groups | $SS_W$ | $df_W$ | $MS_W$ | |
| Total | $SS_T$ | $df_T$ | | |

**Computational form of analysis of variance summary table**

| Source | Sums of squares | Degrees of freedom | Mean square | F |
|---|---|---|---|---|
| Between groups | $\sum \frac{\left(\sum X\right)^2}{n} - \frac{T^2}{N}$ | $k-1$ | $\dfrac{SS_B}{df_B}$ | $\dfrac{MS_B}{MS_W}$ |
| Within groups | $SS_T - SS_B$ | $k(n-1)$ | $\dfrac{SS_W}{df_W}$ | |
| Total | $\sum\sum X^2 - \frac{T^2}{N}$ | $N-1$ | | |

Where

| | |
|---|---|
| $\sum X$ | is the sum of scores in each group |
| $\sum\sum X^2$ | is the sum of all scores that have been squared first. |
| $T$ | is the total (sum of all scores). |
| $n$ | is the number of scores/groups. |
| $k$ | is the number of groups. |
| $N$ | is the total number of scores. |

- Alpha
- *df* numerator
- *df* denominator

### 8-5a  Alpha Level

The alpha level is the chance of a Type I error that will be tolerated. This "significance level" is usually set at .05. However, the significance level could be lower, say, .01 or .001. It is common to report the lowest alpha level for which the calculated $F$ statistic is significant. Reporting a lower alpha level than you have adopted doesn't mean that you have changed your alpha level. It simply means you recognize that other researchers who read your report might have a different alpha level. Some $F$ tables present different pages for the different commonly used alpha levels. If this is the case, you must simply choose the right page. Others present the alpha levels as additional nested rows. These tables are more difficult to use, so be careful to know exactly how the alpha is being represented in the table.

### 8-5b  Degrees of Freedom

The *df* numerator is the degrees of freedom associated with the numerator of the $F$ ratio. In this case, the *df* numerator is the *df* between groups. You may wonder why the columns on Table 8-4 aren't called the *df* between. The reason is that the analysis of variance has many applications for more complex experimental designs. The numerator of the $F$ ratio depends on the particular design and is not always the $MS$ between groups. (This will be illustrated in Chapter 9, "Repeated Measures One-Factor Designs," with the analysis of variance for within subjects designs). The *df* numerator usually represents the columns in the table; therefore, you must find the column that matches your *df* numerator.

Step 1.    Write the formula.

$$SS_B = \Sigma \frac{(\Sigma X)^2}{n} - \frac{T^2}{N}$$

$$SS_W = SS_T - SS_B$$

$$SS_T = \Sigma\Sigma X^2 - \frac{T^2}{N}$$

Step 2.    Determine the quantities that need to be calculated.

They are:

| | | |
|---|---|---|
| $\Sigma X_1$ | $n_1$ | $\Sigma\Sigma X^2$ |
| $\Sigma X_2$ | $n_2$ | $T$ |
| $\Sigma X_3$ | $n_3$ | $N$ |
| $\Sigma X_4$ | $n_4$ | |

Step 3.    Calculate the terms determined in Step 2. (Refer to Table 8-1.)

| | Condition | | | |
|---|---|---|---|---|
| | No arousal | Low arousal | Moderate arousal | High arousal |
| $\Sigma X$ | 96 | 120 | 140 | 92 |
| $\Sigma X^2$ | 1164 | 1812 | 2468 | 1076 |
| $n$ | 8 | 8 | 8 | 8 |

$$N = \Sigma n = 8 + 8 + 8 + 8 = 32$$

$$T = \Sigma(\Sigma X) = 96 + 120 + 140 + 92 = 448$$

$$\Sigma\Sigma X^2 = \Sigma(\Sigma X^2) = 1164 + 1812 + 2468 + 1076 = 6520$$

Step 4.    Substitute terms calculated in Step 3 in formulas (Step 1).

$$SS_B = \Sigma \frac{(\Sigma X)^2}{n} - \frac{T^2}{N} = \left[\frac{96^2}{8}\right] + \left[\frac{120^2}{8}\right] + \left[\frac{140^2}{8}\right] + \left[\frac{92^2}{8}\right] - \frac{448^2}{32}$$

$$= \left[\frac{9216}{8} + \frac{14400}{8} + \frac{19600}{8} + \frac{8464}{8}\right] - \frac{200704}{32}$$

$$= [1152 + 1800 + 2450 + 1058] - 6272 = 6460 - 6272 = 188$$

$$SS_T = \Sigma\Sigma X^2 - \frac{T^2}{N} \left(\text{Note: } \frac{T^2}{N} \text{ calculated above}\right)$$

$$= 6520 - 6272 = 248$$

$$SS_W = SS_T - SS_B = 248 - 188 = 60$$

**Figure 8-4**

*Step-by-Step Example for Calculating the Sums of Squares for a Between Groups Experiment*

The *df* denominator is the degrees of freedom associated with the source that is the denominator of the *F* ratio. These are usually represented in terms of the rows of the table. For the sample experiment, you would find the page of the table that corresponded to alpha = .05.

## 8-5c Finding the Critical *F*

To find the critical *F* in Table 8-4, you first look for the column associated with the degrees of freedom for the numerator. In this case the numerator is between groups and its *df* is 3 (4 conditions – 1). Next, you find the row that is associated with the degrees of freedom for the denominator. In the example the denominator is the within groups variance and the *df* within are 28 (4(8 participants per group – 1)). Therefore, the critical *F* is equal to 2.95. You can write it as follows:

$$F \text{ critical } (df = 3, 28; \alpha = .05) = 2.95$$

| TABLE 8-4 | Analysis of Variance Summary Table for the Arousal Experiment |
|-----------|---------------------------------------------------------------|

| Source | Sums of Squares | Degrees of Freedom | Mean Square | F |
|--------|-----------------|--------------------|-------------|-----|
| Between Groups | 188 | 3 | 62.667 | 29.244 |
| Within Groups | 60 | 28 | 2.143 | |
| Total | 246 | 31 | | |

| TABLE 8-5 | Excerpt of the Table for Critical Values for the F Distribution ($\alpha$ = .05) |
|-----------|-----------------------------------------------------------------------------------|

| Degrees of Freedom Denominator | Degrees of Freedom Numerator | | | |
|--------------------------------|------|------|------|------|
| | 1 | 2 | 3 | 4 |
| 8 | 5.32 | 4.46 | 4.07 | 3.84 |
| 10 | 4.96 | 4.10 | 3.71 | 3.48 |
| 12 | 4.75 | 3.89 | 3.49 | 3.26 |
| 14 | 4.60 | 3.74 | 3.34 | 3.11 |
| 16 | 4.49 | 3.63 | 3.24 | 3.01 |
| 18 | 4.41 | 3.55 | 3.16 | 2.93 |
| 20 | 4.35 | 3.49 | 3.10 | 2.87 |
| 24 | 4.26 | 3.40 | 3.01 | 2.78 |
| 28 | 4.20 | 3.34 | 2.95 | 2.71 |
| 30 | 4.17 | 3.32 | 2.92 | 2.68 |

It is important to present both the *df* and alpha along with the critical *F*. If the critical *F* is less than or equal to the calculated *F*, then the treatment can be said to be statistically significant. That is, there is a statistically significant effect. If the critical *F* is greater than the calculated *F* ratio, then you must conclude that there are no significant differences in the dependent variable due to the independent variable. In other words, the probability is greater than 5% that the observed differences among the means could be due to chance alone.

# 8-6 Interpretation of the Results of ANOVA

If the *F* ratio is statistically significant, it is necessary to present the means for each group and interpret their differences. One good way to present means from a multiple group experiment is to use a figure. Figure 8-5 shows the means for the sample experiment. For a one-factor (one independent variable) experiment, always plot the levels of the treatment on the X-axis and the values of the means for the dependent variable on the Y-axis. The bars represent the means of each treatment group.

Examination of the figure can aid in interpreting the results. Is the pattern of means consistent with the hypothesis tested? The analysis of variance tells you whether there is an overall difference among the treatment means. It does not, however, allow you to conclude that each mean is different from the others. Indeed, to interpret the results fully, you must do an additional analysis, making

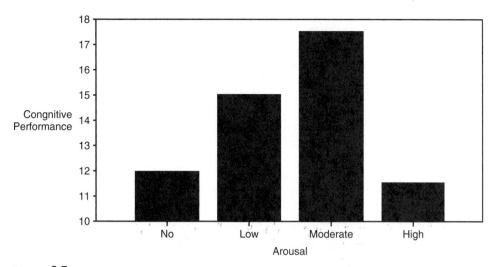

**Figure 8-5**
*Mean Cognitive Performance by Arousal Condition*

comparisons among the means, two by two. These analyses are called *Multiple Comparisons.*

# 8-7 Multiple Comparisons

Using Multiple Comparisons tests is more complex than simply doing repeated Student's t tests for each pair of means. The repeated use of Student's t tests will lead to Type I errors. Therefore, many methods have been devised to keep down the overall experiment-wise Type I error rate. The problem is that the more conservative (low Type I error rate) an inferential statistic is, the less power it tends to have (high Type II error rate). That is why there are so many different multiple comparison techniques. The researcher can choose the specific multiple comparison procedure to use based on his or her preference for power versus precision and the particular types of comparisons desired.

In this chapter only one of the multiple comparison statistical approaches will be presented. This is the honestly significant difference test (called the Tukey **HSD** method, after its creator). The Tukey HSD method depends on a statistic called the *studentized range statistic.* It is represented by the symbol $q$ and basically is defined as the ratio of the difference between two treatment means and an estimate of the variance within those two groups. The distribution of the $q$ statistic is based on the number of means to be compared. You can obtain it from a table of the studentized range statistic based on three parameters:

> **HSD** Honestly significant difference (Tukey) test used to make multiple comparisons while keeping the experiment-wise probability of making a Type I error at alpha.

$\alpha$—Total experiment-wise Type I error rate

$k$— Number of means to be compared (number of treatments)

$df$ denominator—$df$ associated with the denominator of the $F$ ratio

After determining the $q$ statistic from the table, you can use it to calculate Tukey's honestly significant difference (HSD) according to the following formula:

$$\text{HSD} = q_\alpha \frac{\sqrt{\text{MS}_{\text{error}}}}{n}$$

Where $q\alpha$ is the studentized range statistic for the number of means being compared.

$\text{MS}_{\text{error}}$ is the MS used in the denominator of the F test.

n is the number of subject per group.

| Step 1. Write the formula. | Step 2. Find $q_\alpha$ in studentized range table. |
|---|---|
| $$HSD = q_\alpha \frac{\sqrt{MS_{error}}}{n}$$ | Use $\alpha = .05$, k = 4 groups, and df = 28 (use df associated with MSerror-) $q_{.05} = 3.86$ |
| **Step 3. Get MS error from ANOVA Summary Table.** | |
| $MS_{error} = MS_{within} = 2.143$ | |

| Step 4. Substitute quantities into the formula. |
|---|
| $$HSD = 3.86 \sqrt{\frac{2.143}{8}} = 3.86 \sqrt{.2679} = 3.86(.5176) = 1.998$$ |

| Step 5. Compare HSD to the differences obtained for the group means. | | |
|---|---|---|
| Calculations | Difference HSD | Conclusion |
| $\left| \overline{X}_2 - \overline{X}_1 \right| = \left| 15 - 12 \right| = 3$ | 3.0 > 1.998 | Significant |
| $\left| \overline{X}_3 - \overline{X}_1 \right| = \left| 17.5 - 12 \right| = 5.5$ | 5.5 > 1.998 | Significant |
| $\left| \overline{X}_4 - \overline{X}_1 \right| = \left| 11.5 - 12 \right| = 0.5$ | 0.5 < 1.998 | Not Significant |
| $\left| \overline{X}_3 - \overline{X}_2 \right| = \left| 17.5 - 15 \right| = 2.5$ | 2.5 > 1.998 | Significant |
| $\left| \overline{X}_3 - \overline{X}_4 \right| = \left| 17.5 - 11.5 \right| = 6.0$ | 6.0 > 1.998 | Significant |
| $\left| \overline{X}_2 - \overline{X}_4 \right| = \left| 15 - 11.5 \right| = 3.5$ | 3.5 > 1.998 | Significant |

| If the difference between two means is greater than HSD, then they are statistically significantly different. |
|---|

**Figure 8-6**
*Application of HSD Test to Sample Experiment*

The quantity, HSD, represents the smallest difference that any two means can be apart in order for their difference to be considered statistically significant. Figure 8-6 shows the application of the HSD test to the sample experiment.

After you have completed the **multiple comparisons**, you can fully interpret the results. Avoid the temptation to say that results "approached statistical significance." There is no such thing as almost significant. Furthermore, results that are significant with alpha = .05 are not less significant than those that are significant at alpha = .001. The difference in alpha only represents different researchers' decision criteria for placing their own scientific "bets" that the results are not due to chance. (Refer to Chapter 6, "Hypothesis Testing: The Control Group Posttest Only Design," for the discussion of statistical inference). Many students calculate their analysis of variance and multiple comparisons but then go on to explain non-significant effects. If it is not significant in your experiment, don't try to explain it as a significant effect. You can conclude only that the results could be obtained by chance!

**multiple comparisons** Analyses making comparisons among the means, two by two.

# 8-8 Effect Size for ANOVA

Cohen's d is an effective way to estimate the effect size for statistical tests involving only two means. Because analysis of variance is used with comparisons among two or more means, a different estimate of the effect size is needed. Instead of showing the difference between means in a standardized form as d, one method is to estimate the amount of variance in the data that can be attributed to the independent variable. Sometimes the effect size is called $R^2$.

$R^2$ is used in many types of statistical analyses to refer to the amount of variance explained. For the analysis of variance, the effect size is more commonly called $\eta^2$ (pronounced eta squared). $R^2$ is the general term and $\eta^2$ is the specific term for analysis of variance.

Calculating the effect size for an analysis of variance is relatively easy. All of the components of the formula have already been calculated for the analysis of variance summary table. Eta squared is the variance between groups divided by the total variance. In other words,

$$\eta^2 = \frac{SS_{\text{between}}}{SS_{\text{total}}}$$

Now look at the sample experiment for the effects of arousal on problem solving. The $SS_B$ was 188 and the $SS_T$ was 246. That means 76% of the variance in all the data could be attributed to the arousal conditions. The calculation looks like this:

$$\eta^2 = \frac{188}{246} = .76$$

# 8-9 APA Style: Reporting ANOVA Results

The method of reporting results for analysis of variance is similar to that presented for the t tests. You must report

The name and type of statistical test employed

All the information needed to evaluate that statistical test

The descriptive statistics for all statistically significant results

Therefore, when reporting the results of the analysis of variance described in this chapter, you must report

A between groups ANOVA

The $F$, including

Degrees of freedom for the numerator and denominator

Calculated $F$ statistic

Critical $F$ statistic or the significance level, both with alpha

Means and variances for significant effects

Multiple comparison tests showing which means are significantly different from the others

This seems like a large amount of technical information to convey in a report. There are standard ways to report the results that make them concise and still very specific. The $F$ statistic is usually reported with the degrees of freedom in parentheses following the letter $F$. This is just like the $t$ test, except that there are now two numbers. The first is always the degrees of freedom for the numerator of the $F$ ratio. The second is always the degrees of freedom for the denominator. The $p$ values or critical $F$ is also reported in a concise way, usually parenthetically. The following sample shows one way the results of the sample experiment for this chapter could be reported:

A between groups one-way ANOVA showed a statistically significant effect of arousal condition on problem solving ($F(3,28) = 29.24$; $F$ critical ($df = 3,28$; $\alpha = .05$) = 2.95, $\eta^2 = .76$). Tukey's honestly significant difference test showed that the moderate arousal level produced the highest cognitive performance scores ($M = 6.0$, $SD = 1.60$) followed by the low arousal condition ($M = 15.0$,

*SD* = 1.31). The no arousal and high arousal conditions produced the lowest cognitive performances scores (*M* = 12, *SD* = 1.31; and *M* = 11.5, *SD* = 1.60, respectively).

# Summary

One-factor between groups designs are used to investigate the effects of two or more levels of the independent variable on the dependent variable. Each condition is presented to a different group of subjects. The null hypothesis is that all of the group means are equal. The two-tailed alternate hypothesis is that the means of the groups are not equal to each other. A one-tailed alternate hypothesis must specify the relationships expected among all the group means.

The analysis of variance applied to a one-factor between groups design is called a one-way ANOVA. This statistical procedure keeps the experiment-wise probability of a Type I error at alpha. The analysis of variance partitions the variation in the data into its different sources. For the one-factor between groups design, the total variance is partitioned into the between groups variance and the within groups variance. The sum of the squared deviations due to each source is called the sums of squares *(SS)*. The sums of squares are divided by the degrees of freedom for each source *(df)* to produce the mean squares *(MS)*. The mean squares are estimates of the variance due to each source. The *F* ratio for a one-factor between groups design is the ratio of the mean squares between groups to the means squares within groups. The statistical significance of the *F* ratio is evaluated using critical *F* tables or the probability of obtaining the *F* by chance alone derived from the *F* distribution. If a statistically significant effect is found for differences among three or more means, then multiple comparison tests must be computed to determine which means are significantly different. One such multiple comparison test is Tukey's honestly significant difference (HSD) test.

# Exercises for Application

A researcher wanted to test the hypothesis that the meaningfulness of words will increase a participant's ability to remember the words. Three lists of words were developed. The first list was composed of nonsense syllables. The second list was composed of nonrelated but common words. The third list was composed of words all related to football. Participants were randomly assigned to one of the three conditions. The total number of words correctly remembered after a 10-minute filler task was measured for each participant.

1. State the null hypothesis.
2. State the alternative hypothesis.
3. What is the correct inferential statistic to test the hypothesis?
4. Calculate the statistic.
5. Present the descriptive statistics.
6. Make a statistical conclusion based on the data analysis.
7. Interpret the results in one nonstatistical sentence.
8. What is the probability of a Type I error?

**Number of Words Remembered**

| Nonsense Syllables | Unrelated Words | Football Words |
|---|---|---|
| 6 | 9 | 16 |
| 8 | 10 | 17 |
| 4 | 8 | 15 |
| 7 | 11 | 14 |
| 8 | 13 | 17 |
| 7 | 12 | 16 |
| 10 | 8 | 15 |
| 5 | 13 | 17 |

## Practice Quiz

**Note:** You can find the correct answers to these questions by taking the quiz and then submitting your answers in the Online Edition. The program will automatically score your submission. If you miss a question, the program will provide the correct answer, a rationale for the answer, and the section number in the chapter where the topic is discussed.

1. If *t* tests are used to compare all the possible differences, two at a time, among four means, what is the probability of a Type I error?
   a. .05
   b. .15
   c. .30
   d. .50

2. The *F* ratio was named in honor of
   a. Sigmund Freud.
   b. Franklin Gosset.
   c. E. L. Fermicetti.
   d. R. A. Fisher.

3. In a between groups design, the *F* ratio is a ratio of the _____ and the within group variance.
   a. between group variance
   b. residual variance
   c. error variance
   d. total variance

4. The *SS* divided by the *df* equal the
   a. *F.*
   b. *t.*
   c. *RQS.*
   d. *MS.*

5. If you get a negative number when calculating the *SS*, it means that
   a. the null hypothesis is correct.
   b. the within subjects variance is larger than the between subjects variance.
   c. the results are in the opposite direction as predicted.
   d. there is a mistake in your calculation.

6. In a three-group experiment with 6 subjects in each group, the *df* between is
   a. 1.
   b. 2.
   c. 9.
   d. 16.

7. The more conservative an inferential statistic is, the
   a. less power it tends to have.
   b. the higher the probability of a Type I error.
   c. the greater likelihood of significant results.
   d. the lower the *q* value.

8. The initials in Tukey's HSD test stand for
   a. highly statistical difference.
   b. higher standard difference.
   c. Howard's Statistical Deviation.
   d. honestly significant difference.

9. The three parameters that need to be used to obtain a critical *F* value are the
   a. *SS, MS,* and *F.*
   b. alpha, *df* numerator, and *df* denominator.
   c. mean, variance, and *F.*
   d. *k, N,* and *r.*

10. The statistical parameter that adjusts Tukey's HSD for the number of means being compared is the
    a. studentized range statistic, *q.*
    b. Fisher's exact test, *r.*
    c. the *z*-score for pair deviations.
    d. the *df* within.

11. The effect size for a multiple group experiment, eta squared, is really just the
    a. residual sums of squares.
    b. the sum of each Cohen's *d* for pair-wise comparisons.
    c. ratio of the variance accounted for by the effect to the total variance.
    d. the same as the *F* ratio.

12. What is wrong with the following ANOVA result report? $F(3) = 29.24$
    a. *F* ratios can't be larger than 1.0.
    b. There should be another *df* in the parentheses.
    c. The degrees of freedom are in the wrong place.
    d. The *F* should be lowercase.

13. The logic of statistical hypothesis testing means that a *p* value of .06
    a. approaches statistical significance.
    b. is not statistically significant.
    c. is better than a *p* value of .03.
    d. can be interpreted only with the degrees of freedom present.

14. In a between groups design the total variance can be divided among the between groups variance and the
    a. treatment variance.
    b. within groups variance.
    c. alternative variance.
    d. within person variance.

15. In an experiment with three levels of manipulated arousal (low, medium, and high), a one-tailed alternative hypothesis is that the mean dependent variables for the groups are related as

a. low > medium < high.
b. low = medium = high.
c. low <> medium <> high.
d. all of the above.

16. If the degrees of freedom associated with an *F* statistic for a between groups design with an equal number of subjects in each group are 3 and 16, then the study had

a. 4 groups and a total of 20 subjects.
b. 3 groups and a total of 15 subjects.
c. 4 groups with 4 subjects in each.
d. 3 subjects each in 16 groups.

# Repeated Measures One-Factor Designs

## Chapter Outline

## Key Terms

ABA design

between subjects variance

counterbalancing

inter-rater agreement

order effect

randomizing the order of treatments

true control condition

within subjects error variance

within subjects experiment

within subjects treatment variance

within subjects variance

# Learning Objectives

- Be able to specify the null hypothesis and alternate hypothesis for a one-factor repeated measures design.
- Be able to decide how many levels of the treatment should be used to unambiguously test a hypothesis with a repeated measures design.
- Identify and reduce the pitfalls that result from repeated exposure of the same participants to different levels of the independent variable.

- Be able to avoid confounding from the order of treatments in a repeated measures design by using counterbalancing or randomizing the order of treatments.
- Be able to employ an ABA design.
- Understand the partitioning of variance in a repeated measures design and be able to apply it to the analysis of variance summary table.
- Compute and interpret a one-factor repeated measures ANOVA.

## Key Idea

Repeated measures one-factor experiments must be designed to control for order effects and so that the repeated manipulation of the independent variable and repeated measurements of the dependent variable do not produce biased results.

## 9-1 One-Factor Repeated Measures Designs

Chapter 8, "One-Factor Between Groups Design and One-Way ANOVA," presented the between groups design. Each treatment condition was received by a different group of subjects, and each subject received only one treatment (level of the cause). If each subject receives all the treatments, the design is a **within subjects experiment**. This design is an extension of the two-treatment repeated measures design discussed in Chapter 7, "Hypothesis Testing: Pretest Posttest Design and Related Measures $t$ Test." You will recall that the pretest posttest design involves the measurement of the dependent variable at two times—once before the treatment and once again after the treatment:

$$O_1 \ X \ O_2$$

The extension of this design to a repeated measures one-factor experiment is that it can be used for two *or more* levels of the independent variable. For example, the pretest posttest design is one type of repeated measures design. It is a one-factor design with two levels of the independent variable (also called the *factor*). The two levels are *pre* and *post*. That is, the dependent variable is measured before the hypothesized cause is presented to the participants and also after it is presented. The one-factor repeated measures design can have more than two levels of the cause. It can be notated as follows:

$$X_1 \ O_1 \ X_2 \ O_2 \ ... \ X_k \ O_k$$

Each $X$ represents a different treatment condition (level of the independent variable), and each $O$ represents a measurement of the dependent variable. The number of different treatment conditions is $k$. Consider the following sample research. Dion, Berscheid, and Walster (1972) showed that "what is beautiful is good," at least in some situations. The theory basically is that all other things being equal, or unknown, a physically attractive individual will be perceived as better than one who is less physically attractive. One of my students, Lauren, wanted to extend the "what is beautiful is good" theory to perceptions of future

**within subjects experiment**
Experiment in which each subject receives all the treatments.

success based on the research of Hatfield and Sprecher (1986). Before we look at how Lauren might have tested her hypotheses, let's look at the simplest one-factor design for this example.

### 9-1a Determining the Levels of the Factor

Lauren's hypothesis was that more attractive people will be perceived by others to have greater success in the future (Dewey, 2000). In this hypothesis the dependent variable is perceived future success. The independent variable is physical attractiveness. There are many ways to operationally define physical attractiveness. If there are only two levels of attractiveness, they could be

- Highly attractive compared to no information
- Highly attractive compared to highly unattractive
- Highly attractive compared to moderately attractive
- Moderately attractive compared to highly unattractive

As the researcher, you would choose to operationally define the independent variable with the number of levels that best address the hypothesis. In this case whatever *two* levels you choose, you can't really answer the question about attractiveness well. That's why Lauren (Dewey, 2000) chose to define attractiveness at three levels:

- Highly attractive
- Moderately attractive
- Highly unattractive

Each of the conditions presents a specific level of the hypothesized cause. Sometimes a **true control condition** in which the cause is absent will also be informative. In this research, for example, a true control condition would be a condition with no information about physical attractiveness. Lauren's interest was in perceptions of future success as they relate to employment. She embedded the manipulation of attractiveness in a resume evaluation task. If she had wanted to know how future success is evaluated in the absence of physical attractiveness information (a true control condition), she would have added a condition with a resume that included no information about physical attractiveness.

A major part of Lauren's research was operationally defining attractiveness and producing the highly attractive, moderately attractive, and highly unattractive materials. She began by producing a set of photographs of "typical" college students. All the photographs were of students from another college and taken in the same place with background, lighting, and distance kept constant. Each of these controls was employed to reduce confounding. If the photographs had been of students from the same campus as her experimental participants, then there could be a relationship between how well recognized the person is and the person's level of attractiveness. Therefore, all the persons represented in the photographs had to be strangers to the research participants. The quality and background of all the photographs had to be the same to avoid confounding those qualities with the physical attractiveness of the person in the photograph.

To select the highly attractive, moderately attractive, and highly unattractive photographs, Lauren enlisted a group of students similar to those who would participate in her experiment to judge the attractiveness of all the photographs. They were the raters in her experiment. The raters individually sorted the photographs into high, medium, and low attractiveness categories. They then rank-ordered the photographs in each category from most to least attractive.

**true control condition**
Condition in which the cause is absent.

**inter-rater agreement**
Correlation among different raters of the same stimuli.

Lauren's criterion for selecting the photographs was **inter-rater agreement**. She selected three photographs that were judged by all the raters as highly attractive to represent that condition. She selected the three that were judged by all the raters as unattractive for that condition. The three that were in the middle for all judges were the moderately attractive stimulus pictures. The photographs that received mixed reviews (some raters thought they were attractive while others did not) were not used in her experiment.

### 9-1b Choosing to Use a Repeated Measures Design

Having paired the photographs with a mock resume and developed a multiple-item measure of perceived future success, Lauren was ready to design the procedure of her study. Should she use a repeated measures design or a between groups design? The answer to that question is based on the same principles that were first introduced in Chapter 6, "Hypothesis Testing: The Control Group Posttest Only Design," and Chapter 7, "Hypothesis Testing: Pretest Posttest Design and Related Measures *t* Test." What are the threats to the validity of the experiment? Can Lauren use a repeated measures design without strong threats to its validity from history, testing, or maturation? Is there so much individual variation in perceptions of future success that she needs to have each participant act as his or her own comparison?

If Lauren chose to use a repeated measures one-factor design instead of a between subjects design, she could increase the statistical power of her research. Remember that power is the ability to detect a cause-effect relationship when it is in fact true. One method of increasing the power of research is to increase the amount of data available. In this case, Lauren could have three times as much data from the same number of participants by using a repeated measures design. Obviously, there are some important trade-offs; otherwise, all research would be repeated measures. Those trade-offs are the threats to the internal validity of the design.

Imagine that you are one of Lauren's research participants. You've been given an informed consent form that describes the experiment as a person perception study. You are asked to read a job description and then given a set of resumes to review. Each resume includes information about the applicant's education, job experience, community service, and a photograph of the applicant. After reading each resume, you are asked to evaluate the applicant it describes on a number of dimensions related to likelihood of future success. You read the first resume and make the ratings. So far, so good. But then you get to the second resume and see that it is basically the same information as the previous resume with a different picture. In a between groups experiment, the resumes' contents would be identical and only the photographs would change. The participants are unlikely to notice anything unusual about the photograph and resume because they read only one resume and see only one photograph. In a repeated measures experiment, the resumes can't be identical; otherwise, the participants will become aware of the hypothesis. This outcome is bad because it increases the demand characteristics of the experiment. Therefore, the researcher must come up with similar but not identical resumes. To avoid confounding, each resume must be counterbalanced with each level of the independent variable.

### 9-1c Counterbalancing in Repeated Measures Designs

**counterbalancing** Presenting each of the contexts equally across all levels of the independent variable.

**Counterbalancing** is presenting each of the contexts (in the example, resumes) equally across all levels of the independent variable (highly attractive, moderately attractive, and highly unattractive). Obviously, if you were a participant in the experiment, you would not expect to see three people with different

| TABLE 9-1 | Three Stimulus Sets That Counterbalance Resume Content with Physical Attractiveness Manipulation | | |
|---|---|---|---|
| **Stimulus Set** | **Highly Attractive** | **Moderately Attractive** | **Highly Unattractive** |
| A | Susan White | Sally Wilson | Sandra Webster |
| B | Sally Wilson | Sandra Webster | Susan White |
| C | Sandra Webster | Susan White | Sally Wilson |

photographs and the same resume information. There would have to be three names associated with the three photographs (e.g., Susan White, Sally Wilson, and Sandra Webster) and three sets of resume contents. As long as each resume is presented to different participants an equivalent number of times across all the attractiveness levels, then the content of the resume should be counterbalanced with the manipulation of physical attractiveness. So you might evaluate the Susan White resume with the attractive photograph, the Sally Wilson resume with the moderately attractive photograph, and the Sandra Webster resume with the highly unattractive photograph. The set of materials could be called stimulus set A. Another participant would rate the same resumes but with the pictures switched so that Susan White would have the moderately attractive photograph, Sally Wilson would have the highly unattractive photograph, and Sandra Webster would have the highly attractive photograph. These materials could be called set B. One other combination of resumes and photographs is required to counterbalance the resumes across the three levels of attractiveness (set C). Each combination should be presented to an equal number of participants to keep the potential effects of the resume content balanced across all of the treatment conditions. Table 9-1 shows the stimulus set for each photograph resume combination.

**order effect** Specific effect that occurs depending on the order in which multiple treatments were presented to the subject.

### 9-1d Order Effects

Put yourself in the place of the research participant again. If you first evaluate the resume of a very attractive individual, will that make a difference in how you perceive the next photograph attached to a resume? Do you think the moderately attractive photograph would seem better if you saw the unattractive photo first? Do you think your evaluations would be influenced by the order in which you saw them? The **order effect** is a consequence of both maturation and testing effects that were discussed before. One way to attempt to neutralize order effects is to present all possible orders of the conditions to the participants. This is really just counterbalancing the order of the repeated factor treatments. In the sample experiment, that would mean each set of stimulus materials should be presented in each possible order. Let's go through the example with Set A. The possible orders are as follows:

Order 1: Attractive Susan, Moderate Sarah, Unattractive Sandra

Order 2: Attractive Susan, Unattractive Sandra, Moderate Sarah

Order 3: Moderate Sarah, Attractive Susan, Unattractive Sandra

Order 4: Moderate Sarah, Unattractive Sandra, Attractive Susan

Order 5: Unattractive Sandra, Moderate Sarah, Attractive Susan

Order 6: Unattractive Sandra, Attractive Susan, Moderate Sarah

Thus, there are 6 possible orderings of three levels of attractiveness needed to counterbalance the order effect. And if Lauren had chosen a repeated measures design, she would need to counterbalance the other two stimulus sets as well. There would be a grand total of 18 different orderings of the three sets.

**Randomizing the order of treatments** is another way of controlling order effects. Instead of using all the possible orders of treatment conditions with an equal number of participants, the order of treatments is randomly determined for each participant. You can assume that randomization results an approximately even number of times each treatment is presented in each order. It is less important whether order effects are eliminated by counterbalancing or by randomizing order than that the order effects are controlled. Otherwise, the results of the treatments will be confounded by the order in which they were presented.

This section has used Lauren's hypothesis extensively. By now, you are probably wondering whether the addition of an attractive photograph really improves a person's chance for a positive resume evaluation, especially in terms of expected future success. In reality, Lauren hypothesized that the effects of physical attractiveness are different for women and men. That means she also varied the gender of the person presented in the resume. That makes her experiment a factorial design (more than one factor). You are probably still curious about the results; therefore, we'll pick up this study in Chapter 10, "When There Is More Than One Cause: Between Groups Factorial Experiments."

You may also be suspecting by now that the study is very complicated using a repeated measures design. Lauren decided, based on some pilot testing, that the threats to internal validity in her study were too great to use a repeated measures design. The carryover effects of reviewing multiple resumes were too great, and viewing multiple photographs that varied on attractiveness made the hypothesis of her study obvious to participants (increased demand characteristics). Therefore, Lauren used a between groups design. Each participant in her experiment evaluated only one resume in one of the three physical attractiveness conditions.

### 9-1e ABA Designs

The pretest posttest design is very liable to order effects because it involves the measurement of the same behavior at two points in time. One improvement to the design involves adding a third observation:

$$O_1 \ X \ O_2 \ O_3$$

This design is useful when the hypothesized effect is temporary and is sometimes called an **ABA design**. In this design one treatment is designated by A (which could be the control condition or pretest), and the other treatment is designated by B. Because the effect of B is temporary, the second measurement in the A condition should show a return to the same level as the first measurement in the A condition. If that first condition was the pretest (A1), then the second measurement can show a return to baseline (A2). This design allows you to rule out the possible confound that the effect of B was the result of order of treatments because it both follows and precedes treatment A. It also allows you to rule out maturation confounds. As mentioned at the beginning of this paragraph, the ABA design is useful for temporary effects. If the cause produces a permanent change in the effect, you could not expect a return to baseline with the third measurement of the effect (second A).

The ABA design is very useful for certain types of field research that don't allow for a control group. Suppose a classroom teacher wanted to find out if the use of praise is better than criticism. For one month she measured children's performance on their math homework using the standard grading method of making check marks for all the wrong answers and counting off for the number of points missed. During the next month she changed the

---

**randomizing the order of treatments** Randomly determining the order of treatments for each participant.

**ABA design** Repeated measures design in which a pretest is given with no treatment (A), the treatment is given and its effect is measured (B), and a third measurement is taken without the treatment (A).

grading procedure to checking the correct answers and adding up the points earned. During the third month she returned to the standard grading style of checking the mistakes and subtracting the total. This would be an applied ABA field experiment. If the children improved their performance with positive feedback but returned to the baseline level of performance with negative feedback, the teacher would be able to conclude that positive feedback is better for her class. She could make her conclusion even stronger by continuing to measure students' performance as she uses the positive feedback grading system for another month, making her design an ABAB design. If the students improved again when receiving the positive feedback, she could really be confident of the effectiveness of positive feedback.

# 9-2 Partitioning the Variance

Just as with the *t* tests covered in Chapters 6 and 7, the partitioning of the variance is different for a repeated measures design than it is for a between groups design. Figure 9-1 shows the partitioning of variance for the within subjects design. Notice that the treatment effect is not estimated from differences between groups of subjects, but rather from differences within the same subjects. That is the essence of a repeated measures design. The treatment effects can be observed for each participant as his or her own baseline.

# 9-3 Analysis of Variance Summary Table

Table 9-2 shows the analysis of variance summary table for a repeated measures design. It is the same as the between groups summary table, except the sources of variance are different. In this case the **between subjects variance** is listed first. It represents the difference among all the subjects, and it isn't relevant for the hypothesis test because that test relies on comparisons of each subject's changes in response to the repeated treatments. The between subjects variance is calculated to remove it as a source of variability from further consideration.

**between subjects variance** Difference among all the subjects.

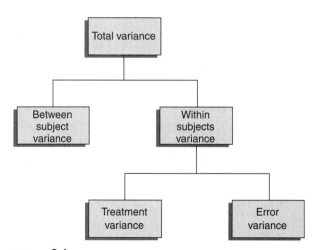

**Figure 9-1**
*Partitioning of Variance for a Within Subjects Experiment*

| TABLE 9-2 | Analysis of Variance Summary Table for a Repeated Measures (Within Subjects Design) |

| Source | Sum of Squares | Degrees of Freedom | Mean Square | F |
|---|---|---|---|---|
| Between Subjects | $SS_S$ | $df_S$ | | |
| Within Subjects | | | | |
| Treatment (IV) | $SS_{IV}$ | $df_{IV}$ | $MS_{IV}$ | F |
| Error | $SS_E$ | $df_E$ | $MS_E$ | |
| Total | $SS_T$ | $df_T$ | | |

**within subjects variance**
Differences within the subjects due to the treatment and error variance.

**within subjects treatment variance** Within subjects variance that can be attributed to the treatment.

**within subjects error variance** Variation within each subject that cannot be attributed to the treatment.

There are two sources of **within subjects variance**. The first is that which can be attributed to the treatment (IV) (**within subjects treatment variance**). The second is the variation within each subject that cannot be attributed to the treatment; it's called the **within subjects error variance**. The ratio of these two variances, within subjects treatment variance to within subjects error variance, is the $F$ statistic. The final row of the table is the total variance.

### 9-3a  Degrees of Freedom for the Within Subjects Design

The degrees of freedom for the within sources are calculated differently than they were for the between groups one-way ANOVA:

- $df_S = N - 1$, where $N$ is the number of subjects
- $df_{IV} = k - 1$, where $k$ is the number of treatment conditions
- $df_E = (N - 1)(k - 1)$
- $df_T = kN - 1$

### 9-3b  Mean Squares for the Repeated Measures Design

The mean squares *(MS)* are calculated as in the one-way between groups ANOVA by dividing the sums of squares *(SS)* by the degrees of freedom *(df)*. It is only useful to calculate the mean squares that will be used to determine the $F$, so there is no reason to compute a mean square for the between subjects variance or the total variance.

# 9-4 Calculation of the Sums of Squares in a Repeated Measures Design

The formulas for calculating the sums of square *(SS)* and degrees of freedom *(df)* for the within subjects (repeated measures) analysis of variance are as follows:

$$SS_{Subjects} = SS_S = \sum \frac{\left(\sum_p X\right)^2}{k} - \frac{T^2}{N}$$

$$SS_{Treatment} = SS_{IV} = \sum \frac{\left(\sum_j X\right)^2}{n} - \frac{T^2}{N}$$

$$SS_{Total} = SS_T = \sum \sum X^2 - \frac{T^2}{N}$$

$$SS_{Error} = SS_E = SS_T - SS_{IV} - SS_S$$

$df_S = n - 1$

$df_{IV} = k - 1$

$df_T = N - 1$

$df_E = (n - 1)(k - 1)$

Where:

$$\sum_p X = \text{Total for Person(p)}$$

$$\sum_j X = \text{Total for Treatment(j)}$$

$n = $ Number of Subjects

$N = $ Number of Scores

$T = $ Total of Scores

$$\sum \sum X^2 = \text{Total of all Squared Scores}$$

$k = $ Number of Treatments

These formulas are similar to those that were used for the one-way analysis of variance for the between groups design. Summing the total for each treatment and the total of all the scores is the same. But, as in the repeated measures $t$ test, there is a combination of scores for each subject. In the repeated measures $t$ test, difference scores were used. Because there may be more than two scores from each subject in the repeated measures design, the scores from each individual are summed across all the treatments that individual received. That way, the individual variation can be partitioned (and removed) from the variance estimates of the error term.

The ABA field experiment that was proposed in section 9-1e is a good example to show for the calculation of the one-factor repeated measures analysis of variance (ANOVA). The hypothesis was that positive feedback grading (checking and counting the correct arithmetic homework problems) would produce better arithmetic performance than would the standard negative feedback grading (checking the incorrect answers and subtracting the number wrong from the total number of problems to produce a score). This example used an ABA design that had a baseline of one month with negative scoring (A) followed by one month of positive scoring (B) and then another month of negative scoring (A). In this example the hypotheses can be stated as follows:

$H_0$: Negative (A) = Positive (B) = Negative (A)

$H_1$: Negative (A) < Positive (B) > Negative (A)

Figure 9-2 shows a step-by-step example of the analysis. The data in the table represent the monthly average scores for six children on homework sets of 15 problems. As you can see, the children didn't do very well in the first month but did improve over time. The $F$ test (ANOVA) will indicate whether the changes over the 3 months are statistically significant.

**Step 1.** Calculate the $SS_S$ (sum of scores for each person) and the $SS_{IV}$ (sum of scores for each treatment).

| Subject | Treatment 1 (Neg.) | Treatment 2 (Pos.) | Treatment 3 (Neg.) | | Step 2. Calculate the $T$ (sum of all scores) and the $\Sigma\Sigma X^2$ (sum of all squared scores). |
|---|---|---|---|---|---|
| 1 | 6 | 10 | 13 | 29 | |
| 2 | 5 | 11 | 14 | 30 | |
| 3 | 3 | 9 | 11 | 23 | |
| 4 | 6 | 12 | 13 | 31 | |
| 5 | 4 | 10 | 14 | 28 | |
| 6 | 5 | 9 | 12 | 26 | |
| $\Sigma X^2$ | 29 | 61 | 77 | $167 = T$ | |
| $\Sigma X^2$ | 147 | 627 | 995 | $1769 = \Sigma\Sigma X^2$ | |
| $\overline{X}$ | 4.83 | 10.17 | 12.83 | | |

**Step 3.** Calculate the sum of squares.

$$SS_S = \left[\frac{29^2}{3} + \frac{30^2}{3} + \frac{23^2}{3} + \frac{31^2}{3} + \frac{28^2}{3} + \frac{26^2}{3}\right] - \frac{167^2}{18}$$

$$= [280.33 + 300 + 176.33 + 320.33 + 261.33 + 225.33] - 1549.39$$

$$= 1563.65 - 1549.39 = 14.26$$

$$SS_{IV} = \left[\frac{29^2}{6} + \frac{61^2}{6} + \frac{77^2}{6}\right] - 1549.39$$

$$= [140.17 + 620.17 + 988.17] - 1549.39 = 1748.51 - 1549.39 = 199.12$$

$$SS_T = 1769 - 1549.39 = 219.61$$

$$SS_E = 219.61 - 199.12 - 14.26 = 6.23$$

**Step 4.** Fill sums of squares into ANOVA table.

| Source | Sums of squares | Degrees of freedom | Mean squares | $F$ |
|---|---|---|---|---|
| Between subjects | 14.26 | 5 | | |
| Within subjects | | | | |
| Treatment (IV) | 199.12 | 2 | 99.56 | 159.807 |
| Error | 6.23 | 10 | 0.623 | |

**Step 5.** Evaluate the significance of $F$ by determining $F$ critical from the table.

$F_{critical}$ (2,10; $\alpha = .05$) = 4.10

Because the obtained $F$ is greater than the critical $F$, the effect of the treatment is significant.

**Step 6.** Calculate Tukey's HSD for 3 means.

$$HSD = q_\alpha\sqrt{\frac{MS_{error}}{n}} = 3.88\sqrt{\frac{.623}{6}} = 3.88\sqrt{.1038} = 3.88(.322) = 1.25$$

Compare differences between means to the HSD.

$\overline{X}_2 - \overline{X}_1 = 10.17 - 4.83 = 5.34 > HSD$

$\overline{X}_3 - \overline{X}_2 = 12.83 - 10.17 = 2.66 > HSD$

$\overline{X}_3 - \overline{X}_1 = 12.83 - 4.83 = 8 > HSD$

Therefore, the differences between all the means are statistically significant at $\alpha = .05$.

**Figure 9-2**

*Step-by-Step Example of Calculating a Repeated Measures Analysis of Variance*

## **9-5** Interpretation of the Results of ANOVA

The principles of interpreting the analysis of variance are the same for the repeated measures design as they were for the between subjects one-way ANOVA. If the calculated $F$ is greater than the critical $F$ found in the table of critical values (see Chapter 8), then the means of the treatment conditions are statistically significantly different. That does not mean that the specific one-tail alternate hypothesis is supported by the results. In fact, in this case, although you can clearly reject the null hypothesis ($F(2,10) = 159.81$; $p < .05$), the results do not support the use of positive grading to improve children's arithmetic performance. The average performance for the children was higher during the positive grading period ($M = 10.17$) than during the first negative grading period ($M = 4.83$). However, it was less than the children's average performance in the second negative grading period ($M = 12.83$). The children were improving over time, and the Tukey HSD test shown as step 6 in Figure 9-2 shows that each month's scores were significantly better than the previous scores. The teacher, or the children, or both are definitely doing something good, but from these results we cannot conclude that the improvement was due to the grading method.

## **9-6** Effect Size for Repeated Measures ANOVA

The effect size, eta squared ($\eta^2$), is the proportion of variance that can be attributed to the effect of the independent variable within subjects. It is estimated in much the same way as was the effect size for a one-way between groups ANOVA. In the within subjects case, the effect size of the treatment is the ratio of the within subjects treatment variance to the total variance. The formula is

$$\eta^2 = \frac{SS_{\text{within\_IV}}}{SS_{total}}$$

For the sample experiment the effect size is calculated as follows:

$$\eta^2 = \frac{SS_{\text{within\_IV}}}{SS_{total}} = \frac{199.12}{199.12 + 6.23 + 14.26} = \frac{199.12}{219.61} = .91$$

Notice that the total sums of squares was calculated by adding together the between subjects sums of squares and both within subjects sums of squares (treatment and error).

## **9-7** APA Style: The Title Page

The title page of a report in APA style contains the running head for publication, the title, authors' names, and their institutional affiliation. A running head is a short form (50 characters or fewer) of the title that will be used at the top of each page in the published article. The title should describe the experiment. A reader should be able to tell the main topic of study from the title. The title of a report of an experiment should make the independent and dependent variables clear. Following the title, the authors' names appear in the order of their contribution to the work. Each author's institutional affiliation is also listed. Figure 9-3 shows a sample title page for the experiment presented in this chapter. Note that the example was hypothetical; therefore, the title page is for a research report that does not exist.

Positive and Negative Feedback 1

Running head:  POSITIVE AND NEGATIVE FEEDBACK ON MATH

The Effects of Positive and Negative Feedback on
Fourth Grade Children's Math Performance
Julia M. Jones
Westminster College

• Number the title page and use short form of running head.
• Capitalize the full running head.
• Center title in the top half of the page.
• Double space title, author names, and affiliations.
• Maintain 1-inch margins throughout the report.

**Figure 9-3**
*APA Style Title Page*

# Summary

The repeated measures one-factor design is appropriate for experiments that are not liable to threats to internal validity from repeated treatments on the same subjects. Research methods for reducing the threats of repeated measurements of the same subjects include counterbalancing or randomizing the order of the treatments. The ABA design involves three repeated measures. The effect of treatment A is measured, followed by measurement of the effect of treatment B. Then another measurement of the effect of treatment A is taken. The ABA design can separate the effect of treatment B from maturation or testing effects.

The analysis of variance for a repeated measures design involves partitioning the within subjects variance into treatment variance and error variance. The $F$ ratio for the repeated measures one-factor design is the ratio of the within subjects treatment variance to the within subjects error variance. Multiple comparisons and effect size estimates are done for any statistically significant treatment effects that involve more than two treatments.

## References

Dewey, L. (2000). The effects of physical attractiveness on perceived life success on graduating college seniors. Paper presented at the Mind Conference, Heidelberg College, Tiffin, OH.

Dion, K., Berscheid, E. & Walster, E. (1972). What is beautiful is good. *Journal of Personality and Social Psychology*, 24(3), 285–290.

Hatfield, E. & Sprecher, S. (1986). *Mirror, mirror ....The importance of looks in everyday life.* New York: State University of New York Press.

## Exercises for Application

Some words are concrete. They are associated with images (e.g., *apple*), whereas others are abstract (e.g., *moral*). In addition some words have multiple meanings (homonyms). One of those meanings can be associated with an image (e.g., *figure* as in Figure 9-1), and the other is more abstract (e.g., "you are going to try to figure out this problem"). It was hypothesized that memory is better for words that have images associated with them than for those that do not. It was not clear whether words that have two meanings, one associated with a visual image, would be remembered better or worse than the concrete words. To test the hypothesis, participants were given a set of 30 words to remember. Ten of the words were concrete, 10 were abstract, and 10 were homonyms that had at least one concrete meaning. The order of the words was randomized. After a 2-minute acquisition period, the participants completed a 3-minute math task (to prevent rehearsal to the words) and then recalled as many of the words as they could by writing them down. The data are as follows:

1. State the null hypothesis (or hypotheses) to be tested.

2. State the alternative hypothesis (or hypotheses) to be tested.

3. Choose the correct inferential and descriptive statistics to test the hypothesis (or hypotheses).

4. Use the correct formulas to calculate the statistics.

5. Determine the statistical significance of the appropriate inferential statistic and draw a statistical conclusion.

6. Present the descriptive statistics needed to explain any significant effects.

7. State the probability of making a Type I error.

8. State the conclusion of the analysis without using statistical terms. (Say what the analysis means without using any numbers or statistical concepts.)

| Participant # | Concrete | Homonym | Abstract |
|---|---|---|---|
| 1 | 6 | 6 | 4 |
| 2 | 5 | 4 | 2 |
| 3 | 6 | 5 | 2 |
| 4 | 5 | 6 | 3 |
| 5 | 4 | 5 | 4 |
| 6 | 2 | 3 | 2 |
| 7 | 9 | 7 | 5 |
| 8 | 5 | 4 | 3 |

# Practice Quiz

*Note:* You can find the correct answers to these questions by taking the quiz and then submitting your answers in the Online Edition. The program will automatically score your submission. If you miss a question, the program will provide the correct answer, a rationale for the answer, and the section number in the chapter where the topic is discussed.

1. A repeated measures design is appropriate when

    a. individual differences in the dependent variable make it desirable for each subject to act as his or her own control.
    b. there is a clear threat from maturation.
    c. the respondents are randomly assigned to treatment condition.
    d. there aren't enough participants for a complete between subjects design.

2. Making sure that each level of the independent variable is presented in each order the same number of times across all the participants is called

    a. confounding.
    b. counterbalancing.
    c. regression toward the mean.
    d. residual variance.

3. The ABA design is an improvement on the pretest posttest design because it can show a

    a. cause-effect relationship.
    b. problem due to order effects.
    c. significant effect.
    d. return to baseline after the treatment condition.

4. In a repeated measures design, the treatment variance is part of the

    a. between subjects variance.
    b. within subjects variance.
    c. error variance.
    d. residual variance.

5. The *F* ratio is formed in a repeated measures design by dividing the treatment mean squares by the

    a. total mean squares.
    b. within subjects mean squares.
    c. error within subjects mean squares.
    d. degrees of freedom within subjects.

6. What are the degrees of freedom for treatment in a within subjects design using three repeated measures with six participants?

    a. 2
    b. 5
    c. 4
    d. 12

7. Providing the same subject with all the treatment conditions can

    a. decrease between subject variance.
    b. improve the internal validity of the experiment.
    c. be a way to counterbalance treatments.
    d. increase the demand characteristics of the experiment.

8. The proportion of variance that can be attributed to the effect of the independent variable within subjects is called

    a. eta squared.
    b. Cohen's *d*.
    c. delta prime.
    d. alpha.

9. The order of authors on the title page is determined

    a. by the amount of contribution to the work.
    b. by alphabetical order.
    c. by seniority, with the most senior last.
    d. randomly.

10. Tukey's honestly significant difference test should be used whenever

    a. there are comparisons to be made among three or more groups.
    b. the *F* ratio was significant.
    c. the experiment-wise Type I error rate should be kept below alpha.
    d. all of the above.

11. The number of levels of the independent variable should be ideally determined by

    a. the number of available participants.
    b. the number of levels that best address the hypothesis.
    c. the statistical tests that you know how to do.
    d. there should always be at least three.

12. If there are too many different orders of treatments to use counterbalancing, another good approach is to

    a. randomize the order of the treatments.
    b. use a yoked-control group.
    c. have all participants receive the same order of treatments.
    d. make sure the control condition is always the first treatment.

13. One of the main differences in calculating a repeated measures ANOVA from calculating the between groups ANOVA is the

    a. $SS_{Total}$.
    b. $SS_{Treatment}$.
    c. $SS_{Subjects}$.
    d. $SS_{Error}$.

14. A short form of the title that is used at the top of each page in a published article is called the

    a. running head.
    b. brief title.
    c. title abstract.
    d. page header.

15. The statistical power of a repeated measures design may be higher than that of a between groups design because

    a. it is easier to get more data when each participant receives each treatment.

    b. the between groups variance is smaller.
    c. the chance of a Type I error is higher.
    d. the probability of demand characteristics is reduced.

16. A treatment in which the hypothesized cause is absent is

    a. a pretest.
    b. a true control condition.
    c. a placebo effect.
    d. an experimental condition.

# When There Is More Than One One Cause: Between Groups Factorial Experiments

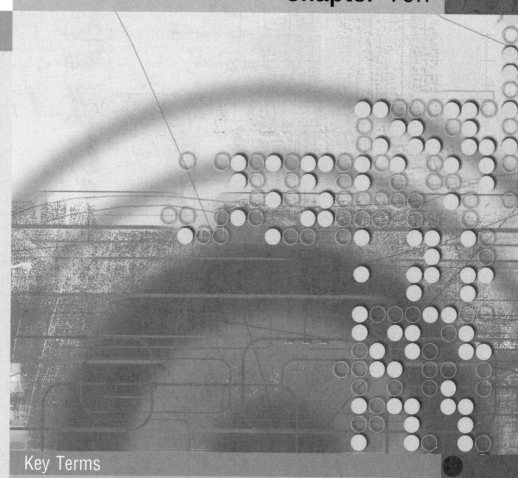

## Chapter Outline

## Key Terms

between groups
cell
cell totals
demand characteristics
factorial design
interact

interaction
main effects
marginal totals
residual variance
two-factor ANOVA

# Learning Objectives

- Be able to explain what it means for two causes to interact.
- Diagram a between groups factorial experiment.
- Graph the main effects and interactions from a factorial experiment.

- Partition the variance in a between groups factorial design.
- Calculate and interpret the analysis of variance for a between groups factorial design.

## Key Idea

Factorial experiments are used when two or more independent variables are hypothesized to cause the effect. A main effect is the influence of one independent variable alone. An interaction occurs if the effect of one independent variable is different for different levels of the second independent variable.

## 10-1 When There Is More Than One Cause

Behavior is very complex. There can be more than one cause at any given time. With humans, probably very few things have only a single cause. Many factors must be taken into account to be able to understand behavior. When you consider more than one factor in the same experiment, this design is called a **factorial design**.

Consider the behavior of eating. People eat because they are hungry. That is one factor. Hunger itself can be determined by many different factors. But can hunger alone explain why you ate pizza last week with your friends? No! There were other important factors. People also eat because of pleasure; people eat because they enjoy the flavor of food. So, there are at least two important factors that must be taken into account to explain eating behavior. But there are many more. You probably would not have eaten the pizza all alone last week. Eating it together with your friends was important. People often eat because of the social function it provides. Now you have three factors to consider to explain eating behavior. How many more can you think of? There are many.

Consider a researcher who believes that more than one factor is the cause of a particular behavior. The researcher must choose between one of two approaches to design an experiment. The simplest approach is to study one factor at a time. The researcher might design a one-factor experiment to study the effects of hunger on eating behavior. After determining the effects of hunger, she or he might go on to the next important factor. Then the researcher would design an experiment about the relationship of flavor of food to eating behavior. After the researcher had completed that experiment, she or he would go on to study the relationship of other factors to eating behavior, one by one. With this approach, a series of related one-factor experiments, the researcher can learn the effects of each factor, alone, on the behavior being studied.

The problem with the series approach is that factors don't occur alone. In fact, people eat based on hunger, taste preferences, and the social context all the time. Therefore, a series of experiments that manipulate one factor at a time cannot approximate the real effects of the *combined factors* on eating behavior.

Furthermore, some factors **interact** with each other. That means their effect when presented in isolation is different from their effect when they are presented together with another factor. For example, hunger may be a good indicator of eating behavior when a person is alone, but hunger may have no effect on eating when the person is in a social context. The amount of eating behavior may be determined solely by the type of social situation. A very hungry person is unlikely to eat *during* a formal social event such as a wedding or graduation ceremony. On the other hand, even a person who is not hungry will eat some of the refreshments served *after* the wedding or

**factorial design** A design in which more than one factor is considered in the same experiment.

**interact** Factors' effect when presented in isolation is different from their effect when they are presented together with another factor.

170

graduation (and the hungry person will eat even more). Hunger interacts with social context to affect eating behavior. Another way to say this is, "The effect of hunger on eating behavior depends on the particular social situation." Can you think of ways that hunger might interact with flavor of food to affect eating behavior? If so, you can see that hunger could interact with both of the other factors. A series of single-factor experiments cannot show the interaction between the factors.

# 10-2 Two or More Factors in the Same Experiment

To test for interactions among factors, researchers design factorial experiments. In a factorial experiment, each of the hypothesized factors is manipulated independently of the other, but they are presented together to the subjects. Thus, there is a factorial design. Think about the simplest factorial design first: That is the $2 \times 2$ factorial design. This design has two factors. The first number 2 represents the number of levels (or treatments) for the first factor. The second number 2 represents the number of levels (or treatments) for the second factor.

The design for a factorial experiment can be diagrammed as shown in Figure 10-1. If the experiment has two factors, then the design must be shown in two dimensions. Each dimension is marked off with as many levels as there are conditions for that factor. The resulting combination of levels shows all the specific treatments. In Figure 10-1, the height dimension represents Factor A, and the width dimension represents Factor B. You can think of the height as the rows and the width as the columns. Because each dimension has two levels, they combine to form four unique treatments. Each of the combined treatments is called a **cell** in the design.

In a factorial design experiment, subjects are randomly assigned to receive one of the treatment combinations. We sometimes say they are randomly assigned to the cells of the design. That makes it sound as though they are being sentenced to prison! In reality, we mean that each subject will be randomly assigned to receive a particular combination of treatments.

Taking a Closer Look 10-1 describes a two-factor sample experiment designed to test the effects of hunger and flavor on eating behavior. The experiment was carefully designed so that all other things were kept constant, and only hunger and food flavor were experimentally manipulated. There were two levels of hunger: not hungry and hungry. They were combined with two levels of flavor: normal and bad. In this example, the $2 \times 2$ factorial design will mean that there are two levels of hunger (none and high) and two levels of flavor (normal and bad). Figure 10-2 shows the design diagram for the sample experiment. The four cells of the design are

- No Hunger + Normal Flavor
- No Hunger + Bad Flavor
- High Hunger + Normal Flavor
- High Hunger + Bad Flavor

**cell** Each of the combined treatments in the design for an experiment.

**Factor B**

|  | Level 1 | Level 2 |
|---|---|---|
| **Level 1** | $A_1B_1$ | $A_1B_2$ |
| **Level 2** | $A_2B_1$ | $A_2B_2$ |

**Factor A**

**Figure 10-1**

*Diagram of a Two-Factor Design*

## Sample Experiment: 2 × 2 Between Groups Experiment

Imagine that a researcher hypothesized that both hunger level and the palatability (flavor) of food affect the amount of food a person will eat. Furthermore, these two factors were hypothesized to interact. It was hypothesized that the effect of hunger on eating behavior depends on the flavor of the food present.

Potential participants were informed that study participation could involve fasting for 12 hours and that after fasting they would be able to break their fast with a snack provided during the second portion of the study. Because some potential participants may have food allergies, they were all forewarned that the snacks provided could include peanuts. Those participants who agreed to the conditions that were described in the informed consent form were asked to report for a study on the effects of certain foods on artistic creativity. Participants in the hungry condition were asked to fast for 12 hours. Participants in the not hungry condition were asked to eat normally before the experiment. When a participant reported for the experiment, she or he was asked to make a collage from art materials and fill out a questionnaire that assessed mood.

After completing the first part of the experiment, the participant was told that the experiment was over and that

another experimenter would soon debrief the participant. The participant was asked to wait in a comfortable room in which a bowl of peanuts was placed on the table along with reading materials. For half the participants, the bowl contained normal peanuts (good flavor condition). For the remaining participants, it contained peanuts that had been treated with quinine (bad flavor condition).

Each participant was asked to make herself or himself comfortable while waiting for the debriefing. After 10 minutes, the participant was completely debriefed by a second experimenter, who explained the real purpose of the experiment and answered questions about the experiment. After the participant left, the experimenter determined the amount eaten by counting the number of peanuts remaining in the bowl. The experimenter had placed a specific number of peanuts in the bowl before the participant was asked to wait. She or he determined the number the participant ate by subtracting the number remaining from the number originally placed in the bowl.

The numbers of peanuts each participant ate during the 10-minute waiting period are presented in Table 10-5 later in this chapter.

**demand characteristics**
Aspects of the research situation that produce effects in the participants that would not occur outside the experimental setting.

To make all the groups equivalent (on average) in terms of the personality and experience differences the participants bring with them to the experiment, the experimenters randomly assigned participants to one of the four treatment conditions. All other possible factors, such as time of day, social context, and physical setting, were kept the same for each of the four experimental groups through counterbalancing and controlling the setting.

The procedure of the experiment was designed to reduce **demand characteristics**. Participants who know they are in an eating experiment are likely to change their eating behavior just because they know that eating is being studied. To reduce those demand characteristics, the experimenters used a cover story. Because this is a factorial experiment, half the hungry participants will have good-flavored food with them, whereas the other half will have the awful-flavored food. Likewise for the nonhungry participants—half will have the normal-flavored food, and half will have

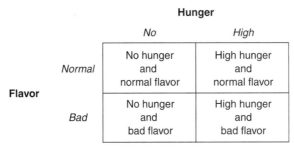

**Figure 10-2**
*Factorial Design Diagram for the Sample Experiment*

the awful-flavored food available. Although these four combinations of treatments are referred to as the four groups, the subjects participate in the experiment individually. In a well-designed study, a participant is not aware of the other treatment conditions because such awareness can produce demand characteristics.

Now let's extend the design notation to more complex designs. A $3 \times 2$ factorial design also has two factors. The only difference between it and $2 \times 2$ design is that in a $3 \times 2$ design the first factor has three different conditions (remember, they are the same as levels or treatments). A $2 \times 2 \times 2$ factorial design is one in which three different causes (factors) are manipulated, each with two conditions.

The total number of cells in any design is the product of the levels of each factor. For example, in the sample experiment, 2 levels of hunger $\times$ 2 levels of flavor = 4 cells.

This principle of multiplying the number of conditions for each factor together to determine the number of cells of the design works for all factorial designs. Thus, the $3 \times 2$ factorial design has six cells. The $2 \times 2 \times 2$ factorial design has eight cells.

In an experiment testing the effects of one cause, there is a null hypothesis to be tested and an alternative hypothesis. In a factorial experiment, there are null hypotheses for each main effect and for each interaction. Thus, there are the following null hypotheses:

$H_{0a}$: There is no main effect of Factor A on the dependent variable.

$H_{0b}$: There is no main effect of Factor B on the dependent variable.

$H_{0ab}$: There is no combined effect of Factors A and B on the dependent variable.

Each null hypothesis will have a corresponding alternative hypothesis. The factorial analysis of variance (ANOVA) tests all the null hypotheses simultaneously, while keeping the probability of a Type I error (alpha) at acceptable levels.

# 10-3 Partitioning the Variance

Just as you partition the variance for a single-factor experiment, you also do so for the factorial experiment. The difference is that you have more sources of variance. Now the data from an experiment can be grouped according to each of the three null hypotheses stated in section 10-2. They are as follows:

- Factor A: Level 1 compared with level 2.
- Factor B: Level 1 compared with level 2.
- Factor A interacting with Factor B: Level 1,1 compared to level 2,1 compared to level 1,2 compared to level 2,2.

Each of these comparisons for effects is a source of variance, as illustrated in Figure 10-3. In a two-factor between groups experiment,

Total variance = Factor A variance + Factor B variance + Interaction between
Factors A and B variance + Within groups variance

## 10-3a Main Effects

The two sources of variance that rely on only one factor are called **main effects**. Factor A has a main effect if, overall, there is a difference between the data in the level 1 group of Factor A compared to those in the level 2 group. This is the alternative hypothesis to the first null hypotheses stated in section 10-2. In the sample experiment, the experimenters are testing the main effect of hunger on eating behavior. If they find that, on average, those in the high hunger group eat more than those in the no hunger group and that this difference is larger than

**main effects** The sources of variance that rely on only one factor.

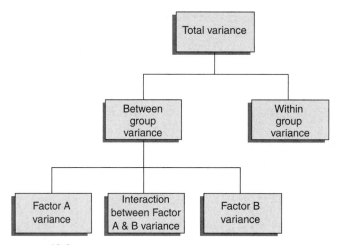

**Figure 10-3**

*Partitioning the Variance for a Two-Factor Between Groups Experiment*

they would expect by chance alone, then they can conclude that there is a main effect of hunger on eating behavior.

Likewise, the experimenters can test for the main effect of flavor on eating behavior. If the average number of peanuts eaten in the normal flavor conditions exceeds the average number eaten in the bad flavor conditions, they would have a main effect of flavor on eating behavior. Thus, they could reject the second null hypothesis.

In any factorial experiment, you have the same number of main effects as you have factors in the experiment. However, a major reason for doing a factorial experiment is to test the interactions of the factors.

## 10-3b Interactions

**interaction** The effect of either factor depends on the level of the other.

**residual variance** Variance not attributed to any factor or interaction.

**between groups** The source of variance between experimental groups.

An **interaction** occurs when the effects of either factor depend on the level of the other. In a two-factor experiment, the difference among all the groups in the experiment is compared to the **residual variance** (that not attributed to any factor or interaction). This difference is used to estimate the **between groups** variance due to the interaction of the variables. In a $2 \times 2$ factorial design, the four cell means are compared. With two means, as in the case of the main effects of a variable that has two levels, you can easily see that the variance is the difference between the two means. With four or more means, the same concept of variance applies, but it is estimated by taking the average difference between each mean and the grand mean of all the data. So if the groups were all equal, their means would all equal the grand mean, and there would be no between groups variance. However, if they were very different from each other, some would be much greater than the grand mean, whereas others would be much smaller. Their squared differences from the grand mean would be an indicator of how much they vary from each other.

A main purpose for doing a factorial experiment is to test the interaction effect. Some factorial experiments are done to efficiently test two main effects even though no interaction is hypothesized. However, testing for interactions is important even when they are not hypothesized because you don't always find what you expect, and the interaction can be an important source of variation. In the sample experiment, the experimenters have hypothesized that hunger and flavor interact to affect eating behavior. The form of the alternative hypothesis is as follows:

$H_1$ : High hunger and normal flavor > No hunger and normal flavor =

High hunger and bad flavor = No hunger and bad flavor

Often, understanding the hypothesized interaction in terms of general group differences is difficult. It is better to make graphs of projected means to communicate exactly what is being hypothesized. This will also help you, the student researcher, with interpretation of results after completion of the data analysis.

# 10-4 Graphing and Interpreting the Results of Two-Factor Experiments

Graphs are seldom used with one-factor experiments because most people can easily compare two numbers, or even three, to each other without seeing them graphically represented. However, it is not easy to make the many comparisons of the four interaction group means and the four main effects group means without a picture. The complexity increases as the number of levels or factors in the design increases. Therefore, graphs are almost always used to represent the results of factorial experiments.

In graphing a factorial experiment, it is typical to graph the interaction cell means. You infer the main effects by comparing these means as well. Figure 10-4 shows the hypothesized interaction of hunger and flavor on eating behavior. The dependent variable is graphed on the Y-axis. In the example, the Y-axis represents the number of peanuts eaten. One of the two factors is represented on the X-axis; it really doesn't matter which one. In this case, the flavor factor is presented on the X-axis. Now you have run out of axes, but there is still another factor to represent. You do so by making different lines on the graph for each level of that factor. Therefore, in the example, one line represents the hypothesized means for the high hunger conditions, and the other represents the hypothesized means for the no hunger conditions.

Graphs of interactions are very useful in understanding the effects of each of the factors and of both of the factors together. You seldom make graphs of main effects alone. If you did, they would look like those presented in Figure 10-5. The first graph shows what would happen if the first level were greater than the second level for Factor A. The second shows the opposite effect in which $\overline{X}_2 > \overline{X}_1$. The steeper the line between the two points on the graph, the larger the difference between the means. The third graph in Figure 10-5 shows no effect of Factor A. Because the

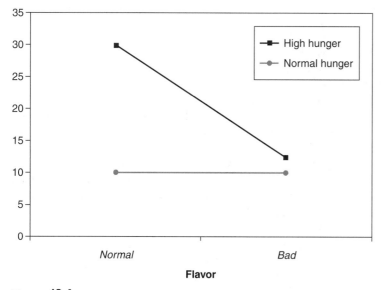

**Figure 10-4**

*Hypothesized Interaction Between Hunger and Flavor on Eating Behavior*

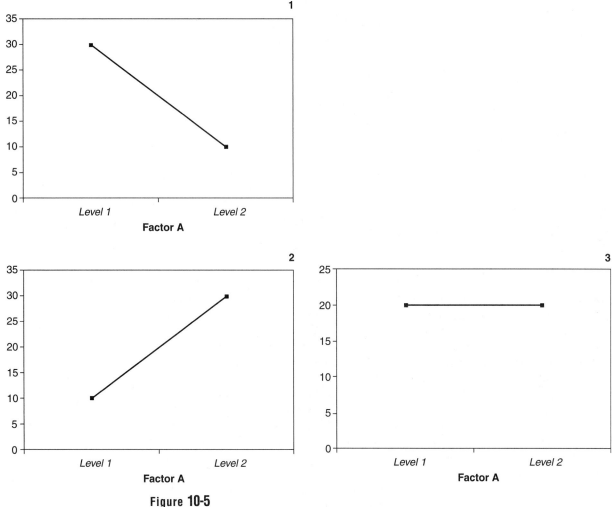

**Figure 10-5**
*Graphic Representations of Main Effects*

means are the same, the line between them is horizontal. The less the effect of Factor A, the flatter the line.

The same principles of slope (flat to steep lines) apply to interactions. Figure 10-6 shows some possible graphs of interactions. The first sample graph shows what a graph might look like when there are main effects but no interaction between factors. The two lines in the graph are roughly parallel. This means that the effect of the second factor is the same amount for each level of the first factor. For example, if you measured the amount of force that could be exerted by two strong men, you could imagine that one man represents Factor A. In level 1, he is exerting force. In level 2, he is not exerting force. Likewise, the other man could be represented by Factor B. The top point in the graph is the amount of force exerted by both men together. The lowest amount of force is exerted when neither man pushes. Each man exerts a main effect. However, there is not an interaction. Each man exerts the same amount of force whether or not the other man is pushing.

Often, both main effects and interactions are present in data, as illustrated in Figure 10-7. Because the lines are not parallel, you can conclude that the factors interact in some way. Closer inspection reveals that the effects of one variable depend on the other. In the first sample graph, the effect of Factor A depends on the level of Factor B. To illustrate this, consider the cohesion produced by the different chemical agents in an epoxy. Neither agent alone produces a strong bond. But when both

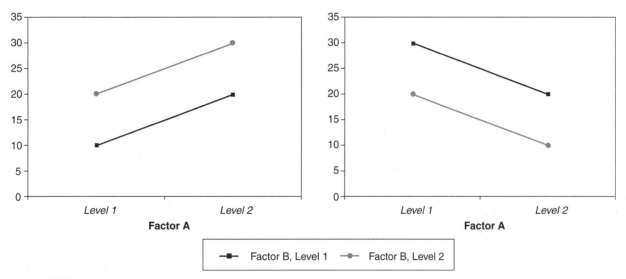

**Figure 10-6**

*Graphic Representations of Cell Means When No Interactions Are Present*

agents are present together, the cohesive bond is very strong. They interact, but neither has a main effect! However, the strength of the interaction may produce a statistically significant main effect. Therefore, when both main effects and interactions are significant, the main effects are interpreted in light of the interactions.

The graphs in Figure 10-8 also show interactions. These graphs show effects of both factors, but depending on the combination with the other factor, they show opposite effects. Pay special attention to the second sample graph: This is the example of an interaction with no main effects. The X form of the graph signifies that there are opposite effects of the Variable A at the two levels of Variable B. An example of this type of effect was shown in a student experiment in which the number of candies eaten was studied as a function of the participant's gender (Factor A) and the gender of a confederate (Factor B). The results showed that women ate more when a woman was present than when a man was present. For men, the results were just the opposite. Men ate fewer candies when a woman was present than when a man was present. The graph of these results was similar to the X shown in Figure 10-8. Note that this example uses a combination of a subject variable (participant

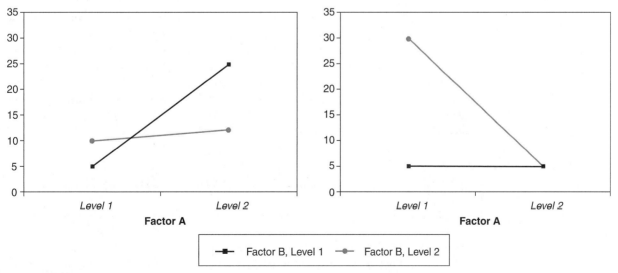

**Figure 10-7**

*Graphic Representations of Interactions and Main Effects*

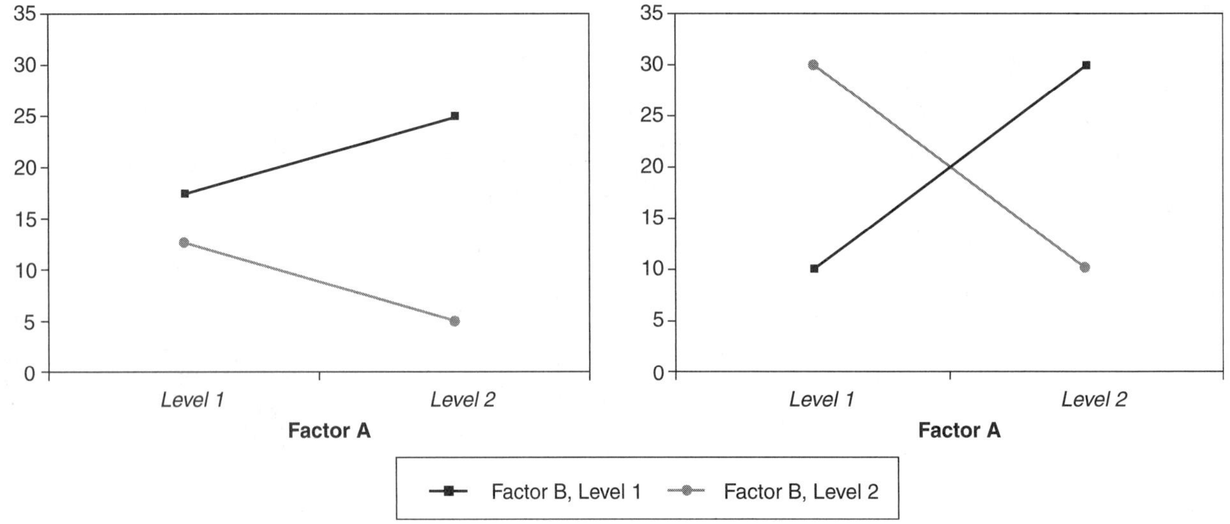

**Figure 10-8**
*Graphic Representations of Cell Means When No Main Effects Are Present*

gender) and an independent variable (gender of the confederate). Care should be taken in interpreting the results because gender was not manipulated.

# 10-5 ANOVA for Two-Factor Experiments

**two-factor ANOVA** Analysis of variance for a two-factor design.

Performing a **two-factor ANOVA** (analysis of variance) for a factorial design is just an extension of the single-factor analysis of variance (which is often called a one-way ANOVA). The major differences are the result of partitioning the variances more than one way. Thus, instead of calculating one $F$ statistic, you calculate an $F$ for each source of hypothesized variance. That means that there is an $F$ statistic to calculate for each main effect and interaction in the design.

As with the one-way ANOVA, calculation of the $F$ statistics for a two-factor design is best done by starting at the end. First, construct the analysis of variance summary table, leaving blank all the terms that must be calculated. This process is a way of defining the problem that will help you keep all the various steps and their results organized. Next, be sure to organize the data in a clear way. After you complete these two steps, the ANOVA is merely the process of applying statistical formulas to the data to fill in the ANOVA summary table. This plan of action is the same for all types of experimental designs. However, each design has its own particular partitioning of the variance and formula for obtaining the statistics. The remainder of this chapter will describe the between subjects two-factor design. Chapter 11, "Repeated Measures and Factorial Experiments," will describe the analysis when one or both of the factors is a repeated measures manipulation.

# 10-6 Between Subjects Two-Factor Designs

Recall that in a one-factor design *between subjects* means that each subject in the experiment received only one treatment and that the effects of the treatments are determined by comparing the means between groups of different subjects. The same principle holds true in factorial designs, except that each subject receives a different combination of treatments. That means there are different subjects in each of the cells of the design. The statistical comparisons to determine the effects of the

| TABLE 10-1 | Analysis of Variance Summary Table for a Two-Factor Between Group Design |
|---|---|

| Source | Sums of Squares | Degrees of Freedom | Mean Square | F |
|---|---|---|---|---|
| Main Effects | | | | |
| Factor A | $SS_A$ | $df_A$ | $MS_A$ | $F_A$ |
| Factor B | $SS_B$ | $df_B$ | $MS_B$ | $F_B$ |
| Interaction | | | | |
| A × B | $SS_{AB}$ | $df_{AB}$ | $MS_{AB}$ | $F_{AB}$ |
| Within Cells | $SS_W$ | $df_W$ | $MS_W$ | |

independent variables are still made between means based on different subjects. The partitioning of the variance for this design was illustrated in Figure 10-3.

To construct an analysis of variance summary table for a factorial experiment, you begin just as you would construct a one-way ANOVA summary table. You define the columns of the table in the same way, as shown in Table 10-1. Recall that the organization of the ANOVA summary table makes it easy to calculate the *F* statistics after the first three columns are completed because the mean squares (*MS*, fourth column) are calculated by dividing the sums of squares (*SS*, second column) by the degrees of freedom (*df*, third column).

When you are constructing the ANOVA summary table for a factorial experiment, however, the rows of the table representing the sources contain more sources than were present in the one-way ANOVA. Each one of the sources of variance has its own row. It is typical to present the main effects first and follow those by the interaction between factors. Last, you list the residual variance (the error variance, within cell variance) and total variance. (Note that some computer statistics programs present subtotals for the variances as well as the individual sources listed in Table 10-1. Their output contains rows of results for all between treatments variances, for the combined main effects, and for the combined interactions. Thus, a table with three sources of variance may have six rows of numbers representing those three sources. I often think of this as computer redundancy. Programs give the same results in many different ways because different users want to see different things. This means that you have to look at a lot more output to get the few numbers that are meaningful to you. Having so many repetitive numbers can be confusing, but you just have to look for the sources you have designed and ignore the rest.)

Notice that in Table 10-1, the next-to-last row has been labeled as the Within Cells source of variance. This is also called the *residual variance* or *error variance*. This source of variance will serve as the denominator for the *F* ratios for both main effects and for the interaction in a between groups factorial design. Remember that the purpose of an ANOVA is to evaluate the effects of a treatment against the normal variation of the behavior. To estimate that normal variation, the amount of variability among subjects in each of the treatment combinations (cells of the design) is estimated and pooled together. The *F* ratio represents the difference between groups of subjects based on the treatments compared to the baseline variation within the cells.

As with the one-way ANOVA, the last row of the table is put on as a check. The sums of squares and degrees of freedom for all the sources, when added together, should equal the totals that have been calculated independently.

It is very important to organize the data from research according to the design. A general data organization is shown in Table 10-2. The matrix form keeps information about each treatment level for both factors very clear.

Analysis of the data will be easier if you calculate a totals summary table from the raw data. The generalized form for such a table is shown in Table 10-3. The table represents the subtotals of data from a two-factor design in which one factor is called

| TABLE 10-2 | Data Matrix for a Two-Factor Between Groups Design |
|---|---|

| | | Factor B | | |
|---|---|---|---|---|
| **Factor A** | **Level 1** | **Level 2** | . . . | **Level $b$** |
| Level 1 | $X_{111}$ | $X_{121}$ | . . . | $X_{1b1}$ |
| | $X_{112}$ | $X_{122}$ | . . . | $X_{1b2}$ |
| | $X_{113}$ | $X_{123}$ | . . . | $X_{1b3}$ |
| | . | . | . . . | . |
| | . | . | . . . | . |
| | | . | . . . | |
| | $X_{11n}$ | $X_{12n}$ | . . . | $X_{1bn}$ |
| Level 2 | $X_{211}$ | $X_{221}$ | . . . | $X_{2b1}$ |
| | $X_{212}$ | $X_{222}$ | . . . | $X_{2b2}$ |
| | $X_{213}$ | $X_{223}$ | . . . | $X_{2b3}$ |
| | . | . | . . . | . |
| | . | . | . . . | . |
| | . | | . . . | . |
| | $X_{21n}$ | $X_{22n}$ | . . . | $X_{2bn}$ |
| . | . | . | | . |
| . | . | . | | . |
| . | . | . | | . |
| Level $a$ | $X_{a11}$ | $X_{a21}$ | . . . | $X_{ab1}$ |
| | $X_{a12}$ | $X_{a22}$ | . . . | $X_{ab2}$ |
| | $X_{a12}$ | $X_{a23}$ | . . . | $X_{ab3}$ |
| | . | . | . . . | . |
| | . | . | . . . | . |
| | . | . | . . . | . |
| | $X_{a1n}$ | $X_{a2n}$ | . . . | $X_{abn}$ |

| TABLE 10-3 | AB Totals Table for Use in Calculating Two-Factor ANOVA |
|---|---|

| | | Factor B | | | |
|---|---|---|---|---|---|
| **Factor A** | **Level 1** | **Level 2** | . . . | **Level $b$** | |
| Level 1 | $AB_{11}$ | $AB_{12}$ | . . . | $AB_{1b}$ | $A_1$ |
| Level 2 | $AB_{21}$ | $AB_{22}$ | . . . | $AB_{2b}$ | $A_2$ |
| . | . | . | | . | . |
| . | . | . | | . | . |
| . | . | . | | . | . |
| Level $a$ | $AB_{a1}$ | $AB_{a2}$ | . . . | $AB_{ab}$ | $A_a$ |
| | $B_1$ | $B_2$ | | $B_b$ | T |

**marginal totals** Totals in the margins of the table.

**cell totals** The totals for all the data for all subjects who received the same combination of treatments.

A and the other is called B. The number of levels of each factor is represented by the lowercase letter of the factor name. So, there are $a$ levels of Factor A and $b$ levels of Factor B. These same letters with subscripts represent the total for a particular level of that factor. For example, $A_2$ is the total of all the scores obtained by subjects who received the second treatment level of Factor A. Likewise, the totals for each Factor B condition are shown on the bottom row of the table and are represented by a subscripted B (e.g., $B_1$). These totals are sometimes referred to as **marginal totals** because they are in the margins of the table. Within the boxes are the **cell totals**; they are the totals for all the data for all subjects who received the same combination of treatments. Cell totals are represented by both letters with a double subscript. Thus, $AB_{34}$ would represent the total for the third level of A when combined with

| TABLE 10-4 | Computational Form of Analysis of Variance Summary Table for a Two-Factor Between Groups Design |
|---|---|

| Source | Sum of squares (see formula below) | Degrees of freedom | Mean square | F |
|---|---|---|---|---|
| Main Effect | | | | |
| A | $SS_A$ | $a - 1$ | $SS_A/df_A$ | $MS_A/MS_W$ |
| B | $SS_B$ | $b - 1$ | $SS_B/df_B$ | $MS_B/MS_W$ |
| Interactions | | | | |
| A × B | $SS_{AB}$ | $(a - 1)(b - 1)$ | $SS_{AB}/df_{AB}$ | $MS_{AB}/MS_W$ |
| Within cells | $SS_W$ | $ab(n - 1)$ | $SS_W/df_W$ | |
| Total | $SS_T$ | $N-1$ | | |

**Computational formula for sum of squares**

$$SS_A = \frac{\sum_{i=1}^{a} A_i^2}{bn} - \frac{T^2}{N}$$

$$SS_B = \frac{\sum_{j=1}^{b} B_j^2}{an} - \frac{T^2}{N}$$

$$SS_{AB} = \frac{\sum_{i=1}^{a}\sum_{j=1}^{b} AB_{ij}^2}{n} - \frac{\sum_{i=1}^{a} A_i^2}{bn} - \frac{\sum_{j=1}^{b} B_j^2}{an} + \frac{T^2}{N}$$

$$SS_W = \sum_{i=1}^{a}\sum_{j=1}^{b}\sum_{k=1}^{n} X_{ijk}^2 - \frac{\sum_{i=1}^{a}\sum_{j=1}^{b} AB_{ij}^2}{n}$$

the fourth level of Factor B. Of course, the cell totals can be added across to produce the row totals (Factor A totals), and they can be added down to produce the column totals (Factor B totals). The sums of the column totals equal the grand total (represented by T). This is also true of the row totals. Their sum is equal to the grand total.

It is now common practice to do most statistics by computer. However, if you use a calculator for this analysis (such as on an exam), you can speed up the process by using the statistical functions of your calculator on the data in each cell of the design. In this case, you should write down all the statistics produced automatically by the calculator in an organized summary table similar to the totals table. Using this organization and the statistical functions of the calculator will increase both the accuracy and the speed of the analysis.

After you have organized and summarized the data, then it is time to apply the formula for the ANOVA. The computational formulas for the two-factor between groups ANOVA are shown in Table 10-4 in the context of the ANOVA summary table. These calculations are similar to those completed for the one-way ANOVA. The major difference is that in the two-factor design it is essential to use subscripts and keep the three different sources of between groups variance straight. Notice that the formula for the AB interaction sums of squares has four terms. The reason is that

| TABLE 10-5 | Data from Sample Experiment on the Effects of Hunger and Flavor on Eating Behavior |
|---|---|

| | Flavor | |
|---|---|---|
| **Hunger** | **Normal** | **Bad** |
| None | 10 | 1 |
| | 0 | 2 |
| | 10 | 3 |
| | 8 | 6 |
| | 3 | 1 |
| | 14 | 4 |
| | 0 | 0 |
| | 11 | 2 |
| | 11 | 0 |
| | 13 | 1 |
| High | 22 | 5 |
| | 30 | 1 |
| | 23 | 6 |
| | 28 | 12 |
| | 33 | 11 |
| | 21 | 2 |
| | 20 | 9 |
| | 29 | 3 |
| | 23 | 0 |
| | 21 | 11 |

the interaction variance is estimated by comparing the cell means to the grand mean and subtracting the variance for the two main effects.

The data from the sample experiment on the effects of hunger and flavor on eating behavior have been organized for the two-factor ANOVA and are shown in Table 10-5. Figure 10-9 provides a step-by-step example of calculating the sums of squares using this data. Table 10-6 shows the ANOVA summary table based on these data. The obtained $F$ statistics are evaluated for statistical significance by comparing them to the critical $F$ for the specified degrees of freedom and alpha level. Because this is a $2 \times 2$ design, all three obtained $F$s have the same degrees of freedom because $a - 1 = b - 1 = (a - 1)(b - 1)$. When the factors have different levels, you need to use different critical $F$ statistics for each different set of degrees of freedom. As you can see in the table, both the main effects of hunger and flavor are statistically significant, as is their interaction. The interaction is shown in Figure 10-10.

# 10-7 Beyond Two Factors

Although the preceding sections probably seem complex enough to you, two-factor designs are the simplest of the factorial designs. Statistically, you can compute an analysis of variance for just about any design as long as you have enough data. (If not, you "run out of degrees of freedom.") However, practically speaking, it is seldom wise to move beyond the two-factor experiment because there is a great possibility of being unable to comprehend and explain what all the interactions mean. Remember, the purpose of design and statistics is to help you understand behavior. A four-factor experiment has four main effects (A, B, C, and D), six two-way interactions (A × B, A × C, A × D, B × C, B × D, and C × D), three three-way interactions (A × B × C, A × B × D, and B × C × D), and one four-way interaction (A × B × C × D). That is a total of 14 $F$ ratios to interpret. It is better to conceptualize carefully and design manageable experiments than to try to include all possible factors.

a)

**Step 1.    Write the formulas.**

$$SS_A = \frac{\sum_{i=1}^{a} A_i^2}{bn} - \frac{T^2}{N} \qquad SS_B = \frac{\sum_{j=1}^{b} B_j^2}{an} - \frac{T^2}{N}$$

$$SS_{AB} = \frac{\sum_{i=1}^{a}\sum_{j=1}^{b} AB_{ij}^2}{n} - \frac{\sum_{i=1}^{a} A_i^2}{bn} - \frac{\sum_{j=1}^{b} B_j^2}{an} - \frac{T^2}{N}$$

$$SS_W = \sum_{i=1}^{a}\sum_{j=1}^{b}\sum_{k=1}^{n} X_{ijk}^2 - \frac{\sum_{i=1}^{a}\sum_{j=1}^{b} AB_{ij}^2}{n} \qquad SS_T = \sum_{i=1}^{a}\sum_{j=1}^{b}\sum_{k=1}^{n} X_{ijk}^2 - \frac{T^2}{N}$$

**Step 2.    Determine the quantities that need to be calculated.**

They are:

| | |
|---|---|
| $A_1$ | $n$ |
| $A_2$ | $a$ |
| $B_1$ | $b$ |
| $B_2$ | $N$ |
| $AB_{11}$ | $T$ |
| $AB_{21}$ | $\sum_{i=1}^{a}\sum_{j=1}^{b}\sum_{k=1}^{n} X_{ijk}^2$ |
| $AB_{12}$ | |
| $AB_{22}$ | |

**Step 3.    Calculate the terms determined in Step 2. Use data in Table 10-5 to form summary tables as follows:**

Totals for table example experiment.
(Raw data presented in Table 10-5)

Flavor

| Hunger | Normal | Bad | |
|---|---|---|---|
| None | $AB_{11} = 80$ | $AB_{12} = 20$ | $A_1 = 100$ |
| High | $AB_{21} = 250$ | $AB_{22} = 60$ | $A_2 = 310$ |
| | $B_1 = 330$ | $B_2 = 80$ | $T = 410$ |

b)

Other useful cell statistics

Flavor

| Hunger | Normal | Bad | |
|---|---|---|---|
| None | $\sum_{k=1}^{k} X_{11}^2 = 880$ $\bar{X}_{11} = 8$ $S_{11} = 5.16$ | $\sum_{k=1}^{10} X_{12}^2 = 72$ $\bar{X}_{12} = 2$ $S_{12} = 1.89$ | $\sum_{j=1}^{2}\sum_{k=1}^{10} X^2 = 952$ |
| High | $\sum_{k=1}^{10} X_{21}^2 = 6438$ $\bar{X}_{21} = 25$ $S_{21} = 4.57$ | $\sum_{k=1}^{10} X_{22}^2 = 542$ $\bar{X}_{22} = 6$ $S_{22} = 4.50$ | $\sum_{j=1}^{2}\sum_{k=1}^{10} X^2 = 6980$ |
| | $\sum_{i=1}^{2}\sum_{k=1}^{10} X^2 = 7318$ | $\sum_{i=1}^{2}\sum_{k=1}^{10} X^2 = 614$ | $\sum_{i=1}^{2}\sum_{j=1}^{2}\sum_{k=1}^{10} X_{ijk}^2 = 7932$ |

From the data presented in Table 10-5

$$a = 2 \qquad b = 2 \qquad n = 10 \qquad N = 40$$

**Figure 10-9**

*Step-by-Step Example for Calculating the Sums of Squares for a Two-Factor Experiment (Figure continued on next page)*

**Figure 10-9**
*Continued*

Step 4.    Substitute terms calculated in Step 3 into formula (Step 1) and calculate.

$$SS_{A \, (Hunger)} = \frac{\sum_{i=1}^{a} A_i^2}{bn} - \frac{T^2}{N} = \frac{100^2 + 310^2}{2(10)} - \frac{410^2}{40} = \frac{10000 + 96100}{20} - \frac{168100}{40} = \frac{106100}{20} - 4202.5 = 5305 - 4202.5 = 1102.5$$

$$SS_{B \, (Flavor)} = \frac{\sum_{j=1}^{b} B_j^2}{an} - \frac{T^2}{N} = \frac{330^2 + 80^2}{2(10)} - 4202.5 = \frac{108900 + 6400}{20} - 4202.5 = \frac{115300}{20} - 4202.5 = 5765 - 4202.5 = 1562.5$$

$$SS_{AB} = \frac{\sum_{i=1}^{a} \sum_{j=1}^{b} AB_{ij}^2}{n} - \frac{\sum_{i=1}^{a} A_i^2}{bn} - \frac{\sum_{j=1}^{b} B_j^2}{an} + \frac{T^2}{N}$$

(Note: The last three terms have been calculated above.)

$$= \frac{80^2 + 20^2 + 250^2 + 60^2}{10} - 5305 - 5765 + 4202.5 = \frac{6400 + 400 + 62500 + 3600}{10} - 5305 - 5765 + 4202.5 = \frac{72900}{10} - 5305 - 5765 + 4202.5 = 422.5$$

$$SS_{W} = \sum_{i=1}^{a} \sum_{j=1}^{b} \sum_{k=1}^{n} X_{ijk}^2 - \frac{\sum_{i=1}^{a} \sum_{j=1}^{b} AB_{ij}^2}{n} = 7932 - 7290 = 642 \text{ (Calculated for } SS_{AB}) \qquad SS_{T} = \sum_{i=1}^{a} \sum_{j=1}^{b} \sum_{k=1}^{n} X_{ijk}^2 - \frac{T^2}{N} = 7932 - 4202.5 = 3729.5$$

| TABLE 10-6 | Analysis of Variance Summary Table for the Hunger and Flavor Sample Experiment |
|---|---|

| Source | Sums of squares | Degrees of freedom | Mean square | F |
|---|---|---|---|---|
| Main effects | | | | |
| Hunger | 1102.5 | 1 | 1102.5 | 61.824* |
| Flavor | 1562.5 | 1 | 1562.5 | 87.619* |
| Interaction | | | | |
| Hunger X Flavor | 422.5 | 1 | 422.5 | 23.692* |
| Within cell | 642 | 36 | 17.833 | |
| Total | 3729.5 | 39 | | |

*$F_{critical}(1,36; \alpha = .05) = 4.11$
*$F_{critical}(1,36; \alpha = .01) = 7.35$

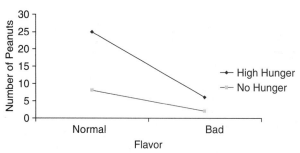

**Figure 10-10**
*The Effects of Hunger and Flavor on Eating Behavior*

# 10-8 Limitations of the Analysis Presented

This chapter has presented the factorial ANOVA in the most basic form. Many important considerations go into the analysis of variance. For example, the formulas used here assume that the factors are fixed and not random factors. This assumption is usually true for experiments in behavioral science but may not be true for other areas, such as quasiexperiments, meteorology, or economics.

All the formulas in this chapter are for use only when you have an equal number of observations in each cell of the design. That is, they are the equal *n* formulas. Often you have unequal *n* because of missing data. Perhaps participants dropped out of the study or failed to answer all the questions. There are many different approaches to solving the problem of unequal *n*. For you, the student researcher, usually the best way to solve the problem is to replace the data by running another participant.

Finally, there is an important assumption that the data are normally distributed. This is the same assumption needed for the *t* test and the one-way ANOVA. Most dependent variables in behavioral experiments are normally distributed. If, however, the descriptive statistics show that the data are not normally distributed, you should either attempt to transform the data statistically so that they approximate the normal distribution, or use some other inferential statistic. Typical transformations of data include using the log of the data, the square root, or the arcsine. As always, it's most important to understand why the data are the way they are. What caused the distribution of the data to be different than was expected?

All of these limitations can be overcome. Advanced research design and analysis books deal with these issues in detail. Most computer software also allows the researcher to specify alternate analysis methods, when appropriate. The computer program, however, will not know when the standard approach isn't appropriate. You have to know that by using your calculator or a computer. When you have complex designs or think that you may be facing some of the limitations presented here, talk with your research advisor. He or she is likely to direct you to his or her favorite advanced statistics book. That means you will be able to get help with concepts that are new to you because they will be familiar to your advisor.

# 10-9 APA Style: Graphs

Graphs are one type of figure used in the American Psychological Association Publication style (APA, 2001). The descriptive statistics for a factorial experiment, especially one with statistically significant interactions, may be best depicted with graphs. Although line graphs are usually used only to show relationships between two quantitative variables, they may be used to illustrate an interaction between two independent variables if the interpretation of the interaction is improved by seeing the slope of the

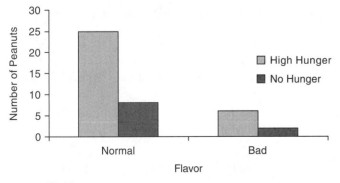

**Figure 10-11**

*The Effects of Hunger and Flavor on Eating Behavior*

lines in the graph. Figure 10-10 showed the results of the sample experiment as a line graph. The same results could be presented in bar graph form, as shown in Figure 10-11. You make the choice to use one type of graph or the other by considering which type best conveys the results to be interpreted. You can see from Figure 10-11 that the most peanuts were eaten, on average, in the normal flavor + high hunger condition and that the least were eaten on average in the bad flavor + low hunger condition. However, it is not as easy to see that the effect of flavor is weaker in the low hunger condition than it is in the high hunger condition. The bar graph displays exactly the same information as the line graph, but it is often not as easy to interpret.

## Summary

Factorial designs involve two or more causes of the same effect. In the same experiment, the effects of each single cause taken alone (main effects) and the effects of the causes acting together (interactions) can be studied. The two-factor design is designated using the form A × B, in which A is the number of levels of the first independent variable and B is the number of levels of the second independent variable. The product of A and B is the number of combinations of treatments to be studied. The treatment combinations are called the cells of the design.

An interaction is present when the effect of one independent variable is dependent on the level of the other independent variable. Line graphs can show the relationships of the means for each group of data in a factorial design. The Y-axis represents the dependent variable. The X-axis represents one of the independent variables. Different lines are used to represent the second independent variable. If the lines are parallel, then there is no interaction between the two independent variables. The steeper the slope of a line, the stronger is the effect it is representing.

The analysis of variance for a between groups two-factor design involves partitioning the variance into sources for each main effect, their interaction, and the residual variance. Calculating the sums of squares, degrees of freedom, and mean squares is similar to the one-way ANOVA with the addition of the interaction effect and its removal from the residual variance.

## References

American Psychological Association. (2001). *Publication manual of the American Psychological Association*. Washington, DC: Author.

## Exercises for Application

For each of the next two problems, use the stepwise approach of analysis:

a. Determine the type of statistical analysis that is appropriate for the research design presented.

b. State the null hypothesis (or hypotheses) to be tested.

c. Choose the correct inferential and descriptive statistics to test the hypothesis (or hypotheses).

d. Use the right statistical formula to calculate the descriptive and inferential statistics.

e. Determine the statistical significance of the appropriate inferential statistic.

f. Draw a statistical conclusion about the null hypothesis (or hypotheses).

g. State the probability of a Type I error for the inferential statistic you performed.

h. Graph the significant effects.

i. Perform multiple comparisons tests, where appropriate.

j. State the conclusion of the analysis (what it all means) in non-jargon terms.

Problem I

A researcher wanted to find out whether the effect of arousal on an aggressive response was mediated by the relationship of the participant to the presumed instigator of the arousal. To test this hypothesis, the researcher randomly assigned children visiting Santa Claus to one of four conditions (2 arousal × 2 relationship). Arousal was manipulated by either (a) requiring the child to wait 2 minutes before receiving the obligatory candy cane (low arousal) or (b) having the candy cane taken back from the child after the 2-minute wait (high arousal). The relationship of the participant to the instigator of the arousal was manipulated by having either (a) Santa give or take back the candy cane (close relationship) or (b) Santa's elf give or take back the candy cane (remote relationship). A photographer videotaped each child's responses, which were later coded by trained raters for aggressiveness. The following scores were obtained. (The higher the score, the greater the aggression.)

| Santa | | Elf | |
|---|---|---|---|
| Arousal | | Arousal | |
| Low | High | Low | High |
| 4 | 9 | 6 | 1 |
| 5 | 7 | 6 | 3 |
| 3 | 9 | 5 | 2 |
| 4 | 8 | 7 | 2 |
| 4 | 7 | 6 | 1 |

Problem II

Lauren's study on the effects of physical attractiveness on perceptions of future success was described in Chapter 9, "Repeated Measures One-Factor Designs." Because of the problems of studying two factors with a repeated measures design, Lauren used a factorial between groups design. The following data are not from Lauren's study because she really had three factors (attractiveness of the target person, gender of the target person, and gender of the participant). She also had many measures of perception of future success. These data, however, do produce the same result as Lauren did for one of her hypotheses. Her hypothesis was that physical attractiveness would be positively related to perceptions of future success for female job applicants but that physical attractiveness would have no effect on the perceptions of future success for male job applicants.

| | | Attractiveness | | |
|---|---|---|---|---|
| | | High | Moderate | Low |
| Target Gender | Male | 8 | 8 | 6 |
| | | 6 | 7 | 5 |
| | | 7 | 7 | 7 |
| | | 6 | 6 | 5 |
| | | 5 | 8 | 8 |
| | Female | 9 | 5 | 7 |
| | | 8 | 8 | 4 |
| | | 8 | 7 | 5 |
| | | 7 | 6 | 5 |
| | | 9 | 6 | 6 |

## Practice Quiz

*Note:* You can find the correct answers to these questions by taking the quiz and then submitting your answers in the Online Edition. The program will automatically score your submission. If you miss a question, the program will provide the correct answer, a rationale for the answer, and the section number in the chapter where the topic is discussed.

1. There is an interaction when the effect of one independent variable

    a. is statistically significant at alpha = .05.
    b. depends on the level of the other factor.
    c. occurs for three or more levels of that factor.
    d. is attributed to the error variance.

2. How many cells are there in a 3 × 3 factorial design?

    a. 6
    b. 9

    c. 12
    d. 4

3. In a between groups factorial design, the denominator of the *F* ratio is the

    a. between subjects variance.
    b. Factor A variance.
    c. Factor B variance.
    d. within subjects variance.

4. When there is no interaction between two factors, the graph of the interaction would be

    a. a scatter plot.
    b. two crossed lines.
    c. parallel lines.
    d. made of lines with different slopes.

5. How many *F* ratios must be interpreted in a two-factor design?

   a. 1
   b. 2
   c. 3
   d. 4

6. All groups are made equivalent (on average) in a between groups factorial design by

   a. random assignment to condition.
   b. repeated measures on all treatments.
   c. statistical equivalence through covariance analysis.
   d. using *z*-scores in the analysis.

7. What are the degrees of freedom for the interaction in a $3 \times 2$ factorial design?

   a. 1
   b. 2
   c. 4
   d. 6

8. Sometimes a cover story is used in an experiment in order to

   a. increase the ethical credibility.
   b. make sure that both independent variables are present.
   c. reduce demand characteristics.
   d. increase the sample size.

9. In a study of the effects of delay and type of interference on memory, which of the following is a main effect null hypothesis?

   a. The longer the delay, the worse the memory.
   b. Proactive interference has a greater effect than retroactive interference.
   c. The effect of delay depends on the type of interference.
   d. There is no difference in memory due to delay.

10. When is a line graph preferred to a bar graph using APA style?

   a. When there are more than six means to compare
   b. When the interaction is easier to interpret looking at lines
   c. When the graph will be presented in black and white only

   d. When there are no significant interactions in the data

11. In a factorial between groups design, the between groups variance is partitioned into _____ sources.

   a. two
   b. three
   c. four
   d. no

12. The main reason to do a factorial experiment is to

   a. efficiently test two main effects.
   b. get twice as much information from one experiment.
   c. rule out the interaction between two main effects.
   d. test for the interaction of two independent variables.

13. The problem of representing three variables on a two-dimensional surface is usually solved in graphing by using different lines to represent

   a. one of the independent variables.
   b. one of the dependent variables.
   c. each cell mean for the interaction.
   d. the main effects.

14. When there are no main effects, then

   a. there can be no interaction effect.
   b. a graph of the cell means shows two parallel lines.
   c. there may be an interaction shown by a graph with lines that form an X.
   d. there is always an interaction.

15. In a totals summary table, the term $AB_{23}$ refers to

   a. the total of all scores summed across the first two levels of A and the first three levels of B.
   b. the interaction of A with B at levels two and three.
   c. the total of all the scores in the second A level and third B level treatment condition.
   d. the difference of $AB_{46}$ and $AB_{23}$.

16. ANOVA is appropriate only if

   a. the data are normally distributed.
   b. there are more than two groups.
   c. the independent variable is measured on at least an ordinal scale.
   d. a *t* test won't work.

# Repeated Measures and Factorial Experiments

## Chapter Outline

## Key Terms

mixed design
multiple treatment interference

# Learning Objectives

- Be able to avoid the problems associated with multiple treatment interference.
- Partition the variance for a repeated measures design and for a mixed factorial design.

- Calculate and interpret the analysis of variance for a repeated measures design and a mixed factorial design.
- Calculate and interpret the multiple comparisons for significant interactions in a factorial design.

## Key Idea

Repeated measures and mixed factorial experiments are used when two or more independent variables are hypothesized to interact together to cause the effect and at least one of them is a within subjects variable.

# 11-1 Within Subjects Factorial Designs

Sometimes it is desirable to use each participant in an experiment as his or her own control, even in a two-factor design. Such a design is called a *within subjects factorial design*. However, all the cautions against the effects of repeated testing that were described with the one-factor repeated measures design also apply in the two-factor case. In particular, these designs are very liable to testing, history, and maturation effects. In addition, repeated measures factorial designs are liable to a threat to validity called **multiple treatment interference**. In the simplest case, each subject in the repeated measures design would participate in four different treatment combinations. There is a great chance that the effects of earlier treatments will carry over and have an effect in addition to the later treatments. That is, they will interfere with future treatments. This is called a *carryover effect*.

**multiple treatment interference** A threat to validity that occurs in repeated measures factorial designs when carryover effects of early treatments interfere with later treatments.

### 11-1a Multiple Treatment Interference

In many mystery novels, the killer is shown as establishing an alibi for poisoning his victim by eating the poisoned food with the victim. Both the culprit and the victim get sick, but the victim dies and the culprit recovers. How can this be? The answer lies in an understanding of a particular multiple treatment interference. Some poisons, when taken in multiple doses, lead to a tolerance. Thus, after multiple treatments of the small doses, a larger dose is not lethal. The previous treatments interfered with the otherwise lethal dose that was taken with the victim.

Although multiple treatment interference may make for a good mystery plot, it is not desirable in an experiment. Suppose you wanted to learn the effects of music tempo and volume on emotional response. Using the repeated measures approach would seem desirable because emotional response to music is very individual—it would seem good to use each participant as his or her own control. However, there is bound to be a carryover effect of the first treatment, say loud music with a fast tempo, which will influence the effects of the later treatments. If the participant were irritated or aroused by the loud music, the second treatment of soft music would have to overcome the carryover effect from the first treatment. One approach to try to overcome this problem, as well as the problems of maturation and testing, is to counterbalance the order of treatment combinations across participants. Counterbalancing would mean that, not only do all participants get all treatments, but that all orders of treatments are given to different participants. With four combinations of treatments, there are 4! orders. To determine whether there has been multiple treatment interference, maturation, or testing effects, you need to analyze the data also for order of presentation. This means that you need a sufficient number of individuals who participate in each order to statistically estimate the effects of order.

## 11-1b Demand Characteristics

Providing the same participant with all treatment combinations can increase the demand characteristics of an experiment. A frequently used attribution research paradigm is one in which the independent variable is manipulated by changing a few words in a written description (often called a *scenario*). Suppose that the in-group/out-group status of an alleged criminal is manipulated in the scenario. If the same participants read the same accounts of the crime, with the only difference being in account A the defendant is described as a member of their own in-group and in account B he is described as a member of the out-group, then the participants are almost certain to guess the hypothesis. When they understand that the researcher is studying their attributional prejudices based on the alleged criminal's characteristics, they may attempt to answer the "right way," or they may not. Either way, the participants' behavior has been influenced by their knowledge of the experiment. This example illustrates why repeated measures designs are used less often than between subjects designs.

If the repeated measures processes described here seem complicated to you, they are! The simple solution may seem to be to use a between groups design. Nevertheless, some behaviors are typically studied with a repeated measures approach. These behaviors are characterized by brevity of response and a lack of carryover effects. These behaviors also are resistant to demand characteristics (participants knowing the manipulations are not likely to affect the outcome). The sample experiment in Taking a Closer Look 11-1 includes just such a behavior. The perception of a visual illusion is a product of the visual stimuli presented. There is sufficient resting

---

**Taking a Closer Look 11-1** — *Repeated Measures Two-Factor Sample Experiment*

In this experiment, the researcher was testing the effects of angle of orientation, either oblique or perpendicular (see below), and the size of the stimuli (6, 12, and 18 cm) on subjective contour. A repeated measures approach was used. Each participant served as his or her own control. Participants were first dark-adapted by spending 10 minutes in a darkened room. Then each of the experimental stimuli was presented to the participant. The order of presentation was randomized among the eight experimental participants. Each stimulus was presented for exactly 1 minute at a distance of 2 meters from the participant's focal plane. There was a 2-minute resting period between each stimulus presentation. Participants were to press a button for as long as they perceived the subjective contour produced by the illusion. The total amount of time, in seconds, that the illusion persisted was measured for each of the stimuli.

Perpendicular

Oblique

time between trials to reduce a maturation effect and to reduce multiple treatment interferences. Knowledge of the independent variables does not alert participants to the hypotheses. Participants who see a square and a diamond are not likely to base their behavior on their own expectations of what the experimenter wants. Finally, although not described in the sample experiment, research paradigms that use repeated measures often have several blocks of trials so that the order of presentation is counterbalanced within participants. For example, an individual would participate in a block of trials with all combinations of the treatments, and then the same participant would participate in a second block of trials with a different order. The number of blocks of trials varies from experiment to experiment, but seems mostly determined by participant fatigue. Research should not have so many repeated trials that participants are made overly tired.

# 11-2 Partitioning the Variance in a Repeated Measures Factorial Design

In a repeated measures design, each subject acts as his or her own baseline. That means, for the analysis of variance, that you partition the variance of the data in a totally different way than you do for the two-factor between groups design. As shown in Figure 11-1, the total variance can still be partitioned into the between subjects variances and the within subjects variances. However, in a repeated measures factorial design, the between subjects variance answers no questions of importance. All you find out from the between subjects variance is about individual differences. Although individual differences are important, they are not relevant for the three hypotheses being tested in a repeated measures two-factor design. Because each subject acts as his or her own baseline, all the treatment variance (due to the manipulated factors) and all the error variance needed to test the hypotheses are within subjects variance.

The within subjects variance is further partitioned into the treatment effects and the interaction effects of those treatments within the subjects. Thus, as shown in Figure 11-1, there are six sources of variance within subjects:

| | |
|---|---|
| Factor A | Factor A × Subjects |
| Factor B | Factor B × Subjects |
| A × B interaction | A × B × Subjects |

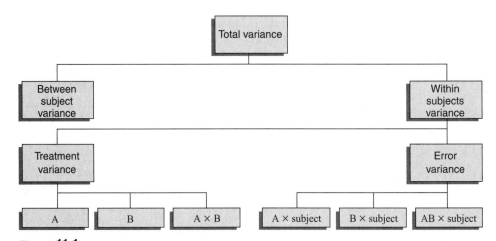

**Figure 11-1**

*Partitioning the Variance for a Two-Factor Repeated Measures Experiment*

| TABLE 11-1 | Analysis of Variance Summary Table for a Repeated Measures Two-Factor Design |
| --- | --- |

| Source | Sums of Squares | Degrees of Freedom | Mean Square | F |
| --- | --- | --- | --- | --- |
| Between subjects | $SS_P$ | $df_P$ | | |
| Within subjects | | | | |
|    Factor A | $SS_A$ | $df_A$ | $MS_A$ | $F_A$ |
|    Factor A $\times$ Subject | $SS_{AP}$ | $df_{AP}$ | $MS_{AP}$ | |
|    Factor B | $SS_B$ | $df_B$ | $MS_B$ | $F_B$ |
|    Factor B $\times$ Subject | $SS_{BP}$ | $df_{BP}$ | $MS_{BP}$ | |
|    A $\times$ B Interaction | $SS_{AB}$ | $df_{AB}$ | $MS_{AB}$ | $F_{AB}$ |
|    A $\times$ B Subject | $SS_{ABP}$ | $df_{ABP}$ | $MS_{ABP}$ | |
| Total | $SS_T$ | $df_T$ | | |

# 11-3 Repeated Measures Factorial ANOVA Summary Table

Each source of variance must be included in the analysis of variance summary table. As you can see in Table 11-1, there are eight sources of variance: the between subjects, total, and the six variance sources within the subjects. The columns of the table are the same as for the between groups ANOVA. It is convenient to organize the rows as they are shown in Table 11-1, with each main effect and the interaction followed by its own error term, because this is the denominator for the particular $F$ ratio. The use of different error terms is the biggest difference between the within groups ANOVAs and the between groups ANOVA (in which all $F$ ratios were calculated with the same error term in the denominator). It requires the use of more than one critical $F$ to test each $F$ ratio because they will usually have different degrees of freedom associated with their denominators.

# 11-4 Computing the Repeated Measures Factorial ANOVA

Computing the repeated measures two-factor ANOVA is more complicated than the between groups example, but the logic to do so is the same. First, construct an ANOVA summary table, leaving blank the spaces that need to be calculated. Second, organize the data into a form that will make calculations both quicker and more accurate. The sample analysis illustrates the application of summary totals table for the repeated measures case. Third, use the calculational formula given in Table 11-2 to calculate the sums of squares, degrees of freedom, mean squares, and $F$ ratios. Fourth, compare the obtained $F$ ratios to the critical $F$ ratios obtained from the $F$ tables. Lastly, graph and interpret the means of those effects that were statistically significant.

The data from the sample experiment on the effects of angle of orientation and size of stimulus on persistence of subjective contours is shown in Table 11-3. Notice that some summary statistics appear at the bottom of the table. It is a good practice to calculate these statistics routinely and think about what they mean. Thinking about what the numbers mean as you do the analysis will help you both discover calculational errors and interpret the results after you complete the analysis. The cell means presented at the bottom of the table tell you that there was variation among the treatments in the persistence of a subjective contour ranging from 15 to 24 seconds. The standard deviations for each cell show you that there was also a range in

| TABLE 11-2 | Computational Form of Analysis of Variance Summary Table for a Two-Factor Repeated Measures Design |
|---|---|

| Source | Sums of squares (see formula below) | Degrees of freedom | Mean square | F |
|---|---|---|---|---|
| Between subjects | $SS_P$ | $p - 1$ | | |
| Within subjects | | | | |
|   Factor A | $SS_A$ | $a - 1$ | $\dfrac{SS_A}{df_A}$ | $\dfrac{MS_A}{MS_{A \times Subj.}}$ |
|   Factor A × subject | $SS_{A \times Subj.}$ | $(a - 1)(p - 1)$ | $\dfrac{SS_{A \times Subj.}}{df_{A \times subj.}}$ | |
|   Factor B | $SS_B$ | $b - 1$ | $\dfrac{SS_B}{df_B}$ | $\dfrac{MS_B}{MS_{B \times Subj.}}$ |
|   Factor B × subject | $SS_{B \times Subj.}$ | $(b - 1)(p - 1)$ | $\dfrac{SS_{B \times Subj.}}{df_{B \times subj.}}$ | |
|   A × B interaction | $SS_{AB}$ | $(a - 1)(b - 1)$ | $\dfrac{SS_{AB}}{df_{AB}}$ | $\dfrac{MS_{AB}}{MS_{AB \times Subj.}}$ |
|   A × B × subject | $SS_{AB \times Subj.}$ | $(a - 1)(b - 1)(p - 1)$ | $\dfrac{SS_{AB \times Subj.}}{df_{AB \times subj.}}$ | |
| Total | $SS_T$ | $N - 1$ | | |

### Computational formula for sum of squares

$$SS_P = \frac{\sum\limits_{k=1}^{p} P_k^2}{ab} - \frac{T^2}{N}$$

$$SS_A = \frac{\sum\limits_{i=1}^{a} A_i^2}{bp} - \frac{T^2}{N}$$

$$SS_{A \times Subj.} = \frac{\sum\limits_{k=1}^{p} \sum\limits_{i=1}^{a} AP_{ik}^2}{b} - \frac{\sum\limits_{i=1}^{a} A_i^2}{bp} - \frac{\sum\limits_{k=1}^{p} P_k^2}{ab} + \frac{T^2}{N}$$

$$SS_B = \frac{\sum\limits_{j=1}^{b} B_j^2}{ap} - \frac{T^2}{N}$$

$$SS_{B \times Subj.} = \frac{\sum\limits_{k=1}^{p} \sum\limits_{j=1}^{b} BP_{jk}^2}{a} - \frac{\sum\limits_{j=1}^{b} B_j^2}{ap} - \frac{\sum\limits_{k=1}^{p} P_k^2}{ab} + \frac{T^2}{N}$$

$$SS_{AB} = \frac{\sum\limits_{j=1}^{b} \sum\limits_{i=1}^{a} AB_{ij}^2}{p} - \frac{\sum\limits_{i=1}^{a} A_i^2}{bp} - \frac{\sum\limits_{j=1}^{b} B_j^2}{ap} + \frac{T^2}{N}$$

$$SS_{AB \times Subj.} = \sum\limits_{k=1}^{p} \sum\limits_{j=1}^{b} \sum\limits_{i=1}^{a} X_{ijk}^2 + \frac{\sum\limits_{i=1}^{a} A_i^2}{bp} + \frac{\sum\limits_{j=1}^{b} B_j^2}{ap} + \frac{\sum\limits_{k=1}^{p} P_k^2}{ab}$$

$$\frac{\sum\limits_{k=1}^{p} \sum\limits_{i=1}^{a} AP_{ik}^2}{b} - \frac{\sum\limits_{k=1}^{p} \sum\limits_{j=1}^{b} BP_{jk}^2}{a} - \frac{\sum\limits_{j=1}^{b} \sum\limits_{i=1}^{a} AB_{ij}^2}{p} - \frac{T^2}{N}$$

$$SS_T = \sum\limits_{k=1}^{p} \sum\limits_{j=1}^{b} \sum\limits_{i=1}^{b} X_{ijk}^2 - \frac{T^2}{N}$$

Where:

$a$ = Number of levels of Factor A.

$b$ = Number of levels of Factor B.

$p$ = Number of persons (or subjects).

$A_i$ = Total of scores for the ith level of Factor A.

$B_j$ = Total of scores for the jth level of Factor B.

$P_k$ = Total of scores for person k.

$AB_{ij}$ = Total of scores for the ij interaction cell.

$AP_{ik}$ = Total of scores for the person k over level i of Factor A.

$BP_{jk}$ = Total of scores for person k over level j of Factors B.

$T$ = Total of all scores.

$$\sum\limits_{k=1}^{p} \sum\limits_{j=1}^{b} \sum\limits_{i=1}^{a} X_{ijk}^2 = \text{Sum of all squared scores.}$$

| TABLE 11-3 | Data from the Sample Experiment on the Effects of Angle of Orientation and Stimulus Size on Persistence in a Subjective Contour | | | | | |
|---|---|---|---|---|---|---|
| | **Perpendicular size** | | | **Oblique size** | | |
| **Subj.** | **6 cm** | **12 cm** | **18 cm** | **6 cm** | **12 cm** | **18 cm** |
| 1 | 10 | 21 | 14 | 15 | 17 | 17 |
| 2 | 20 | 30 | 21 | 23 | 22 | 18 |
| 3 | 15 | 21 | 20 | 18 | 19 | 20 |
| 4 | 17 | 25 | 20 | 20 | 19 | 23 |
| 5 | 19 | 25 | 17 | 19 | 20 | 21 |
| 6 | 13 | 23 | 18 | 22 | 20 | 20 |
| 7 | 11 | 24 | 18 | 24 | 18 | 24 |
| 8 | 15 | 23 | 16 | 19 | 17 | 17 |
| $\Sigma X$ | 120 | 192 | 144 | 160 | 152 | 160 |
| $\Sigma X^2$ | 1890 | 4666 | 2630 | 3260 | 2908 | 3248 |
| $\bar{X}$ | 15 | 24 | 18 | 20 | 19 | 20 |
| $s$ | 3.59 | 2.89 | 2.33 | 2.93 | 1.69 | 2.62 |

$$\Sigma\Sigma\Sigma X^2 = 18602$$

the variability (1.69 to 3.59) but that none of the standard deviations is particularly large or small given the scale of measurement and the behavior being studied.

Figure 11-2 illustrates the process of calculating the sums of squares for the example, and Table 11-4 shows the completed ANOVA summary table.

The statistically significant interaction of angle of orientation and stimulus size is graphed in Figure 11-3. The main effect for size of stimulus was also statistically significant. If both a main effect and an interaction involving that main effect are significant, the main effect is interpreted in the context of the interaction. The reason is that, as you can see in the figure and by examining the means shown at the bottom of Table 11-3, stimulus size was not important for the oblique stimuli, but was for the perpendicular ones. Averaging the perpendicular and oblique trials for each of the three stimulus sizes shows the highest marginal mean for the 12 cm stimuli, but that number is totally due to the high persistence of the 12 cm perpendicular stimulus. Likewise, the lower marginal means of subjective contour persistence for stimuli of 6 cm and 18 cm result from the perpendicular stimuli only.

# 11-5 Mixed Designs

The third two-factor design to be covered in this chapter is the **mixed design**. In this design, there are repeated measures on one of the two factors, while the other factor is a between subjects factor. Before we go into the formula, consider a mundane example. Suppose you had a friend whose hobby is cooking. This friend decided to have a dinner party and invited many guests. When the guests arrived, they were asked to pick a slip of paper out of a hat. Half the slips read "Chinese," and the remaining half read "French." Those with the "Chinese" slips were served an eight-course Chinese meal. Those with the "French" slips were served an eight-course French meal. At the end of each course, each guest had to rate the food she or he was served. It seems your friend has serious aspirations to be a great chef and was taking a scientific approach. In this example, the type of meal, French or Chinese, was a between

**mixed design** A design in which there are repeated measures on one of the two factors, while the other factor is a between subjects factor.

Step 1.    Write the formula for the sums of squares.

(See Table 11-2.)

Step 2.    Determine the quantities that need to be calculated.

$$\sum_{k=1}^{p}\sum_{j=1}^{b}\sum_{i=1}^{a}X_{ijk}^{2} \qquad \sum_{j=1}^{b}B_{j}^{2} \qquad \sum_{k=1}^{p}\sum_{i=1}^{a}AP_{ik}^{2} \qquad \sum_{j=1}^{b}\sum_{i=1}^{a}AB_{ij}^{2} \qquad p$$

$$\sum_{i=1}^{a}A_{i}^{2} \qquad \sum_{k=1}^{p}P_{k}^{2} \qquad \sum_{k=1}^{p}\sum_{j=1}^{b}BP_{jk}^{2} \qquad a \qquad T$$

Step 3.    Make the totals tables needed to calculate the above quatities by summing the raw data across the conditions of the factors.

Subject by angle of orientation totals table (AP)

| Person | Angle of orientation | | Total |
|---|---|---|---|
| | Perpendicular | Oblique | |
| 1 | 45 | 49 | 94 |
| 2 | 71 | 63 | 134 |
| 3 | 56 | 57 | 113 |
| 4 | 62 | 62 | 124 |
| 5 | 61 | 60 | 121 |
| 6 | 54 | 62 | 116 |
| 7 | 53 | 66 | 119 |
| 8 | 54 | 53 | 107 |
| Total | 456 | 472 | 928 |

Subject by size totals table (BP)

| Person | Size | | | Total |
|---|---|---|---|---|
| | 6 cm. | 12 cm. | 18 cm. | |
| 1 | 25 | 38 | 31 | 94 |
| 2 | 43 | 52 | 39 | 134 |
| 3 | 33 | 40 | 40 | 113 |
| 4 | 37 | 44 | 43 | 124 |
| 5 | 38 | 45 | 38 | 121 |
| 6 | 35 | 43 | 38 | 116 |
| 7 | 35 | 42 | 42 | 119 |
| 8 | 34 | 40 | 33 | 107 |
| Total | 280 | 344 | 304 | 928 |

Angle of orientation by size total table (AB)

| Angle of orientation | Size | | | Total |
|---|---|---|---|---|
| | 6 cm. | 12 cm. | 18 cm. | |
| Perpendicular | 120 | 192 | 144 | 456 |
| oblique | 160 | 152 | 160 | 472 |
| Total | 280 | 344 | 304 | 928 |

Step 4.    Calculate the quantities listed in Step 2 using the totals obtained in Step 3. Calculate the $\Sigma\Sigma\Sigma X^2$ from the raw data.

$$T = 928$$

$$\sum_{k=1}^{p}\sum_{j=1}^{b}\sum_{i=1}^{a}X_{ijk}^{2} = 18602$$

$$\sum_{i=1}^{a}A_{i}^{2} = 456^{2} + 472^{2} = 207936 + 222784 = 430720$$

$$\sum_{j=1}^{b}B_{j}^{2} = 280^{2} + 344^{2} + 304^{2} = 78400 + 118336 + 92416 = 289152$$

$$\sum_{k=1}^{p}P_{k}^{2} = 94^{2} + 134^{2} + 113^{2} + 124^{2} + 121^{2} + 116^{2} + 119^{2} + 107^{2} = 8836 + 17956 + 12769 + 15376 + 14641 + 13456 + 14161 + 11449 = 108644$$

$$\sum_{k=1}^{p}\sum_{i=1}^{a}AP_{ik}^{2} = 45^{2} + 49^{2} + 71^{2} + 63^{2} + 56^{2} + 57^{2} + 62^{2} + 62^{2} + 61^{2} + 60^{2} + 54^{2} + 62^{2} + 5^{2} + 66^{2} + 54^{2} + 53^{2} = 54480$$

**Figure 11-2**
*Step-by-Step Example for Calculating the Sums of Squares of a Two-Factor Repeated Measures Experiment*

**Figure 11-2**
*Continued*

$$\sum_{k=1}^{p}\sum_{j=1}^{b}BP_{jk}^2 = 25^2 + 38^2 + 31^2 + 43^2 + 52^2 + 39^2 + 33^2 + 40^2 + 40^2 + 37^2 + 44^2 +$$

$$43^2 + 45^2 + 38^2 + 35^2 + 43^2 + 38^2 + 35^2 + 42^2 + 42^2 + 34^2 + 40^2 + 33^2 = 36576$$

$$\sum_{j=1}^{b}\sum_{i=1}^{a}AB_{ij}^2 = 120^2 + 192^2 + 144^2 + 160^2 + 152^2 + 160^2 = 146304$$

| Step 5. | Substitute the quantities determined in Step 4 into the terms in the formula and solve. |
|---|---|

$$\frac{T^2}{N} = \frac{928^2}{48} = 17941.33 \qquad \frac{\sum_{j=1}^{b}B_j^2}{ap} = \frac{289152}{(2)(8)} = 18072.00 \qquad \left| \; \sum_{k=1}^{p}\sum_{j=1}^{b}\sum_{i=1}^{a}X_{ijk}^2 = 18602 \qquad \frac{\sum_{k=1}^{p}\sum_{i=1}^{a}AP_{ik}^2}{b} = \frac{54480}{3} = 18160.00 \right.$$

$$\frac{\sum_{k=1}^{p}P_k^2}{ab} = \frac{108644}{(2)(3)} = 18107.33 \qquad \frac{\sum_{k=1}^{p}\sum_{j=1}^{b}BP_{jk}^2}{a} = \frac{36576}{2} = 18288.00 \qquad \left| \; \frac{\sum_{i=1}^{a}A_i^2}{bp} = \frac{430720}{(3)(8)} = 17946.67 \qquad \frac{\sum_{j=1}^{b}\sum_{i=1}^{a}AB_{ij}^2}{p} = \frac{146304}{8} = 18288.00 \right.$$

| Step 6. | Substitute the quantity for each term (determined in Step 5) into the sums of square equations and solve. |
|---|---|

$$SS_{\text{Subjects}} = \frac{\sum_{k=1}^{p}P_k^2}{ab} - \frac{T^2}{N} = 18107.33 - 17941.33 = 166$$

$$SS_A = \frac{\sum_{i=1}^{a}A_i^2}{bp} - \frac{T^2}{N} = 17946.67 - 17941.33 = 5.34$$

$$SS_{A \times \text{Subjects}} = \frac{\sum_{k=1}^{p}\sum_{i=1}^{a}AP_{ik}^2}{b} - \frac{\sum_{i=1}^{a}A_i^2}{bp} - \frac{\sum_{k=1}^{p}P_k^2}{ab} + \frac{T^2}{N} = 18160.00 - 17946.67 - 18107.33 + 17941.33 = 47.33$$

$$SS_B = \frac{\sum_{j=1}^{b}B_j^2}{ap} - \frac{T^2}{N} = 18072.00 - 17941.33 = 130.67$$

$$SS_{B \times \text{Subjects}} = \frac{\sum_{k=1}^{p}\sum_{j=1}^{b}BP_{jk}^2}{a} - \frac{\sum_{j=1}^{b}B_j^2}{ap} - \frac{\sum_{k=1}^{p}P_k^2}{ab} + \frac{T^2}{N} = 18288.00 - 18072.00 - 18107.33 + 17941.33 = 50$$

$$SS_{AB} = \frac{\sum_{j=1}^{b}\sum_{i=1}^{a}AB_{ij}^2}{p} - \frac{\sum_{i=1}^{a}A_i^2}{bp} - \frac{\sum_{j=1}^{b}B_j^2}{ap} + \frac{T^2}{N} = 18288.00 - 17946.67 - 18072.00 + 17941.33 = 210.66$$

$$SS_{AB \times \text{Subjects}} = \sum_{k=1}^{p}\sum_{j=1}^{b}\sum_{i=1}^{a}X_{ijk}^2 + \frac{\sum_{i=1}^{a}A_i^2}{bp} + \frac{\sum_{j=1}^{b}B_j^2}{ap} + \frac{\sum_{k=1}^{p}P_k^2}{ab} - \frac{\sum_{k=1}^{p}\sum_{i=1}^{a}AP_{ik}^2}{b} - \frac{\sum_{k=1}^{p}\sum_{j=1}^{b}BP_{jk}^2}{a} - \frac{\sum_{j=1}^{b}\sum_{i=1}^{a}AB_{ij}^2}{p} - \frac{T^2}{N} =$$

$$18602.00 + 17946.67 + 18072.00 + 18107.33 - 18160.00 - 18288.00 - 18288.00 - 17941.33 = 50.67$$

$$SS_{\text{Total}} = \sum_{k=1}^{p}\sum_{j=1}^{b}\sum_{i=1}^{a}X_{ijk}^2 - \frac{T^2}{N} = 18602.00 - 17941.33 = 660.67$$

subjects factor. Each guest was randomly assigned to eat only one of the meals. The courses, however, were repeated measures. Each guest ate and rated all eight courses, from appetizers to dessert. Therefore, the dinner party was a two-factor mixed design.

## 11-5a Partitioning the Variance in a Mixed Factorial Design

The variance for a mixed design can be partitioned as shown in Figure 11-4. The factor with repeated measures and the interaction between the two factors are both part of the within subjects variation. Their effects will be determined by

| TABLE 11-4 | Analysis of Variance Summary Table for the Angle of Orientation and Stimulus Size Sample Experiment |
|---|---|

| Source | Sum of squares | Degrees of freedom | Mean square | F |
|---|---|---|---|---|
| Subjects | 166.00 | 7 | | |
| Angle of rotation | 5.34 | 1 | 5.34 | 0.790 |
| Angle of rotation × Subject | 47.33 | 7 | 6.76 | |
| Size | 130.67 | 2 | 65.33 | 18.29* |
| Size × subject | 50.00 | 14 | 3.57 | |
| Angle × size | 210.66 | 2 | 105.33 | 29.10* |
| Angle × size × subject | 50.67 | 14 | 3.62 | |

\* > $F_{critical}$ (2.14, $\alpha$ = .01) = 6.51

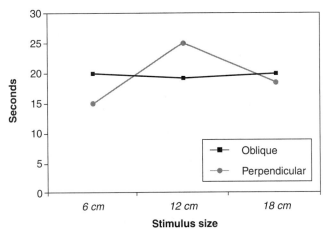

**Figure 11-3**
*The Effects of Angle of Orientation and Stimulus Size on Persistence of a Subjective Contour*

comparing the ratio of their variance to the variance due to the interaction between the repeated measures factor and the subjects within the groups. The between subjects factor, on the other hand, can be compared to the subjects within groups variation. The organization of the analysis of variance summary table for a two-factor mixed design parallels the partitioning of variance, as shown in Table 11-5.

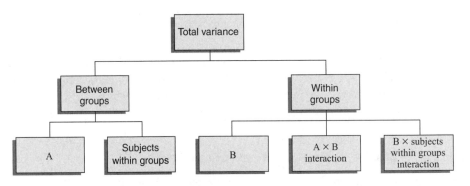

**Figure 11-4**
*Partitioning the Variance for a Two-Factor Mixed Design (Repeated Measures on Factor B)*

| TABLE 11-5 | Analysis of Variance Summary Table for a Two-Factor Mixed Design (Repeated Measures on Factor B) |
|---|---|

| Source | Sums of Squares | Degrees of Freedom | Mean Square | F |
|---|---|---|---|---|
| ***Between Subjects*** | $SS_P$ | $df_P$ | | |
| Factor A | $SS_A$ | $df_A$ | $MS_A$ | $F_A$ |
| Subjects within groups | $SS_{Sub}$ | $df_{Sub}$ | $MS_{Sub}$ | |
| ***Within Subjects*** | $SS_{Within}$ | $df_{Within}$ | | |
| Factor B | $SS_B$ | $df_B$ | $MS_B$ | $F_B$ |
| A × B | $SS_{AB}$ | $df_{AB}$ | $MS_{AB}$ | $F_{AB}$ |
| B × subject within groups | $SS_{B \times Sub}$ | $df_{B \times Sub}$ | $MS_{B \times Sub}$ | |

In many cases, a mixed design is desirable. Often one factor is repeatable without causing subject fatigue, interference, or demand characteristics. Taking a Closer Look 11-2 describes a possible experiment with music type and tempo. The type of music is a between subjects factor, with half the participants being randomly assigned to hear melody, while the other half the hear rhythm. The tempo of the music is a repeated measures or within subjects factor. Each participant hears all three tempos, with order of tempo presentation being counterbalanced across 30 trials. This experiment could have been designed as a totally between subjects experiment if each participant heard only one of the three tempos

**Taking a Closer Look 11-2**    *Mixed Design Two-Factor Sample Experiment*

It was hypothesized that tempo and type of music (rhythm vs. melody) interact to affect linguistic decision accuracy. Specifically, rhythm was predicted to decrease accuracy in deciding if a combination of letters formed a word, but melody was not. Furthermore, it was hypothesized that very slow rhythms would produce the greatest decrements, while normal and fast rhythm tempos would have lesser effects. Tempo was hypothesized not to affect decision accuracy when only melody was present.

Participants were randomly assigned to either the melody group or the rhythm group. They were trained in the word decision task that was presented on a microcomputer. First, a signal would appear; then the screen would be blank and 20 seconds of "music" would be generated by the computer. In the rhythm-only condition, the "music" consisted of complex rhythmic patterns that were unfamiliar to the participants. In the melody conditions, the music consisted of unfamiliar complex melodies that had no discernable rhythmic component. After 20 seconds, a set of letters would be displayed in the center of the screen for 1 second. The participant was to decide whether the letters formed a correctly spelled word. If the letters formed a word, the participant was to indicate the

response by pressing the up-arrow key on the computer keyboard. If not, the participant was to press the down-arrow key. After the participant pressed the arrow key, the music stopped. There was a 30-second interval until the next trial. The amount of time from the display of the letter set to the key press was recorded, as was the latency of the response. In addition, if the participant responded that the letters formed a word, he or she was to type the word on a sheet of paper. Each participant trained in the task with no music present until the reaction time did not continue to decrease and at least 7 out of 10 trials were correct.

During the experimental trials, participants completed three blocks of 10 trials. The only difference between the blocks was the tempo of the music presented. In the slow tempo condition, the music was played at a tempo of 60 beats per minute. In the normal tempo condition, the music was played at a tempo of 90 beats per minute, and in the fast tempo condition, the tempo was played at 120 beats per minute. All participants participated in all three tempo conditions, but the order of presentation was counterbalanced across the two music type treatment groups. The results were summarized in terms of the number of correct word decisions of each of the 10 trials per block in Table 11-7.

for 10 trials. This would have resulted in the same amount of data with three times as many participants. Because the instruction time and debriefing time would be approximately the same for each participant, the amount of time required to complete data collection would be more than tripled. Because of this, experimenters would like to use mixed and repeated measures designs to be able to get more data in less time. However, the convenience of data collection should always be a secondary consideration to the validity of the design. Such designs should be used only if the threats to validity associated with them can be minimized.

### 11-5b  Computing the Mixed Factorial ANOVA

The computation of analysis of variance for the mixed design is much like that in sections 11-3 and 11-4; only the formula and the error terms have changed. Table 11-6 presents the computational form of the analysis of variance for a mixed design. Remember to make sure which factor is the between subjects factor (Factor A in the table) and which factor is the within subjects factor (Factor B in the table).

The data from sample experiment B are presented in Table 11-7.

These data are used in a step-by-step analysis in Figure 11-5, and Table 11-8 presents the analysis of variance summary table for the sample experiment. (Notice that these data, by chance, gave a very unusual result: Both $F$s for the main effects are the same number. They must be compared against different critical $F$s because they have different degrees of freedom for both their numerators and denominators.) The only statistically significant effect was the interaction between music type and tempo.

The interaction means have been plotted in Figure 11-6.

# 11-6  Multiple Comparisons for Factorial Experiments

The results of the third sample experiment illustrate the difficulties of interpreting factorial experiments if you don't get precisely what you expect. It was hypothesized that tempo would affect accuracy only for the rhythm groups. It appears from Figure 11-6 that it did. Accuracy was lowest for the slow tempo condition with rhythm. This was somewhat consistent with the hypothesis. However, the graph shows that tempo had the opposite effect for the melody conditions. The slow tempo produced the greatest accuracy. No effect of tempo for the melody condition was hypothesized. The significant interaction $F$ between melody and tempo indicates that some of the six means are different, but not which ones.

Whether the results are as predicted or not, it is appropriate to complete multiple comparisons whenever more than two means are involved in any significant effect. However, there are many forms of these multiple comparisons, including the simple main effects tests, orthogonal contrasts, and many more. One simple approach for interactions is to apply the Tukey Honestly Significant Difference Test (described in section 8-7, "Multiple Comparisons"). Use the mean squares associated with the interaction term. The $n$ is the number of observations per interaction cell. Applying the Tukey HSD formula to the last example, you would obtain HSD = 1.86. Thus, you can conclude that the slow tempo melody produced significantly more accurate word identification than did the slow tempo rhythm; however, with normal and fast tempos, the music type did not significantly influence accuracy. Comparison across the three melody

**TABLE 11-6** Computational Form of Analysis of Variance Summary Table for a Two-Factor Mixed Design (Repeated Measures on Factor B)

| Source | Sums of squares (see formula below) | Degrees of freedom | Mean square | F |
|---|---|---|---|---|
| Between subjects | $SS_{Between}$ | $na - 1$ | | |
|    Factor A | $SS_A$ | $a - 1$ | $\dfrac{SS_A}{d_A}$ | $\dfrac{MS_A}{MS_{Sub}}$ |
|    Subject within group | $SS_{Sub}$ | $a(n - 1)$ | $\dfrac{SS_{Sub}}{df_{Sub}}$ | |
| Within subject | $SS_{Within}$ | $na(b - 1)$ | | |
|    Factor B | $SS_B$ | $b - 1$ | $\dfrac{SS_B}{df_B}$ | $\dfrac{MS_B}{MS_{B \times Sub}}$ |
|    A × B interaction | $SS_{AB}$ | $(a - 1)(b - 1)$ | $\dfrac{SS_{AB}}{df_{AB}}$ | $\dfrac{MS_{AB}}{MS_{B \times Sub}}$ |
|    B × subj. w. groups | $SS_{B \times Sub}$ | $a(b - 1)(n - 1)$ | $\dfrac{SS_{B \times Sub}}{df_{B \times Sub}}$ | |

Computational formula for sum of squares

$$SS_{Between} = \frac{\sum_{k=1}^{p} P_k^2}{b} - \frac{T^2}{N}$$

$$SS_A = \frac{\sum_{i=1}^{a} A_i^2}{nb} - \frac{T^2}{N}$$

$$SS_{Sub} = \frac{\sum_{k=1}^{p} P_k^2}{b} - \frac{\sum_{i=1}^{a} A_i^2}{nb}$$

$$SS_{Within} = \sum_{k=1}^{n}\sum_{j=1}^{b}\sum_{i=1}^{a} X_{ijk}^2 - \frac{\sum_{k=1}^{p} P_k^2}{b}$$

$$SS_B = \frac{\sum_{j=1}^{b} B_j^2}{na} - \frac{T^2}{N}$$

$$SS_{AB} = \frac{\sum_{j=1}^{b}\sum_{i=1}^{a} AB_{ij}^2}{n} - \frac{\sum_{i=1}^{a} A_i^2}{nb} - \frac{\sum_{j=1}^{b} B_j^2}{na} + \frac{T^2}{N}$$

$$SS_{B \times Sub} = \sum_{k=1}^{n}\sum_{j=1}^{b}\sum_{i=1}^{a} X_{ijk}^2 - \frac{\sum_{j=1}^{b}\sum_{i=1}^{a} AB_{ij}^2}{n} - \frac{\sum_{k=1}^{p} P_k^2}{b} + \frac{\sum_{i=1}^{a} A_i^2}{nb}$$

Where:

$N$ = Number of scores.

$a$ = Number of levels of Factor A.

$b$ = Number of levels of Factor B.

$p$ = Number of persons (or subjects).

$n$ = Number of persons in each level of A (between groups factor).

$A_i$ = Total of scores for level i of Factor A.

$B_j$ = Total of scores for level j of Factor B.

$P_k$ = Total of scores for person k.

$AB_{ij}$ = Total of scores for the ij cell of design.

$T$ = Total of all scores.

$\sum_{k=1}^{p}\sum_{j=1}^{b}\sum_{i=1}^{a} X_{ijk}^2$ = Total of all squared scores.

| TABLE 11-7 | Data from Sample Experiment on the Accuracy of Word Identification as a Function of Music Type and Tempo | | | | |

| | | Tempo | | | |
| | Subject | Slow | Normal | Fast | Total |
|---|---|---|---|---|---|
| Rhythm group | 1 | 6 | 7 | 7 | 20 |
| | 2 | 5 | 5 | 8 | 18 |
| | 3 | 2 | 4 | 6 | 12 |
| | 4 | 5 | 4 | 7 | 16 |
| Melody group | 1 | 7 | 5 | 5 | 17 |
| | 2 | 8 | 6 | 7 | 21 |
| | 3 | 9 | 6 | 5 | 20 |
| | 4 | 9 | 7 | 6 | 22 |
| | Total | 51 | 44 | 51 | 146 |
| | $\Sigma X^2$ | 365 | 252 | 333 | |
| | $\bar{X}$ | 6.375 | 5.5 | 6.375 | |

**Step 1.** Write the formula.

(See Table 11-6.)

**Step 2.** Determine the quantities that need to be calculated.

They are:

| $P_1$ | $P_2$ | $P_3$ | $P_4$ |
|---|---|---|---|
| $A_1$ | $A_2$ | | |
| $B_1$ | $B_2$ | $B_3$ | |
| $AB_{11}$ | $AB_{12}$ | $AB_{13}$ | |
| $AB_{21}$ | $AB_{22}$ | $AB_{23}$ | |
| $T$ | | | |

$$\sum_{k=1}^{n}\sum_{j=1}^{b}\sum_{i=1}^{a} X_{ijk}^2$$

| $n$ | $a$ | $b$ | $N$ |

**Step 3.** Calculate the terms determined in Step 2. Use data in Table 11-7 to form summary tables as follows:

Total tables for mixed design example experiment (Raw data presented in Table 11-7)

| | Tempo | | | |
| | Slow | Normal | Fast | |
|---|---|---|---|---|
| Rhythm group | 18 | 20 | 28 | 66 |
| Melody group | 33 | 24 | 23 | 80 |
| | 51 | 44 | 51 | 146 |

Other usefull cell statistics

| | Slow | Normal | Fast |
|---|---|---|---|
| Rhythm group | $\Sigma X^2 = 90$ <br> $\bar{X} = 4.5$ <br> $s = 1.73$ | $\Sigma X^2 = 106$ <br> $\bar{X} = 5$ <br> $s = 1.41$ | $\Sigma X^2 = 198$ <br> $\bar{X} = 7$ <br> $s = 0.82$ |
| Melody group | $\Sigma X^2 = 275$ <br> $\bar{X} = 8.25$ <br> $s = 0.96$ | $\Sigma X^2 = 146$ <br> $\bar{X} = 6$ <br> $s = 0.82$ | $\Sigma X^2 = 135$ <br> $\bar{X} = 5.75$ <br> $s = 0.96$ |

$a = 2$     $b = 3$     $n = 4$     $N = 24$     $\Sigma\Sigma X^2 = 950$

**Figure 11-5**

*Step-by-Step Example for Calculating the Sums of Squares for a Two-Factor Mixed Design*

Step 4.    Substitute terms calculated in Step 3 into the formula and calculate.

$$SS_{\text{Between}} = \frac{\sum_{k=1}^{p} P_k^2}{b} - \frac{T^2}{N} = \frac{20^2 + 18^2 + 12^2 + 16^2 + 17^2 + 21^2 + 20^2 + 22^2}{3} - \frac{146^2}{24}$$

$$= \frac{2738}{3} - \frac{21316}{24} = 912.667 - 888.167 = 24.5$$

$$SS_{\text{Type}} = \frac{\sum_{i=1}^{a} A_i^2}{np} - \frac{T^2}{N} = \frac{66^2 + 80^2}{(4)(3)} - 888.167 = \frac{10756}{12} - 888.167 = 896.333 - 888.167 = 8.167$$

$$SS_{\text{Sub}} = \frac{\sum_{k=1}^{p} P_k^2}{b} - \frac{\sum_{i=1}^{a} A_i^2}{nb} = 912.667 - 896.333 = 16.334$$

$$SS_{\text{Within}} = \sum_{k=1}^{p}\sum_{j=1}^{b}\sum_{i=1}^{a} X_{ijk}^2 - \frac{\sum_{k=1}^{p} P_k^2}{b} = 950 - 912.667 = 37.333$$

$$SS_{\text{Tempo}} = \frac{\sum_{j=1}^{b} B_j^2}{na} - \frac{T^2}{N} = \frac{51^2 + 44^2 + 51^2}{(4)(2)} - 888.167 = \frac{7138}{8} - 888.167 = 892.25 - 888.167 = 4.083$$

$$SS_{\text{Type}\times\text{Tempo}} = \frac{\sum_{j=1}^{b}\sum_{i=1}^{a} AB_{ij}^2}{n} - \frac{\sum_{i=1}^{a} A_i^2}{nb} - \frac{\sum_{j=1}^{b} B_j^2}{na} + \frac{T^2}{N} = \frac{18^2 + 20^2 + 28^2 + 33^2 + 24^2 + 23^2}{4} - 896.333 - 892.25 + 888.167$$

$$= \frac{3702}{4} - 896.333 - 892.25 - 888.167 = 925.5 - 896.333 - 892.25 + 888.167 = 25.084$$

$$SS_{\text{Tempo}\times\text{Sub}} = \sum_{k=1}^{p}\sum_{j=1}^{b}\sum_{i=1}^{a} X_{ijk}^2 - \frac{\sum_{j=1}^{b}\sum_{i=1}^{a} AB_{ij}^2}{n} - \frac{\sum_{k=1}^{p} P_k^2}{b} + \frac{\sum_{i=1}^{a} A_i^2}{nb} = 950 - 925.5 - 912.667 + 896.333 = 8.166$$

**Figure 11-5**
*Figure continued*

| TABLE 11-8 | Analysis of Variance Summary Table for the Music Type and Tempo Sample Experiment (Mixed Design) |
|---|---|

| Source | Sums of squares | Degrees of freedom | Mean square | F |
|---|---|---|---|---|
| Between subjects | 24.5 | 7 | | |
| Type | 8.167 | 1 | 8.167 | 3.00 |
| Subject within group | 16.334 | 6 | 2.722 | |
| Within subject | 37.333 | 16 | | |
| Tempo | 4.083 | 2 | 2.041 | 3.00 |
| Type × Tempo | 25.084 | 2 | 12.542 | 18.431* |
| Tempo × subject within groups | 8.166 | 12 | 0.681 | |

$F_{\text{critical}}$ (1,6; $\alpha$ = .05) = 5.99
*$F_{\text{critical}}$ (2,12, $\alpha$ = .05) = 3.89

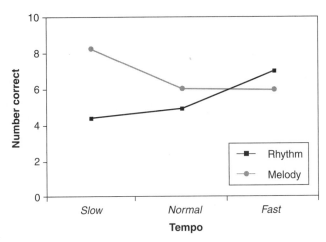

**Figure 11-6**
*The Interaction Between Music Type and Tempo on Word Identification Accuracy*

conditions shows that there is a significant difference between the slow melody condition and the normal and fast melody conditions. Finally, the comparison among the three rhythm tempo conditions reveals the slow rhythm condition produced significantly less accuracy than did the fast rhythm condition.

# 11-7 APA Style: Tables

Section 10-9, "APA Style: Graphs," showed how to illustrate interactions with graphs. A second way to present the means for significant effects in an experiment is to use a table. Tables are often used to summarize both descriptive and inferential statistics. You should use tables if the amount of numerical information in the text is dense and difficult to follow. You should not use them to present a small amount of information (APA, 2001). Follow these rules for the APA table format:

Tables are numbered, and the top of the table is labeled Table *X*, where *X* is the number of the table.

Titles for tables should be brief but clear. The title begins double-spaced after the Table *X* heading.

A table should have good, descriptive headings that are specific to the information it conveys.

Report numbers at the appropriate level of scientific precision for the measurement scales used.

Footnotes explain important information such as sample size, significance level, and specific considerations needed to interpret the information presented in the table.

Figure 11-7 illustrates how to write the results of the music tempo and rhythm sample experiment using a table to present the interaction means. The use of a table allows you to present the exact means along with the information from the Tukey HSD test on which means differ significantly from which other means.

# Summary

A repeated measures factorial design has repeated measures on each of the independent variables. A mixed factorial design has repeated measures on at least one of the independent variables and at least one other independent variable is a between subjects variable. In the two-factor mixed design, that means there is one repeated measures factor and one between subjects factor. In both repeated measures and mixed factorial

Results

The word identification accuracy scores were analyzed with a 2 × 3 (music type by tempos) mixed ANOVA, with repeated measures on tempo. There was a statistically significant interaction between music type and tempo on the number of words identified correctly ($F(2, 12) = 18.43$, $p < .05$). The mean word identification accuracy for each music type by tempo condition is shown in Table 1. The highest word identification accuracy scores were obtained in the slow melody condition, and the lowest word identification accuracy scores were obtained in the slow and medium tempo melody conditions.

Table 1

The Interaction between Music Type and Tempo on Word Identification Accuracy

| Type of Music | Slow | Tempo Medium | Fast |
|---|---|---|---|
| Rhythm | $4.50_a$ | $5.00_a$ | $7.00_a$ |
| Melody | $8.25_{bc}$ | $6.00_{ab}$ | $5.75_{ab}$ |

Note: There were 8 observations per conditions. Means that do not share the same subscript are significantly different at $p < .05$ in the Tukey Honestly Significant Difference comparison.

**Figure 11-7**
*Sample Results in APA Style*

designs, it is important to minimize demand characteristics by designing procedures that reduce carryover effects and other types of multiple treatment interference.

The analysis of variance for repeated measures and mixed factorial designs follows the same logic as that used for the between subjects factorial designs. The important difference is in the partitioning of the variance. For the within subjects factorial design, each factor and the interaction has its own error term based on the repeated measures within that effect. For the mixed factorial design, the between subjects factor error term is the between subjects within groups variance, but within subjects error variance is used for estimating the effects of the repeated measures factor and the interaction.

When both main effects and interactions are statistically significant, the main effects are interpreted in the context of the interactions because strong interactions may produce the appearance of a main effect. To interpret the main effect and not the interaction in such cases can lead to serious errors. Both graphs and tables can be used to illustrate the significant effects of factorial designs.

# References

American Psychological Association. (2001). *Publication manual of the American Psychological Association.* Washington, DC: Author.

# Exercises for Application

For each of the next two problems, use the stepwise approach of analysis:

a. Determine the type of statistical analysis that is appropriate for the research design presented.

b. State the null hypothesis (or hypotheses) to be tested.

c. Choose the correct inferential and descriptive statistics to test the hypothesis (or hypotheses).

d. Use the right statistical formula to calculate the descriptive and inferential statistics.

e. Determine the statistical significance of the appropriate inferential statistic.

f. Draw a statistical conclusion about the null hypothesis (or hypotheses).

g. State the probability of a Type I error for the inferential statistic you performed.

h. Graph the significant effects.

i. Perform multiple comparisons tests, where appropriate.

j. State the conclusion of the analysis (what it all means) in non-jargon terms.

## Problem I

It was hypothesized that people would be more accurate in detecting deception if it was perpetrated by members of their own gender. To test this hypothesis, a videotape was prepared in which 24 women and 24 men presented two-minute speeches representing their own true opinions about a current social issue. However, half the speakers presented the opinion of another person, which was in disagreement with their own. Participants viewed these tapes and judged each speaker as telling the truth or lying.

An accuracy score was calculated for each participant for each speaker gender based on the number of correct identifications of the deceptions and the truths. These scores are as follows:

|  | Accuracy Score | |
| --- | --- | --- |
|  | *Male Speaker* | *Female Speaker* |
| *Male Participants* | | |
| 1 | 16 | 12 |
| 2 | 21 | 13 |
| 3 | 18 | 16 |
| 4 | 19 | 9 |
| 5 | 16 | 11 |
| 6 | 18 | 11 |
| *Female Participants* | | |
| 1 | 18 | 13 |
| 2 | 22 | 15 |
| 3 | 21 | 14 |
| 4 | 20 | 17 |
| 5 | 23 | 15 |
| 6 | 19 | 12 |

## Problem II

It was hypothesized that the judgments of guilt accorded to an accused rapist would be both a function of the alleged victim's physical attractiveness and that of the accused rapist. To test this hypothesis, mock jurors were asked to read scenarios of nine different rape cases and, assuming the accused was guilty, to assign the years of his imprisonment. Each scenario was accompanied by a pro-

| | Accused Rapist | | | | | | | | |
| --- | --- | --- | --- | --- | --- | --- | --- | --- | --- |
| | **High Attractive Victim** | | | **Medium Attractive Victim** | | | **Low Attractive Victim** | | |
| Participant | *High* | *Medium* | *Low* | *High* | *Medium* | *Low* | *High* | *Medium* | *Low* |
| 1 | 20 | 15 | 13 | 19 | 20 | 17 | 18 | 19 | 11 |
| 2 | 23 | 16 | 15 | 11 | 15 | 12 | 14 | 20 | 16 |
| 3 | 17 | 15 | 21 | 13 | 21 | 5 | 14 | 17 | 11 |
| 4 | 20 | 22 | 16 | 18 | 18 | 4 | 10 | 9 | 7 |
| 5 | 17 | 23 | 14 | 18 | 19 | 9 | 13 | 11 | 16 |
| 6 | 22 | 19 | 17 | 16 | 17 | 7 | 15 | 14 | 14 |
| 7 | 25 | 20 | 15 | 15 | 15 | 10 | 15 | 15 | 15 |
| 8 | 21 | 18 | 14 | 14 | 16 | 11 | 13 | 16 | 13 |
| 9 | 19 | 19 | 20 | 15 | 15 | 10 | 11 | 14 | 15 |
| 10 | 20 | 15 | 13 | 16 | 17 | 12 | 13 | 15 | 14 |

file sheet describing the victim and the accused rapist. To reduce order effects, the pictures were counterbalanced across the scenarios. The photographs had been independently rated in terms of physical attractiveness. Three represented high attractiveness, three were of medium attractiveness, and three were of low attractiveness for both the victim and the accused rapist. The numbers of years of prison assigned are as follows:

## Practice Quiz

*Note:* You can find the correct answers to these questions by taking the quiz and then submitting your answers in the Online Edition. The program will automatically score your submission. If you miss a question, the program will provide the correct answer, a rationale for the answer, and the section number in the chapter where the topic is discussed.

1. Multiple treatment interference can occur when

   a. the effects of earlier treatments carry over.
   b. there is more than one treatment.
   c. there are too many experimenters in the room.
   d. the effects of a pretest influence a posttest.

2. When would you do a Tukey HSD with a 2 × 2 factorial design?

   a. When the main effect of A is significant
   b. When the main effect of B is significant
   c. When the interaction of A and B is significant
   d. When none of the effects is significant

3. A factorial design with repeated measures on one factor and between groups on the other is a

   a. crossed factorial design.
   b. 2 × 3 design.
   c. mixed design.
   d. partial replication.

4. Repeated measures designs are especially appropriate when

   a. knowledge of the independent variable does not alert participants to the hypothesis.
   b. there is a strong possibility of a carryover effect.
   c. an attribution scenario type paradigm is being used.
   d. there is multiple treatment interference.

5. In a repeated measures factorial design, the between subjects variance

   a. serves as the denominator of the *F* ratio.
   b. is partitioned into main effects and interaction sources.
   c. answers no important questions.
   d. is useful to estimate the effects of individual differences.

6. What is the biggest difference when comparing a between groups factorial ANOVA summary table to a repeated measures factorial ANOVA summary table?

   a. The repeated measures table is simpler because it has fewer sources of variation.
   b. The repeated measures table includes a separate error term for each main effect and the interaction.
   c. The repeated measures table has no between subjects source of variance.
   d. The way that the *F* is computed.

7. Thinking about what the numbers mean as you do the calculations for an ANOVA will

   a. help you discover calculation errors.
   b. make interpretation of the results easier.
   c. a and b.
   d. just make the calculations more confusing.

8. In a mixed design, the error term for the interaction is

   a. the MS between groups.
   b. the MS within groups.
   c. the MS total.
   d. the same as that for the repeated measures factor.

9. According to APA style, tables should be used to present

   a. numerical information that would be dense and difficult to follow in the text.
   b. ANOVA summary tables.
   c. numerical comparisons of two groups.
   d. statistically insignificant results.

10. Counterbalancing in a repeated measures factorial design is used to try to reduce or measure the effects of

    a. carryover.
    b. maturation.
    c. testing.
    d. all of the above.

11. The *F* ratio of the interaction in a repeated measures design is composed of the ratio of the $MS_{AB}$ to the

    a. $MS_B$.
    b. $MS_A$.
    c. $MS_{AB}$.
    d. $MS_{ABP}$.

12. If the degrees of freedom for the main effect of factor A are 1 and 7, then you know that there were two levels of A and
    a. 12 subjects.
    b. 8 subjects.
    c. 9 subjects.
    d. 14 subjects.

13. The critical $F$ for 2 and 14 degrees of freedom with alpha = .05 is 3.74. If the calculated $F$ = 3.56, you should
    a. reject the null hypothesis.
    b. fail to reject the null hypothesis.
    c. reject the alternative hypothesis.
    d. fail to reject the alternative hypothesis.

14. If both a main effect and an interaction involving the main effect are statistically significant, you should
    a. ignore the main effect and explain only the interaction.
    b. ignore the interaction because the main effect was more important.
    c. interpret the main effect in the context of the interaction.
    d. look for your mistake because the two effects should match.

15. There are often different critical $F$s for each main effect and interaction on a mixed analysis of variance summary table because they have different
    a. alphas.
    b. degrees of freedom.
    c. significance levels.
    d. sums of squares.

16. When you are making an APA style table, numbers should be reported
    a. with exactly the same number of decimal places as shown on the calculator or printout.
    b. rounded to two decimal places.
    c. at the appropriate level of precision for the scale of measurement used.
    d. with no rounding.

# When the Cause Cannot Be Manipulated: Pre-experimental Design and Chi-square

## Chapter Twelve

## Key Terms

| | |
|---|---|
| ABAB design | posttest only one group study |
| case study | pre-experimental designs |
| chi-square | random sample |
| ideographic approach | selection |
| nomothetic approach | single group observation |
| nonresponder bias | survey instrument |

# Learning Objectives

- Identify hypotheses that should be tested with pre-experimental methods.
- Appreciate the role of single subject research in behavioral science.
- Evaluate the appropriateness of the sample, survey instrument, and survey methods used in particular survey research.
- Calculate and interpret the chi-square statistic.

## Key Idea

Pre-experimental research is done when it is impossible or unethical to manipulate the hypothesized cause but it is desirable to describe the associations among variables.

## 12-1 Hypothesized Causes That Cannot Be Manipulated

What causes personality? This question has engaged psychologists from the beginning of the scientific study of psychology. To use experiments to answer this question, we must first hypothesize the causes and then manipulate those causes in an experiment. We want to know whether personality is the result of experience alone (as in Rousseau's *tabla rasa* theory). Or, is personality an innate, genetically determined aspect of the individual, as suggested by Sir Francis Galton in his study of the heritability of traits (1889)? These two hypotheses have been with us for a long, long time. Yet the method of experiments could not be used to test them. An experiment must involve the manipulation of the hypothesized cause of, in this case, personality. Until recently, genetic manipulation was not possible in humans, so we could not experimentally test Galton's theory. Furthermore, even if such manipulations are possible, researchers do not have the right to tamper with human lives on such a magnitude. The same can be said for the manipulations of the purely environmental conditions. Think about it. One group of participants would be subjected, from birth, to positive experiences. The control group would be raised in isolation from these experiences. Would you volunteer for such an experiment without knowing its outcome? More to the point, would you allow your newborn infant to participate in such an experiment, say as part of the control group—that group which would not experience the environmental conditions hypothesized to be essential for a healthy personality. Science fiction writers have speculated on these types of societal experiments, but they remain in the realm of fiction because either we do not have the means to manipulate the hypothesized causes or because to do so is unethical.

As John Stuart Mill (1874) correctly pointed out, to unambiguously determine the cause of an effect, the cause must be manipulated so that changes in the effect can be observed. In this way, with a carefully designed experiment, we can rule out or minimize alternative explanations for the relationship between the hypothesized cause and effect. There are many important causes, however, that either cannot or should not be manipulated. Think of schizophrenia, which is defined as a collection of symptoms that share a characteristic of incoherent, confused thought patterns. There are many theories of schizophrenia. One theory is that schizophrenia is biologically produced through a genetic disorder (Fowles, 1992). Such a cause cannot be tested experimentally because (a) we do not have the technology to experimentally manipulate human genes, and (b) if we could do so, causing schizophrenia would be unethical. Similarly, the causes of alcoholism, child abuse, personality disorders, and so on are usually impossible to study in a true experiment because the experimenter cannot (or should not!) manipulate them.

Does this mean that behavioral scientists must ignore phenomena for which they cannot manipulate the cause? Clearly, history shows us that the answer is no. However, history also shows us that such areas that cannot be put to the experimental test take much longer for psychologists to obtain clear, empirically supported results. In this chapter, many of the examples focus on the area of personality. By its nature, personality is difficult to study experimentally. Personality is stable and yet dynamic. That means it does change, but usually so slowly that research into its development often spans decades. Furthermore, personality has been studied over the past century with almost every pre-experimental and quasi-experimental design imaginable (see Chapter 13, "Correlational and Quasi-Experimental Designs"). In fact, many advances in statistics have been accomplished to test particular hypotheses about personality. Nevertheless, many conflicting theories developed more than 50 years ago remain current, in part, because they cannot be tested experimentally.

# 12-2 Pre-Experimental Designs

Campbell and Stanley (1966) used the term **pre-experimental designs** to identify research designs that shared much with experiments but that did not involve the manipulation of an experimental treatment. These designs are commonly used when the cause cannot be manipulated, but some empirical evidence of relationship between the variables is desired. They are also often used when researchers have not had proper training in research methods.

**pre-experimental designs** Designs that do not involve the manipulation of an experimental treatment (Campbell & Stanley, 1966).

## 12-2a Case Studies

In a **case study**, a single case is studied in great detail, usually over a period of time. Case studies are done because a particular, unusual case is very interesting, as in Oliver Sacks' (1970) case of the man who mistook his wife for a hat. This memory disorder case was so interesting that it was even used as the basis for an opera. It also has the attributes common to most case studies: It involved a very rare condition, and understanding that condition might aid in understanding normal behavioral processes. Other such famous case studies include Freud's case of Anna O. (Breuer & Freud, 1893–95/1955), the case of multiple personality which inspired the movie *The Three Faces of Eve*, J. B. Watson's case of little Albert (Watson & Raynor, 1920), and Gordon Allport's case study covered in his book, *Letters from Jenny* (1965).

A second reason for studying an individual case, besides the rarity of particular types of cases, is that the in-depth knowledge gained through such study is important to understand behavior. Allport championed the **ideographic approach**, which is the study of an individual, over time, and in detail to get a picture of the whole personality (Allport, 1937). He also used the **nomothetic approach** to personality. This approach involves measuring a large number of individuals on a relatively small number of variables; it is a type of survey research. Both of these methods are pre-experimental because no hypothesized cause is manipulated. They are both discussed in this chapter.

**Selection** is the major problem with case studies. When you study a specific case, it is impossible to isolate the general principles of behavior from individual idiosyncrasies. Without having a comparison condition, there is no way to know if the particular behaviors are causes, effects, or irrelevant. Case studies can offer interesting insights that can provide the hypotheses for further study, but in themselves they are necessarily inconclusive.

**case study** A type of study in which a single case is studied in great detail, usually over a period of time.

**ideographic approach** The study of an individual, over time, and in detail to get a picture of the whole personality (Allport, 1937).

**nomothetic approach** A study that measures a large number of individuals on a relatively small number of variables.

**selection** The threat to external validity that occurs because a sample was selected in such a way that it does not adequately represent the population.

### 12-2b Single Subject Designs

**ABAB design** A single subject study in which the participant acts as his or her own control.

A variation of the case study is the *single subject study* in which the participant acts as his or her own control. This type of research is common in behavior modification. Richard Foxx described an **ABAB design** in the behavior modification of Harry, a self-abusive patient in the film *Harry* (Foxx & DuFresne, 1984). The letters ABAB represent the assessment of behavior without the treatment (A) and under the treatment (B) conditions. If the treatment is effective, then the desired behavior should occur only under the B conditions. Indeed, during the first baseline session, Harry showed a high degree of self-abuse. During the treatment phase (B) that involved reinforcing Harry for nonabusive behaviors, his abusive behavior declined dramatically. During the second control period (A), the abusive behavior was almost as high as the baseline levels. Finally, the return to the treatment (B) showed that the treatment effectively reduced the self-abusive behavior. Based on the single subject research, a program of behavior modification was developed for Harry that reinforced positive behaviors.

As you can see from the preceding example, the single subject design is more limited in scope than a full-blown case study. The reason is that the question asked is more limited. "Will this treatment reduce these symptoms?" is an easier question to answer than "What are the symptoms of this memory disorder and why?" As always, the greater the control and the greater the ability of the researcher to manipulate variables, then the easier it is to determine some causality. Limiting the scope of research is often desirable because it allows more precise answers to specific questions. Nevertheless, even in the single subject study with an ABAB design, you know only that the treatment was effective for this subject at this time. You cannot generalize from one subject to many. In clinical and applied settings, the goal may be to generalize only to the participant at hand (Harry in the preceding case). These types of designs are appropriate in those conditions. As this example shows, single subject research can and should employ the principles of experimental design that have been covered previously in this book.

Inferential statistics play a very small role in most case studies and single subject research. The purpose of statistics is to summarize data. With only one subject, it is not usually useful to attempt to summarize the data. A mean of one observation over many different types of variables makes no sense. Likewise, you cannot do statistical inference on single cases. Assessing the probability of obtaining a single case by chance, again, doesn't make sense. Statistics may be used in single subject experiments. For example, Foxx presented the number of Harry's self-abusive events per time period as well as the number of minutes of nonabusive behavior for each treatment session. In the ABAB design, statistics can be used to determine whether the average of the target behaviors during the treatment conditions differs from that during the control conditions. This type of paradigm has been used for single subject experiments in learning and in memory. Ebbinghaus (1885/1913), the inventor of the nonsense syllable, was his own single subject. Yet he showed statistical analyses for his own forgetting as a function of time.

# 12-3 Survey Research

**survey instrument** The questionnaire that is used to conduct a survey.

Survey research is a major tool of many social sciences. Sociology, in particular, has developed sophisticated survey research techniques. Surveys are useful to describe a particular population. A good survey has a sample designed to adequately represent the population. It is also based on a valid and reliable **survey instrument**. That instrument is administered with the technique that will provide the most accurate response for the given population. The statistical analyses involve descriptive and associational statistics and the inferential techniques appropriate to test the observed measures and associations compared to those expected by chance. Generalizations are made only to those variables measured in the survey.

## 12-3a  Sample Design

Sample design is of utmost importance because the purpose of a survey is to represent a particular population accurately. The sample must be representative. The most representative sample is the **random sample**. There are several types of random samples. In a simple random sample, each member of the population has an equal probability of being selected for the sample. Thus, if there were a population of 100 members of a particular village, a sample of villagers could consist of 10 randomly selected members. The probability of any one villager (of the 100) being in the sample would be .1 (10 sample/100 population). A *stratified* random sample is one that randomly samples all segments of a population according to their proportion in the population. Therefore, if you wanted to stratify based on age, you would need to know the age characteristics of the total population of the village. Assume that the village had 30% of the people below 21 years old, 30% between 21 and 40 years old, 30% between 41 and 60 years old, and the remaining 10% over the age of 60. A stratified random sample of 10 villagers would involve randomly sampling three people under the age of 21, three between 21 and 40, three between 41 and 60, and one over 60 years old. A good sample must also have enough members to provide statistical confidence in generalizing to the population. For example, if the sample consisted of only 10 members, many people would be unwilling to conclude that those 10 adequately represent the village. With a small sample, extreme cases may outweigh the rest. Assuming a representative sample, the larger the sample, the more valid are the results of a survey.

**random sample** A sample in which each member of the population has an equal probability of being selected.

Random samples are very difficult to obtain in behavioral science. First, it is necessary to know and have access to the entire population in order to give each member of the population an equal opportunity to participate in the sample. Across many different types of populations, this is very difficult to achieve. Let's consider a far-fetched example. Suppose you were interested in surveying the personality of dogs. All dogs are not equally accessible. A random sample of dogs would be quite impossible. Some dogs are friendly; others are surly. You would run into difficulty obtaining survey results from a dog that would rather bite the interviewer than be assessed for any traits. Although this example seems far-fetched, ethologists do make generalizations about animal behavior from survey type research. Although they don't ask their participants to answer questions, they do assess particular traits and generalize to a population. Their problem of generalization to the population is similar to that of the opinion pollster. If the sample is not representative of the population, then the results cannot be generalized. If the dog surveyors study only those subjects that are not fearful of human researchers, their results cannot be applied to all members of the species in question. Similarly, if survey researchers poll the opinions of only those people who like to give their opinions (e.g., a call-in talk show poll or magazine response survey) they cannot conclude that those opinions represent the entire population. They are not valid for the large portion of the population that prefers not to participate.

Most survey research involves humans, and although they are not likely to bite the survey researchers, many things interfere with obtaining a random sample. First, the researchers must have an accurate list of the population. Even in developed countries, population census data are inaccurate and out of date. A random sample based on the 2000 U.S. census would not include me. I was out of the country when it was taken. The U.S. and many other countries have highly mobile populations. This makes a census reliable only for that portion of the population that (a) was counted in the first place, (b) remained in the same relative location, or (c) can be traced to their current location. Surveys that are based on the census underrepresent the mobile and difficult-to-reach members of the population.

Some survey researchers attempt to overcome these problems by sampling from the population of telephone numbers or of residential units. One way to represent a community may be to design a random sample of all the residential units in the community. Then even though the people may be moving in and out of the community, or within it, the sample would be representative of the community at the time it was taken. Telephone survey methods are very common. In the United States approximately 97% of all households have telephones. Because not all of these phones are listed in the phone books, a technique called random digit dialing was developed. First, a random sample of all exchanges is developed (area code and the first three digits). Then the last four digits of the phone numbers are randomly determined. Unlisted numbers are as likely to result as are those that are listed in the phone directories. In good samples the phone numbers that are known to represent businesses are removed.

A random sample should not be confused with random assignment to treatment group. Random assignment to treatment group has been the foundation of true between group experiments discussed previously in this book. Participants are randomly assigned to treatments when they have equal likelihood of being placed into any one of the several treatment conditions (e.g., treatment vs. control). On the other hand, a sample is a random sample only if each member of the population has an equal chance of being included in the sample. A random sample is not necessary for a true experiment because the major purpose of the true experiment is to show that the treatments had different effects on similar groups of individuals (made equivalent through random assignment). In a true experiment, an available sample is randomly assigned to treatment conditions. It is best to maximize the internal validity of a study by random assignment and to also increase the external validity by selecting a sample that is similar to the relevant population. Because the purpose of a survey is not to test a cause-effect hypothesis but to accurately describe a population, a random sample is very desirable, as it is the most representative type.

Students often confuse the term random with the concept of haphazard. Random in research design is anything but haphazard. It is precisely defined and operationalized. I believe that humans are unable to do anything in a truly random fashion. If humans could be truly random, the projective techniques of personality assessment and free association would give no insight into our personalities. For humans to produce a random process, we must use randomization devices such as flipping a coin, drawing a card from a deck, or using a random number table. Even the random number table was not developed by having an individual write numbers in a haphazard way. Proper randomization is so complex that survey researchers often employ the services of firms that specialize in producing random samples. Among behavioral and social scientists, sociologists are most respected for their abilities to construct samples that represent populations.

There are other methods of sample construction besides random sampling. They will not be covered here. Rather, remember that as an experiment cannot be valid unless its design is internally valid, a survey is not valid unless its sample is representative. Good research design maximizes both internal and external validity.

After the researcher reaches an individual for survey participation, that individual may not agree to participate in the survey. This is called **nonresponder bias**. Many things can be done to increase survey participation, but even the best survey will have nonresponders. Nonresponder bias is a problem for all types of samples, even the random sample. If possible, a nonresponder analysis is conducted that shows how the nonresponders differ from the responders (perhaps on location, gender, anything that can be determined without their participation in the survey). The format and style of the survey instrument are very important in reducing nonresponder bias.

**nonresponder bias** The outcome that occurs when individuals do not agree to participate in a survey.

### 12-3b Survey Instrument

After a sample is constructed, it is essential that the survey instrument reliably and validly measure the constructs to be surveyed. It must also be designed in such a way as to maximize completion of the survey. Survey participation is voluntary. If the survey takes too much time for the respondent, includes insulting or overly personal questions, or in some way irritates the respondent, it is likely that the survey will be terminated before it is completed. The higher the number of survey respondents who do not complete the survey, the less representative the sample. Furthermore, termination is not likely to be random. Rather it is likely to be systematic. Thus, the survey results will be very unrepresentative.

How can survey instruments be designed to avoid these problems? First, the mode of the survey should match the respondents' style of communication. For example, two students collected data for a survey of consumer satisfaction with outpatient services of a mental health agency. Because many of the consumers were mentally handicapped, the interviewers read the questions on the survey to each respondent. The interviewers also wrote the answers. This technique avoided problems due to literacy of the respondents. Some of the respondents were unable to read the questions correctly. Or they were unable to express themselves fully in writing. The interviewers were trained to present the questions in a neutral but clear manner. Thus, all the consumers not only agreed to be in the survey, but also completed it without frustration.

For some participants, writing their own survey responses may provide better results, particularly if the population is an educated one. The length of the survey and its difficulty are important issues. Each should be within the capacities and expectations of the sample. If the respondents are very interested in the topic of the survey, it is possible to have a longer, more involved survey. Even preschool children can be surveyed if the instrument is short enough, the questions clear, and their responses are recorded via audio or videotape.

The type of question is also important. Generally, it is better to ask many specific questions and form a scale from the responses than to ask a few, broad, open-ended questions. The response options presented to the respondents should be in terms that they understand and are comfortable using. For example, it's probably easier for a person to strongly agree with a statement than to rate level of agreement on a five-point scale and say "5." The researcher can code strongly agree with a "5" for data analysis without confusing or possibly alienating a respondent by requiring the respondent to answer in numbers. If a numeric response is essential, it can be put in the context of a familiar unit. If asked to estimate your grade for a course in z-score units, you would probably have trouble. If asked the same question in terms of a percent of possible points or a letter grade, you would probably have much less difficulty. The reason is that you are more familiar with those scales.

Some questions should not be asked because they will insult or embarrass the respondent. Asking such questions may be possible if confidentiality can be assured and if the questions are asked in a sensitive way. It's a good idea to ask sensitive questions near the end of the interview also. For example, many people are sensitive to questions about their income. However, such questions may be relevant for defining the sample. These questions will produce fewer problems if asked at the end of the survey, and if broad categories of response are available, rather than requiring respondents to specify a dollar amount. As in all research involving humans, the participant has the right to stop the study at any point. Surveys should be designed so that participants willingly complete them.

## 12-3c Survey Administration

The most important functions of survey administration are to obtain reliable and valid information from the respondents. The interviewer, if there is one, should not bias the results in any way. It is better to have respondents complete surveys individually because group discussions can influence results.

# 12-4 Chi-square ($\chi^2$) Analysis

**chi-square** A test of
independence between
variables that are each
measured on a nominal scale.

The results of surveys are often presented in tables of percentages or frequencies. Many statistical techniques can be applied. They all answer questions about the particular sample and how well it represents a specific population. A very common statistical technique that is applied to survey results is the **chi-square** ($\chi^2$). The chi-square statistic is a test of independence between variables that are each measured on a nominal scale.[1] Another way of describing a chi-square is that it is a measure of the goodness of fit between the observed frequencies and those that would be expected if the two nominal variables were independent. It is the most commonly used nonparametric statistic. (Recall that nonparametric statistics are those that are used on data that have not been measured with quantitative scales—interval or ratio scales.) Chi-square is usually used to determine whether there is a significant association between two nominal variables. Generally, more complex relationships (associations among three or more variables) should be evaluated with other types of nonparametric statistics.

Consider the example presented in Taking a Closer Look 12-1 Both leadership and birth order have been measured with nominal scales. The null hypothesis to be tested is that the two measures are independent of each other. In other words, the null hypothesis is that there is no relationship between leadership and birth order. The formula for the chi-square ($\chi^2$) raw score form is as follows:

$$\chi^2 = \sum_{j=1}^{r} \sum_{i=1}^{c} \frac{\left(O_{ij} - E_{ij}\right)^2}{E_{ij}}$$

Where $O_{ij}$ is the obtained cell frequency, and

$E_{ij}$ is the expected cell frequency for each cell in a frequency contingency table.

**Taking a Closer Look 12-1**    *Sample Survey: Relationship between Birth Order and Leadership*

It was hypothesized that first-born children would hold more leadership roles in college student organizations than would latter-born children or only children. To test this hypothesis, a survey was developed that determined the birth order of all 100 registered officers at a small liberal arts college. For purposes of the survey, *leader* was defined as president, vice president, secretary, or treasurer of the organization. *Other officer* was defined as any committee chair or other formal office. The results of the survey were tabulated to form the frequency contingency table shown in Table 12-1.

---

1. Coming up with an example of chi-square analysis involving personality variables has been my hardest task so far in writing this book. The chi-square analysis is most appropriate for nominal scale data. Although it is often applied to categories that have been artificially created from interval or ratio scale data (e.g., median splits), such analyses are very much weaker than the appropriate parametric statistics. I searched through the many recent personality studies at my disposal. In each case, I came to the same conclusion: The personality variables measured should not be presented as nominal. The bottom line is that I believe that all personality traits are normally distributed and should be measured parametrically. The controversy between personality trait and personality type theorists has long been concluded. People differ on the number of traits they possess, but not by qualitative type. Therefore, the example has been totally fabricated with variables that could be operationalized in parametric terms but are easy to think about as nominal scales. If I truly conducted research as described in Box 12-1, I would use more precise measures of both birth order and leadership behaviors.

| **TABLE 12-1** | Frequency Contingency Table | | | |
|---|---|---|---|---|
| | | **Birth Order** | | |
| **Organizational Role** | **First Born** | **Latter Born** | **Only Child** | |
| Leader | 12 | 2 | 6 | 20 |
| Other Officer | 12 | 6 | 12 | 30 |
| Member Only | 4 | 24 | 22 | 50 |
| | 28 | 32 | 40 | 100 |

This statistic basically compares the observed frequencies ($O_{ij}$) to those that would be expected ($E_{ij}$) if there were no relationship between the two variables. The $\chi^2$ is the sum of all the squared differences between the observed frequency and expected frequency with each squared difference divided by the expected frequency before they are all added together. Because the $\chi^2$ is an inferential statistic, it has degrees of freedom ($df$) associated with it. Conceptually, the degrees of freedom for a chi-square are the number of cells of the contingency table that could be determined randomly while keeping the marginal totals constant. This number is simply the number of rows less one, multiplied by the number of columns less one. The formula for the degrees of freedom for the $\chi^2$ is as follows:

$$df = (r - 1)(c - 1)$$

Where    $r$  is the number of rows, and

$c$ is the number of columns.

To calculate the $\chi^2$, you must calculate the expected frequencies. Table 12-2 shows the definitions for the expected frequencies ($E_{ij}$). You obtain the expected frequency for a particular cell of the contingency table by first multiplying the total frequency for the row that it is in by the total frequency for the column it is in. Next, you divide this product by the grand total. The sum of the expected frequencies for the cell in any row must equal the total observed frequency for that row (marginal total). Likewise, the sum of the expected frequencies for all the cells in a column must equal the total observed frequency for that column (marginal frequency). Although this is true by definition, it is useful to add up the expected frequencies for the rows (and/or columns) as a check before you complete the $\chi^2$ analysis. An error detected early in the analysis can prevent much unnecessary work later. Even worse, an undetected error could lead to false conclusions!

A step-by-step example of $\chi^2$ analysis is provided in Figure 12-1. The calculations are relatively simple, but there are many of them. The general procedure is identical to the procedures used for other inferential statistics (e.g., $t$ test and $F$). Let's review the general steps to inferential statistics after the particular inferential statistic has been selected. They are

- Write the formula.
- Organize the data in a form convenient for analysis.
- Find all the parts to the equations.
- Calculate the equations.
- Obtain the critical statistic from a table.
- Compare the obtained inferential statistic to the critical value to make an inference.
- Interpret results as they either support the alternate hypothesis (reject $H_O$) or do not (fail to reject $H_O$).

**TABLE 12-2**     Frequency Contingency Table for Chi-Square Analysis

|  | Column 1 | Column 2 | ... | Column j |  |  |
|---|---|---|---|---|---|---|
| Row 1 | $O_{11}/E_{11}$ | $O_{12}/E_{12}$ | ... | $O_{1j}/E_{1j}$ | Row 1 Total | $R_1$ |
| Row 2 | $O_{21}/E_{21}$ | $O_{22}/E_{22}$ | ... | $O_{2j}/E_{2j}$ | Row 2 Total | $R_2$ |
| ☐ | ...☐ | ☐ | ☐ | ☐ | ☐ | ☐ |
| Row i | $O_{i1}/E_{i1}$ | $O_{i2}/E_{i2}$ | ... | $O_{ij}/E_{ij}$ | Row j Total | $R_i$ |
|  | Column 1 Total C1 | Column 2 Total C2 | ... | Column j Total $C_j$ | Grand Total T |  |

Where

$O_{ij}$ represents the observed frequencies,

$R_{ij}$ represents the total frequencies for row i $\left( \sum_{j=1}^{c} O_{ij} = R_i \right)$

$C_j$ represents the total frequencies observed for column j
$\left( \sum_{i=1}^{r} O_{ij} = C_j \right)$

T is the total frequency, and

$E_{ij}$ represents the expected frequency, if the two variables are independent $\left( \Sigma_{ij} = \dfrac{R_i {}^* C_j}{T} \right)$.

The critical values for $\chi^2$ for the first five degrees of freedom are presented in Table 12-3. $\chi^2$ is almost always performed as a two-tailed test. The null hypothesis to be tested with $\chi^2$ analysis is that there is no association between the two variables that have been categorized. To justify a one-tailed test, you must make very specific alternate hypotheses, a priori, regarding the frequencies in each cell of the contingency table. For most research, such precise predictions are not warranted. Consider the example in Box 12-1. Although the hypothesis is fairly clear about first-born individuals relative to latter-born, it is ambiguous about only children's leadership behavior. It is seldom possible to make exact predictions for all cells in a contingency table. There are, however, some cases in which a one-tailed $\chi^2$ is entirely appropriate. If there are very specific predictions for relatively few cells in a contingency table, then you should use a one-tailed $\chi^2$. For example, suppose the hypothesis was that an extroverted individual is more likely to be hired for a job than an introverted individual. If a survey of interviewers were conducted to determine both the personality of the applicants (introverted or extraverted) and their employment outcome, a one-tailed chi-square would be appropriate. In that case, the critical values for the $\chi^2$ should come from the column in the table with alpha equal to .10 rather than .05.

Nonparametric statistics in general and $\chi2$ in particular are not very powerful, especially if the sample size is small. It has been standard practice for $\chi2$ to use an alternative, more conservative formula when the expected value for any cell in the contingency table was less than 5. One commonly used alternative is Yate's correction factor. Recently, however, concern over the high number of Type II errors that result from the more conservative approaches has led some to recommend that the

a)

**Step 1.    Write the formula.**

$$x^2 = \sum_{j=1}^{r}\sum_{i=1}^{c} \frac{(O_{ij} - E_{ij})^2}{E_{ij}}$$

**Step 2.    Form the frequency contingency table.**

(See Box 12-1.)

**Step 3.    Calculate the expected values for each cell ($E_{ij}$)**

|  | Birth order | | | |
|---|---|---|---|---|
| Organizational role | First born | Latter born | Only child | Row totals |
| Leader | 12/5.6 | 2/6.4 | 6/8 | 20 |
| Other officer | 12/8.4 | 6/9.6 | 12/12 | 30 |
| Member only | 4/14 | 24/16 | 22/20 | 50 |
| Column totals | 28 | 32 | 40 | 100 |

$$E_{ij} = \frac{R_i \times C_j}{T} \qquad E_{11} = \frac{R_1 \times C_1}{T} = \frac{20 \times 28}{100} = \frac{560}{100} = 5.6$$

$$E_{12} = \frac{R_1 \times C_2}{T} = \frac{20 \times 32}{100} = \frac{640}{100} = 6.4$$

$$E_{13} = \frac{R_1 \times C_3}{T} = \frac{20 \times 40}{100} = \frac{800}{100} = 8$$

**CHECK!**    $\sum_{j=1}^{3} E_{1j} = R_1 \qquad 5.6 + 6.4 + 8 = 20$

If not, there is an error. Redo calculations.

$$E_{21} = \frac{R_2 \times C_1}{T} = \frac{30 \times 28}{100} = \frac{840}{100} = 8.4$$

$$E_{22} = \frac{R_2 \times C_2}{T} = \frac{30 \times 32}{100} = \frac{960}{100} = 9.6$$

$$E_{23} = \frac{R_2 \times C_3}{T} = \frac{30 \times 40}{100} = \frac{1200}{100} = 12$$

**CHECK!**    $\sum_{j=1}^{3} E_{2j} = R_2 \qquad 8.4 + 9.6 + 12 = 30$

$$E_{31} = \frac{R_3 \times C_1}{T} = \frac{50 \times 28}{100} = \frac{1400}{100} = 14$$

$$E_{32} = \frac{R_3 \times C_2}{T} = \frac{50 \times 32}{100} = \frac{1600}{100} = 16$$

$$E_{33} = \frac{R_3 \times C_3}{T} = \frac{50 \times 40}{100} = \frac{2000}{100} = 20$$

b)    **CHECK!**    $\sum_{j=1}^{3} E_{3j} = R_3 \qquad 14 + 16 + 20 = 50$

For ease in calculating the $x^2$, write the expected values in the corresponding cells of the contingency table, below a diagonal line. This has already been done in the above table.

**Step 4.    Use observed and expected values to calculate chi-square ($x^2$).**

$$x^2 = \sum_{j=1}^{c}\sum_{i=1}^{r} \frac{(O_{ij} - E_{ij})^2}{E_{ij}}$$

$$x^2 = \frac{(12-5.6)^2}{5.6} + \frac{(2-6.4)^2}{6.4} + \frac{(6-8)^2}{8} + \frac{(12-8.4)^2}{8.4} + \frac{(6-9.6)^2}{9.6}$$

$$+ \frac{(12-12)^2}{12} + \frac{(4-14)^2}{14} + \frac{(24-16)^2}{16} + \frac{(22-20)^2}{20}$$

$$x^2 = \frac{(6.4)^2}{5.6} + \frac{(-4.4)^2}{6.4} + \frac{(-2)^2}{8} + \frac{(3.6)^2}{8.4} + \frac{(-3.6)^2}{9.6} + \frac{(0)^2}{12} + \frac{(-10)^2}{14} + \frac{(12)^2}{2} + \frac{(2)^2}{20}$$

**Figure 12-1**

*Step-by-Step Example of Chi-Square Analysis (Figure continued on next page)*

**Figure 12-1**
*Continued*

| | |
|---|---|
| **CHECK!** | Count the terms to make sure you included all cells of the design. $(r)(c) = (3)(3) = 9$. |

$$x^2 = \frac{40.96}{5.6} + \frac{19.36}{6.4} + \frac{4}{8} + \frac{12.96}{8.4} + \frac{12.96}{9.6} + \frac{0}{12} + \frac{100}{14} + \frac{64}{16} + \frac{4}{20}$$

$$x^2 = 7.314 + 3.025 + 0.5 + 1.543 + 1.35 + 0 + 7.143 + 4 + 0.20$$

$$x^2 = 26.875$$

**Step 5.** Calculate the degrees of freedom.

$$df = (r-1)(c-1) \qquad df = (2)(2)$$
$$df = (3-1)(3-1) \qquad df = 4$$

**Step 6.** Use a table to obtain the critical $x^2$ with $df$ and alpha ($\alpha$)

$$x^2_{critical} (df = 4, \alpha = 0.05) = 9.49$$

Compare obtained $x^2$ to critical $x^2$. Because $x^2 = 34.875 > 9.49 = x^2_{critical}$ reject the null hypothesis. The association between birth order and organizational role is statistically significant.

standard formula be applied in all cases (Ferguson & Takane, 1989). My position on this issue remains as it has been: The researcher is responsible to design research that will minimize both types of errors. Therefore, an adequate sample size should be obtained to assure that all statistics have both power (low probability of a Type II error) and precision (low probability of a Type I error) to provide unambiguous results. The statistical problem of what to do with small sample sizes is usually best addressed by increasing the sample size rather than adjusting the formula.

Chi-square is a measure of the association between two nominal variables. It is, itself, a nominal measure. That is, it merely allows the researcher to conclude that two variables are probably related (significant $\chi^2$) or that they probably are not (not significant $\chi^2$). The $\chi^2$ itself has no information regarding causality. Only the research design can provide evidence for a cause-effect relationship. Survey research, because it only measures variables and does not manipulate them, cannot provide evidence for a cause-effect relationship. Consider the example from Box 12-1. The $\chi^2$ showed that birth order and leadership were significantly associated. It did not show why they are associated. There are several possible explanations: (a) birth order may cause leadership; (b) leadership may cause birth order; or (c) something else may cause parts of each of them. Although alternative b is not plausible in this case, it does not follow that alternative a is true. Just because one event precedes another event in time (as birth order precedes leadership), you cannot conclude that first event is the cause of second event. A fever precedes the appearance of the pox associated with chicken pox. They are highly associated. Yet, it is clearly wrong to conclude that the cause of the chicken pox is the fever. A third variable (the chicken pox virus) caused both symptoms.

| TABLE 12-3 | Excerpt of the Table for Critical Values for the $\chi^2$ Distribution | |
|---|---|---|
| | **Critical Value** | |
| **df** | **α=.05** | **α=.10** |
| 1 | 3.84 | 2.71 |
| 2 | 5.99 | 4.60 |
| 3 | 7.82 | 6.25 |
| 4 | 9.49 | 7.78 |
| 5 | 11.07 | 9.24 |

Chi-square analysis is relatively simple to compute with a calculator. Yet, even this analysis is usually performed with a computer. Most statistical analysis packages provide $\chi^2$ as an option on the contingency table procedure (sometimes called the *crosstabs*). Computerized spreadsheets also often include options for conducting $\chi^2$ analysis. A word of caution about the sheer number of $\chi^2$ statistics that can be performed this way is in order: It is possible for a computer printout to contain literally hundreds of $\chi^2$ analyses. Each significant $\chi^2$ has the probability of being incorrect (Type I error) equal to alpha (.05). Thus, it is likely that some of the significant associations are not really valid. The problem is that you don't know which ones. Survey results, like all other research, should not be analyzed by "wholesale" strategies that test for every possible relationship. Rather, they should be thoughtfully analyzed, based on a clear understanding of the area under study, with specific hypotheses identified and tested. Just because it is as easy to do 200 $\chi^2$ analyses by computer as one, that is no reason to do them!

# 12-5 APA Style: Reporting the Chi-Square

The reporting of nonparametric statistics follows the same principles as those given for parametric inferential statistics. You must

- Describe the statistical test used.
- Present the obtained statistical value along with the degrees of freedom and the probability of obtaining it by chance alone or the significance level.
- Present the descriptive statistics to show the relationship.

In the case of chi-square, the descriptive statistics are likely to be tables of frequencies or proportions. Bar graphs may also be used. Figures 12-2 and 12-3 show how the leadership and birth order sample study are presented so that you can see two ways of presenting the same information. Either is acceptable, but you should choose to use only one of them.

# 12-6 One Group Studies

One group studies are pre-experimental because there is no proper control. Campbell and Stanley (1966) listed three such designs. They are

- Single group observation
- Posttest only one group study
- Pretest posttest study

The **single group observation** is a study of one group. It is like a survey in that respect. If its goal is to describe the behavior only of that one group, it may be able to reach that goal. However, it is often used to either explain a cause-effect relationship, which it cannot, or it is used to describe a population for which it is not an adequate sample. This, too, it cannot do. The student of research design should learn to recognize such studies for what they are. They may suggest causal hypotheses, but these should be tested with the appropriate experimental research designs. Furthermore, they may suggest interesting attitudes and opinions. Survey research with representative samples should be conducted to test whether such generalizations can be made. Thus, this type of research is pre-experimental. It leads up to experiments, but it cannot answer the causal questions posed by experiments.

**single group observation** A study of one group.

Results

A chi-square analysis was conducted on the relationship between birth order and leadership of campus organizations. This analysis revealed a statistically significant association between the two variables ($\chi^2(4) = 34.87$, $p < .05$). Table 1 shows that although the first-born students composed only 28% of the sample, they were 60% of the leaders. Latter-born students made up 32% of the sample but 48% of the members only. Only children seemed to be represented about the same in the sample and in the three leadership categories.

Table 1

Leadership Status and Birth Order of Members of Student Organizations

| | Birth Order | | |
|---|---|---|---|
| Organizational Role | First Born | Latter Born | Only Child |
| Leader | 12 | 2 | 6 |
| Other Officer | 12 | 6 | 12 |
| Member Only | 4 | 24 | 22 |

**Figure 12-2**
*Example 1*

---

**posttest only one group study** A type of study in which a treatment condition is administered to a single group.

The **posttest only one group study** is done when a treatment condition is administered to a single group. Following the treatment, measurement of the specific effect is done. There is no pretest and no control group. Although the measured effect follows the manipulation, there is no way to know whether the manipulation really was the cause of the effect. For example, a study that showed the effect of subliminal suggestion on popcorn and Coke buying used this design. A few frames that displayed the words "Drink Coke" or "Buy popcorn" were spliced into a movie several minutes before intermission. Then the amounts of Coke and popcorn purchased during the intermission were measured. The problem is that without a control group, there is no way to conclude that the subliminal stimuli had any effect on snack food purchasing. This type of design has no redeeming value. At the very least, there should be a pretest before the treatment is delivered.

The one group pretest posttest design is discussed at length in Chapter 7, "Hypothesis Testing: Pretest Posttest Design and Related Measures *t* Test." It is an improvement on both of the other two **pre-experimental designs** in that at least the pretest may be able to serve as the appropriate control. As described in Chapter 7, there are serious threats to the internal validity of this type of design. The most important threats to validity of the pretest posttest design are history, maturation, and testing.

Results

The relationship between birth order and leadership of campus organizations is statistically significant ($\chi^2(4) = 34.87$, $p < .05$). As shown in Figure 1, first-born students are likely to be leaders or other officers, and latter-born children are likely to be members but much less likely to be leaders or other officers. Only children hold leadership positions in about the same proportion as those positions are available (e.g., 20% of the positions are leadership positions, and 15% of the only children hold such positions).

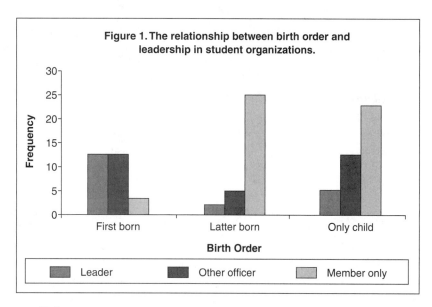

Figure 1. The relationship between birth order and leadership in student organizations.

**Figure 12-3**
*Example 2*

# Summary

Pre-experimental designs are those in which no independent variable is manipulated. They may be useful in describing particular phenomena that cannot be practically or ethically manipulated in an experiment. Case studies are in-depth analyses of many variables on a single case. Single subject designs also use a single case (subject) but are focused on a more specific set of variables and may involve the manipulation of an independent variable as a repeated measure. Survey research measures many individuals on a limited set of variables.

One of the most important characteristics of a valid survey is a representative sample. A random sample is one in which every member of the population has an equal probability of being selected for the sample. The survey instrument and administration methods should be designed to reduce responder bias and attrition. An adequate sample is representative and large enough to statistically represent the population.

Chi-square is a nonparametric statistical test used to measure the association of two nominal variables. If the chi-square statistic is statistically significant, then the variables are probably not independent. The chi-square statistic can be used for all types of research. Causal conclusions are drawn based on the design, and not on the statistic. Causal conclusions are inappropriate for pre-experiments because the alternative explanations of relationships between variables cannot be ruled out by the design.

## References

Allport, G. W. (1937). *Personality: A psychological interpretation.* London: Constable.

Allport, G. W. (1965). *Letters from Jenny.* New York: Harcourt, Brace & World.

Breuer, J. & Freud, S. (1893–1895). *Studies in hysteria.* In J. Strachey (Ed. & Trans.) *The standard edition of the complete psychological works of Sigmund Freud, vol. 2.* London: Hogarth, 1955.

Campbell, D. T. & Stanley, J. C. (1966). *Experiments and quasi-experimental designs for research.* Chicago: Rand McNally.

Ebbinghaus, H. (1913). *Memory: A contribution to experimental psychology* (H. A. Ruger & C. E. Bussenius, Trans.). New York: Teachers College, Columbia University. (Original work published in 1885)

Ferguson, G. A. & Takane, Y. (1989). *Statistical analysis in psychology and education* (6th ed.). New York: McGraw-Hill.

Fowles, D. C. (1992). Schizophrenia: Diathesis-stress revisited. In M. R. Rosenzweig & L.W. Porter (Eds.), *Annual Review of Psychology, 43,* Palo Alto, CA: Annual Reviews, Inc.

Foxx, R. & DuFresne, D. (1984). "Harry": The use of physical restraint as a reinforcer, timeout from restraint, and fading restraint in treating a self-injurious man. *Analysis and Intervention in Developmental Disabilities, 4,* 1–13.

Galton, F. (1889). *Natural inheritance.* London: Macmillan.

Mill, J. S. (1874). *A system of logic, ratiocinative and inductive: Being a connected view of the principles of evidence and the methods of scientific investigation* (8th ed.). New York: Harper & Brothers.

Sacks, O. (1970). *The man who mistook his wife for a hat and other clinical tales.* New York: Simon & Schuster.

Watson, J. B. & Raynor, R. (1920). Conditioned emotional responses. *Journal of Experimental Psychology, 3,* 1–14.

## Exercises for Application

1. One of the methods that Abraham Maslow used in developing his theory of self-actualization was the case study. He did in-depth interviews of many famous individuals who seemed to be self-actualized. What valid conclusions could be drawn using this approach? What conclusions cannot be supported by a group of case studies?

2. Suppose that you believe that adequate sleep (8 hours or more per night) is important for optimal cognitive performance. You decide to use yourself as the participant in a single subject design. How would you design your intervention? How would you measure cognitive performance? What are the strongest conclusions that you can draw from your research? Can you definitively conclude that adequate sleep improves cognitive performance? Why or why not?

3. What would you want to know to be able to assess the validity of the claim that almost 2 women in 3 is either dieting or exercising in order to control her weight?

4. Imagine that a survey were conducted to determine the association between music preferences and major. The survey results are summarized in the following table. What is the strongest conclusion that can be drawn about music preference and major?

|  | Psychology | Sociology | Economics | Political Science | Physics |
|---|---|---|---|---|---|
| Rock | 50 | 60 | 20 | 80 | 40 |
| Jazz | 25 | 35 | 40 | 20 | 30 |
| Classical | 25 | 5 | 40 | 0 | 30 |

## Practice Quiz

*Note:* You can find the correct answers to these questions by taking the quiz and then submitting your answers in the Online Edition. The program will automatically score your submission. If you miss a question, the program will provide the correct answer, a rationale for the answer, and the section number in the chapter where the topic is discussed.

1. Who said that in order to unambiguously determine the cause of an effect, the cause must be manipulated so that changes in the effect can be observed?
   a. Socrates
   b. John Stuart Mill
   c. Sigmund Freud
   d. B. F. Skinner

2. Research designs that share much with experimental design but that do not involve the manipulation of an independent variable are called
   a. confounded designs.
   b. pre-experimental designs.
   c. post-experimental designs.
   d. quasi-experimental designs.

3. An intensive study of one individual over time is a
   a. case study.
   b. nomothetic study.
   c. pretest posttest study.
   d. survey.

4. The main problem with the single subject ABAB design is that
   a. there is no baseline.
   b. the hypothesized cause isn't manipulated.
   c. there's no operational definition for the effect.
   d. the results can't be generalized to other subjects.

5. A good example of nomothetic research is the
   a. case study.
   b. single subject ABAB design.
   c. pretest posttest design.
   d. survey.

6. The most representative sample for a survey is a
   a. convenience sample.
   b. bell weather sample.
   c. random sample.
   d. quota sample.

7. In designing a survey instrument, it is generally better to
   a. ask a few, broad, open-ended questions.
   b. ask many specific questions that can be formed into a scale.
   c. ask personal questions first to get them out of the way.
   d. make sure that an undecided response is always available.

8. A chi-square is a test of independence between variables that are measured on a _____ scale.
   a. nominal
   b. ordinal
   c. interval
   d. ratio

9. The expected frequencies used in calculating a chi-square come from
   a. the researcher's prior odds estimates of the frequencies.
   b. multiplying the column total by the row total and dividing by the grand total.
   c. asking participants about their expectations for the categories measured.
   d. a chi-square table.

10. The degrees of freedom for a chi-square are
    a. $N - 1$
    b. $r * c$
    c. $(r - 1)(c - 1)$
    d. $n(rc)$

11. A one-tailed chi-square hypothesis test is appropriate if
    a. the number of frequencies exceeds 100.
    b. the two-tailed test failed to be significant.
    c. the relationship between the two variables is one of independence.
    d. specific hypotheses have been made for the frequencies of each cell.

12. Because a chi-square has low power when the sample size is small, it is best to
    a. use a special formula that takes into account the small sample size.
    b. expect to tolerate a high Type II error rate.
    c. use a $t$ test instead.
    d. design your study with a large enough sample to test the hypothesis well.

13. The proper use of a one group study is to
    a. test cause-effect hypotheses.
    b. describe the behavior of one group.
    c. make generalizations from the group to a larger population.
    d. assess the posttest results.

14. The posttest only one group study has
    a. limited applications for testing new products.
    b. the same problems as any survey research.
    c. value when a control group is impossible.
    d. no redeeming value because the results have nothing to compare to.

15. Which of the following is *not* a meaning of "random" in research design and statistics?
    a. participants have an equal probability of being assigned to a treatment group.
    b. all members of a population have an equal probability of being selected for a sample.
    c. a table of numbers that have no patterns.
    d. haphazard and without forethought.

16. Pre-experimental designs may be especially useful in
    a. describing behavior and suggesting hypotheses for future experimental research.
    b. explaining cause-effect relationships with causes that are impossible to manipulate.
    c. explaining cause-effect relationships with causes that are unethical to manipulate.
    d. capitalizing on chance relationships in the data.

# Correlational and Quasi-Experimental Designs

## Chapter Thirteen

## Key Terms

mortality
Pearson's product moment correlation coefficient (*r*)
quasi-experiments

scatter plot
selection
selection by maturation interaction
static group comparison design

# Learning Objectives

- Identify hypotheses that should be tested with quasi-experimental or correlational methods.
- Describe three major limitations of quasi-experimental research designs.

- Construct and interpret scatter plots.
- Explain why correlation does not imply causation.
- Calculate and interpret Pearson's product moment correlation coefficient.

## Key Idea

Quasi-experimental designs have treatment and comparison conditions, but there are systematic differences between the conditions in addition to the hypothesized cause that limit the causal inference which can be drawn. Correlation is a measure of the association between two quantitative variables.

# 13-1 Quasi-Experimental Designs

Chapter 12, "When the Cause Cannot Be Manipulated: Pre-Experimental Design and Chi-Square," dealt with pre-experimental designs. Such designs are called *pre-experimental* because no variable is manipulated. Designs that have some of the features of true experiments but cannot claim to have all things equivalent between treatment groups other than the independent variable are called **quasi-experiments** (Campbell & Stanley, 1966). A treatment may be provided and comparisons may be made to groups of individuals who did not receive the treatment, but the assignment to treatment condition was not random. One of the most commonly used quasi-experimental designs will be covered in this chapter.

**quasi-experiments** Designs that have some of the features of true experiments but cannot claim to have all things equivalent between treatment groups other than the independent variable (Campbell and Stanley, 1966).

### 13-1a Static Group Comparison Design

Sometimes a natural experiment occurs. That is, two groups in nature are very similar except that one receives the hypothesized cause, and the other does not. These natural experiments are based on static groups—groups that were not assigned or under the control of the experimenter. In some cases, the experimenter does have control of the treatment; in others, he or she merely can measure the treatment as it is present at different levels in the two static groups. Often program evaluation and educational research use the **static group comparison design**. A new program or technique is tried out with one existing class or client group, while another group or class acts as the control. Similarly, research on personality that assesses people on personality and then compares the effects of a treatment on those personalities is a static group comparison design. The researcher did not assign participants to a personality condition but took what the participant brought to the experiment. Thus, a class project done by one of my students in which participants were assessed on their introversion-extraversion and then the effects of a treatment, caffeine, is a type of static group comparison design. Although half of the extroverted participants were randomly assigned to the placebo condition (decaffeinated coffee), as were half of the introverted participants, the personality dimension was not manipulated by the experimenter. She had to take what the participants brought to the experiment and make assessments based on that subject variable. When participants are assigned to an experimental group based on any trait (personality, gender, experience, age, etc.), the resulting groups are static groups.

**static group comparison design** A study design in which a new program or technique is tried out with one existing class or client group, while another group or class acts as the control.

The problem with static group comparison designs is that the groups always differ in more ways than the one of interest to the researcher. In my experience of research, the most troubling quasi-experimental design was one on the relationship between marijuana and female reproductive hormonal functioning among reproductive-age women (Dornbush, Kolodny, Bauman & Webster, 1978). This study used a static group comparison design in which healthy young women were recruited to participate. They were asked to record their behaviors daily. They were also asked to provide blood samples on a regular schedule throughout two months. Based on their daily behavior records, the participants were divided into two groups: those who smoked marijuana and those who did not. The two groups did indeed differ significantly on hormonal profiles. They also differed on their use of alcohol, other illegal drugs, and sexual activity. As the project statistician, I had to emphasize that any of these variables, or some that we had not measured, could be the cause of the hormone differences. It is even possible that the hormonal differences caused the different patterns of drug use. No amount of statistical analysis could separate the effects because they were tied together in the design.

The preceding example is especially good because it clearly shows the problems with quasi-experimental research. However, it is also an example of a research problem for which there is no other better design. A true experiment is impossible for this particular problem because it is unethical (and illegal) to give a potentially hazardous substance to women who may bear children liable to the effects of that substance much later. (Consider the long-term effects of Agent Orange on the children of Vietnam War veterans). Even though it would be easy to randomly assign participants to treatment group, it would be unethical to give the treatment. It is irresponsible to ignore the question, though, because of its social importance. Furthermore, although animal research can provide some evidence of effects, it is limited in its generalizability to humans. The strongest possible ethical design is the static group comparison design. Yet the conclusions must be restricted to those of association. Ultimate causation cannot be concluded.

# 13-2 Threats to Validity of Pre-Experimental Designs

Pre-experimental designs cannot support causal conclusions, but even these designs can produce useful information when the threats to their validity are minimized. Strong pre-experimental designs avoid the particular threats of selection, mortality, and the selection x maturation interaction. These threats and suggestions for minimizing them in pre-experimental designs are discussed in sections 13-2a through 13-3c

## 13-2a Selection

**Selection** is an important threat to the validity of research when there is differential selection into the treatment groups. Because the pre-experimental designs have no treatment groups, there would seem to be no threat from this source. However, there is usually an implicit comparison group. That could be the perceived status quo or some other normative figures. Often the single group studied is available for study because it is not like the status quo—it is not the norm. Therefore, even one-group experiments are liable to have a selection bias, if the results of the one group are to be compared to some perceived base rate.

The threat from selection may be estimated by carefully measuring the static group members' characteristics on a number of known variables and comparing

**selection** An important threat to the validity of research when there is differential selection into the treatment groups.

them to known norms for the population. For example, I was asked to teach a pilot course that used laptop computers in the classroom. Ideally, we would test the new program by randomly selecting the students for the class. However, students didn't like being told that they were selected for a new program that required them to purchase a specific computer and use that computer for all class activities. Therefore, the students for the new program were volunteers. By measuring their motivation and previous academic achievement, we could assess how different they were from the population of students. They were more motivated, had higher high school grades and college entrance exam scores, and had more high school leadership positions than the other students. Therefore, the strongest conclusion that could be drawn from the pilot program was that it worked well with highly motivated, intelligent, hard-working students. This conclusion was important because, before the pilot program was done, it wasn't clear that the program could work at all, even with good students and faculty.

### 13-2b Mortality

**mortality** The threat to validity that occurs when subjects fail to complete the experiment.

**Mortality** is the threat to validity that occurs when subjects fail to complete the experiment. This is usually the problem when the conditions are different between the treatments. For example, comparisons of one group to another are problematic if the treatment in group one causes many people to drop out of the program. The results are then biased because you cannot tell what the results would have been had those who dropped out been included.

The threat from mortality can be assessed by comparing the characteristics of the individuals who leave the study early to those who remain to its completion. If mortality is likely to be an issue because of the length of the treatment, then it would be wise to measure the participant characteristics early during the program. Then, if the characteristics of those who leave are similar to those who remain, the sample may have little bias from experimental mortality. A second way to minimize the threat from experimental mortality is to design studies that are easy for participants to complete. Pilot testing can help researchers understand the stress, boredom, or other negative factors associated with participation. They can then design programs that reduce the negative aspects.

Mortality can be an especially strong threat for the no treatment control groups of therapy studies. People may stop study participation for two main reasons. First, they may have spontaneously recovered as a function of the passage of time. Because they no longer need the promised future treatment, they leave the study. Second, they may be unwilling to wait for treatment and seek it elsewhere. In either case, their departure from the study will make the no treatment comparison group even less comparable to the treatment group than it had been.

### 13-2c Selection by Maturation Interaction

**selection by maturation interaction** The treatment effect is different for the selected groups because of their different rates of maturation.

In many static group comparison designs, the two groups are not equivalent on their type of maturation. The **selection by maturation interaction** occurs when the treatment effect is different for the selected groups because of their different rates of maturation. For example, comparing fifth graders to first graders could produce problems. The first graders are developing at a quicker rate than the fifth graders and may show a stronger effect of a treatment. On the other hand, they tire more quickly and may show fatigue effects that could interfere with the treatment.

One way to manage the selection by maturation threat is to have control groups for each static group that are maturing at the same rate. The control groups allow you to estimate the effects of maturation alone.

# 13-3 Drawing Conclusions from Quasi-Experimental Research

Quasi-experimental research is often used as the basis for many practical applications. The temptation to overgeneralize from quasi-experimental research is strong because it is often conducted under conditions that are very similar to the desired "real world" applications. Such research seldom is criticized for its artificiality, as is laboratory research. However, the lack of internal validity for most quasi-experimental research negates its external validity. If the conditions of data collection were not well controlled, it is very risky to apply those results. A second temptation with the quasi-experimental research is to infer a causal relationship. Yet the statistical measures are those of association. As Mill (1874) so aptly stated, correlation is a necessary prerequisite to show causation, but it is not sufficient. Only a carefully designed program of experiments can yield evidence for a causal conclusion.

There is a solution to the paradox posed by the complementary strengths and weaknesses of experimental designs (which are artificial but do show causality) and quasi-experimental designs (which often are realistic but show only associations). That solution is to base your understanding of a phenomenon on both experimental and quasi-experimental research. Bandura's (1965) excellent experimental work on children's modeling of aggressive behavior is much more compelling when taken in the context's of Eron's (1986) quasi-experimental research on the long-term effects of viewing violence on subsequent aggressive behaviors. Together, the different types of research provide stronger results than they do separately.

# 13-4 Pearson's Correlation Coefficient

Karl Pearson, who perfected the chi-square statistic, also developed a statistical technique to measure the association between two variables measured on an interval or ratio scale (Stigler, 1986). This technique carries his name, the **Pearson product moment correlation coefficient ($r$)**. The statistic is referred to with the lowercase $r$ almost universally. The Pearson $r$ is very useful. Not only does it tell whether the association between the two variables is significant, but also the direction and degree of that association. Correlations are descriptive statistics. Like all other descriptive statistics, statistical inferences can be made about them. They range between +1.0 to −1.0. A correlation of 1.0 is a perfect correlation; it means that the two variables show identical patterns of variation. One of them could be used to accurately predict the other one. Think about the association of your height measured in inches and your height measured in centimeters. If the measurements were accurate, then the correlation would be 1.0. Both variables measure the same construct—your height. A correlation of −1.0 is also a perfect correlation. It means that the two variables have patterns that are in the opposite directions. If one is high, you can predict that the other is low. For example, imagine that you are traveling from school to your home. At any point on the journey, you can measure the distance from school and the distance to your home. As the distance from school increases, the distance to your home decreases. Their correlation is −1.0. Correlations are often illustrated with scatter plots.

**Pearson's product moment correlation coefficient ($r$)** The statistic used to tell whether the association between two variables is significant, but also the direction and degree of that association.

## 13-4a Graphing Relationships: Scatter Plots

A **scatter plot** shows the relationship between two variables by having a point on the plot represent each pair of variables. If the variables are related, a pattern is

**scatter plot** A graph that shows the relationship between two variables by having a point on the plot represent each pair of variables.

visible among the points. Figure 13-1 shows three different scatter plots. One scatter plot is of a positive relationship between two variables. When Variable A is low, Variable B also tends to be low. Likewise, when Variable A is high, Variable B is higher. The two variables are positively correlated. Examples of variables that tend to be positively correlated include height and weight; age and income; IQ and grades; and health and education. In each case, there is a close association between the variables. But the association does not necessarily imply causation. Nevertheless, if you know someone weighs 170 pounds, you could make a fairly good guess about that person's height. Conversely, if you knew the person's height, say 6 feet, you could guess the weight within a certain range (160 to 230 pounds). You can do so because of the correlation between the two variables. Correlations allow you to make predictions about one variable based on knowledge of the other.

Correlations that are negative show scatter plots similar to that in the negative association plot in Figure 13-1. A negative association means that as one variable is high, the other tends to be low. In the figure, you can see points for Variable B with values of 4, 5, and 6 that are associated with values of Variable A of 1 and 2. The high B values are associated with the low A values and conversely. Negative correlations are present among variables such as speed and accuracy; individuals' golf and basketball scores; ambient temperature and the amount of clothing worn; and physical fitness and the hours of television viewed. Negative

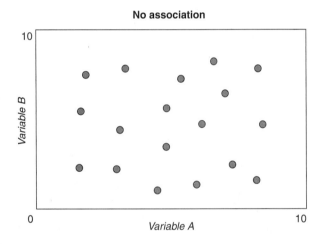

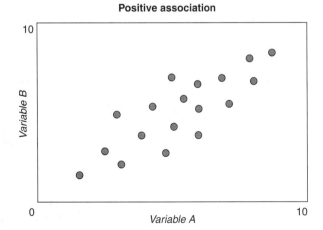

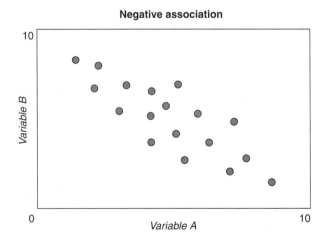

**Figure 13-1**
*Associations Depicted by Scatter Plots*

correlations can be just as informative as positive ones. If you know your friend has spent the last 72 hours without sleep, you can predict that your friend will not perform well on an exam. The reason is that sleeplessness is negatively correlated with test performance. As with all correlations, there may be individual exceptions, but in general the relationship holds.

When there is no relationship between two variables, the scatter plot looks like that shown in the remaining portion of Figure 13-1. The points are scattered throughout the space with no pattern at all. They may center on the middle of the graph or be dispersed throughout. If there is no correlation, you can make no good guesses about one variable based on knowledge of the other. Consider trying to predict personality traits from knowing a person's shoe size. There is no correlation. A person with a big foot may be as likely to be friendly, intelligent, and energetic as a person with a small foot.

The examples presented in Figure 13-1 were fabricated to show clear patterns. Real data often don't show such clear patterns. The stronger the correlations (close to either positive or negative 1), the clearer is the pattern in the scatter plot. Such patterns also show up better with more points. The power of the correlation statistic depends on the number of cases measured. Scatter plots with more points are also more revealing.

Correlations are also stronger if the variables are measured on their full range. One reason that the correlations between shyness and other social behaviors such as self-monitoring may appear low is that the very shy individuals do not volunteer for the study. Thus, the correlation between shyness and self-monitoring would not include the high end of the shyness scale. Whenever the sample is very homogenous (all alike), it is difficult to show correlations among the variables on which they are similar. Restriction of the range of the scale should be recognized when it exists. Pay careful attention to the range of possible scores and the norms that exists for those scores. The restriction of range problem occurred in research I did attempting to predict college students' graduation rate from their coping styles as incoming first-year students. The graduation rate for that class was extremely high (79%), leaving me little to predict. To understand student outcomes better, I had to find additional measures of academic success that did not have such a restricted range.

Figure 13-2 shows some scatter plots that were prepared with the SPSS statistical software from real data. SPSS uses the number of observations at each point to represent that point. Thus, the 3 on the graph indicated three people had exactly the same scores on both variables. Lisa Langsdorf (1993) hypothesized that there are relationships among moral and religious development. Although she found no significant correlations between moral development of college students and religious orientation, she did find correlations among two of the three scales of religious orientation developed by Batson and Ventis (1982). The top scatter plot in Figure 13-2 shows the relationship between external religious orientation (religion as a means) and internal religious orientation (religion as a belief system). These two orientations are positively correlated. This may indicate that religious college students tend to be oriented toward both the social aspects of their religion and the belief aspects. A third orientation suggested by Batson and Ventis is the quest orientation. This orientation represents the search for knowledge of God, with an open mind. It was not significantly correlated to either of the other two orientations. The bottom scatter plot in Figure 13-2 shows a nonsignificant association.

It is possible to have very high correlations with few observations. Figure 13-3 illustrates the case of a positive correlation between SAT math scores and final college GPA (grade point average) of 10 psychology majors. Although the correlation is very high, the low number of observations suggests caution be used in interpreting the relationship. The lower portion of Figure 13-3 is also based on real data. With three times the observations, the lower correlation (−.4899) is probably more reflective of the relationship. Note the pattern of the scatter plot for a negative relationship. The lower scatter plot shows the relationship between two scale scores that were

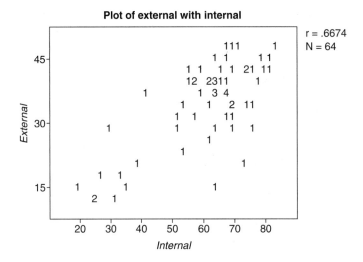

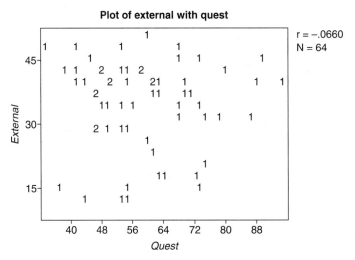

**Figure 13-2**
*Associations between External, Internal, and Quest Religious Orientations*

developed from the experiment presented in Taking a Closer Look 13-1 The variable *DYS* stands for the dysphoria subscale. It is a measure of negative mood. *PAS* is a measure of positive mood. These two scores are negatively correlated. For most participants, if they had a high positive mood score, they had a low negative mood score, and conversely. Note that some participants had either low or moderate scores on both negative and positive moods; they showed essentially no mood. Hence, the correlation is an intermediate one (–.4899).

### 13-4b Calculating the Pearson *r*

Unlike the chi-square, the calculation of the Pearson *r* is not quick and simple. Few people, when given the opportunity to use a computer, choose to do this calculation by hand, especially when there are many observations. Because the power of all associational techniques is directly dependent on the sample size—the more observations, the more powerful the statistic—most correlations are calculated on many numbers. (This is also true for the inferential statistical tests of differences among means. One way statistical power is increased is through an increase in sample size.)

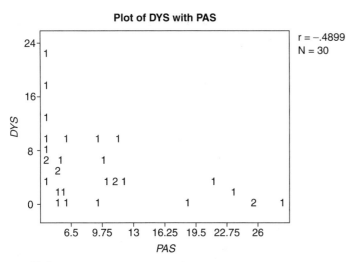

**Figure 13-3**

*Scatter Plots from Small Samples*

Nevertheless, the formula and procedures for the Pearson product moment correlation coefficient *r* are as follows:

$$r = \frac{N\Sigma XY - \Sigma X \Sigma Y}{\sqrt{\left[N\Sigma X^2 - (\Sigma X)^2\right]\left[N\Sigma Y^2 - (\Sigma Y)^2\right]}}$$

Where

**N**   is the number of subjects,

Σ**X**   is the total for variable $X$,

Σ**Y**   is the total for variable $Y$,

Σ**XY**   is the sum of the products of $X$ and $Y$,

Σ**X²**   is the sum of all the $X$ score squared first, and

Σ**Y²**   is the sum of all the $Y$ scores squared first.

df = N−2

**Taking a Closer Look 13-1** — *Sample Data to Show Correlations among Mood Scales*

Thirty participants were measured on their current mood using the Multiple Affect Adjective Check List (Today Form) as part of an experiment. The moods measured were anxiety (A), depression (D), hostility (H), positive affect (PA), and sensation seeking (SS). It was hypothesized that the moods would be correlated. The data are as follows:

| SUB | A | D | H | PA | SS |
|-----|---|---|---|-----|-----|
| 1 | 0 | 0 | 0 | 18 | 7 |
| 2 | 1 | 1 | 3 | 0 | 5 |
| 3 | 1 | 0 | 3 | 0 | 4 |
| 4 | 1 | 1 | 1 | 10 | 1 |
| 5 | 0 | 0 | 0 | 4 | 1 |
| 6 | 1 | 0 | 3 | 20 | 1 |
| 7 | 3 | 2 | 4 | 4 | 2 |
| 8 | 4 | 3 | 10 | 0 | 4 |
| 9 | 1 | 0 | 1 | 5 | 1 |
| 10 | 2 | 2 | 0 | 7 | 4 |
| 11 | 1 | 1 | 6 | 0 | 4 |
| 12 | 0 | 0 | 0 | 5 | 4 |
| 13 | 1 | 1 | 2 | 10 | 2 |
| 14 | 0 | 0 | 0 | 11 | 7 |
| 15 | 0 | 0 | 0 | 18 | 7 |
| 16 | 4 | 1 | 4 | 2 | 7 |
| 17 | 0 | 0 | 0 | 2 | 4 |
| 18 | 2 | 2 | 0 | 6 | 4 |
| 19 | 2 | 4 | 4 | 3 | 8 |
| 20 | 0 | 4 | 2 | 1 | 3 |
| 21 | 2 | 3 | 8 | 0 | 4 |
| 22 | 4 | 1 | 2 | 0 | 5 |
| 23 | 3 | 2 | 4 | 0 | 4 |
| 24 | 2 | 0 | 3 | 1 | 4 |
| 25 | 0 | 0 | 2 | 1 | 4 |
| 26 | 0 | 0 | 0 | 20 | 8 |
| 27 | 2 | 0 | 0 | 12 | 11 |
| 28 | 0 | 2 | 4 | 0 | 4 |
| 29 | 4 | 1 | 2 | 4 | 6 |
| 30 | 5 | 7 | 10 | 1 | 3 |

The formula itself is somewhat like that for standard deviation, except there are two variables. The additional component is the *product term*. That is, the product of each pair of scores is obtained. These products are then summed. The product term $\Sigma XY$ is the only thing new in this formula. The degrees of freedom for a correlation coefficient are simply the number of pairs of scores ($N$) minus 2.

It is very instructive to be familiar with the procedures to calculate $r$ because the procedures themselves show how the two variables are related. Most students cannot appreciate this measure of relationship by reading the formula or cranking out the statistic with a computer program. Figure 13-4 shows a step-by-step example using data from the sample study presented in Box 13-1. Although five different mood scales were measured, the example deals only with the correlation between D (depression) and H (hostility). The steps for calculating $r$ follow the same pattern as used in previous analyses. Start by writing the formula. Next, organize the data in a way that will minimize errors and facilitate calculation. Because you start with the raw data for two variables ($X$ and $Y$), and must calculate the square of each of these ($X^2$ and $Y^2$) and their product ($\Sigma XY$), you need five columns. The arrangement suggested in Figure 13-4 is one efficient way to organize the data.

In actually calculating the r, it is essential to keep straight which variable is which. The correlation will be the same regardless of which variable you call X and which you call Y. But if you get mixed up within the formula, the result will be wrong. The only way to avoid errors with r is to check your work. Even then, some errors are likely to result. However, it is good to remember that r must be between +1.0 and −1.0. Any result outside these limits is wrong. Also, remember to pay attention to the numbers as you calculate the r. Sometimes you can detect a calculation error because the statistical results aren't consistent with the "feel" of the data. If you obtain significant and unexpected results, the first thing to do is to look for the error.

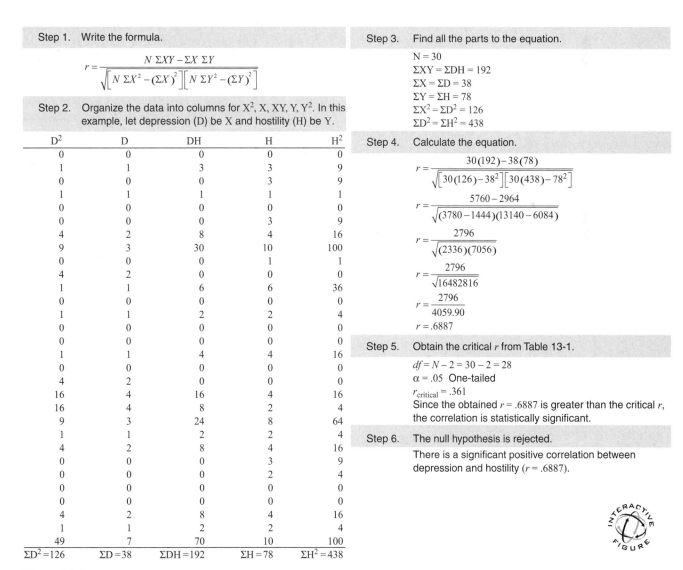

**Figure 13-4**

*Step-by-Step Example for Calculating Pearson's Product Moment Correlation Coefficient (r)*

| | TABLE 13-1 | Selected Critical Values of Pearson's Product Moment Correlation Coefficient ($r$) |

| *df* | $\alpha$ (two-tailed)* | |
|---|---|---|
| (*N* − 2) | .10 | .05 |
| 13 | .441 | .514 |
| 14 | .426 | .497 |
| 18 | .378 | .444 |
| 22 | .344 | .404 |
| 28 | .306 | .361 |
| 40 | .257 | .304 |

*For one-tailed test
$\alpha_{1\text{-tailed}} = \alpha_{2\text{-tailed}}$ divided by 2

Using computers for analysis will reduce some types of calculation errors. Even computer programs are liable to error, though. A good program for beginning data analysts will generally fail when an inappropriate analysis is requested (such as a Pearson correlation between a nominal variable and a ratio variable). However, most computer programs will do whatever they are programmed to do, whether the calculation makes sense or not. I have seen computer programs that print impossible statistical results when the research design is specified incorrectly. The point to remember is that whether you calculate the statistic by hand or with a supercomputer, you have to do the thinking.

The correlation coefficient is a descriptive statistic. Yet a statistical inference also accompanies it. Whenever a correlation is calculated, the null hypothesis is that there is no relationship between the two variables measured. In this example, the null hypothesis is that depression and hostility are unrelated. Another way to say the same thing is to say that they are independent of each other. Formally, the null hypothesis is that the correlation between the two variables is not significantly different from zero:

$$H_0 : r = 0$$

This null hypothesis is statistically tested by comparing the obtained $r$ with a critical value of $r$. The critical value of $r$ is dependent on the degrees of freedom and alpha. Table 13-1 has selected critical values for the sizes of research designs that beginning students might conduct. In the example, $N$ is 30. Therefore, the degrees of freedom equal 28. The alternate hypothesis was that hostility and depression are positively correlated. Thus, a one-tailed test is in order. The table presents two-tailed alpha values. To obtain the one-tail critical value for $\alpha = .05$, use the column of the two-tailed probability with $\alpha = .10$. The critical value in the example is .306. Because the obtained (calculated) $r$ is greater than the critical value, the null hypothesis is rejected. The correlation of .6887 is significantly greater than zero. The interpretation is that depression is positively associated with hostility in the experiment.

Another interpretation for correlation is that the correlation coefficient, when squared, shows the proportion of the variation in one of the variables that can be accounted for by the other. Although this is a confusing concept, it is very useful. Consider the example of the relationship between hostility and depression. Within the experimental situation, the proportion of variance in depression that can be accounted for by hostility is $r^2$ ($.6887^2 = .47$). That means that almost half of depression could be accounted for by hostility (or vice versa). It must be reiterated that correlation does not imply causation. It does, however, imply shared variation.

| TABLE 13-2 | Sample Correlation Matrix |
|---|---|

Correlations: EXTERNAL INTERNAL QUEST

| | | | |
|---|---|---|---|
| EXTERNAL | 1.0000 | .7207** | .0038 |
| INTERNAL | .7207** | 1.0000 | −.0650 |
| QUEST | .0038 | −.0650 | 1.0000 |

Minimum pairwise $N$ of cases: 60
1-tailed Signif: * − .01 ** − .001

" . " is printed if a coefficient cannot be computed.

Correlation coefficients are often calculated and interpreted for many pairs of variables simultaneously. The most common way to display these results is to use a correlation matrix. Table 13-2 contains the correlation matrix obtained from the Langsdorf (1993) study. A careful inspection of the table will show you that the variables represented in the rows are the same as the variables represented in the columns. Thus, the first correlation coefficient in the table is the correlation of the first variable with itself. The second correlation in the second row is the correlation of the second variable with itself, and so forth. All of the self-correlations are, of course, equal to 1.0 because anything is perfectly correlated with itself. The line of 1.0s in the matrix is referred to as the *diagonal*. The correlation coefficients above the diagonal are redundant with those below the diagonal. The reason is that the correlation between $x$ and $y$ is the same as that between $y$ and $x$, but both are in the matrix. Often only half the matrix is presented (either above or below the diagonal). Sometimes, especially in large correlation matrices, only the statistically significant correlations are printed. In some matrices, the probabilities of each correlation occurring by chance are also printed.

### 13-4c Associations among Nonparametric and Parametric Data

Association statistics also can be calculated when one variable is not really a number (nominal) and the other is parametric (measured numerically as in interval or ratio scales). These techniques take into account the nature of measurement for each variable. Rank data have special problems because they violate the assumption of independence between data. There are statistics used to measure associations among rank (ordinal measurement scale) data. When you are designing research, it is best to operationalize variables in the most precise way possible. If associations between nominal and parametric data are necessary, seek the proper statistical analyses from a book on nonparametric methods.

# 13-5 APA Style: Reporting Correlations

Correlations can be reported in the results section of an experimental report in the text. Remember to name the statistic and to provide the degrees of freedom and statistical significance level. The sample problem could be reported as follows.

> There was a statistically significant positive correlation between depression and hostility ($r(28) = .69$; $p < .05$).

Tables are often used to present many correlations. Table 13-3 shows the APA style for the correlations presented in Table 13-2. Notice that the APA (2001) style is not the same as the computer output. The correlations are not repeated; therefore, only the portion of the table above the diagonal is presented. The self-correlations are also not presented. Therefore, the three subscales are reduced to two rows (A and B) and two columns (B and C) that allow for comparisons among all three subscales (A with B, A with C, and B with C). Finally, the correlation coefficients are rounded to the

| TABLE 13-3 | Intercorrelations between Subscales of Religious Orientation (*N* = 60) | |
| --- | --- | --- |
| **Subscale** | **Internal** | **Quest** |
| External | .72* | .00 |
| Internal | | .07 |

Note: *\*p < .001*

scientifically significant digits. That resulted in the very low correlations of .0038 being reported as .00. Also note that the information in this table could be efficiently presented in the text, especially because only one of the correlations is significantly different from zero. However, the principles of table construction apply to larger correlation matrixes and can be understood as applied to the simplest case.

# Summary

Quasi-experiments are natural or field experiments that involve comparisons among treatment conditions in which some things in addition to the independent variable are different. One type of quasi-experiment is the static group comparison design. Existing groups are studied. One of these groups receives the treatment, and the other serves as a comparison group. Because the groups differ on more than the treatment, the conclusion drawn from the results of the research must be restricted.

Three threats to validity of an experiment are particularly liable for the static group comparison design. Selection is a threat if the comparison group differs from the treatment group in some systematic way. Mortality is a threat if participants leave the experiment in one condition more so than in the other condition, and if those who leave are systematically different from those who complete the study. Selection by maturation is a threat when the static groups differ in their maturation rates, thus confounding a maturation effect with a treatment effect.

Pearson's product moment correlation coefficient (r) is a measure of association between two interval or ratio scale measures. Correlations may be illustrated by the patterns shown on scatter plots. A positive correlation is shown by a pattern of points that increase on both variables. As one increases, the other is also likely to increase. A negative correlation is shown by a pattern of points that moves down the scatter plot from left to right. As one of the variables increases, the other decreases. A scatter plot that shows points all over in no discernable pattern represents zero correlation between two variables.

Pearson's r is calculated by summing the product of the two variables for each participant and adjusting for the variation within each of the variables. Statistical inferences are made about the likelihood of obtaining the computed r by chance alone if there is no association between the two variables.

# References

American Psychological Association. (2001). *Publication manual of the American Psychological Association.* Washington, DC: Author.

Bandura, A. (1965). Influence of model's reinforcement contingencies on the acquisition of imitative responses. *Journal of Personality and Social Psychology, 1,* 589–595.

Batson, C. D. & Ventis, W. L. (1982). *The religious experience: A social-psychological perspective.* New York: Oxford University Press.

Campbell, D. T. & Stanley, J. C. (1966). *Experiments and quasi-experimental designs for research.* Chicago: Rand McNally.

Dornbush, R., Kolodny, R., Bauman, J. E. & Webster, S. K. (1978). Human female chronic marijuana use and endocrine functioning. *Neuroscience Abstracts, 4,* 490.

Eron, L. (1986). Intervention to mitigate the psychological effects of media violence on aggressive behavior. *Journal of Social Issues, 42*(3), 155–169.

Langsdorf, L. M. (1993). *Moral development, religious orientation and helping behavior.* Honor's thesis, Westminster College, New Wilmington, Pennsylvania.

Mill, J. S. (1874). *A system of logic, ratiocinative and inductive: Being a connected view of the principles of evidence and the methods of scientific investigation* (8th ed.). New York: Harper & Brothers.

Stigler, S. M. (1986). *The history of statistics: The measurement of uncertainty before 1900.* Cambridge, MA: Belknap Press.

## Exercises for Application

1. Consider each of the following research descriptions. Identify the type of quasi-experimental design used. Then explain the particular problems associated with the research. If possible, suggest improvements for the research methods. Finally, outline the strongest possible conclusion that could be drawn from the research.

   a. Research on homosexuality often compares a sample of homosexual men to heterosexual men and to women. A variety of physical and personality characteristics have been measured. If the averages on any of these variables are different between homosexual men and heterosexual men, and the homosexual men average more similar to that of women than do the heterosexual men, the researchers conclude that the particular physical or personality characteristic is the cause of homosexuality.

   b. Two in-depth group interviews (focus groups) were conducted with individuals who are chronically depressed. Analyses of the interview tapes showed that many of the individuals had a life-long experience of depressive episodes that they associated with conflict, particularly between their parents. The researchers concluded that reducing parental conflict may reduce depression.

   c. A sample of women who had recently undergone mastectomies was surveyed along with their significant others over a period of 5 years. Attitudes toward social support and sexuality were correlated to recovery.

2. Calculate and interpret the correlations among the remaining variables (other than D and H), presented in Box 13-1. Make a scatter plot of two of the variables.

## Practice Quiz

*Note:* You can find the correct answers to these questions by taking the quiz and then submitting your answers in the Online Edition. The program will automatically score your submission. If you miss a question, the program will provide the correct answer, a rationale for the answer, and the section number in the chapter where the topic is discussed.

1. A quasi-experiment is like a true experiment *except*
   a. the independent variable isn't manipulated.
   b. groups are not equivalent on control variables.
   c. there is no dependent variable.
   d. there is no control condition.

2. Groups that were not assigned or that were not under the control of the experimenter are called

   a. convenience groups.
   b. reality groups.
   c. permanent groups.
   d. static groups.

3. Why was the relationship between marijuana use and female reproductive hormones difficult to determine?

   a. The static comparison groups also differed on other drug use and lifestyles.
   b. There was no pretest before marijuana use began.
   c. The study was stopped because it was illegal to have participants smoke marijuana.
   d. Participants' self-reports of their marijuana use were unreliable.

4. Including volunteers of new programs into research can result in a
   a. selection threat to the study validity.
   b. mortality threat to the study validity.
   c. sample that is too large.
   d. maturation threat.

5. It is important to design studies that are easy for subjects to complete to reduce the threat of
   a. selection.
   b. mortality.
   c. maturation.
   d. selection × maturation interaction.

6. A selection by maturation interaction is likely to be a problem when
   a. there are differences between the groups in terms of their maturity.
   b. the groups are changing at different rates.
   c. old people are used in the study.
   d. only people of specific ages are included in the study.

7. The major criticism of experimental research is that it is
   a. artificial.
   b. correlational.
   c. not able to show causation.
   d. weak on internal validity.

8. The correlation statistic was developed by
   a. Fisher.
   b. Pearson.
   c. Tukey.
   d. Student.

9. A scatter plot that shows points which are evenly distributed all over the graph would be likely to represent a _____ correlation.
   a. −1.0
   b. −0.5
   c. 0.0
   d. +0.45

10. A correlation may appear lower than it should be because of
    a. heterogeneity in the sample.
    b. a monotonic relationship between the variables.
    c. restriction of range on one or both variables.
    d. too much data.

11. A negative correlation between positive affect and dysphoria shows that as positive affect increases, dysphoria is likely to
    a. increase.
    b. stay the same.
    c. decrease.
    d. increase at first but then decrease.

12. The only "new" ingredient for the Pearson correlation coefficient formula that wasn't used to calculate the variance is the
    a. sum of all the $X$ scores.
    b. sum of the products of all the $X$ and $Y$ scores.
    c. sum of all the squared $X$ and squared $Y$ scores.
    d. the number of scores.

13. The degrees of freedom for a correlation are
    a. $N - 1$.
    b. $N - 2$.
    c. $X - Y$.
    d. $(X - 1)(Y - 1)$.

14. The null hypothesis for a correlation is that
    a. the mean of $X$ = the mean of $Y$.
    b. $r = 1.0$.
    c. $r = -1.0$.
    d. $r = 0.0$.

15. If the correlation between two variables is −.5, then the proportion of variance that they share is
    a. .50.
    b. −.50.
    c. −1.0.
    d. .25.

16. APA style correlation tables are likely to show a lot of empty cells because
    a. all the variables are listed twice.
    b. only statistically significant variables are presented.
    c. self-correlations and redundant correlations are omitted.
    d. white space is easy on the eyes.

# Glossary

## A

**ABA design**  Repeated measures design in which a pretest is given with no treatment (A), the treatment is given and its effect is measured (B), and a third measurement is taken without the treatment (A).

**ABAB design**  A single subject study in which the participant acts as his or her own control.

**alpha**  Accepted level of probability of a Type I error, typically .05.

**alternative hypothesis**  Hypothesis that the cause has an effect.

**analysis of variance**  Statistical comparison of all the variance in the data that can be attributed to the independent variable compared to all the remaining variance in the data.

**ANOVA**  Acronym for analysis of variance.

**ANOVA summary table**  Table that shows the sources of variance for a given experiment, estimates of those variances *(SS, df, MS)*, and the ratios of the variances *(F)*.

**APA ethical principles**  A set of ethical principles published by the American Psychological Association that mandate avoiding harm while actively benefiting psychological clients, research subjects, and society in general.

**APA reference style**  Specific guidelines for citing sources in research published by the American Psychological Association.

**APA style**  Specific format for manuscripts submitted to the American Psychological Association for publication.

**a priori hypothesis**  Hypothesis that is made before data collection.

**atheoretical**  No theory.

**authorship**  Inclusion as authors of the written report those individuals who made substantial contributions to a piece of research, with the major contributor being the first author.

## B

**bar graph**  A graph in which a bar is drawn to the height of the frequency for each category.

**beta**  Probability of a Type II error.

**between groups**  The source of variance between experimental groups.

**between subjects**  Experimental design in which each participant receives only one treatment.

**between subjects variance**  Difference among all the subjects.

**bipolar**  Measurement approach in which labels at the ends of the scales are the two opposite "poles."

**Boolean search**  An online search that connects a set of key words with the Boolean operators (and, or, not) to limit the search to specific interests.

## C

**case study**  A type of study in which a single case is studied in great detail, usually over a period of time.

**cell**  Each of the combined treatments in the design for an experiment.

**cell frequency**  Count (frequency) that occurs in one cell of a cross-tabulation table.

**cell totals**  The totals for all the data for all subjects who received the same combination of treatments.

**chi-square**  A test of independence between variables that are each measured on a nominal scale.

**citing sources**  Listing sources for all ideas in a research report.

**Cohen's *d***  Number of standard deviations between two sample means.

**concomitant variation**  Change in one variable that occurs as a result of a change (manipulation) in the other variable.

**condition**  The method of manipulating the independent variable at one of its levels.

**confederate**  An assistant to the experimenter who is playing the role of a research participant.

**confidence interval**  Range within which a statistical result is confidently accepted as probably not due to chance.

**confidentiality**  The use of data provided by research participants only for the purpose of the research and not presented as information about the participants for any other purpose.

**confound**  Factor varies systematically with treatment of the independent variable.

**control**  Condition in which the cause is absent.

**control group**  Group of participants who are equivalent to a treatment group except that they do not receive the independent variable.

**counterbalancing**  Presenting each of the contexts equally across all levels of the independent variable.

**counterbalancing**    Keeping the numbers of participants with a particular attribute equivalent across the treatment conditions.

**cross-tabulation table**    Frequency table that shows the counts in the cells based on two variables (rows and columns).

**curiosity**    Characteristic often found in scientists, whereby they want to know what makes things work and why.

# D

**data falsification**    The act of making up data to produce desired results.

**debriefing**    Clear and complete feedback about the experiment and its results.

**deception**    The active misleading of a participant by either false information and/or the presence of confederates in the experiment.

**deduction**    The logical process of going from a general rule to specific applications.

**degrees of freedom**    Number of different ways that the data could have produced the group means that were obtained simply through random sampling from a population.

**demand characteristics**    Aspects of the research situation that lead people to act differently than they would if they were not in the research.

**demand characteristics**    Aspects of the research situation that produce effects in the participants that would not occur outside the experimental setting.

**dependent variable**    An effect to be measured by the experimenter.

**deprivation**    The act of withholding food or water from animals.

**descriptive statistics**    Summaries of the data in terms of central tendencies and spread.

**determinism**    The value that every effect has a cause.

**dichotomy**    Type of nominal scale in which you can divide any variable into two, and only two, classes.

**discussion section**    Section of a research report in which the results of the research are discussed.

**dispersion**    Spread of the numbers that make up the data within a data set.

# E

**empiricism**    The practice of relying on observable facts.

**ethics**    Principles of right action.

**experiment-wise error**    All the sources of error (e.g., Type I) that can occur in one experiment with multiple statistical tests.

**experimental design**    The plan of an experiment that includes how the cause will be manipulated, how the effect will be measured, and how other variables will be controlled.

**experimental treatment**    Condition in which the cause is present.

**explicit values**    Values that individuals have consciously developed and accepted as their own.

**external validity**    Degree to which results may be applied outside the experimental setting.

# F

**$F$ ratio**    Inferential statistic that will allow the researcher to estimate the probability of getting the obtained results by chance alone.

**factorial design**    A design in which more than one factor is considered in the same experiment.

**frequency distribution**    A table showing the number of entries for each type, or category, of data.

**frequency histogram**    A type of graph similar to a bar graph, except that the X-axis represents a continuous variable, not one that is defined in categories.

**full citation**    Complete bibliographic information, including author(s), year of publication, title, journal name or publisher, volume number and pages, and place of publication.

# H

**history**    "The specific events occurring between the first and second measurement in addition to the experimental variable" (Campbell & Stanley, 1963, p. 5).

**HSD**    Honestly significant difference (Tukey) test used to make multiple comparisons while keeping the experiment-wise probability of making a Type I error at alpha.

**hypothesis**    A more specific application of a theory to predict a particular outcome.

**hypothetico-deductive method**    A method used in science to test the ideas that derive from our curiosity in an organized way.

# I

**ideographic approach**    The study of an individual, over time, and in detail to get a picture of the whole personality (Allport, 1937).

**implicit values**    Values developed over time through socialization that individuals may not consciously recognize as values.

**independent variable**    A cause to be manipulated by the experimenter.

**induction**    A form of logic in which a general conclusion is drawn from the observation of many specific events or facts.

**inferential statistics**    Probability estimates of obtaining the specific results by chance alone.

**informed consent**    The approval received after potential participants are given a clear and accurate description of the time and tasks required by participation before they decide to become involved in the research.

**Institutional Review Boards (IRBs)**    The formal review panels convened by a college, university, or other research supporting institution to review the ethical aspects of proposed research sponsored by the institution and/or conducted at it.

**interact**  Factors' effect when presented in isolation is different from their effect when they are presented together with another factor.

**interaction**  The effect of either factor depends on the level of the other.

**internal validity**  Ability to logically rule out explanations for the effect observed (dependent variable) other than the manipulated cause (independent variable).

**inter-rater agreement**  Correlation among different raters of the same stimuli.

**interval**  Amount of space or distance between two things.

**interval scale**  Scale of measurement in which the intervals between the points are known.

**ipsative**  Within any individual participant, the scores sum to a constant.

## K

**key word searches**  Searches of *PsychInfo* or *Psychological Abstracts* using key, or relevant, words.

## L

**levels of the independent variable**  Different amounts or types of the cause.

**Likert scale**  Ordinal scale that requires ratings organized in order of strength—e.g., strongly agree, somewhat agree, neither agree nor disagree, somewhat disagree, or strongly disagree.

**line graph**  A graph that shows the same information as a frequency histogram, with points placed vertically to represent the frequency for each category.

**literature review**  The process of reading and evaluating reports of previous research and using deduction to form hypotheses. Also used to describe the portion of a research report introduction that summarizes the previous research and theory relevant to the hypotheses tested in that report.

## M

**magnitude of effect**  Measure of the size of the differences.

**main effects**  The sources of variance that rely on only one factor.

**marginal frequencies**  Frequencies for the two nominal variables, without regard to their cross-tabulation.

**marginal totals**  Totals in the margins of the table.

**matching**  Determining, before the experiment is conducted, which psychological variables are important for the particular causal relationship under study and matching the participants on those variables.

**materials and/or apparatus**  Questionnaires, scales, equipment, and so forth that are needed to conduct research.

**maturation**  "Processes within the respondents operating as a function of the passage of time per se, including growing older, growing hungrier, growing more tired, and the like" (Campbell & Stanley, 1963, p. 5).

**mean**  Average of a set of data.

**mean squares (MS)**  Sums of squares divided by the degrees of freedom for each source of variance.

**measures of central tendency**  Descriptive statistics such as the mean, median, and mode that describe the center of a set of data.

**median**  The middle score from a set of data.

**methods section**  Section of an APA style paper that describes the participants, materials and/or apparatus, and the procedures of the study.

**minimal risk**  The temporary physical discomfort, emotional stress, or social pressures experienced by research participants.

**mixed design**  A design in which there are repeated measures on one of the two factors, while the other factor is a between subjects factor.

**mode**  The most frequent score from a set of data.

**mortality**  The threat to validity that occurs when subjects fail to complete the experiment.

**multiple comparisons**  Analyses making comparisons among the means, two by two.

**multiple treatment interference**  A threat to validity that occurs in repeated measures factorial designs when carryover effects of early treatments interfere with later treatments.

**multiple treatment interference**  Threat to internal validity of an experiment that occurs when multiple treatments are present and interfere with each other.

## N

**nominal scale**  Scale of measurement in which the variable is defined according to different "names."

**nomothetic approach**  A study that measures a large number of individuals on a relatively small number of variables.

**nonparametric statistics**  Statistics that are used on nominal data.

**nonresponder bias**  The outcome that occurs when individuals do not agree to participate in a survey.

**normal distribution**  Hypothesized probability density function that resembles the bell-shaped curve and is assumed to represent the measurement of a variable in a population.

**null hypothesis**  Hypothesis that a change in the independent variable has no observable effect on the dependent variable.

## O

**odds**  Probability of an outcome to occur in a given situation.

**one-tailed hypothesis**  Alternate hypothesis that specifies the direction of the difference between the means.

**one-tailed test**  Statistical inference technique used for a one-tailed hypothesis.

**operational definition**    A definition that is specific enough to be used to actually perform an experiment.

**order effect**    Specific effect that occurs depending on the order in which multiple treatments were presented to the subject.

**ordinal scale**    Scale of measurement that allows quantitative comparisons in terms of which is more.

# P

**paradigm**    A standard method of conducting research that has been developed over a number of studies as demonstrated to be effective.

**parameter**    Numeric value used in a formula.

**parametric tests**    Tests that require data (the parameter) that have been measured with quantitative scales.

**participants**    Human subjects of the research.

**partitioning the variance**    Dividing the variance according to source.

**Pearson's product moment correlation coefficient ($r$)**    The statistic used to tell whether the association between two variables is significant, but also the direction and degree of that association.

**peer reviewers**    Colleagues who review a researcher's study for potential risks of participation.

**peripheral search**    An examination of the items near to the target. For example, reviewing those surrounding one located in *Psychological Abstracts* in case they also are useful.

**pie chart**    A circle divided into wedges, with the area of each wedge proportional to the frequency of each category represented.

**pilot study**    A part of the research study in which the researcher conducts the experiment (or specific parts of it) in order to see how well the procedures work.

**placebo**    Treatment that has every appearance of the cause, but not the hypothesized causal agent.

**plagiarism**    The act of using another person's idea without giving credit to its source.

**pooled standard deviation**    Standard deviation estimated from two samples.

**population**    The group of individuals to whom research can be generalized.

**post hoc hypotheses**    Hypotheses created after the data have been collected and analyzed.

**posttest only design**    Design that involves measuring the dependent variable only once, after the treatment has been presented to participants in the treatment group.

**posttest only one group study**    A type of study in which a treatment condition is administered to a single group.

**power**    Ability to statistically find relationships among variables.

**pre-experimental designs**    Designs that do not involve the manipulation of an experimental treatment (Campbell & Stanley, 1966).

**premise**    A general rule or a specific fact that is used in logical deduction.

**pretest posttest design**    Design that uses each participant as his or her own control.

**probability**    Likelihood of anything happening.

**probability density function**    Set of probabilities calculated for each possible result in a particular experimental design.

**PsychInfo**    An electronic form of *Psychological Abstracts* available on the Internet.

**Psychological Abstracts**    Sets of thousands of abstracts of psychological reports published each year.

# Q

**quasi-experiments**    Designs that have some of the features of true experiments but cannot claim to have all things equivalent between treatment groups other than the independent variable (Campbell and Stanley, 1966).

# R

**random assignment**    Method by which each participant has an equal chance of being assigned to each treatment condition.

**random number table**    Table of numbers that has been derived through a random process and that can be used for random assignment.

**random sample**    A sample in which each member of the population has an equal probability of being selected.

**randomizing the order of treatments**    Randomly determining the order of treatments for each participant.

**ranking scale**    Scale in which participants are asked to rank their preference for a number of different objects or alternatives.

**ratio scale**    Scale that has equal intervals between its points and that contains a true zero.

**related measures $t$ test**    Inferential statistic to test the difference between two means that are related by being from the same participant (repeated measures) or in some other way (e.g., matching).

**reliable**    Gives the same result every time.

**replicate**    To duplicate an experiment with the hope of obtaining the same results.

**residual variance**    Variance not attributed to any factor or interaction.

**results section**    Section of a research report that contains all the descriptive and inferential statistics needed to test the hypotheses.

**risk**    The negative outcome(s) that might occur to a research subject or participant as a result of study participation.

**risk/benefit ratio**    The weighing of benefits to risks in a research study.

# S

$s$    Statistical notation for the standard deviation.

$s^2$    Statistical notation for the variance.

**samples**    The individuals selected from a population to be included in research.

**sampling distribution of the mean**    Set of all possible samples of a given size $(n)$ from a population.

**scales of measurement**    Types of measurement used, whether nominal, ordinal, interval, or ratio.

**scatter plot**    A graph that shows the relationship between two variables by having a point on the plot represent each pair of variables.

**selection**    An important threat to the validity of research when there is differential selection into the treatment groups.

**selection**    The threat to external validity that occurs because a sample was selected in such a way that it does not adequately represent the population.

**selection by maturation interaction**    The treatment effect is different for the selected groups because of their different rates of maturation.

**significance level**    Probability of obtaining the results by chance alone.

**single group observation**    A study of one group.

**skew**    The effect of extreme scores on the mean and variance.

**standard deviation**    Square root of the variance.

**standard error of the mean**    Measure of variance equal to the standard deviation divided by the square root of $n$.

**standard scores**    Scores that have been made uniform in terms of center and variance.

**static group comparison design**    A study design in which a new program or technique is tried out with one existing class or client group, while another group or class acts as the control.

**statistical inference**    Process of using statistics to make decisions about the hypotheses (null and alternative) based on the data collected in the experiment.

**statistical power**    Ability of the statistical test to reveal differences that actually exist.

**statistical precision**    Ability of a statistical test to reveal only differences that actually exist, thus avoiding Type I error.

**statistics**    Tools for understanding data.

**student's *t* test**    Statistical test used to determine whether the means of two groups are significantly different.

**subject search**    A search of the subject index.

**subject variance**    Variance due to individual differences in the subjects.

**sums of squares (SS)**    Sums of the squared scores for each of the sources of variance.

**survey instrument**    The questionnaire that is used to conduct a survey.

**syllogism**    The combination of premises and deduction that lead to a logical conclusion.

# T

**terminate**    End study participation.

**testing**    Effects of taking a test upon the scores of a second test.

**theory**    An organized, systematic explanation of a phenomenon.

**threats to internal validity**    Any aspect of the research design that produces a confound with the independent variable that weakens the logical link between it and the hypothesized effect.

**treatment**    Presence of the cause.

**treatment group**    Group of participants who receive the independent variable.

**treatment variance**    Variance due to the independent variable.

**true control condition**    Condition in which the cause is absent.

**two-factor ANOVA**    Analysis of variance for a two-factor design.

**two-tailed hypothesis**    Alternate hypothesis that specifies the means will be different, but not in which direction.

**two-tailed test**    Statistical inference technique used for a two-tailed hypothesis.

**Type I error**    Null hypothesis is true and based on the statistics of the experiment it was rejected.

**Type II error**    Null hypothesis is false and was not rejected with the statistics of the experiment.

# U

**uniform distribution**    Flat distribution in which each score occurs with about equal frequency.

**unobtrusive research**    Observation of public behaviors without the express knowledge of the participants.

# V

**valid**    Measures what it is designed to measure.

**values**    Beliefs held by an individual that influence the individual's thoughts, emotions, and overt behaviors.

**variability**    Amount of difference within a data set.

**variance**    Measure of how all the scores in a set of data deviate from the mean.

# W

**within subjects**    Experimental design in which each participant receives all the levels of the independent variable.

**within subjects error variance**    Variation within each subject that cannot be attributed to the treatment.

**within subjects experiment**    Experiment in which each subject receives all the treatments.

**within subjects treatment variance**    Within subjects variance that can be attributed to the treatment.

**within subjects variance**    Differences within the subjects due to the treatment and error variance.

# Z

**z-score**    Form of individual score that has a mean of zero and standard deviation of one.

# Index